Divided Jerusalem

ALSO BY THE SAME AUTHOR

The British in Palestine
Britain and the Jews of Europe 1939–1945
The Secret Lives of Trebitsch Lincoln
Herbert Samuel
Vanishing Diaspora
Secret War in Shanghai

Divided Jerusalem

The Struggle for the Holy City

Bernard Wasserstein

P

PROFILE BOOKS

First published in Great Britain in 2001 by
Profile Books Ltd
58A Hatton Garden
London EC1N 8LX
www..profilebooks.co.uk

Typeset in Lapidary 333 by MacGuru
info@macguru.org.uk

Printed and bound in Great Britain by
St Edmundsbury Press, Bury St Edmunds

A CIP catalogue record for this book is available from the British Library.

ISBN 1 86197 355 1

For Teddy, Sarah and Miriam

Contents

Preface   x
Acknowledgements   xvi
List of Tables   xviii
List of Maps   xix

Prologue: The Heavenly City   1
Jerusalem of the Jews
Jerusalem of the Christians
Jerusalem of the Muslims

1 **The Wars of the Consuls**   14
The holy places
Egyptian rule in Jerusalem
The Protestant bishopric
War clouds over the tomb of Christ

2 **Old City, New City**   45
Beyond the walls
Spiritual imperialism
Jerusalem promoted
'A Christmas present for the British nation'

3 **Jerusalem under the Mandate**   82
From military government to mandate
Christian triumphalism
The rise of the mufti
Towards partition
'A glorified cockpit'

4 Division   132
Mandatory abdication
Spontaneous partition
Pantomime across the Jordan
Collapse of corpus separatum
A king for Jerusalem
'Will the Vatican send an army here?'

5 Two Jerusalems   179
Divide and rule
Jerusalem demoted
Christians in a divided Jerusalem
New consular wars
Cul-de-sac capital

6 Annexation   205
Conquest
Unification
Jerusalem under Israeli rule
Arab resistance
World reaction

7 Towards Palestinian Autonomy   239
Diplomacy by declaratory gesture
Jerusalem: an American problem?
Palestinians and Jerusalem
Intifada *and after*

8 Christian Jerusalem in Eclipse   266
Christians under Jewish rule
Reds and whites

9 Creeping Partition   287

The Beilin-Abu Mazen agreement
Palestinian elections
The siege of Orient House
Camp David and beyond

10 Trouble on the Temple Mount   317

Palimpsest
Riots at the Wailing Wall
The Temple Mount under Israeli rule
The battle of the muftis
The logic of haggle

Epilogue: The Earthly City   345

Jigsaw-puzzle solutions
The Clinton legacy
Israeli and Palestinian public opinions
Demographic diktat?
Must heaven wait?

Notes   360
Sources   390
Index   401

Preface

'Jerusalem,' wrote Herman Melville after a visit there in 1860, 'is besieged by an army of the dead.' The city is said to have been conquered thirty-seven times between its foundation and the capture of its ancient heart by the Israelis in 1967. When Arthur Koestler went there during the war of 1948, he despaired at the 'international quarrelling, haggling and mediation' that seemed in store. 'No other town,' he wrote, 'has caused such continuous waves of killing, rape and unholy misery over the centuries as this Holy City.'[1] Horrifying numbers of Jerusalem's citizens have suffered violent death and injury since those melancholy observations of Melville and Koestler. In particular, the period since 1967 has seen a succession of terrorist bombings, riots, rebellion and repression.

The violence reflects the lack of a consensual polity. The 'eternally unified capital' of the state of Israel is the most deeply divided capital city in the world. Its Arab and Jewish residents inhabit different districts, speak different languages, attend different schools, read different newspapers, watch different television programmes, observe different holy days, follow different football teams – live, in almost every significant respect, different lives. In a poll a few years ago 70 per cent of Israelis confessed that they had never set foot in Arab areas of Jerusalem outside the old city. Arabs enter Jewish districts only in order to perform certain assigned roles within the Israeli economy, as construction workers, waiters or general labourers, though they are gradually being squeezed out of such jobs by a labour reserve army of non-Jewish immigrants to Israel: Russians, Filipinos, Turks, Romanians, Ghanaians and others who do not present the same security risks in the eyes of their employers. Arabs and Jews in

Jerusalem mix socially even less than blacks and whites in Johannesburg. Marriages across the line are legally difficult and socially taboo. Above all, Arabs and Jews inhabit different mental worlds, informed by fundamentally different ideological axioms, infected with profound collective suspicions of each other and infused with a mutual dread that has repeatedly exploded into hate-filled aggression.

The Jerusalem question in its current form contains two separate elements: sovereignty over the city and the status of the holy places. The former is contested by two national groups, the latter by three religions. But such a taxonomy, while it serves the purpose of analysis, does not altogether fit the real world. The issues of sovereignty and of the holy places, of nationalism and religion, are in Jerusalem, more than anywhere else on earth, inextricably tangled. If it were otherwise, the matter would probably have been settled long ago.

Like a Russian doll, the struggle for the holy city is a microcosm of larger global conflicts and at the same time contains within itself a seemingly interminable series of ever more petty quarrels. Jerusalem lies at the crux of the historic antagonism between the eastern and western Churches. Within the Orthodox Church, Hellene battled against Arab, Russian against Greek, 'red' against 'white'. Nor were Protestants behindhand in challenging Catholics, or Jesuits in contesting the pretensions of Franciscans. As Sir Ronald Storrs, the first governor of Jerusalem under the British mandate, put it, 'The local and indigenous Christian communities needed – alas! – for their fratricidal tumults no outside provocation.'[2] All three great religions have been riven in Jerusalem by sectarian rivalries that pit Coptic monk against Ethiopian priest, Ashkenazi versus Sephardi Chief Rabbi, Palestinian-appointed versus Jordanian-appointed mufti, and so on almost without end.

The *odium theologicum* is seldom even worthy of the name, for the issues of dispute have more often been material than spiritual. The controversies over such matters as who might carry how many candles down which passageway in the Church of the Holy Sepulchre at what hour on which day have brought Armenians, Greeks and Latins to blows for centuries. As if seeking to emulate the Christians, Jews and Muslims over the past century have resorted to bitter, often murderous brawling over such issues as whether benches may be placed before the Western ('Wailing') Wall or whether a tunnel may be drilled under the Temple Mount.

In some respects the Jerusalem question bears comparison with the Roman question, which famously agitated European diplomacy and engaged the anxious attention of European chancelleries for more than half a century. When the modern Kingdom of Italy was established by a mixture of war and diplomacy in 1861, Rome, which remained under the temporal authority of the Pope, did not form part of the new national state; papal sovereignty was protected by a French garrison until the eve of the collapse of the second French empire in 1870. On 20 September 1870 Italian troops entered the city, thus completing and crowning the Risorgimento. Thereafter the eternal city became the capital of a kingdom which the Pope, an Italian and religious leader of nearly all Italians, refused to recognize. As a result, successive Popes remained virtual prisoners in the Vatican until the conclusion of the Lateran Treaty of 11 February 1929, which for the first time established a basis of mutual recognition between the (by that time fascist) Kingdom of Italy and the sovereign Vatican state.

The Roman, like the Jerusalem, question involved issues of spiritual and temporal authority, of the disputed location of the capital of a new nation state, of the connection between a holy city and universal faith. The love-hate relationship between the leaders of the Risorgimento and Rome compares in many respects with the mixture of disgust and pride in Jerusalem that animated early Zionists. *Mutatis mutandis*, Giuseppe Mazzini's justification of the defence of the Roman Republic in 1849, might have been uttered by the Israeli Prime Minister David Ben Gurion at the time of the Arab siege of Israeli Jerusalem a century later:

As the seat of a form of faith now extinct, and only
outwardly sustained by hypocrisy and persecution ... her
people, although full of noble and manly pride,
necessarily ignorant ... Rome was regarded by some with
aversion, by others with disdainful indifference. A few
individual exceptions apart, the Romans had never shared
that ferment, that desire for liberty which had constantly
agitated Romagna and the Marches. It was therefore
essential to redeem Rome; to place her once again at the
summit, so that Italians might again learn to regard her as
the temple of their common country.[3]

Substitute Tel Aviv and the Valley of Jezreel for Romagna and the
Marches, the Temple Mount for the Vatican and the 'old *yishuv*' (the
pre-Zionist Jewish community in Palestine) for the Roman establishment so despised by Mazzini, and you have a precise statement of the
early Zionist attitude to Jerusalem.

Yet the striking parallels between the Roman and Jerusalem questions are outweighed by the differences. In the case of Rome it was a
matter of one religion and one Church; the Jerusalem question concerns three religions and multiplicities of sects, particularly of Christianity. In the case of Rome, a single state faced a single religious
potentate; several states have claimed rights in Jerusalem over the
past century. And by contrast with the Pope's divisions defending the
Vatican, few but relatively disciplined, the cause of Jerusalem has mobilized imposing formations of feuding muftis, rabbis and Christian
clerics. Above all, of course, Jerusalem, even more than Rome, lies at
the heart of a political conflict that, beyond its own inhabitants, has
engaged great human masses across many continents.

Jerusalem today is more than ever a divided city. If any doubt remained over the hollowness of Israeli claims since 1967 to have unified the city under its exclusive sovereignty, that was finally expunged
by the eruption of the 'al-Aqsa *intifada*' on 28 September 2000. After

that date the invisible curtain between Arab and Jewish districts of the city redescended, Palestinian and Israeli peacemakers were cowed or overwhelmed by the cacophony of hate-mongers, and politicians on both sides resumed their old habits of talking past rather than to each other. Whether all this was a temporary false turning or part of a deeper historical logic remains undetermined. What is certain, and what this book seeks to demonstrate, is that the struggle for Jerusalem can be resolved only when there dawns some genuine recognition of the reality and legitimacy of its plural character, spiritually, demographically and – all claims to sole possession notwithstanding – politically.

Psychiatrists who know the city have diagnosed a 'Jerusalem syndrome' that afflicts visitors (and some writers on the subject), leading them into soaring flights of fancy and endowing them with delusions of mystical experiences and powers. Of course, it must be recognized that, as one exasperated diplomat put it in 1967, 'Jerusalem is not just a problem, it's an *emotion*.'[4] Above all, it has been an object of religious emotion. Veneration for Jerusalem by Jews, Christians and Muslims runs deep and it is the duty of the historian to notice and record that – to record but not to succumb. Much of what has been written about Jerusalem over the centuries has been inspired by religious fervour. The sincere faith of multitudes of Muslims, Christians and Jews has often been shabbily exploited, both in polemical literature and in daily life, for brazen political ends. One of the central purposes of this book is to demonstrate how Jerusalem as 'an emotion' has been instrumentalized by politicians of all religions – as well as by those 'of no particular faith', as the Welsh Baptist David Lloyd George described his countrymen when justifying British rule in Jerusalem in 1917.

This is not a history of Jerusalem. Nor, *a fortiori*, is it a history of the Arab-Israeli conflict. This book seeks rather to isolate for special attention the 'question of Jerusalem' in international diplomacy. I have dealt with the internal political, social and demographic history of the city only to the limited extent necessary for an understanding of the diplomatic issues. Jerusalem today is at the core of continuing negotiations between Israel and the Palestinian Arabs and of the larger Arab-Israeli relationship. But it has been on the international diplomatic agenda at least since the second quarter of the nineteenth century. Why is the question of Jerusalem so apparently insoluble? Why has it outlasted even the intractable Roman question as a focus for international wrangling? What are the different elements of it that have entangled so many powers and interests? What is the explanation for the profound divisions among the different groups in the city's population. Can these ever be overcome? These are the issues that this book sets out to address.

Acknowledgements

Some parts of this book were delivered, in an embryonic version, as the Sherman Lectures at Manchester University in May 1998. I am very grateful to Professor Philip Alexander for his invitation to deliver those lectures.

I have been fortunate over the past two decades in enjoying financial support for my research on this subject from a number of bodies: the United States Information Agency, the British Academy, the University of Sheffield Research Fund, the American Philosophical Society and the Brandeis University Sachar Fund all awarded me small grants at the early stages of the project. Two major grants, from the United States National Endowment for the Humanities and the American Council of Learned Societies, helped move work forward during sabbatical years. Brandeis University, the Oxford Centre for Hebrew and Jewish Studies and the University of Glasgow provided substantial further aid.

My research also benefited from the hospitality and facilities made available by many institutions of learning. Much of the work was conducted while I was a Faculty Associate of the Center for Middle East Studies at Harvard University between 1983 and 1993 and I want to express my appreciation of the support I received there. My investigations in the Ottoman archives in Istanbul were made possible by a period of residence at the American Research Institute in Turkey. I am also grateful to All Souls College, Oxford, where I worked on this subject as a Visiting Fellow in 1995, and to the Middle East Centre at St Antony's College, Oxford, with which I have enjoyed fruitful intellectual connections for many years. In addition to the archives and repositories listed in the sources, I particularly wish to thank Brandeis

University Library, the British Institute of Archaeology in Ankara, the Institute for Jewish Policy Research, the Jewish National and University Library in Jerusalem, the University of Glasgow Library, Pusey House Library, Oxford, and the Mitchell Library, Glasgow. Mr Mike Shand of the University of Glasgow's cartography unit drew all the maps.

My publisher, Andrew Franklin, has been a source of perpetual encouragement and infectious enthusiasm. Penny Daniel and Lesley Levene helped turn the manuscript into publishable form. Bruce Hunter of David Higham Associates, my literary agent, is without peer in his profession. My indebtedness to individual experts and colleagues is so great that I hope that they will forgive me if I express gratitude to them collectively rather than to each individually. It is no less heartfelt for that. I must, however, pay special tribute to the contribution of two citizens of Jerusalem, my mother and sister, who hunted down errors and infelicities, and helped in many other ways. My greatest debt is to my brother, Professor David Wasserstein of Tel Aviv University, who read and commented on the manuscript before it went to press and from whose advice and wide-ranging scholarship I benefited at every stage.

List of Tables

1 Population of Jerusalem by religion (1563–1995)   46
2 Participation of east Jerusalem Palestinians
  in municipal elections (1969–93)   221
3 Population of old city of Jerusalem (1914–99)   347
4 Population of old city of Jerusalem by quarter (1997)   351

List of Maps

1 Late Ottoman administrative divisions in Palestine 67
2 The Sykes-Picot plan (1916) 73
3 Palestine under the British mandate 91
4 Royal Commission partition plan for Palestine (1937) 111
5 Jewish Agency partition plan for Jerusalem (1937) 113
6 Sir William Fitzgerald's proposal for Jerusalem (1945) 123
7 United Nations partition plan for Palestine (1947) 129
8 United Nations *Corpus Separatum* plan for Jerusalem (1947) 130
9 Israel (1949–67) 166
10 Divided Jerusalem (1949–67) 168
11 Jerusalem since 1967 214
12 Jerusalem: the old city 321

Prologue   The Heavenly City

Jerusalem, we are often told, is a holy city to three world religions. But the holiness of Jerusalem is neither a constant nor an absolute. It may be conceived as divinely inspired or as a human attribution. What is undeniable is that, considered as a historical phenomenon, the city's sanctity has waxed and waned according to social, economic and cultural conditions, and, perhaps above all, political influences.

Three religions, Judaism, Christianity and Islam, claim to venerate Jerusalem as holy – and no doubt the adherents of each make the claim with full sincerity and zeal. But in the case of the first, religious devotion did not carry with it, until very recently, a demand for restoration of sovereignty. As for the two successor faiths, of each it can be demonstrated that the holiness of Jerusalem was a late historical development rather than present *ab initio*. In all three cases, the dispassionate observer is compelled by the evidence to conclude that the city's sanctity arose as much from political as from purely spiritual sources.

Jerusalem of the Jews

Two Jewish voices. The first is that of Ananus, the oldest of the priests of Jerusalem on the eve of the destruction of the Second Temple in the year 70. According to the account of his contemporary Josephus, Ananus, speaking with tears in his eyes and casting his eyes towards the Temple, which had been seized by the party of Jewish extremists known as Zealots, said: 'Certainly it had been good for me to die before seeing the house of God full of so many abominations, or those sacred places that ought not to be trodden upon at random filled with the feet of these blood-shedding villains.'[1] The second voice is that of the proto-Zionist Moshe Leib Lilienblum. Writing in 1882 of the future Jewish state in Palestine, he declared, 'We do not need the walls of Jerusalem, nor the Jerusalem temple, nor Jerusalem itself.'[2] Two Jewish voices, two Jewish views of Jerusalem.

The Jewish presence in the Holy Land may, as we are often told, have remained continuous throughout the period between the end of the second Jewish Commonwealth and the rise of Zionism. The contention is sometimes extended to an allegedly continuous Jewish presence in Jerusalem: for example, the first President of Israel, Chaim Weizmann, in a speech in Jerusalem in 1948, referred to 'the unbroken chain of Jewish settlement in this city'.[3] And a public statement issued by the Israeli Foreign Ministry on 14 March 1999 claimed that 'the Jewish presence in Jerusalem remained constant and enduring'. Whatever the truth of such a claim for Palestine in general, the evidence for it in the case of Jerusalem is questionable. Jews were forbidden even to enter the city throughout the periods of Roman and Byzantine rule.[4] Although some Jewish pilgrims appear to have visited it, there is no evidence of a Jewish community there between the second and the seventh centuries.

Jews resumed residence in Jerusalem after the first Arab conquest of the city in 638. A number of documents in the Cairo *geniza* (a store of old manuscripts uncovered at the end of the nineteenth century) record financial contributions by Jews in Egypt, Syria and Sicily towards the support of poor Jews and towards the maintenance of a synagogue next to the Western ('Wailing') Wall in Jerusalem.[5] Such dependence on outside financial support was to become a characteristic feature of Jerusalem's Jewish community until the early twentieth century.

When the Crusaders conquered Jerusalem in 1099, the Jews were once more thrown out of the city.[6] Only after 1260, under the government, based in Egypt, of the Mamluk Sultans, did they slowly return – although they came into conflict with Christians particularly over Mount Zion. The conquest of the city by the Ottoman Turks in 1516 created conditions for secure Jewish settlement and slow demographic growth. But in the seventeenth century the estimated Jewish population was still only a thousand souls, perhaps 10 per cent of the population. In that period the main centre of Jewish life, certainly of Jewish intellectual life, in Palestine was not Jerusalem but Safed. For a long time in the eighteenth century Jewish bachelors and persons under sixty were forbidden by the Jewish 'Istanbul Committee' to settle in Jerusalem. The object of the ban was to limit the size of the community, which, it was feared, would otherwise be too large to support.[7] The earliest community records of the Jews in Jerusalem, as distinct from records elsewhere about them, date from no earlier than the eighteenth century. As Jacob Barnai has written, 'The lack of material reflects the lack of organic continuity in these communities during the late Middle Ages and the Ottoman period.'[8]

Yet if Jewish settlement in Jerusalem for much of the pre-modern period was sparse and patchy, Jerusalem has nevertheless always been central to the thought and symbolism of Judaism: the resting place of its holy tabernacle, the site of its temple, the capital of its monarchy, the subject of lamentation from the year 70 down to our own time. Jews faced Jerusalem when they prayed. They called it 'the navel of the earth'. Biblical literature, halakha (Jewish law), aggada (non-legal rabbinic teaching), tefilla (liturgy), kabbala (mystical writings), haskala (the Hebrew enlightenment of the eighteenth and nineteenth centuries) and Jewish folklore all celebrated Jerusalem's ancient glory and mourned its devastation. In medieval Spain Yehuda Halevi and Shlomo ibn Gvirol wrote poignant verses expressive of yearning for Jerusalem. In eastern Europe a picture of Jerusalem traditionally hung on the eastern wall of the Jewish house. In our own day Shmuel Yosef Agnon rejoiced in the renewal of Jewish creativity in the city whose 'hills spread their glory like banners to the sky'. Throughout the ages Jerusalem remained the foremost destination of Jewish pilgrimage. Above all, Jerusalem carried for Jews an overwhelming symbolic freight as the focus of messianic hope and the locus of the imminently expected resurrection.

At the same time, Judaism differentiated between the heavenly Jerusalem (*Yerushalayim shel ma'lah*) and the earthly or everyday one (*shel matah*). Religious devotion to the city was not regarded as involving any duty to regain Jewish sovereignty over it. Indeed, when the idea of such a restoration first began to be discussed in the nineteenth century, the dominant strain of religious opinion was strongly opposed. This remained true until the destruction of the religious heartland of Jewry, located in eastern Europe, between 1939 and 1945. At least until then, most orthodox Jewish authorities opposed Zionism as a blasphemous anticipation of the divine eschatological plan. And on this point they found common cause with most early leaders of Reform Judaism – though the two groups would have shrunk with horror from any thought of commonality. Orthodox Zionists were a relatively insignificant stream within the Zionist movement – and equally so within orthodox Judaism. Zionism, until long after the establishment of the state of Israel in 1948, remained predominantly and often aggressively secular.

Early Zionist thinkers generally avoided attributing special importance to Jerusalem. The exponent of 'spiritual' Zionism, Ahad Ha-am, was repelled by his first encounter with the Jews of Jerusalem in 1891; when he later moved to Palestine, he chose rather to settle in Tel Aviv. The founder of political Zionism, Theodor Herzl, was shocked by Jerusalem's filth and stench when he first visited it in 1898.[9] When Arthur Ruppin set up the Zionist Organization's first Palestine Office in 1908, he did so in Jaffa, not Jerusalem. The early Zionist settlers in Palestine from the 1880s onwards, and particularly the socialist Zionists, who arrived in large numbers after 1904, looked down on Jerusalem and all it stood for in their eyes by way of obscurantism, religiosity and squalor. In particular, they despised what they saw as the parasitism of Jerusalem's Jews and their dependence on the *halukah* (charitable dole) from co-religionists in Europe and north America.[10] David Ben Gurion, who was later, as Israeli Prime Minister, to declare Jerusalem Israel's capital, did not bother to visit it until three years after his immigration to Palestine.

Modern Hebrew literature too contained deeply contradictory tendencies regarding Jerusalem: in the last two decades of the nineteenth century writers of the *ahavat Zion* (love of Zion) school tended to extol Jerusalem and sing its praises; modernist poets and novelists from Haim Nahman Bialik onwards took a more harshly realistic view. In the first half of the twentieth century, a stream of writing hostile to Jerusalem, loathing it, demystifying it, even stressing its irrelevance (Yosef Haim Brenner, Nathan Alterman, Avraham Shlonsky, the early Uri Zvi Greenberg), shaped a profoundly negative view of Jerusalem in the Hebrew literary imagination.[11] Of course, this was only one stream of thought – but in its time perhaps the most influential and truly expressive of the Zionist revolution against Jewish traditionalism.

Thus spiritual values exalting Jerusalem competed with, and were overshadowed by, other religious, social, political and intellectual forces in forming the ambivalent modern Jewish view of Jerusalem.

Jerusalem of the Christians

Two Christian voices. First, St Jerome (337–420), who went on pilgrimage to the Holy Land and spent the last thirty-four years of his life in a monastery in Bethlehem. He argued that it was part of the Christian faith 'to adore where His feet have stood and to see the vestiges of the nativity, of the Cross, and of the passion'.[12] The second voice is that of St Gregory of Nyssa (fourth century), who wrote to a disciple, 'When the Lord invites the blest to their inheritance in the Kingdom of Heaven, he does not include a pilgrimage to Jerusalem among their good deeds.'[13] Two Christian voices; two Christian views of Jerusalem.

For Christians the sanctity of Jerusalem derives wholly from the events associated with the life, death and resurrection of the Saviour in that city. Historically speaking, however, there is no evidence of any particular sanctity attached to Jerusalem by Christians until the fourth century and it is only then that we encounter the first recorded account of a Christian pilgrimage to Jerusalem.

Recent scholarship has focused on the ecclesiastical struggle in fourth-century Christianity between those who affirmed the holiness of Jerusalem and those who tended to play it down. As P. W. L. Walker writes, 'Jerusalem and the "holy places" showed from the outset that, despite their capacity to be focuses for Christian unity, they also had great potential for division.'[14] Walker lays stress on the 'largely negative and dismissive' views of Eusebius, metropolitan bishop of Caesarea (c. 260–339), regarding Jerusalem's holiness. Eusebius' opinion may have derived in part from competition between his episcopal see and that of Jerusalem.[15] Beyond that, it has been argued, his view was born out of a desire to combat an incorrect emphasis on the physical, earthly Jerusalem – an error attributed to the Jews.[16]

By contrast, and in opposition to Eusebius, Bishop Cyril of Jerusalem (c. 320–c. 386) maintained that the 'prerogative of all good things was in Jerusalem'.[17] This became, indeed, a dominant view in the Church. Just as Eusebius' somewhat negative view of Jerusalem has been connected to his attitude towards Jews, the more affirmative Christian attitude to Jerusalem in the early Middle Ages was also bound up with hostility to the Jews: 'The complete destruction of Jewish Jerusalem and its transformation into a Christian city, with the resultant expulsion, dispersion and subjugation of the Jews, was seen as a Divine punishment and as an essential stage on mankind's road to complete salvation.'[18] The triumph of the Christian theological view of Jerusalem's holiness was, however, an outcome not only of debate among the Church Fathers but of the political triumph of the Emperor Constantine, who ruled Jerusalem from 324. The celebrated journey of his mother, Helena, to Jerusalem to identify the sites of the crucifixion and resurrection marked a critical turning point in the

Christian history of the city. The Anastasis (later known as the Church of the Holy Sepulchre), erected over the tomb at Constantine's command and inaugurated in 335, replaced a temple to Aphrodite at the same location. Like so many other holy places and shrines in Jerusalem, the Anastasis thus from its very outset gave physical expression to competitive religious spirit – in this case between Christianity and paganism.

With Helena's visit, Jerusalem became firmly established as a centre of veneration and pilgrimage for Christians. The *Itinerarium Burdigalense*, an account of a pilgrimage to Jerusalem from Bordeaux in 333, is one of the earliest examples of what became a common literary genre. Christian glorification of Jerusalem was briefly challenged in 363, when the pagan emperor Julian the Apostate proposed to rebuild the Jewish Temple in Jerusalem. But after his death in battle later that year it resumed with even greater momentum. It was in full flood by the last two decades of the century when Egeria, probably a Spanish nun, wrote a narrative of her pilgrimage to Jerusalem – still widely read today.

External financial support for Christian institutions in Jerusalem, as for Jewish ones, is a long-standing feature of the city's history, extending back in the case of the Christians to the Byzantine period. During the first period of Muslim rule over the city, non-Muslims almost certainly still formed a majority of the population of the city. At one point in the early Arab period there is even said to have been a Christian governor of the province. On Christmas Day 800, coronation day of Charlemagne in Rome, the new emperor is reported to have received the key to the Church of the Holy Sepulchre and the flag of the holy city as tokens of respect from the Patriarch of Jerusalem (or, according to another account, from the Muslim Caliph Harun al-Rashid). Charlemagne and his son Louis built a number of new Christian institutions in Jerusalem. This new construction work gave rise to some conflict. In 827, for example, Muslims complained that Christians had built a bigger dome over a church than that over the Muslim shrine of the Dome of the Rock. Similarly, competition in pilgrimages, a feature of religious and commercial life in the city throughout the ages and into modern times, is recorded very early. These pilgrimages and the holy days with which they were associated were frequently occasions of communal violence. On Palm Sunday 937 or 938 a Christian procession was attacked and the Church of the Holy Sepulchre was burnt to the ground. On Pentecost in 966 a number of churches were pillaged and on 28 September 1009 the Holy Sepulchre was again destroyed by order of the mad Caliph al-Hakim. It was not rebuilt until 1048.

The conquest of Jerusalem by the Crusader forces of Godfrey de Bouillon on 15 July 1099 inaugurated a new period of terror against Muslims and Jews, all of whom were driven out of the city, their mosques and synagogues destroyed.[19] The Muslim shrines on the Temple Mount were turned into Christian churches. The Latin kings carved the city into separate districts based on the nationality of the Christian settlers, the knightly orders and the various eastern Christian communities. The Orthodox Patriarch was packed off to Constantinople and the Latins – that is, Roman Catholics – assumed the *praedominium* (right of pre-eminence) over the holy places.

After the final ejection of the Crusaders from Jerusalem in 1244, Christians were compelled to translate their conception of Jerusalem from an earthly to a heavenly sphere. Christian pilgrimages, however, continued: Chaucer's Wife of Bath went to Jerusalem three times. And books of *Laudes Hierosolymitanae* (praises of Jerusalem) were produced in large quantities. The Christian struggle for Jerusalem now assumed a new form. Having lost the war against the Infidel, Christians embarked on a war against each other. This internecine conflict had indeed begun earlier, in 1204, when the Fourth Crusade sacked Constantinople.

Now began in earnest the great contest between the eastern and western Churches for control of the holy places, above all the Church of the Holy Sepulchre in Jerusalem and the Church of the Nativity in

Bethlehem. Unable to agree among themselves, the squabbling Christian sects were compelled by the Muslim authorities in or before 1289 to hand over the keys of the Church of the Holy Sepulchre to a Muslim family for safekeeping. When the last Crusader fortress in Palestine, at Acre, fell in 1291, the only remaining Latin institutional presence in Palestine was that of the Franciscans, who had first arrived in 1217. In the early fourteenth century, the Pope appointed them to the 'Custody of the Holy Land' (*Custodia Terrae Sanctae*). This little outpost of Roman Christianity saw as its primary task the battle against the pretensions of the eastern Churches to proprietorship of the holy places. It fought by every means to uphold the enduring rights in Jerusalem of the true Rome. The fight carried on into modern times and, in modified form, endures still. It coloured every aspect of Christian life in Jerusalem, as well as the diplomacy of the Christian powers in relation to the holy city.

Thus for Christians, as for Jews, though in different ways, Jerusalem was both a symbol of unity and a fault line of profound internal schism.

Jerusalem of the Muslims

Two Muslim traditions. The first is a statement attributed to the Prophet Muhammad, according to which he said, 'He who performs the pilgrimage to Mecca and visits my grave [in Medina] and goes forth to fight [in a holy war] and prays for me in Jerusalem – God will not ask him about what he [failed to perform of the prescriptions] imposed on him.'

The second tradition concerns Umar, the second Muslim Caliph, who reigned at the time of the first Muslim conquest of Jerusalem in 638. Umar, it is said, was in a camel enclosure when two men passed by. He asked where they came from and they said Jerusalem. Umar hit them with his whip and said, 'Have you performed a pilgrimage like the pilgrimage to the Kaaba [in Mecca]?' They said, 'No, O

Commander of the Faithful, we came from such and such a territory and passed [Jerusalem] by and prayed there.' To which Umar said, 'Then so be it', and let them go.[20] Two Muslim voices; two Muslim views of Jerusalem.

For Muslims the holiness of Jerusalem derives primarily from its identification with the 'further mosque' (al-masjid al-aqsa), mentioned in the Quran as the place to which the Prophet was carried on his 'night journey' from Mecca. From here he ascended to the seventh heaven.

There is some evidence, however, to suggest that the attribution of sanctity to Jerusalem was, at least in part, connected to the city's central position in the two precursor religions that Islam claimed to supersede. According to Muslim tradition, Jerusalem was the first qibla (the direction of prayer) before it was changed to Mecca in 624. The practice is not attested in the Quran but it is engrained in Muslim tradition – and survived in the practice of occasional elderly worshippers in the Dome of the Rock in Jerusalem within living memory (as witnessed by the present author in 1969).

In the earliest period of Islam there appears to have been a tendency to emphasize the holiness of Mecca and Medina and to stress the importance of pilgrimages to those cities rather than to Jerusalem. There were also, however, some contrary views and it was not until the second Islamic century (719–816 of the Christian era) that a general acceptance developed of the holiness of all three cities.[21] A decisive point came during the Caliphate of Abd al-Malik b. Marwan (685–705): he was engaged in conflict with a rival Caliph, Abd Allah b. al-Zubayr, who was installed at Mecca. Abd al-Malik built Jerusalem's most impressive surviving religious monument, the Dome of the Rock – often wrongly called the 'Mosque of Umar': it is, in fact, a shrine, not a mosque, and has nothing to do with Umar. One authority has argued that the Dome of the Rock was not merely a memorial to the ascension of the Prophet: 'Its extensive inscriptions indicate that it is a victory monument commemorating triumph over the Jewish and Christian religions.'[22] The great orientalist Ignaz Goldziher argued that Abd al-Malik's motive in building the shrine and reaffirming the city's sanctity was to compete with the rival Meccan Caliph and divert the pilgrim trade to his own dominions.[23] This view has been widely accepted, although S. D. Goitein disagreed, suggesting that Abd al-Malik's object was to create a structure that could match the magnificent churches of Jerusalem and other Syrian towns.[24] What unites all these interpretations is the attribution of an underlying competitive motive to the Caliph. The Arabic name of the city, al-Quds ('the Holy'), first appears only in the late tenth century.[25]

Surprisingly, the conquest of Jerusalem by the Crusaders was greeted at first by Muslim indifference rather than fervour for its recapture. Even those Muslims who called for a holy war against the invading Franks refrained, with few exceptions, from stressing the sanctity of Jerusalem – which seems in this period to have been neither widely diffused nor deeply implanted in Muslim thought.[26] A change of attitude emerges only in the mid-twelfth century – as so often in the history of Jerusalem, heightened religious fervour may be explained in large measure by political necessity. In the 1140s Zenki, ruler of Mosul and Aleppo, with his son and successor Nur al-Din, called for an all-out war against the Crusader state. Their official propagandists consequently placed a sudden new emphasis on the holiness of Jerusalem in Islam. This tendency was further accentuated under the leadership of Saladin who used the sanctity of Jerusalem as a means of cowing potential opponents. In the late twelfth century the idea of the holy city was invoked no less in internal Muslim quarrels than in the external conflict with Christendom.[27] The Muslim reconquest of Jerusalem, on 2 October 1187, was greeted with an outburst of enthusiasm and rejoicing in the Islamic world. Saladin's victory was hailed in letters, poems and messages of congratulation. During the following years the existing literature in praise of Jerusalem (*Fadail Bayt al-Maqdis*) was hugely amplified and extended. Muslims were encouraged to resettle there and to go on pilgrimage.

Returning pilgrims carried to their homes the concept of the sanctity of Jerusalem. 'Intimately connected to the idea of *jihad* [holy war], [it] acquired a place of honour in the religious consciousness of pietist circles and popular strata.'[28]

Henceforth Muslim rule over the city came to be regarded as a veritable act of faith. In 1191 Saladin wrote to Richard the Lionheart, in the course of armistice negotiations, that even if he were personally disposed to yield the city, the crusading English king 'should not imagine that its surrender would be possible; I would not dare even to utter the word in front of the Muslims.'[29] Jerusalem was nevertheless returned to the Christians by the Treaty of Jaffa in 1229. Under this agreement, Jerusalem, Bethlehem and Nazareth were handed over to the Holy Roman Emperor, Frederick II, though the Muslims were permitted to retain their holy places there. At the same time the walls of the city were demolished in order that it would no longer serve as a fortified point. The result was that for many years it was vulnerable to military attack and to raids from nomads. The treaty was to last for ten years. After that, fighting broke out again and in 1244 the city was sacked by invading Kharezmian Tartars. Only after 1260 was order restored under the Mamluks.

Under Mamluk rule Jerusalem was not a place of any political importance.[30] The division of the city into four quarters – Muslim, Christian, Jewish and Armenian – had its origins in this period. Islamic institutions were established and the Muslim character of the city enhanced, though, unlike the Christians, Muslims tolerated the presence of other faiths. Religious groups tended to settle around their most important shrines and holy places: Muslims north and west of the Haram al-Sharif (literally 'noble sanctuary' – the name given to the Temple Mount), Armenians in the south-west near their Cathedral of St James, the other Christians in the north-west near the Holy Sepulchre and the Jews in the south near the Western Wall. By the dawn of the modern era, divided Jerusalem was a geographical as well as a spiritual fact.

So we see that within Judaism, Christianity and Islam there have been countervailing positive and negative tendencies regarding Jerusalem – and in each case political considerations have played a significant part in the affirmation or qualification of Jerusalem's holiness. Competition among the faiths has repeatedly focused on Jerusalem. Each tried to outbid the other two in claiming Jerusalem as a central religious symbol, often by means of hyperbolic special pleading. Yet each religion has been ambivalent or fractured in its relationship to Jerusalem, its degree of holiness, its holy places and its function in this world and the next. These lines of division determined the history of the earthly city in the modern period. They form the subject of this book.

1   The Wars of the Consuls

Divided Jerusalem is a product of external pressures at least as much as of internal dynamics. Above all, it is a product of competition among the great powers to gain and extend authority in and through the holy city. While they sought an intangible, sometimes almost metaphysical prestige, they used what were often crude methods of influence-building: exploitation of religious sentiment, patronage of local protégés, construction of dependent institutions – churches, monasteries, convents, hospitals, orphanages, schools and colleges. By the mid-nineteenth century they had created a quasi-imperial regime in which their local agents, the consuls, acquired the status of virtual colonial governors, each exercising power over his own nationals, institutions and protected persons, each waging an unceasing struggle against both the Ottoman government and rivals in the consular corps.

When it was captured by the Ottoman Turks in late 1516, Jerusalem was an obscure, provincial backwater with a population of fewer than 15,000. Under the Ottomans for the next four centuries, as under their predecessors, it was not a major administrative centre. For much of the period it was the capital of a district (*sanjak*) that formed part of the province of Damascus. Under the rule of the Sultan Sulayman I ('the Magnificent', 1520–66), Jerusalem's greatest secular monument, the girdle of walls around the city, was built – or rather rebuilt. This huge protective shield, still almost intact today, enabled the Ottomans to resist invaders and defend the city against bedouin attacks from the neighbouring countryside. The walls defined the contours of the city until the late nineteenth century and the Ottomans attached great importance to their maintenance. One reason for this that has been advanced is that they feared a renewal of Crusader-type attacks by European powers.[1]

Although Muslims had ruled Jerusalem for more than 700 of the previous 900 years, the city had never acquired an exclusively Islamic character. Under the Ottomans, the various sects continued to huddle together in their separate areas, although it was not until the nineteenth century that these crystallized into the quarter divisions familiar today (see Map 12, page 321). The notion of quarters was geographical rather than mathematical: the Muslim quarter was by far the largest in area and until around the start of the nineteenth century Muslims remained an absolute majority of the population. A government survey in 1560 showed 1,933 Muslim, 281 Christian and 237 Jewish heads of houses in the city.[2] The quarters should not be thought of as hermetically sealed; there were no physical markers separating them and residence was to some extent mixed. Muslims, in particular, lived in all four quarters.[3]

Religious groups in Ottoman Jerusalem tended to conduct their own affairs and administer their institutions with little interference from the government. Although the system of *millets* (autonomous communities, organized on an empire-wide basis throughout the realm) was not fully formed and so named until the nineteenth century, its essence in local administration could be observed as early as the sixteenth.[4] Christians and Jews suffered from a number of discriminatory laws and in a sense were second-class citizens. But they had a recognized status in society and to a certain degree could rely on the protection of the law.

The holy places

The Jerusalem question in its modern form first emerged as a by-product of the slow meltdown of the Ottoman Empire. Its central feature in its first phase was the struggle over the Christian holy places. Although French traders appeared in the coastal plain in the early seventeenth century, trading links with Europe and other external influences remained minimal until the late Ottoman period. Nevertheless, the beginnings of international, that is primarily Christian, diplomatic interest in Jerusalem can be traced as far back as the first years of Ottoman rule. Among the earliest *firmans* (decrees) issued by Sulayman I were several guaranteeing the rights and privileges of Christians. A *firman* of 1521, for example, dispatched to the governor of Jerusalem, states that 'the community of religious and other kinds of infidel currently residing in Jerusalem' have complained 'that certain individuals have been oppressing and overly interfering with them, preventing them from following their ceremonies according to their ancient custom'. The governor was ordered to look into the matter and prevent such harassment in the future.[5]

The object of the central government seems to have been the natural one of maintaining civil order in an area of mixed religious population, this at a time when the Ottomans were still taking their first steps towards administrative absorption of their new provinces. Yet even at this early stage external as well as internal influences played a role. Succeeding *firmans* go some way towards clarifying the nature of the nuisances allegedly suffered by Christians, the identities of victims and perpetrators, and, most importantly, the process by which such disputes came to the attention of the Sultan. A *firman* of 1525 notes a complaint that Christians in the Convent of Zion had been forcibly expelled from quarters and gardens they had long occupied. Another, of 1528, reports that the Venetian bailiff (diplomatic representative) at the Ottoman court had sought imperial intervention in favour of Latin Christians in the Church of the Holy Sepulchre, whose rights were being interfered with by Georgians. The following year we hear of 'certain individuals of the Arab nation' said to be bothering priests; and in 1536 we learn that the Venetian envoy had again intervened, this time accusing 'a Jew named Salomon and certain Christian hangers-on of the Georgian nation' of 'molesting and bothering' Latin Christians at the Convent of Zion. They were even said to be carrying away marble-work and columns from the Church of the Holy Sepulchre and other Christian sites.[6] No more is heard of the Jew Salomon but the theme of internecine Christian conflict remained audible throughout the next four centuries.

The very frequency of *firmans* enjoining the local governor to prevent such vexations is evidence that they continued – or, at any rate, that disputes remained unresolved. Out of such diplomatic representations arose the treaty system known as the Capitulations. The first capitulatory treaty was an agreement between Sulayman and King Francis I of France in 1535 whereby French merchants were granted certain privileges in the Ottoman Empire. That treaty did not mention Jerusalem or the holy places. But in 1542 France and Turkey signed a formal treaty of alliance and, during the long war of the Turks against the Holy Roman Emperor and Venice, the French took over from the Venetians the role of protectors of the Latin Christians in the Holy Land. In 1572, after the Battle of Lepanto, in which the Turks suffered a crushing naval defeat by the allied Christian fleet of Don John of Austria, the Franciscans in Jerusalem were arrested and taken as prisoners to Damascus. It was the intervention of the king of France that secured their release.

The first capitulatory treaty to mention Jerusalem was signed with France in 1604 by the Sultan Ahmed I. In this he agreed that subjects of the French king and of his allies might 'visit under his protection freely the holy places of Jerusalem without any hindrance being put in their way'. The treaty added that 'the monks who live in Jerusalem and serve in the Church of the Holy Sepulchre of our Lord Jesus Christ may stay there and come and go securely without trouble or disturbance'.[7] These treaty obligations were faithfully reflected in further directives issued by the emperor to his officials. No fewer than thirty-three *firmans* concerned with Jerusalem were issued between 1604 and 1621, attempting in particular to address renewed complaints from the Latins of 'usurpations' by Orthodox Armenians.

Evidently seeing in these monkish controversies a lever for influence-building, the French decided to send a permanent representative to Jerusalem. In 1621 the first consul of any foreign power in Jerusalem was appointed by Louis XIII. The king himself took a personal interest in the matter, writing to his ambassador in Constantinople, 'I have considered it appropriate, for the glory of God and the comfort of pious persons who go devoutly to visit the holy places, to appoint Mr Lempereur to exercise the responsibility of consul for the French nation in Jerusalem.'[8] The incident that precipitated this decision by the French king was an alleged assault on the rights of Latins by Armenians, who had taken the daring step of hanging and lighting two lamps in the Grotto of the Nativity in Bethlehem.

Jean Lempereur, a Parisian lawyer who had previously visited Jerusalem as a pilgrim, wrote that the king defined his mandate as the defence of Cordeliers (Franciscan Recollects) and Catholic pilgrims visiting the holy places 'in order that they not be tyrannized and insulted by the Turks as they have been in the past'. Lempereur had secured the position through the good offices of his cousin, who was secretary to the Constable of France. He was provided with an allowance of 12,000 écus. The king did not, however, pay this sum himself. It was to be diverted from revenues of the abbeys of the Gallican Church: Lempereur was obliged to write to a Jesuit friend to ask for the intervention of the Pope to ensure that the money would actually be paid.[9]

Behind the appointment of the consul, and its financial arrangements, lurked political intrigue as well as purely spiritual motives. Its originators were Jesuits ambitious to oust the Franciscans from their position as sole representatives of the Roman Church in Jerusalem. Indeed, the Society of Jesus privately harboured even wider ambitions. They hoped, as Lempereur explained, to found a college in Jerusalem that would 'subjugate and re-establish in pristine splendour all the Christian schismatics, who have been altogether diverted from the true path'.[10] Lempereur realized the delicacy of introducing the Jesuits into territory that the Franciscans had hitherto regarded as peculiarly theirs. He therefore urged that the plan for a college be kept secret, pending his arrival in Jerusalem. The Jesuits secured the powerful support of Cardinal La Rochefoucauld, who recommended the project to the king. 'Don't worry at all about the Cordeliers,' the prelate reassured a Jesuit associate. 'They know very well that, if it came to it, I could find a way of ousting them from their position.'[11]

In order to pave the way for Lempereur, the king sent a special ambassador, Louis des Hayes, Baron de Courmenin, to visit Constantinople and Jerusalem. In the Turkish capital des Hayes threw his (or his royal master's) weight around in an imperious manner. By dint of unrelenting pressure, he secured letters from the Turkish government addressed to the governor of Jerusalem and the local mufti (an authoritative Muslim jurisconsult). Armed with these, he set out for the Holy Land. Upon landing at Jaffa, he sent word ahead to Jerusalem as to how he, as representative of the king of France, expected to be received. Word came back that officials in the holy city were much embarrassed. On the one hand, they wished to follow the instructions of their superiors; on the other, they felt obliged to point out that the law of the country forbade Christians to enter Jerusalem on horseback or bearing arms. Des Hayes had earlier planned (so he said) to enter the holy city on foot, but he now chose to regard this message as an affront to his monarch. He therefore insisted that he would arrive in Jerusalem on horseback and wearing his sword. In the event of any attempt to stop him, he would go back to Constantinople to lodge a complaint with the government and he assured the officials in Jerusalem that they 'would have occasion to repent'. The threat worked. As the French ambassador approached the holy city, the under-pasha met him to offer a choice of several horses for his ceremonial entrance. His sword flashing, des Hayes rode into the city on one of these mounts, 'to the great contentment of the resident Christians'. The Franciscans accompanied him in procession to their convent, where they sang a *Te Deum* for their deliverance from usurpation by the Armenians and persecution by the Turks. Their joy was to be short-lived.

During his stay in Jerusalem, des Hayes met the governor and other officials and presented his letters from the Ottoman authorities. He recorded that at first he had great difficulty in even being received, because the Armenians, 'foreseeing that the diplomacy of Mr des Hayes would lead to their ruin', had bribed the local officials with 30,000 *livres*. Moreover, the envoy's high-handed behaviour aroused murmurings among the Muslim populace. Nevertheless, the governor and the mufti acquiesced in his demands for the repair of the Church of the Holy Sepulchre, the removal of the Armenians from the holy places and their replacement by Franciscans, and the establishment of Lempereur's consulate.[12]

On his return to Paris, the ambassador congratulated himself on the success of his mission. In a letter to the General of the Jesuit Order, he also disclosed that he had entered into a secret agreement with a young Lebanese amir, Fakhr al-Din, who had earlier found refuge in Tuscany and was planning an attack on the Levant in alliance with Christian powers.[13] But it soon emerged that des Hayes's arrogant conduct and political intrigues had had a counter-productive effect on his Turkish hosts. Hardly was his back turned, than the Sultan issued a *firman* reaffirming the rights of Armenians over Franciscans at the holy places. The ordinance laid down that the Armenians 'should hold their vain ceremonies ... as *ab antiquo*; lighting their candles and suspending their lamps, and paying the dues of the *awqaf* [endowments]. Nobody, neither the Frankish nor any other community of the Christian subjects, should be allowed to interfere or intervene. They should not hinder them. Let this be known. Let them credit my noble sign.'[14]

Lempereur therefore found that, far from easing his path, des Hayes had, if anything, unwittingly queered his pitch. No sooner had Lempereur arrived in Jerusalem in December 1623 and ensconced himself in the Cordeliers' monastery than he quarrelled with his hosts, who ejected him from the building. The quarrel was partly financial, partly the result of the Franciscans' fear (for which, as we have seen, there was sound basis) that the consul would introduce Jesuits into the Holy Land. The Franciscans insisted that, as the recognized 'custodians' of the Holy Land, they had monopoly rights over Latin enterprises in the country. Lempereur also encountered bitter hostility from the Venetian ambassador in Constantinople and from the local Ottoman pasha in Jerusalem. The latter refused to be mollified by the Frenchman's presents and accused him of intriguing with a rebel chieftain in the vicinity. This accusation, as we have seen, was also well justified.

Lempereur's travails coincided and were connected with a landing on the coast of Palestine by Fakhr al-Din. Although defeated in battle near Jaffa, the ambitious amir remained a threat to Ottoman power in the region for several years thereafter. Lempereur was regarded with the utmost suspicion as an associate of the Lebanese and perhaps a spy. Within nine months of taking up his duties, having alienated almost everybody, the representative of the king of France suffered the indignity of being arrested, bundled up and escorted to Damascus as a prisoner. After five days of imprisonment, he bribed his way to freedom. He returned briefly to Jerusalem but failed to re-establish any kind of authority there. In January 1625 he retreated to Constantinople, where he spent the next thirty-five years as secretary of the French embassy – 'an occupation no doubt less perilous than that of consul in the holy city', as one of his twentieth-century successors later observed.[15]

Thus ignominiously ended the first European consular expedition to Jerusalem. Its main themes were to be replicated in subsequent missions over the next three centuries: overweening pride, political ambitions thinly disguised as spiritual, competition between western and eastern Churches and within the Churches, rows with rambunctious wards who balked at the cost to themselves of dubious 'protection', alliances with local rebels against imperial authority. The pattern of the future was set.

Over the following decades, repeated changes took place in control of the holy places as the Ottoman government was swayed by diplomatic winds blowing alternately from east or west. Again and again the Sultan issued *firmans* affirming the rights of this or that Church to this or that holy place. Between 1630 and 1637 alone the *praedominium* is said to have alternated between the Orthodox and the Latins six times.[16]

A successor to Lempereur was not appointed until 1699. The background to this appointment appears to have been commercial rather than spiritual, in particular a desire to ensure the smooth supply to French manufacturers of 'coton de Jérusalem' after a period of trading disruption.[17] Consul Brémond's first meeting with the pasha of Jerusalem, which took place in Acre, was remarkably friendly. The Ottoman official seemed the soul of friendliness and showered him with courtesies.[18] A ruder reception awaited him at the gate of Jerusalem in February 1700: he was challenged by the mufti, who, according to a Franciscan chronicler, shouted very loudly, objecting to the consul's presence and accusing him of being a spy. He had to spend his first night under the protection of his friend the pasha. The following morning, accompanied by thirty soldiers, he arrived at the Cordeliers' convent. There, however, he was greeted with no less suspicion than Lempereur, though the monks 'washed his feet like a pilgrim'. But within forty-eight hours an altercation over precedence erupted, with Brémond insisting that, as a royal envoy, he should sit in the place of honour at table and in church. The argument reached such a pitch that the consul was said to have threatened one of the monks with the bastinado (beating on the soles of the feet) and with 'tearing off the bristles of his beard'. In the course of time his relations with the Ottoman authorities likewise deteriorated. After six months the pasha confessed candidly that his earlier amiability had been motivated solely by hope of financial reward; this not being forthcoming, he ordered Brémond to leave town within three days. A fugitive, the consul took refuge in Bethlehem. While he was there, a demonstration of 'more than ten thousand people' took place on the

Haram al-Sharif, opposing any Christian consular presence in Jerusalem and threatening to turn in anger against the Cordeliers. The pasha ordered Brémond to leave the district altogether. Accompanied by a military escort, for which he was obliged to pay, he fled, losing most of his baggage and even his clothing on the way.[19]

In 1703 a major revolt erupted in Palestine. Rebels captured Jerusalem and locked the gates. They held out against an Ottoman siege for two years until hunger forced them to surrender. In such disturbed conditions no revival of the consulate could be contemplated. In the meantime, the War of the Spanish Succession convulsed Europe. It was not until 1713, just after the Peace of Utrecht, that a third French consul arrived – but he encountered no warmer a welcome than his predecessors. He remained just four months. From 1714 until 1843 the French abandoned the field altogether. The experiences of Lempereur and Brémond and the disputes that led to their downfalls sadly prefigured the struggles and tribulations of many later consuls of various nationalities in the city of peace.

In the course of the eighteenth century these conflicts gradually assumed a menacing diplomatic aspect, as Russia joined France in interesting herself in the Holy Land. Connected with the problem of the holy places was the larger issue of the non-Muslim communities in Jerusalem and, indeed, throughout the Ottoman Empire. In Jerusalem Christians and Jews were subject not only to the *jizya* (the special tax levied on non-Muslims) but to other discriminatory imposts on both individuals and institutions.[20] Russia adopted the role of defender of the eastern Orthodox Church, to which the majority of Palestinian Christians belonged. France, on the other hand, reaffirmed her traditional protection of the Latin Church in the Holy Land. The Latins, much weaker numerically in Palestine than the Orthodox, looked with ever more urgency to the French to redress the balance in their favour.

Meanwhile, the gradual retreat of the Turks from Europe led them to sign a series of treaties with Christian powers in which the patrons of the eastern and western Churches sought to insert advantages for their protégés in Jerusalem. In the Treaty of Carlowitz of 1699, signed following the Turks' defeat by Austria, Venice and Poland, the Catholic powers succeeded in gaining recognition of Latin rights at the holy places. These were confirmed in the Treaty of Passarowitz of 1718. French help for the Turks against Austria and Russia led to a further treaty in 1740 that confirmed Latin rights and in effect recognized France as protector of the Latins. This treaty represented, in Walter Zander's words, 'the high-water mark of French influence in the Ottoman Empire' and came to be regarded as 'a kind of Magna Carta of Latin rights'.[21]

Indeed, by this time, the contest for *praedominium* at the holy places, had become a hardy perennial on the international diplomatic agenda; rather like human rights today, it required ritual treatment in almost any major treaty. As the Catholic historian Paschal Baldi later put it:

> Thus the question of the holy places appeared as one of the great questions of European public right, in which the large Catholic nations considered themselves interested, in such a manner as to make it the object of special agreements with the Government of the Sublime Porte, each time there was question of the stipulation of truces, treaties of peace, pacts or mere commercial conventions.[22]

The existence of such treaties and the issuing of countless *firmans* did not, however, halt hostilities on the ground. These grew ever more serious, as may be seen from the following account of an incident in 1757.

> Incited and armed by their monks, the Greek mob, in the night preceding Palm Sunday, rushed into the basilica [of

the Holy Sepulchre] with clubs, maces, hooks, poniards
and swords; upset the candlesticks, rent the tapestries,
broke the lamps and reduced everything to pieces; then
turned towards the convent of the Minors to kill the poor
friars living there, who had to barricade the doors to
escape the violence of those malefactors 'excited by wine
and debauch'.[23]

This at any rate was the account of Baldi, still blazing with indigna-
tion a century and a half later. The Orthodox, of course, had a different version of the matter and they succeeded in persuading the
Ottoman government to issue a new *firman*, curtailing Latin rights.
The French ambassador's objections were brushed aside by the
Ottoman Grand Vizier with the cynical reflection, 'These places, Sir,
belong to the Sultan and he gives them to whom he pleases; it may
well be that they always were in the hands of the Franks, but today his
Highness wishes that they belong to the Greeks.'[24]

The Treaty of Küçük Kaynarca, signed by Russia and Turkey in
1774 after the Ottoman defeat by the army of Catherine the Great,
gave definitive expression to the Orthodox triumph over the Latins.
In article 7, the Ottoman government promised 'constant protection
to the Christian religion and to the churches of that religion'. Although the western Church retained some rights, the Orthodox were
clearly top dogs. They now had their own 'Magna Carta'.

For a moment, in 1799, when Napoleon led his army from Egypt
into Palestine, it looked as if Jerusalem might again fall under Christian rule. The young general conquered Jaffa, Ramleh and Acre, but
declared the holy city 'not on my line of march' and moved elsewhere
in pursuit of a higher destiny.[25] His English antagonist, Sir Sidney
Smith, by contrast, visited Jerusalem and marched in procession to
the Church of the Holy Sepulchre before, like Napoleon, returning to
his homeland. In themselves trivial, these episodes gave a first inkling
of later Anglo-French estrangements in the area.

In 1808 the Church of the Holy Sepulchre was burnt to the ground in a fire – malicious tongues among the Christian sects accused one another of responsibility. Although the government granted permission for rebuilding, Orthodox and Latins disputed the right to supervise reconstruction and some Muslims sought to prevent it altogether. The outbreak of the Greek war of independence in 1821 led to Muslim attacks on the Greek Orthodox Patriarchate in Jerusalem and there were further troubles, mounting to full-scale revolt. Rebels in the city were bombarded by cannons set up on the Mount of Olives and only the arrival, in 1826, of an Ottoman army, reinforced by bedouin of the Abu Ghosh tribe, quelled the rebellion.

Egyptian rule in Jerusalem

It was not until the 1830s, however, that Jerusalem was thrust forcefully on to the international diplomatic agenda. The precipitant was the conquest of Palestine from the Ottoman Sultan by his over-mighty vassal Muhammad Ali, ruler of Egypt. In December 1831 a 90,000-strong army commanded by Ibrahim, son of Muhammad Ali, entered Jerusalem. An Ottoman force held out in the citadel for a few months and local Muslim notables were at first unwilling to cooperate with the Egyptians. In April 1832 the mufti of Jerusalem was persuaded or coerced to join Ibrahim, but the rest of the Muslim religious hierarchy, fearful of losing their traditional privileges, remained hostile to the invaders.[26]

In 1834 a peasant revolt, based in Nablus but with support also from townspeople and notables in Jerusalem, drove Ibrahim's army out of the city. Among those involved in the revolt were two members of the notable Husayni family (in the next century to produce a number of Palestinian nationalist leaders). Some recent historians have seen this anti-Egyptian movement as a first stirring of Palestinian nationalism.[27] The immediate cause, however, was resistance to conscription. Nor is there any evidence of national feeling that transcended sectarian boundaries; on the contrary, strong hostility was manifested against Christians, who fled to monasteries, and to Jews.[28] The Egyptians reconquered Jerusalem after a short interval and held it in an iron grip with a garrison of 3,000 men, sufficient to overcome any potential resistance, until 1840.

Egyptian rule brought a modernizing spirit to the administration of the country. In Jerusalem this was felt particularly in the improved position of Christians, who were granted equality with Muslims and made eligible for official positions. For the first time since 1289 the three main Christian communities, Latin, Greek and Armenian, were given sets of keys to the Church of the Holy Sepulchre.[29] The position of Jews also improved, although some Jewish shops in Jerusalem were attacked by Muslims during the 1834 revolt.[30]

As Egyptian power grew, fear of total Ottoman collapse drew the European powers into competitive involvement. Britain emerged as the principal champion of the integrity of the Ottoman Empire, while France supported the upstart ruler of Egypt. In 1838 Britain established a consulate in Jerusalem. It used to be said that Lord Palmerston's purpose in doing so was the protection of Jews in Jerusalem, an objective strongly advocated by evangelicals such as the then Lord Ashley, better known to history as the 7th Earl of Shaftesbury. But the late Mayir Vereté argued persuasively that Palmerston's motives were strategic rather than religious in inspiration. Above all, it seems, Palmerston wished to counter growing Russian influence in the region.[31] The French re-established their consulate in 1843, this time on a more permanent basis than before, and these were soon followed by other consulates: Sardinian and Prussian (1843), United States (1844), Austrian (1849) and Russian (1853). In due course, even countries such as Sweden, Norway, Denmark, Portugal, Belgium, the Netherlands and Persia had consulates in Jerusalem.

The eastern question, as it had come to be known, assumed crisis proportions in 1839 when Muhammad Ali threatened to seize Constantinople and take over the Ottoman government for himself. He enjoyed the support of the French but Russia, Britain, Austria and Prussia joined to defend the Sultan. Diplomatic support for the Turks, however, came at a price. In return, the Sultan was obliged, in November 1839, to issue a decree, the 'Noble Rescript of the Rose Chamber', promising equality to non-Muslims in his empire. The decree was part of a wider policy of reform (*Tanzimat*) by which the Ottoman Empire sought to propel itself into modernity.

That 'Noble Rescript' gave an opening to the powers to use the rights of protection enjoyed by consuls, in Jerusalem as elsewhere in the empire, to enhance their influence. Each of the consuls accordingly was on the look-out for potential protégés. The Russians strengthened their patronage of the Orthodox Christians – though their title to do so was later challenged by the Greeks. The French assumed their traditional protectorate of the Latin and Uniate Christians – though their title was subsequently challenged by the Italians. There were few indigenous Protestants in Palestine – but American and British missionaries set about resolutely manufacturing them. To egg the pudding, the British consuls took upon themselves the protection of Druzes as well as of 'Samaritans, Abyssinians, and all Jews in distress'.[32]

On 15 July 1840 Britain, Austria, Prussia, Russia and Turkey signed a convention in London threatening Muhammad Ali with war if he did not withdraw from Syria. He was, however, to be permitted to maintain his rule in Palestine, including Jerusalem. The Egyptian ruler was given ten days to accept or face the consequences. The French were furious and made bellicose noises. Emboldened by French support, Muhammad Ali rejected the four-power proposal. An allied fleet appeared off the coast of Syria and a general uprising against the Egyptians broke out in the country. Ibrahim retreated south in a hurry and his rule in Syria came to an abrupt end.

The French, deeply wounded by this rebuff, brooded on the setback and plotted revenge. The Foreign Minister, Guizot, in a private letter in December 1840, mused optimistically that 'the latest events have by no means destroyed the old preference which the eastern Catholics have always had for us. We shall cultivate it in those very places.' Soon afterwards Lord Granville, British ambassador in Paris, learned that Guizot was secretly contemplating efforts to establish a 'Christian Free City at Jerusalem' rather like the then free city of Cracow.[33] This was the first occasion in the diplomacy of the Jerusalem problem on which the idea of some sort of internationalization was broached. We may note, as one of the many ironies of the question, that Guizot himself, author of this scheme for advancing France's claims by the exploitation of her historic links with the Latin Church in Palestine, was a Protestant. Lord Palmerston did not support Guizot's proposal: 'Religious protections,' he said, 'pave the way for political dismemberments.'[34] Much to the relief of the British, Guizot's royal master pooh-poohed his idea. King Louis Philippe, in conversation with Granville, 'treated as chimerical and absurd the notion of establishing a little independent Christian community in Jerusalem'.[35] Metternich announced that Austria too opposed the creation of any Levantine Cracow. The idea collapsed.

The Protestant bishopric

Shortly afterwards, however, the project, in a revised form, found a new and powerful backer. Frederick William IV had ascended the throne of Prussia in June 1840. The Convention of London, signed the following month, attracted his attention to Palestine and the withdrawal of Muhammad Ali's forces seemed to leave an inviting vacuum. In February 1841 the Prussian king proposed an international agreement on Jerusalem, Bethlehem and Nazareth, providing for an independent government of Christian inhabitants and the creation of a five-power administration (Austria, Russia, France, Britain and Prussia) of the Christian holy places. The Prussians, of course, as Molière's Misanthrope put it, 'had their reasons'. Unlike the French and the Russians, they had few local protégés. There were next to no

Lutherans in Palestine at that period. This was an early manifestation of a rule that was to be repeated later: internationalization as the recourse of the locally weak. Frederick William was sufficiently serious about his proposal to dispatch his brother to Jerusalem to scout out the land.

Catholic Austria and Orthodox Russia soon put paid to the Prussian king's idea. But about the same time he sponsored another project that, unlike the internationalization plan, was realized. This was for a joint Prussian-English bishopric in Jerusalem. The notion might seem strange: it was as if Lutheranism and Anglicanism were somehow the same. In fact, the animating idea in the mind of the Prussian king was indeed that all evangelical Protestants should join together in one Church. Jerusalem, he believed, was 'the place to exhibit the true Unity and Catholicity of the Church of Christ'.[36] The chief Prussian advocate of the proposal was the Chevalier (later Baron) de Bunsen, whom the king sent to England to promote it among English evangelicals such as Shaftesbury. Already in August 1840 Bunsen had written to Gladstone, 'It is surely impossible not to see the finger of God in the foundation of an English church and a congregation of Christian proselytes on the sacred hill of Jerusalem.'[37] Bunsen claimed, in a letter to his wife, to have had some kind of vision 'that it might be the will of the Lord, and probably would be that of the King, that in Jerusalem the two principal Protestant Churches of Europe should, across the grave of the Redeemer, reach to each other the right hand of fellowship'.[38]

Behind ecumenical ideas of this sort lay other motives that helped persuade Bunsen's English interlocutors. One was the long-standing English interest, inherited from the seventeenth-century Puritans, in the Jews as instruments of the coming millennium. In the 1650s, for example, the Baptist Hebrew scholar the Reverend Henry Jessey had collected £300 in England for the Jews of Jerusalem, who, he wrote, were supported by Jews elsewhere 'to keep, as it were possession, or at least some footing in it, and to show their hopes, till a full restitution come'.[39] Evangelical philo-semitism in the nineteenth century, however, barely concealed diplomatic rivalry. Bunsen noted that it was 'notorious' that French missionary activity in the Levant was increasing. The English evangelicals had their own competitive agenda, seeing in the Jerusalem bishopric a cause that might be a rallying point in their battle against the Romanizing trend of the Oxford Tractarians led by John Henry (later Cardinal) Newman. The bishopric seemed to offer a kind of Protestant catholicity to rival that of Rome. And in England too, beyond competitive religious zeal, other more directly political considerations arose. In spite of the withdrawal of Muhammad Ali from Syria, the Ottoman Empire still seemed in danger of breaking up; in that event, it was suggested, the Levant might well become a suitable region for European settlement. All these ideas helped Bunsen secure rapid approval for his scheme from Queen Victoria, the British government, majorities in both houses of Parliament and a preponderant part of the Anglican Church.

The bishopric was set up by a written agreement between the two governments in July 1841, followed by the swift passage of an act of Parliament — necessary as there was no precedent for the appointment of an Anglican bishop in a foreign country to minister to foreign citizens. Frederick William endowed the see with £15,000. The English and Prussian kings were to have alternating rights of nomination to the see. Although commonly called an 'Anglo-Prussian bishopric', strictly speaking it was only Anglican, since the bishop had to be in Anglican orders. The first incumbent of the see was Michael Solomon Alexander, Professor of Hebrew at King's College, London. Born in Prussian Poland, Alexander was a convert from Judaism and had formerly been cantor of the Jewish community of Plymouth. The evangelicals were thrilled by the appointment. Lord Shaftesbury wrote in his diary:

> The Bishop of London told me that he had never known
> the Archbishop so animated as he had been on this

subject during the last few weeks. The whole thing was wonderful, and to those who have long laboured and prayed in the Jewish cause nearly overwhelming, to see a native Hebrew appointed, under God, by the English Church to revive the Episcopate of St James, and carry back to the Holy City the truths and blessings we Gentiles had received from it. [40]

So fevered was Shaftesbury's enthusiasm that his wife mocked him mercilessly: 'You din this perpetually in my ears, and it sets my back up against it, always talking of how wonderful, how wonderful.'[41] The Tractarians were correspondingly disgusted. Newman complained that the bishopric 'actually was courting an intercommunion with Protestant Prussia and the heresy of the Orientals'. This was the 'third blow' that finally shattered Newman's faith in the Church of England and propelled him along the road to Rome.[42] One modern writer has gone much further in extrapolating hypothetically the consequences of the creation of the bishopric:

> Had Pusey followed his own instincts in favour of Bunsen's scheme and not surrendered his judgement to Newman – had Tractarianism not thrown up an impassable barrier to Protestant unity – had the Anglo-Prussian Bishopric in Jerusalem not been a mere flash in the pan – the whole course of the relations between England and Prussia might have been changed, and the European War of 1914 might never have occurred. [43]

Whether the Jerusalem question can realistically be seen as a proximate cause of the Great War is doubtful – but the suggestion by a serious historian faithfully reflects the mix of political and spiritual motives behind the appointment.

Perhaps appropriately, therefore, Bishop Alexander was conveyed to Palestine on a warship, HMS *Devastation*, arriving in Palestine in January 1842. The Admiralty had first offered the frigate *Infernal*, but Alexander did not like that name so the vessel was changed. The motive behind the unusual method of episcopal conveyance was certainly not to signal aggressive designs. But whatever their initial intentions, it was probably inevitable that the Anglicans would be drawn into the mire of ecclesiastical politics in Jerusalem.

The new bishop's duties were defined as the 'superintendence of the English clergy and congregations in Syria, Chaldaea, Egypt and Abyssinia, and of such other Protestant bodies as might wish to place themselves under his episcopal care'[44] – a job description that presumably left him with much time on his hands since such clergy or congregations were thin, verging on non-existent, in those scattered regions. But his primary mission was to the Jews in Jerusalem and he had some initial success in converting a handful of Russian Jews, whom he baptized in an Anglican service performed, interestingly, in Hebrew.[45]

Such proselytizing, however, soon aroused opposition both from the Jewish community and from the Russian consul, who objected to what he saw as a British attempt to poach on his rights of protection over Russian citizens. Nor did the bishop endear himself to the Ottoman authorities by his inaugural sermon, in which he referred to the Muslim government as 'an usurped one'. The British consul-general in Beirut, who was present, required him 'never again to mention such objectionable matters'.[46] The consul in Jerusalem, W. T. Young, reported that the bishop had received a request from Copts in the city to take them under his protection.[47] Diplomatic unease was reported in faraway Vienna, occasioning a typically forthright letter to the Foreign Secretary from one staunch supporter of the bishopric: 'Surely,' wrote Queen Victoria, 'it cannot do harm if we have some share in that part of the world, in the religious influence which the Roman Catholics seem to think they alone have a right to possess.'[48]

Behind these ecclesiastical proceedings, of course, lay far-reaching diplomatic ambitions – as Young pointed out in a dispatch in 1844: 'Jerusalem is now become a central point of interest to France and Russia, because both Governments have adopted, according to their respective Creeds, the character of Protectress of the native Churches – and it is here that their main objects have to be contended for.' France and Russia, Young reported, were seeking to control the internal affairs of their protégé Churches and to assume control of all communications between them and the Ottoman authorities. The French consul, he claimed, 'has adopted the idea that this country has never been conquered, and he delights in dwelling on the spirit of the Crusades, as though his views were bounded by a revival of something similar'.

While warning against French and Russian consular intrigues and efforts to control their respective Churches, Young sought to undermine what he referred to delicately as 'another party, which is looking to Jerusalem and Palestine as the great Theatre on which the fulfilment of Prophecy is speedily to be accomplished respecting the restoration of the Jews.' The consul warned:

> After a residence here of five years, I am induced to come
> to the conclusion that to attempt to shape a course in
> order to meet the views of a popular reading of Prophecy,
> it is necessary to cast plain and obvious duties and sound
> reason overboard. If the Student of Prophecy would
> regard the actual conditions of these countries in a calm
> and practical point of view, endeavouring to respect the
> privileges and prejudices of others equally with his own I
> think he would feel the desirableness of studying the real
> position and wants of their present Inhabitants before he
> indulges in speculative theories regarding a superhuman
> view of the future, which, if ever to be accomplished, he
> is perhaps more likely to retard than hasten by his
> premature zeal.[49]

Who was the unnamed 'Student of Prophecy' so roundly criticized by the British consul? We can have little doubt that it was the head of the English ecclesiastical mission in Jerusalem, Bishop Alexander.

This was merely one of a number of episodes in the course of Alexander's sojourn in Jerusalem in which he and the British consul found themselves in conflict. The following autumn, Young seized the opportunity of disturbances among sheikhs in the neighbourhood of the city to persuade the bishop and his clergy to leave Jerusalem for the coast for their own safety. A year later Alexander went away again. This time he did not return: in November 1845 he died in the desert on his way to Cairo.

As his successor, the king of Prussia selected Samuel Gobat – a Francophone Swiss. He was the only Prussian nominee ever appointed, for the bishopric, like so many multinational schemes in Jerusalem, fell victim to diplomatic rivalries and, as we shall see, was eventually wound up. In the meantime, the British, like the French and the Russians, found that, in sponsoring a religious cause, they had opened something of a diplomatic Pandora's box.

Following the example set by the Protestant powers, both the Orthodox and the Catholics moved swiftly to buttress their ecclesiastical position in Jerusalem. In 1843 the Archimandrite Porfiri Uspenskii was dispatched to the Near East by the Russian government to report on the position of the Orthodox Church there. Two years later, the newly elected Greek Orthodox Patriarch of Jerusalem, Cyril, parted from the non-resident tradition of his predecessors and decided to set up residence in the city. The Latin Patriarchate too, dormant since 1291 (though titular Patriarchs had resided in Rome), was revived in 1847 with the elevation of Monsignor Joseph Valerga. The significance of this may be gauged from the fact that the Jerusalem Patriarch was the only one of the three Latin Patriarchs of the Near East who actually resided within the territorial confines of his patriarchate. At this time there were only an estimated 4,000 Latin Catholics in the whole of Palestine. The primary purpose of Valerga's appointment, like that of his Orthodox colleague, was diplomatic rather than pastoral. The two Patriarchs engaged in what one historian has called 'ridiculous practices' to impress their local clients.[50] Seated on a scarlet divan covered with a leopard-skin, Cyril received visitors wearing black satin robes with diamonds and emeralds surrounding an enamel painting of the Redeemer on his breast. Valerga countered by holding court on a velvet-covered throne.

As the consular corps too expanded, some of the consuls began to assume hardly less inflated pretensions of grandeur. They arrogated to themselves ever-increasing powers to dispense judgement over their subjects in consular courts. They moved round Jerusalem in procession flanked by guards and preceded, like the Patriarchs and the Ottoman pasha, by a *kawas* – a colourfully clad officer wearing a scimitar and wielding a big silver-headed stick that was banged ceremoniously on the paving stones to warn people to get out of the way. Some consuls even began to conduct themselves as if they were the superiors of the Ottoman governor himself. In July 1844, for example, Consul Young reported:

> Yesterday the City was thrown into an uproar in
> consequence of a dispute between the Pacha and the
> Artillery Corps which occupies the Castle. The French
> Consul, as his habit is, immediately interfered and placed
> himself unsolicited by either party, between the Pacha and
> his soldiers; and in the evening he publicly exhibited
> himself on his Terrace surrounded by his people, and a
> party from the Artillery Corps giving his judgement in the
> case.

Young termed his French colleague's behaviour 'a scandal' and suggested that he appeared to be trying to set himself up as 'protector-General and mediator of all differences'.[51]

Yet the French consul was not the only one with delusions of grandeur. The most egregious example of such self-aggrandizement was James Finn, who served as British consul from 1845 to 1862. Finn was a combative, combustible character who got involved in disputes with the Protestant bishop, local rabbis, other consuls and Ottoman officials, as well as with his employer, the Foreign Office. His staunch support for Jews in Jerusalem led him into several excesses of zeal. In 1852 he was reprimanded by the Foreign Secretary for taking under his protection Russian Jews who were claimed by the Russian consul-general in Beirut as his protégés. Finn, a highly undiplomatic personality, disputed his instructions and returned argumentative dispatches to the Foreign Office, occasioning further censure:

> To prevent any future misconception on your part, I have now to state to you that you are not to enter into any Correspondence with the Russian Consulate as to the conditions or the manner in which that Consulate may renounce the protection of Russian Jews; and you are not to take any steps either with the Jewish Rabbis or with individual Jews to encourage those Jews who may be discarded by the Russian Consulate to come to the British Consulate for protection. Her Majesty's Government would much prefer that such Jews should not seek British protection; but Her Majesty's Government will not withhold it from them if they apply for it in the proper manner. [52]

Finn took such rebukes on the chin — then carried on regardless.

In 1850 the Ottoman government recognized the Protestants in the empire as a *millet*, like the Orthodox and the Latins. This recognition led Bishop Gobat to pursue an even more assertive policy, particularly in proselytization, leading to renewed disputes and clashes with heads of other Christian communities, who suspected the Protestants of stealing souls from among their flocks. The Protestants also came into conflict with the Jewish community, who bitterly resisted missionary activity, with the Russian consul, who disputed the British claim to protect Jews of Russian nationality, and with the Turkish authorities, who inevitably found themselves drawn in as arbiters on this as on other controversies among the Churches in Jerusalem.

By now, however, it was the issue of the holy places that was once more in the forefront of ecclesiastical politics and of diplomatic relations among the powers. As one penetrating observer, Karl Marx, noted, 'The Ottoman Porte and its agents, adopting a most troublesome *système de bascule* [system of weights], gave judgments in turn favorable to the Latins, Greeks, and Armenians, asking and receiving gold from all hands, and laughing at each of them.'[53] The system worked for a while, but in the early 1850s it broke down, leading to a major crisis.

War clouds over the tomb of Christ

The origins of the crisis lay in a new quarrel that had arisen in 1847 among the major Christian sects concerning their rights in the holy places. On 31 October the Greek and Latin clergy came to blows in the Church of the Nativity in Bethlehem and the Greeks were joined as allies by their Orthodox brethren the Armenians. In the course of the brawl, a silver star that allegedly marked the exact spot of the nativity disappeared. Greeks and Latins each claimed ownership of the missing star and accused the other of stealing it. Both appealed to the governor of Jerusalem for vindication. The French and Russian consuls took up positions affirming the rights and claims of their respective protégés. The British consul, James Finn, his evangelical predilections notwithstanding, sided with the Latins. The matter was referred to Constantinople and raised to the diplomatic plane with the active involvement of the ambassadors of the powers.

The dispute became acute when the Franciscans, in their capacity as Custodians of the Holy Land, demanded the right to replace the star. The claim was supported by the French consul and the ambassador in Constantinople. In February 1848 the Ottoman government agreed in principle to the restoration of the star but stated that the replacement would be performed by the government. The right to conduct repairs at holy places had been linked, since time immemorial, with rights of ownership, and the Latins therefore demurred at the government's proposal, regarding it as a derogation of their rights.

The government of Louis Napoleon (nephew of the first emperor), elected President of France under the constitution of the second French republic in December 1848, embarked on a pro-Catholic policy in both domestic and international affairs, in the hope of winning conservative support. Privately the French were quite candid about their motives in championing the Latin cause. A French diplomat wrote:

> What is the significance of this quarrel stirred up in
> Constantinople over the holy places? ... I know the
> Orient and I can assure you that Russia will not give in.
> For her it is a question of life and death and it is to be
> hoped that one knows this full well in Paris in case one
> wishes to push the affair to the limit. [54]

The danger of war with Russia was indeed well understood in Paris – but far from leading to restraint, Napoleon and his ministers saw the issue as an opportune pretext. Napoleon's Foreign Minister, Edouard Drouyn de Lhuys, was as cynical in his advocacy of a forward Catholic foreign policy as his Protestant predecessor Guizot. Drouyn later candidly admitted that the question of the holy places was intrinsically 'of no importance whatever to France' but nevertheless useful as a battering-ram with which to destroy the alliance of the powers against France.[55]

In early 1852 the French considered mounting a naval demonstration off Constantinople in order to back Latin claims.[56] They were temporarily mollified by a new *firman* issued by the Sultan on 8 February which reaffirmed the (pro-Orthodox) status quo of 1757 while making some minor concessions to the Latins.[57] The position as laid out in this *firman* became subsequently the *locus classicus* for the definition of the status quo at the holy places and for all claims by the various sects regarding their rights there.

The Turks tried to satisfy the rival contenders by issuing simultaneous diplomatic communications: on the one hand, they informed the French of the concessions made to the Latins; on the other, they sought to reassure the Russians by dwelling on the concessions made to the Orthodox. This double, not to say duplicitous, mode of diplomacy succeeded only in frustrating both Russia and France. The Russian envoy in Constantinople 'expressed himself with unusual vehemence and no small degree of irritation against the proposed arrangement'; the French President was reported to be inclined to 'accept the concessions made to him, keeping open a door for the remainder of his claims, but practically abstaining for the present'.[58]

The French nevertheless continued to apply pressure in Constantinople and eventually they received their reward. Three keys to the Church of the Nativity in Bethlehem, a central item of dispute, were handed over to the Latins; and on 22 December 1852 the Latin Patriarch of Jerusalem ceremoniously placed in position in the church a new silver star that had been provided by the Franciscans and formally delivered to the Ottoman government by the French ambassador. The French, it appeared, had scored a signal triumph. The Russians were furious: Tsar Nicholas I told the British Minister Plenipotentiary, Hamilton Seymour, 'We have on our hands a sick man, a very sick man.'[59] Hence the phrase 'sick man of Europe', which passed into common currency with reference to the Ottoman Empire. Count Nesselrode, the Russian Chancellor and Foreign Minister, declared

> that the acts of injustice towards the Greek Church,
> which it had been desired to prevent, had been
> perpetrated, and, consequently, that now the object must
> be to find a remedy for those wrongs; that the success of
> the French negotiations at Constantinople was to be
> ascribed solely to intrigue and violence.

The rights of the Russian emperor, 'secured to him and to the Greek church', Nesselrode maintained, 'could not be withheld with impunity'.[60] Incidentally, the statesman who thus launched Russia towards war in support of the rights of Orthodox Christians had been baptized at birth a member of the Church of England (his mother was a Protestant). Like Guizot's, Nesselrode's fervour was that of the ruthlessly disinterested diplomat rather than the honest religious fanatic.

Two weeks after the ceremony in Bethlehem, the Russians mobilized an army corps for advance to the Turkish frontier. Prince Menshikov was sent to Constantinople as a special envoy to present an ultimatum to the Turks, offering a secret treaty of alliance, demanding a new *firman*, insisting on a return to the status quo at the holy places (as the Orthodox interpreted it) and reaffirming the right of the Tsar to protect all Orthodox Christians in the Ottoman Empire. In meetings with Turkish leaders, Menshikov also requested permission to build a hospital for pilgrims and a church for Russian priests in Jerusalem, called for two Turkish buildings next to the Church of the Holy Sepulchre to be pulled down and required that the Greek Orthodox Patriarch of Jerusalem should have the right to superintend repairs to the church's cupola. The proposed church and hospital were to be placed 'under the special inspection of the Consul-General of Russia in Palestine and Syria'.[61] Meanwhile, the French fleet had been ordered to sail to Salamis and the British dispatched their ultimate diplomatic weapon, their imperious ambassador Lord Stratford de Redcliffe, who returned to Constantinople on the British naval steamship *Fury*. The Turks, trembling between the menaces of all their prospective allies, tacked first in one direction, then the other.

The British had maintained a scrupulous neutrality on the issue of the holy places. They had no interest in furthering the ambitions of Napoleon III. The Foreign Secretary, Lord John Russell, noted that it was the French who had been 'the first to disturb the *status quo* in which the matter rested' and also 'the first to speak of having recourse to force'. Russell found it 'lamentable' and 'melancholy' that 'armies and fleets [should be] put in motion for the purpose of making the Tomb of Christ a cause of quarrel among Christians'.[62] Stratford de Redcliffe, applying exceptional diplomatic energy, succeeded in bringing together his French and Russian colleagues in Constantinople and on 22 April achieved oral agreement on all contentious aspects of the holy places question.[63] *Firmans* were prepared setting out the terms of the latest redefinition of the status quo and sighs of relief were heard in several of the chancelleries of Europe.[64]

But by this stage both the Russians and the French had the bit between their teeth. Neither government was to be balked of its desire for war merely by the inconvenience of a diplomatic agreement on the supposed issues of difference. In July 1853 the Russians occupied the principalities of Moldavia and Wallachia, nominally still under Turkish suzerainty. In October Turkey declared war on Russia. The British remained reluctant to become involved but they could not countenance Russian control over the Black Sea Straits and thus found themselves drawn ineluctably towards war. The destruction of a Turkish naval squadron by the Russians at Sinope in November led the British to fear a complete collapse of the Ottoman Empire and an advance by Russia to Constantinople. This they were determined to prevent and in March 1854 Britain joined France as an ally of Turkey against Russia.

The Crimean War, of course, really had little to do with the holy places question. Essentially the powers waged war over larger strategic issues – the Russian claim to a protectorate over Christians in the Ottoman Empire, particularly in the Balkans, the British fear of a Russian fleet in the Mediterranean, the French emperor's desire to emulate the military feats of his uncle. For both Russia and France, Jerusalem and the holy places were convenient pretexts rather than issues of vital national interest in their own right.

One might have thought that the outbreak of the war would lead to a truce in the conflicts among the Christian sects and their consular patrons in Jerusalem – at any rate between the Latins and the Protestants. Not so. The French government did indeed issue instructions to all its consular representatives to preserve harmonious relations with their British allies. But as a French diplomat observed at the end of the war, 'It was not always thus and the majority of the French consular agents in the territories of the Sultan, moved by a zeal more ardent than reflective, did not take sufficiently into account the nature of their duties'.[65] At the conclusion of hostilities, the powers, meeting in conference at Paris, reaffirmed the principle of the status quo at the holy places. At the level of international diplomacy, that doused the flames for a while – but in Jerusalem the bickering continued and, as we shall see, burst forth anew at the slightest opportunity in the course of the following century and more.

Given this account of intrigues, disputes, conflicts and antagonisms, one important fact should be stressed. During the whole of the late Ottoman period, that is from the end of the Egyptian occupation until the First World War, there were no significant instances of mass communal violence in Jerusalem.[66] Inter-communal relations of Muslims, Christians and Jews, although sometimes fraught with suspicion and even sectarian contempt, were contained within a framework of law and civil peace. Nevertheless, the consular wars in Jerusalem illustrate the capacity of the Jerusalem question to inflame and aggravate relations between the powers. Seized upon as a sacred cause, Jerusalem proved a handy pretext for warmongers with much larger objectives. In the aftermath of the Crimean War all the major

European powers embarked on a programme of quasi-imperial expansionism in the Near East, particularly in Palestine – and most spectacularly in Jerusalem.

2　Old City, New City

During the final phase of Ottoman rule, between the Crimean and First World Wars, Jerusalem changed dramatically. From an inward-looking, walled hill town, it expanded into a city with some spectacular modern architecture and with international economic and political connections. As the city grew, the character of the Jerusalem question in international diplomacy also evolved. From a struggle for influence among the Christian sects over rights at the holy places, it became the arena of larger conflicts and claims of all three monotheisms as well as the territorial ambitions of several of the powers. The Jerusalem question was also shaped by the importation from Europe of a new secular religion that won adherents among Christians, Muslims and Jews alike: nationalism.

Beyond the walls

Jerusalem's population doubled from about 11,000 in the 1830s to 22,000 by 1870. By 1914 it had more than tripled again, reaching an estimated 70,000 (see Table 1, page 46). From mid-century significant numbers of Christians, Jews and Muslims, broadly speaking in that order, moved outside the walls. In 1914 it was estimated that half the population lived in this 'new city'.[1]

The largest contribution to this population surge was made by Jews, who came by the early 1880s to form a majority of the city's residents.[2] In 1690 the Jewish community had numbered no more than about 1,000, constituting some 10 per cent of the total number of inhabitants. But by 1752 a local Jewish sage wrote that gentiles were complaining 'that too many [Jews] are coming'.[3] Until the

Table 1 **Population of Jerusalem by religion (1563–1995)**

Year	Jews	Muslims	Christians	Total
1563	1,434	11,802	1,830	15,066
1800	2,250	4,000	2,750	9,000
1850	6,000	5,400	3,600	15,000
1910	45,000	12,000	12,900	69,900
1922	34,000	13,500	14,600	62,500
1931	51,200	19,900	19,300	90,500
1946	99,300	33,700	31,400	164,400
1967	196,800	58,100	12,900	267,800
1983	306,300	108,500	13,700	428,500
1995	417,100	182,700	14,100	617,000

Note: There are many problems in presenting the population of Jerusalem. The figures for 1563 are estimates by Professor Amnon Cohen, based on Ottoman surveys: see Amnon Cohen, *Jewish Life under Islam: Jerusalem in the Sixteenth Century* (Cambridge, Mass., 1984), pp. 12–17. Cohen suggests, however, that these numbers may understate, somewhat, the true picture. Ottoman censuses, which were conducted only from the late nineteenth century onwards, counted only Ottoman citizens and therefore give only a partial picture. The first reasonably reliable census was conducted by the British in 1922. All the pre-1922 figures, as well as those for 1946, are estimates. The Israeli census figures are held by many Palestinians to undercount Arab residents since they count only the so-called '*de jure* population', i.e. persons who were, in Israeli eyes, legally resident. On the other hand, the figures for the 1995 census, given above, were later corrected by the Israeli census bureau and both Jewish and non-Jewish numbers were reduced because persons who had been *de facto* present had wrongly been counted (the Jewish figure was actually reduced proportionately *more* than the non-Jewish). Account should also be taken of the changes in municipal boundary of Jerusalem over the past century. Apparent discrepancies in the 'total' column reflect the presence of small numbers of persons whose religion was classified as 'other' or 'unknown'. For all these reasons, the above figures should be regarded as generally indicative rather than precise. For discussion of Jerusalem's demography in the nineteenth and early twentieth centuries, see the works by Yehoshua Ben-Arieh, Justin McCarthy and U. O. Schmelz cited in the Sources. The most up-to-date discussion of Jerusalem's current and projected demography is Sergio DellaPergola, 'Jerusalem's Population, 1995–2020: Demography, Multiculturalism and Urban Policies', to appear in *European Journal of Population* (2000). I am grateful to Professor DellaPergola for making an advance copy of this paper available to me.

1760s, most Jewish immigrants had been Sephardim (descendants of Jews expelled from the Iberian peninsula at the end of the fifteenth century); thereafter the majority were Ashkenazim (Jews from Germany and eastern Europe). In 1777 a small but significant number of hasidim from Poland and Russia began to arrive. Until the end of the eighteenth century the Jewish community in Jerusalem limited immigration by the so-called 'bachelor' regulation.[4] The effect was to stunt natural increase as well as immigration. Nevertheless, Jewish numbers increased both absolutely and relatively, perhaps reaching 6,000 out of a total population of 15,000 in the 1850s. After that there was steady growth as a result of immigration from Europe (later also from Yemen), as well as of improvements in living conditions outside the crowded confines of the old Jewish quarter.[5] By 1914 there were an estimated 45,000 Jews in Jerusalem out of a total population of 70,000. Jerusalem at that point was the home of a majority of the Jews in Palestine, who numbered at most 85,000 out of an estimated total population of 790,000.

Hardly less spectacular than the growth of the Jewish population in the city was the increase in the number of Christians. From an estimated 3,000 in 1835 they grew more than fourfold to around 13,000 by 1910. This was a faster rate of growth than that of Muslims in the city.[6] Indeed, Christians came to surpass Muslims in absolute numbers in Jerusalem, probably for the first time since the Crusades. According to a recent painstaking analysis of Ottoman census records, the 11,500 Christians (18.4 per cent of the population) in Jerusalem in 1905 just outnumbered the 11,000 Muslims (17.6 per cent).[7]

This rapid population growth led inevitably to the geographical expansion of the city. The process was aided by the general growth in security, particularly from bedouin raids, in the later part of the century. The decrepit, filthy, smelly hill town, depicted in memorably unprepossessing terms by such visitors as A. W. Kinglake and Mark Twain, began its transformation into a modern city. The chief motor of urban development was not the Ottoman government but rather foreign capital, in particular the financial inflow associated with religious institutions, both Christian and Jewish, supported by foreign powers operating under the protective capitulatory regime. As the population began to move out of the old city, characteristic geographical lines of separation appeared that to some degree are still visible today: Muslims moved mainly to the north and south of the city, Jews primarily to the west.

Christians were the first to move outside the walls. One of the earliest to do so was the British consul James Finn, who built a summer house in the early 1850s at Talbieh, a hillside facing the western side of the city. Shortly afterwards Bishop Gobat built a school on Mount Zion. In 1860 a German Protestant missionary, Johann Ludwig Schneller, established an orphanage near the village of Lifta, to the north-west of the city. And in 1867 a German nobleman, von Keffenbrink, donated money for the founding of a leper hospital near the Mamilla pool, outside the Jaffa Gate. A Carmelite convent and church were built on the Mount of Olives in 1868 with funds from the Princess de la Tour d'Auvergne, a relation of Napoleon III. In the late 1870s the massive Ratisbonne monastery of St Pierre was established in what is now the Rehavia district. And the even more gargantuan Notre Dame hospice of the Assumptionist Fathers, just opposite the New Gate to the old city, opened in 1887.[8]

Among the earliest Christian neighbourhoods established in the 'new city' was the German colony, a settlement of the Templers, a pietist sect founded in 1854 in southern Germany (not to be confused with the Templar order of knights). From 1868 they established a number of pioneering colonies in Palestine which imported European agricultural techniques, implements and machinery (incidentally, in this regard predating the Zionists' similar efforts). In Jerusalem they built a little neighbourhood of solid German-style houses that still retains traces of its original character, though its German inhabitants were deported by the British during the Second World War.

Jewish expansion outside the walls up to the First World War had little to do with proto-Zionism. Jewish immigration to Jerusalem was inspired primarily by religious motives and most of the newcomers, like the established Jewish community, had no interest in, or sympathy for, Jewish nationalism. Even after the influx of Zionists to Palestine started in the 1880s, few came to Jerusalem. The headquarters of the Hovevei Zion (Lovers of Zion) was in Jaffa. The newcomers preferred to settle there or in agricultural settlements in the coastal plain. Jerusalem, the capital of the so-called 'old *Yishuv*', was regarded, particularly by secular Zionists, as the home of all that was primitive and backward-looking in Judaism. Far from viewing Jerusalem with affection, they despised it and all it stood for, particularly the traditional dependence of Jews there on *halukah*.

Population pressure in the crowded Jewish quarter and fear of moving outside the walls led some Jews in the 1870s to settle in the Muslim quarter. Some *yeshivot* (talmudical colleges), schools and other institutions were established there and the Hebrew newspaper *Havatzelet* was published there. Jewish shops were to be found in both the Muslim and Christian quarters.[9] Eventually pressure of numbers forced Jews to build new neighbourhoods outside the old city. The first was Mishkenot Shaananim, almshouses set up south-west of the Jaffa Gate by the English-Jewish philanthropist Moses Montefiore in 1855, but for many years these were uninhabited because Jews feared to live there. The Meah Shearim ('Hundred Gates') district, so called because the original subscribers to the founding cooperative numbered 100, was established in 1873 by orthodox Jews. A decade later 2,000 Jews were living outside the walls. Theodor Herzl, on his visit in 1898, mused in his diary that an entirely new city would have to be built outside the walls. 'Old Jerusalem would remain Lourdes, Mecca, and Yerusholayim. A very beautiful and elegant city would be quite feasible next to it.'[10] His vision soon began to be realized. By 1914 nearly twice as many Jews lived in the new city as in the old (29,000 as against 16,000).[11]

Muslim construction outside the walls was later and less extensive than that of Christians and Jews. Around 1870 the Husayni quarter, comprising a number of handsome villas owned by the notable family of that name, began to be developed near the Sheikh Jarrah mosque, to the north of the Damascus Gate. One of these later became the core of the American Colony, first a mission, then a hospital, today a hotel. Other wealthy Jerusalem notable families, such as the Nashashibis and Jarallahs, built large houses nearby, with the result that Sheikh Jarrah became the most fashionable Muslim district of Jerusalem. Lower-class Muslims tended to remain in the Muslim quarter of the old city (still today one of its poorest areas) and it is estimated that by 1914 barely a fifth of the Muslim population of Jerusalem lived outside the walls.[12]

Spiritual imperialism

The creation of the new city was a product not only of demographic pressure but of outside interest – touristic, spiritual, archaeological and also imperialist.

Jerusalem had begun to appear on the itinerary of the Grand Tour in the 1830s. Among the earliest visitors was Benjamin Disraeli – though whether the visit can be connected with his occasional proto-Zionist utterances is doubtful.[13] The future British Prime Minister was followed by a stream of crowned and coroneted heads of Europe. Archduke Maximilian of Bavaria arrived in 1838 and, a few years later, his ill-fated fellow Archduke Maximilian, the future emperor of Mexico. In April 1841 the brother of the king of Prussia spent eight days in the city. With the introduction of the steamship into commercial service in the Mediterranean in the 1840s, the opening of the Suez Canal in 1869 and of the Jaffa–Jerusalem railway in 1892, such royal tourism became commonplace. In 1855 the Duke of Brabant arrived and in 1859 the Russian Grand Duke Konstantin came as a pilgrim at the Tsar's request. The Prince of Wales, the future Edward VII, visited in 1862, as did his grandson, the future Edward VIII, in 1913. The most famous such visit was paid by Kaiser Wilhelm II in 1898, when he entered the city on horseback through a gap specially cut in the city wall next to the Jaffa Gate (*Punch* described the pilgrim monarch cruelly as 'Cook's crusader'). By the end of the century Jerusalem had become a frequent destination not only for the European aristocracy but also for large numbers of ordinary tourists and humble pilgrims.

Many of the eminent persons who embarked on the pilgrimage to the holy city took a personal interest in the construction of churches and monasteries there. The most impressive was the Kaiserin Augusta Victoria Stiftung on Mount Scopus, initially projected at the time of the Kaiser's visit in 1898 and dedicated in 1910. The building's fortress-like aspect and strategically dominant position on Mount Scopus gave rise to suspicions that it had been established for a military rather than an eleemosynary purpose.[14] It was never used as planned: in 1909 the roof blew off; its opening in 1914 was postponed because of the outbreak of the Great War; it later served as the first official residence of the British High Commissioner. After a purpose-built Government House was completed in the 1930s, it was agreed that the building would be made available to the German Deaconesses' Hospital. The date set for its opening was September 1939 ...

Even the Jews profited from royal philanthropy: the king of Prussia contributed to the building of the Hurva synagogue, opened in 1863, and his name was inscribed above the entrance with those of other benefactors. When the Austrian Emperor Franz Josef, among whose many titles was 'King of Jerusalem', visited the city in 1869 he donated funds for the gate to the Batei Mahseh area in the Jewish quarter.

Much of this constructive philanthropy was no doubt stimulated by the purest of spiritual motives. But almost always behind this lurked the genie of *odium theologicum*, which gave expression to diplomatic rivalries and imperialist ambitions.

The Treaty of Paris, signed at the conclusion of the Crimean War, sealed the status quo at the holy places, as defined in the *firman* of

8 February 1852. This became the permanent basis for resolution of all disputes on the subject. But the dependence of the Turks on their allies in the war enabled these Christian powers to upset another aspect of the status quo – the discriminatory legal regime under which non-Muslims still laboured in the Ottoman Empire. The emancipatory Noble Rescript of the Rose Chamber, granted by the Sultan as a result of Anglo-French pressure in 1839, provoked a conservative reaction felt throughout Syria and Palestine, including Jerusalem, and was not fully enforced. The crisis of the mid-1850s offered Britain and France a renewed opportunity to press for satisfaction. Even before the outbreak of war, the British Foreign Secretary the Earl of Clarendon pointed out to Stratford de Redcliffe that 'every fair advantage should be taken of the present situation of the Turkish Empire to press upon the Sultan and his ministers the importance of removing all civil distinctions between the Christian and Mahomedan subjects of the Sultan'.[15]

Accordingly the Sultan issued a number of new decrees, culminating, on 18 February 1856, in an Imperial Rescript which confirmed the equality of all Ottoman citizens. The Rescript stipulated that no obstacle was to be raised to the repair of houses of worship, schools, hospitals or cemeteries and that 'a minimum of administrative obstacles' should be placed in the way of permission for the construction of new edifices by non-Muslims.[16] The position of Christians and Jews, at any rate those who were Ottoman citizens, was further strengthened by the *millet* law of 1865. These legal changes inaugurated the next phase of involvement by the powers in the Jerusalem question, the phase of spiritual imperialism.

This was most frequently bound up with missionary activity, the beginnings of which dated back to the 1820s. The first missionary to arrive in Jerusalem was probably James Connor, an Oxford graduate operating on behalf of the Church Missionary Society. He went there in 1819 but left after a short time, having decided that it was too dangerous to stay. In 1820 a Swiss pastor, Melchior Tschoudy, an agent of the London Society for Promoting Christianity among the Jews, visited the city and arrived at slightly more favourable conclusions. He was followed by an American, Levi Parsons, who spent several months in Jerusalem in early 1821. But it was not until 1833, following the advent of Egyptian rule, that the London Society set up a permanent establishment in the city, headed by the Reverend John Nicolayson, a Dane.

One point on which the western powers failed to secure compliance from Turkey in the period of the *Tanzimat* related to freedom of conversion from Islam. Missionary interests pressed strongly for an end to the sanctions, sometimes involving death, inflicted on such converts. The Ottoman government undertook that apostates would no longer be executed.[17] But fearful of Muslim reaction, it resisted pressure from the powers to withdraw other penalties. Consequently missionaries in Jerusalem, as elsewhere in the Ottoman Empire, generally refrained from attempting to proselytize among Muslims. Instead they were driven back to the only safe constituencies – Jews and members of rival Christian sects. But their efforts among the former provoked vigorous resistance, sometimes even violence, from orthodox Jews. And rival Christian sects resented attempts to poach in what they regarded as their spiritual territory. The number of converts was disappointingly small: by 1852, the five European missionaries in Jerusalem could claim a total of only 131 'Hebrew Christian' adherents.[18]

Diplomatic competition among the powers, reflected in controversies over the holy places, rumbled on throughout this period. Coenobitic blood flowed after battles between Greek and Latin monks in Bethlehem in 1873 and Jerusalem in 1901 – to mention just two of the more serious confrontations. Rather than resolving disputes or clarifying rights, the doctrine of the status quo ensured that disputes would never be resolved, rights never clarified. This state of constant uncertainty and endless conflict suited the powers perfectly: it afforded them a continuous supply of grievances on the basis of which they might vindicate their claim to protective authority.

The French protectorate over the Latins was affirmed seamlessly by succeeding regimes of all political colours. In 1851 the second French republic had pleaded the cause of the Latins 'in the name of the entire Catholic world'.[19] Under the Second Empire the policy reached its apogee. But following the fall of Napoleon III in 1870 his republican successors adopted without question the historic mantle of protectors of Latin Christendom.

They did so against new rivals in the Catholic world. The creation in 1861 of a unified kingdom of Italy had already aroused French fears of a challenge to the protectorate. At first, the Italians held back. They were under some obligation to the French for help in the recent war of liberation against Austria. And they were also conscious of the presence of a French garrison protecting the Pope's little island of secular power in Rome. The French consul in Jerusalem was authorized in 1862 to accord protection to Italian citizens in order to maintain the 'unity of the protectorate'.[20] The establishment in 1871 of an Italian consulate, at a moment of sudden French enfeeblement following defeat by Prussia at Sedan, awoke French fear of displacement by the Italian newcomer. Alluding to this danger, the French ambassador in Constantinople warned his consul in Jerusalem, 'While instructing you to maintain the most friendly relations with M. de Rege-Donato, I beg you, Sir, to take great care lest the cordiality of your relations serves to permit the encroachments against which we have daily to struggle.'[21] In 1878 the French thought to secure their position afresh by article 62 of the Treaty of Berlin, which declared (*inter alia*), 'The rights possessed by France are expressly reserved and it is well understood that no alterations can be made in the *status quo* in the Holy Places.'

The Italians, however, persisted in exercising the right to protect their own citizens, pointing to another sentence in the same clause of the treaty that recognized 'the right of official protection by the

Diplomatic and Consular Agents of the Powers ... both as regards [ecclesiastics] and their religious, charitable, and other establishments in the Holy Places and elsewhere'.[22] Given that the Latin Patriarch and many senior Latin ecclesiastics in Palestine were generally Italians, this clause gave an opening to Italian diplomacy that its consuls in Jerusalem eagerly exploited. In 1891 the French ambassador to the Holy See warned the Quai d'Orsay that the Italian government did 'not weary of trying indirectly by every means to strip us of the prerogatives of the Religious Protectorate in the Orient'.[23] In the same year, no doubt with a view to enhancing the primacy they claimed among the foreign consuls, the French raised their representation in Jerusalem to the level of consul-general.

When, in the early years of the next century, France adopted a rigorously anti-clerical policy, this was strictly for internal consumption; externally the republic continued to pursue a Catholic foreign policy. The French consul put it trenchantly in a newspaper interview in November 1902: 'At home France can be whatever she wants but in the Orient she is Catholic, she is the secular arm of the Holy See and the representative of Latinity.'[24] In one respect, the two went together: the legal measures against religious congregations taken by the governments of Waldeck-Rousseau and Combes led thousands of monks and nuns to leave France – in many cases thereby augmenting the French membership of Catholic orders in the Levant.

The reassertion of French prerogatives was deemed necessary after a series of untoward incidents and exchanges with the Italians. First there had been acrimonious communications in 1902 between the Father Custodian of Terra Sancta, Frediano Giannini, and the acting French consul, Ferdinand Wiet. The French consul complained bitterly that, following a '*bagarre*' with some Greeks on the parvis of the Church of the Holy Sepulchre, some monks of the Franciscan Custody had sought the intervention of the Italian consul rather than the proper protecting authority – himself. This, he declared, was a 'deliberate blow against our protectorate'.[25] Shortly afterwards, the

Italian consul, Carletti, took deft advantage of a visit to Jerusalem by a group of Italian pilgrims accompanying Cardinal Ferrari of Milan. The cardinal was accorded a magnificent welcome by Carletti, who sent a carriage to bring him to Jerusalem, held a grand reception for him in a tent flying the Italian flag and then sent him off in procession through the city accompanied by a band of Salesian Fathers playing the royal anthem. The *Giornale d'Italia* complimented the consul on his 'skill and timeliness' in thus affirming the Italian right of protection. The paper further reported that the French consul, evidently offended, had behaved with discourtesy towards the distinguished visitor. 'Eyewitnesses' were said to have testified that when the French consul met the cardinal he had barely doffed his hat, had spoken in a haughty manner and had not even descended from his horse. The cardinal had responded *'seccamente'*, whereupon the consul rode off *'al gran trotto'*.[26] Fierce polemics ensued between the French and Italian press, with the latter demanding 'emancipation' of Italian ecclesiastical establishments in the Holy Land.[27] The French consul hardly helped matters by giving an interview to a correspondent for the *Osservatore Cattolico* of Milan in which he declared, 'Whether you want it or not, whether it's to your liking or not, we are proud to protect you and to transmit to our descendants the secular heritage of France.'[28]

In 1904 the Vatican severed diplomatic relations with France in protest against the French President's visit to the capital of the kingdom of Italy. The French held that this did not affect in any way their protectorate over the Latins in the Holy Land, but their ambassador in Berlin, Jules Cambon, commented in 1909, 'Whatever our protestations in this respect, there is a certain contradiction on our part in claiming to continue the traditional Catholic protectorate in the Orient when we maintain no representation at the Holy See, even though Orthodox Russia and Protestant Prussia judge it necessary to have one.'[29]

Rome was not the only potential threat to French rights in the holy city. 'Protestant Prussia' had been the bogey of all French diplomats since the disaster of 1870. The arrival in Jerusalem in 1873 of a new German consul, the young and energetic Baron Thankmar von Münchhausen, lent some substance to French fears. Münchhausen set about extending German influence by every means possible and, in the course of his seven years in the post, particularly encouraged Jewish institutions to use the German language.[30] In 1878 the Deutsche Palästina Verein was founded. Ostensibly devoted to scholarly-cum-religious purposes, like parallel Russian, French and British voluntary groups this also served the purposes of spiritual imperialism, German-style.

Münchhausen's appointment evoked ominous reflections from the French consul. In a long dispatch, outlining the success of the Templer colonies in Palestine, he warned:

> The day serious complications were to threaten the
> existence of the Turkish empire, is it not to be feared that
> the numerous German subjects and the interests that
> they represent would paralyse our liberty of action? ... I
> do not agree with those who say that the northern races
> cannot acclimatise themselves in this country and that the
> Germans are set to disappear after two or three
> generations. In the plains perhaps, but on the hills a
> European race, constantly augmented by migration, could
> perpetuate itself since the climate there is not too
> different from that of central Europe ... We cannot,
> therefore, look without disquiet upon German
> immigration growing so much; the enmity that that race
> has devoted to us, an enmity that appears everywhere that
> theirs have a presence next to ours, must preoccupy us,
> especially in a land where religious passions can give rise
> at any moment to serious conflicts.

Unfortunately, he continued, the French could not compete with

the Germans in the same way since 'our compatriots hardly emigrate
... It is only with the indigenous Catholic element that we can try to
counterbalance the Germans – a bad element, it is true, but one from
which the actually existing religious institutions have not drawn
proper advantage, in my view.' The consul therefore urged that one of
the French teaching orders be encouraged to work in the Holy Land.
In particular he suggested that the Abbé Ratisbonne, rather than surrounding himself with foreign teachers in his new school, should
instead employ French citizens who 'by their zeal and spirit of patri-
otism' would 'little by little attract around them the greater part of
the Catholic population, and even those of other rites'.[31] The dispatch represented a dominant trend in French diplomatic thinking.
In line with such ideas French Catholic institution-building in
Jerusalem and elsewhere in Palestine intensified over the four
decades up to the outbreak of the First World War.

One sign that the French consul's fears regarding German designs
on the Holy Land were not far-fetched was the decision by the German government in 1882 to denounce the agreement of 1841 with
England concerning the Protestant bishopric in Jerusalem. When the
Anglican Bishop Barclay died in that year, the right of nomination of
a new bishop fell, according to the agreement, to the Prussian crown.
But Frederick William IV's dream of union of the Lutheran and Anglican Churches remained unfulfilled. Since the 1840s a substantial
Lutheran congregation had grown up in Jerusalem and the German
government decided that it would be impractical to maintain the
agreement whereby the Protestant bishop must be in Anglican holy
orders. After four years of negotiations it was decided in December
1886 to put aside the agreement by mutual consent.[32] The following
year the bishopric was reconstituted as a purely Anglican see –
although, in the hope of avoiding offence to the Orthodox, the incumbent was henceforth known as bishop *in* rather than *of* Jerusalem.
Can we detect in this formulation a prefiguring of the Jewish National
Home that was to be established, as the Balfour Declaration of 1917

stated and the Churchill White Paper of 1922 explicitly noted, *in* Palestine? St George's Cathedral, initially known as St George's Church, was begun in 1896. Characteristically Anglican in its design, it was the most significant British contribution to the ecclesiastical construction boom in Jerusalem in this period. The neighbouring St George's College, opened in 1899, was modelled on English cathedral schools. Its pupils included not only Anglicans but other Christians, upper-class Muslims and even a few Jews.

The new-found independence of the Lutherans in Jerusalem was marked in 1898 by the central event of the Kaiser's visit to the city: his opening in the Christian quarter of the old city of the Church of the Redeemer, for which his father had laid the foundation stone in 1869. The visit occasioned anxious telegraphic instructions from Paris to the French consul-general. He was ordered under no circumstances to fly the German flag. If the consuls met to consider whether to put up illuminations to mark the visit, he was to point out that no such illuminations had been put up at the embassies in Constantinople and it would be best to follow their example. If a majority of consuls nevertheless decided on illuminations, and if all of them were lit, then the French consulate was to be lit in a very restrained way 'to avoid any appearance of sulking [*bouderie*]'. The religious communities under French protection were to fly only the French flag and they were not to put up illuminations at all; in case of necessity they were to be reminded that the Pope had recommended that they adopt a reserved attitude. The French consul was to be present at all visits by the Kaiser to protected institutions. As for the monarch's visit to the Church of the Holy Sepulchre, the consul was instructed to be present 'without being conspicuous'.[33]

Meanwhile, after their setback in the Crimean War, the Russians renewed their efforts at spiritual empire-building in Palestine. In 1857 some 800 Russian pilgrims arrived; thereafter the number grew steadily year by year. A steamship service was established between Odessa and the Syrian coast that carried the pilgrims, generally simple peasants, to visit the holy places. In January 1858 a permanent Russian ecclesiastical mission arrived in Jerusalem, headed by Bishop Cyril of Melitopolsk. A Russian Foreign Ministry memorandum delineated the aims of this mission:

> We must establish our 'presence' in the East not politically but through the church ... While our influence was still strong we could afford to conceal our activities and thus avoid envy, but now that our influence in the East has weakened we, on the contrary, must try to display ourselves so that we do not sink in the estimation of the Orthodox population ... Jerusalem is the centre of the world and our mission must be there.[34]

Nesselrode's successor as Russian Foreign Minister, Prince Gorchakov, was careful to reassure the French chargé d'affaires in St Petersburg that the new Russian mission would 'abstain from all proselytism and avoid any attitude or démarche that might excite the susceptibilities of other Christian communions, in particular those of the Latin clergy'.[35] But the French somehow obtained a copy of the mission's secret instructions. These adjured its members:

1 Not to look at the affairs of the Church, as was done in the past, 'through a Greek prism' but to be concerned primarily with Russian interests;
2 To act above all on the indigenous element oppressed by the Greeks, in order to maintain the Arabs within Orthodoxy and prevent their conversion to the Latin faith ... [36]

The French and their wards the Latins duly maintained their guard against the threatened spiritual aggression.

The Russians, however, encountered a number of obstacles. There were squabbles between rival groups of enthusiasts in Russia as well as rows between Russian consuls and ecclesiastics. The Greek clergy put up fierce resistance to Russian pretensions to order them around. 'The patriarch,' wrote a member of the Russian church mission in 1858, 'would very much like to crush us to his bosom and suffocate us in his embrace.'[37] Just as the Latin clergy in Palestine, in particular the Franciscans, were jealous of their right of custody of the Holy Land, and resisted the overlordship of would-be guardians from the seventeenth century to the twentieth, so the Greeks were not disposed to hand over direction of their affairs to the Russians.

Nevertheless, Russia was able to show significant returns on its investment in Jerusalem. The most notable was the Russian cathedral and compound on the *maidan*, the former Turkish military parade-ground (today in the central business district of west Jerusalem). Construction began in the 1850s – it was the first really large-scale development outside the walls – leading one historian to write that 'the New City was thus a Russian invention, and not a British or French one'.[38] The cathedral was dedicated in the presence of Grand Duke Nikolai Nikolaievich in October 1872. Ten years later the Russians launched a great new endeavour, the Orthodox Palestine Society, under the patronage of the Tsar – the prefix 'Imperial' was added in 1889. The society inspired a renewed upsurge in Orthodox building and activity in Jerusalem and in the numbers of Russian pilgrims. In 1888, when 2,250 arrived, the onion-domed Orthodox Church of Gethsemane, perhaps the most beautiful of all Jerusalem's nineteenth-century landmarks, was opened on the Mount of Olives by the Grand Duke Sergei Aleksandrovich.

The huge spate of Russian activity alarmed the other powers, especially the French, and was in no way diminished by the conclusion of the Franco-Russian alliance, given final approval on 4 January 1894. The French Foreign Ministry later the same month warned its consul-general in Jerusalem that France could not be indifferent to this 'powerful organization [the Imperial Orthodox Palestine Society] from the point of view of maintaining our influence and the exercise

of our religious protectorate in the Levant'.[39] When a press inter-
viewer suggested to the French consul in 1902 that the French were
often constrained in their protection of the Latins for fear of trouble
with the Russians, the consul interrupted and said, 'Excuse me, but
that's not so. Our interests in Palestine are diametrically opposed to
those of Russia and we know how to uphold them against our ally of
the Occident [sic]. Russia regards Jerusalem as an oriental Rome; she
wants to supplant Latin influence there in order to possess an
absolute hegemony there, but we resist as energetically as we can.'[40]

As the British and the French thus became increasingly concerned
over the threat of Russian and German expansion towards the Near
East, they began to shore up their positions. The British were determined, above all, to protect the flank of the Suez Canal, opened in
1869, the lifeline to their empire in the east. In 1882 they occupied
Egypt and in 1905 extended Egyptian rule across the Sinai peninsula
to the border of Palestine. The French concentrated their efforts in
Syria, where they established a shadow protectorate over the
autonomous Christian province of Lebanon. Throughout the Levant
they built railways and funded schools, hospitals, churches and
monasteries. A colonialist pressure group grew up demanding 'compensation' in the Near East for France's grievous loss of Alsace and
Lorraine in 1871. 'The question is wrongly put,' wrote Etienne
Flandin, a leader of this lobby, in 1916, 'if one asks "Should Palestine
be French?" For Palestine, like the rest of Syria, is already French.'[41]

As in other parts of the world, imperialism marched hand in hand
with exploration, mapping and surveying – in the case of Palestine,
also with archaeology. In this sphere too the French had been first in
the field. Pierre Jacotin, a geographer in Napoleon's army of Egypt,
had drawn the first modern maps of Palestine, and in 1863 the
archaeologist de Saulcy excavated the so-called Tombs of the Kings
north of the Damascus Gate, mistakenly identifying them as the
tombs of the House of David. In the later part of the century, however, it was the British who became pre-eminent in the field.

In 1865 Captain Charles Wilson, R E, of the Topographical Department of the War Office, produced the *Ordnance Survey of Jerusalem*
'made with the sanction of the Right Hon. Earl de Grey and Ripon,
Secretary of State for War'. Wilson's expedition not only surveyed
the city but also conducted some excavations – at the Ottoman governor's insistence, these were at all times overseen by a *zapti* (policeman). Wilson's survey was received in England with enthusiasm and
helped bring about the foundation in the same year of the Palestine
Exploration Fund, with Queen Victoria as its patron. At its inaugural
meeting, the President, William Thompson, Archbishop of York,
made a speech that included a succinct assertion of English spiritual
imperialism: 'This country of Palestine belongs to you and me. It is
essentially ours.'[42] Headed by Wilson, the PEF undertook a series of
further digs and surveys. For a long time, however, its activities were
hampered by religious and political suspicions. In 1869, for example, Colonel Charles Warren tried to obtain permission from the
Ottoman government, through the British Embassy in Constantinople, to examine the Haram al-Sharif, but the reply was given that
this would be impossible 'because of the state of local feeling in
Jerusalem'.[43]

The early PEF surveys had a strong intelligence dimension, realized
mainly by officers of the Royal Engineers. To the general public the
mapping of Palestine in general and Jerusalem in particular was connected with scholarly controversies over the correct location of the
holy places (especially the Holy Sepulchre). War Office interest was
stimulated more by concern for the security of the Suez Canal.
Among the officers engaged in such mapping in the 1870s and 1880s
was the young Herbert Kitchener who, as Secretary of State for War
in 1914, was to be responsible for the British war effort against the
Ottoman Empire; and in 1913–14 the young T. E. Lawrence, in the
guise of archaeologist, carried out further cartographic work that
helped pave the way for his guerrilla campaign against the Turks in
Palestine three years later.

The role of British army officers in these enterprises could not but arouse the suspicions of the Turks. In the 1870s an expedition headed by Claude Conder, that resulted in his book *Tent Work in Palestine* (1878), produced a riot and trouble with the Turkish authorities.[44] Ottoman wariness of British intentions intensified with the crisis in Egypt in 1882. In February that year Conder, who was later to serve in the British expeditionary force in Egypt, went to Constantinople, where he had an interview with the British ambassador, Lord Dufferin. He requested the ambassador's help in getting a new *firman* from the Ottoman government that would enable him to conduct further survey work in Palestine. Dufferin sympathized with Conder's difficulties but

> stated that the obstacle lay in the fact that the Sultan was at present in a state of suspicion 'amounting to frenzy' concerning the design of France on Egypt and of England on Syria [*sic*]. The Turks, he thought, had become aware of the fact (which I already knew) that Russian officers had succeeded in making maps of the whole of Northern Syria and I understood his Lordship to consider that the Sultan's suspicions had been increased by the presentation of the Society's map of Western Palestine by Sir Charles Wilson. It was in his opinion the making of maps which specially aroused apprehension on the part of the Turks.[45]

In 1883, as Turkish apprehensions intensified, a new disturbing element, one of the emblematic figures of the British idea of empire, suddenly arrived in Jerusalem – Charles 'Chinese' Gordon, the God-fearing British general.

In his savagely satirical portrait of Gordon in *Eminent Victorians*, Lytton Strachey opens with a snapshot of the 'solitary English gentleman ... wandering, with a thick book under his arm, in the neighbourhood of Jerusalem'. In the course of his meanderings, Gordon made what he considered to be the important discovery of the tomb of Christ – situated not, as the Empress Helena and most Christians since her time had thought, in the Church of the Holy Sepulchre but some distance away outside the city walls. Although the historical authenticity of Gordon's discovery was by no means generally accepted, some Protestants pilgrims began to venerate this 'Garden Tomb'. Strachey was no doubt correct in depicting Gordon's mission to Jerusalem as that of a biblically inspired *naïf*. But his activities were followed with a mixture of awe and suspicion by the French consul. The English general, he surmised darkly, was engaged in neither a pleasure trip nor a scientific expedition: 'He wants to study the country, men, things and situations, to study it above all from the military point of view.' Gordon's appearance, the consul feared, indicated 'quite clearly that the English believe in the possibility, if not the imminence of military action in this country and that they are actively preparing for that eventuality.'[46]

As the powers, through their consuls, exerted ever-growing influence, Ottoman officials were brought to the brink of despair. In 1883 Rauf Pasha, then governor of Jerusalem, found it necessary to repair to Constantinople 'to consolidate his position at the Sublime Porte which had been greatly shaken by his enemies of the Russian Party' – this, at any rate, was the interpretation of the French consul.[47] Successive governors voiced similar concerns, the more so as Jerusalem grew in political weight in the late Ottoman period.

Jerusalem promoted

The consuls' influence was felt not only in the governorate but in the *majlis al-shura*. Originally established by the Egyptians in the 1830s, this appointed advisory council was retained by the Ottomans upon their return in 1840. Most of its members were Muslims, though in 1840 there were also two Armenian representatives and one Jew.[48]

Initially this body had little power, but it slowly acquired a political role and in 1867 an elected municipality was established (a *firman* ordering its creation had been issued in 1863).[49] The franchise remained extremely limited and most councillors were members of prominent notable families. Muslims were always in the majority but consular pressure led to the admission of some Christian and Jewish councillors. The mayor was always drawn from one of the half-dozen leading Muslim notable families. Nevertheless, the large number of non-Ottoman citizens in the city gave the consuls a lever that they did not hesitate to use in interfering in municipal decision-making. As a Turkish official in Jerusalem put it, in a letter to the Grand Vizier in Constantinople in 1906, 'In a country where more than half its inhabitants are foreign nationals, it is impossible, in matters relating to the municipality, to regard the foreigners as though they do not exist. That is why the consuls endeavour first of all to participate in practice in the affairs of the municipality.'[50]

One sign of Jerusalem's new political significance was its promotion in 1841 to the status of an 'unattached district'. This meant that the pasha in Jerusalem was no longer under the authority of the provincial governor in Damascus but reported direct to the imperial government in Constantinople (see Map 1, page 67). Under later Ottoman administrative reorganizations, Jerusalem was known as an 'independent sanjak', reinforcing its autonomous position. These changes had social as well as political consequences. In particular, they enhanced the standing of the Muslim notables of Jerusalem, who tended to monopolize offices in the government and the religious and judicial establishment. Families such as the Alamis, Husaynis, Asalis and Dajanis, long regarded as local leaders, now began to acquire authority well beyond the confines of the city, a process that was facilitated by their ownership of agricultural land, often at some distance from the city, and their supervision of *awqaf* (endowments). Forging alliances with notable families in other areas, they began to elaborate interlocking clan networks and loyalties that became characteristic

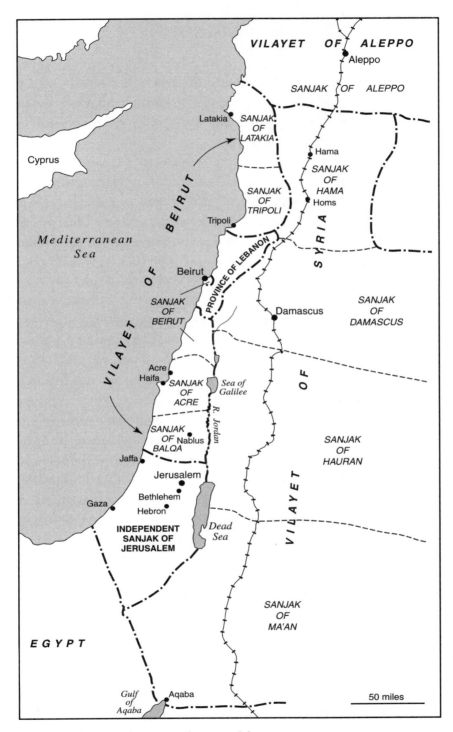

Map 1: Late Ottoman administrative divisions in Palestine

features of Arab politics in Palestine.[51] In particular, members of such families were among the first to express concern about a new threat to their position – and potentially to Muslim predominance in Jerusalem and in Palestine as a whole.

In 1899 Yusuf Diya al-Khalidi, a member of one of the leading Jerusalem Muslim families (he had served as a deputy in the first, short-lived Ottoman parliament in 1877–8 and as President of the Jerusalem Municipal Council) wrote a private letter to Chief Rabbi Zadoc Kahn of France in which he expressed a reasoned opposition to Zionist aims in Palestine. Khalidi conceded that the Zionist idea was 'completely natural, fine and just'. Indeed he went further: 'Who can challenge the rights of the Jews on Palestine? Good Lord, historically it is really your country.' But he warned that Zionism was bound to evoke opposition from Muslims and Christians in Palestine. It was therefore necessary for the Zionist movement to 'stop'.[52] Khalidi's was an isolated, though prescient statement. But within a decade his voice had been joined by many more.

The 1908 revolution in Turkey and the ensuing elections to the revived Ottoman parliament quickened political mobilization throughout the empire – and in Jerusalem too. The political atmosphere in the city at that time is reflected in the recently published dispatches and other official documents of Ekrem Bey, who served as governor from 1906 to 1908.[53] He records irritation with the pretensions of foreign consuls, frustration at his own lack of real power, opposition to Zionist immigration – and no sense of the impending downfall of the four-century-old imperial structure.

The Turkish official also noted a new political phenomenon: stirrings of Arab nationalist feeling. As befitted its leading political position, Jerusalem played a significant role in this development, contributing more members to the various small proto-nationalist groups than Haifa, Gaza and Nablus put together – thirty-five as against thirty-four for the other three towns. Members of the notable Husayni family were particularly active: Jamal al-Husayni was prominent in the Cultural Club (al-Muntada al-Adabi); Said al-Husayni founded a Jerusalem branch of the moderate Decentralization Party; and Shukri al-Husayni served as Treasurer of the Arab-Ottoman Brotherhood.[54] These societies did not, in general, demand full independence for the Arabs. The call was rather for autonomy or – particularly favoured in Jerusalem – annexation to British-ruled Egypt.[55]

Opposition to Zionism was already an effective political rallying cry. When the revived Ottoman parliament met, an Arab member representing Jerusalem raised the issue of Jewish immigration. The matter was referred to the Ottoman Council of Ministers, whose minutes recorded that reports and memoranda had been received from a number of sources, including the *mutasarrif* (governor) of Jerusalem. According to these reports, 'in the sphere of administration in Jerusalem problems were encountered because, after the declaration of the constitutional regime, some classes of the population dared to try and obtain the aspirations and political and religious interests they had nourished since times past'. In the light of this, the Council decided to prepare measures 'that would make absolutely certain that Jews would be prevented from settling in the places that are considered to be the Land of Palestine'.[56] In 1911 the issue was raised again by Ruhi al-Khalidi and Shukri al-Asali, deputies for Jerusalem.[57] In the parliamentary election of 1914, Ragheb Nashashibi, who was elected with a large majority as a deputy for Jerusalem, promised his constituents to 'devote all my energies day and night to remove the harm and danger awaiting us from Zionism and the Zionists'.[58]

By 1914, when the Germans raised the status of their representation in Jerusalem to consulate-general, they had made considerable progress in extending their influence in Jerusalem. Unlike the Russians, French and British, the Germans had no territorial aspirations in the region and were therefore better able to secure Turkish confidence – and eventually alliance. One of their consular achievements was in taking over protection of the Jews from the British. This original function of the British consulate had gradually lapsed after the departure of Consul Finn in 1862. In 1890 British protection of Russian Jews formally ended and soon after that protection was limited to those Jews who could legitimately claim British nationality.[59] By the eve of the Great War, according to the last British consul in Jerusalem, 'protection of Jews, as such, had not only long lapsed, but had been entirely forgotten'.[60] Consular records show that only nineteen Jews were registered in Jerusalem as naturalized British citizens in 1913.[61] German influence among the Jews, by contrast, was so great that, in the years immediately before the outbreak of the Great War, German was a serious rival to Hebrew in the 'language war' that rent the *yishuv*. Nevertheless, the British consul reported in 1913 that, notwithstanding articles in the British press 'on the supposed pro-German and pro-Ottoman sympathies of the Jews in Palestine', he had been reliably assured that 'they had always striven to secure the protection of the British flag for their institutions, being convinced that under no other auspices could they hope to attain their object, viz., the settlement of a Hebrew-speaking Jewish population in the land of their fathers'.[62]

Unexpectedly, after all the efforts devoted over the previous century to Christian institution-building in Jerusalem, it was the protectorate of the Jews that, over the next few years, became the focal point of diplomatic manoeuvring.

'A Christmas present for the British nation'

The entry of the Ottoman Empire to the First World War, as an ally of Germany and Austria-Hungary, at the end of October 1914 brought immediate and far-reaching changes in the diplomacy of the Jerusalem question. In an effort to capitalize on the sanctity of the holy cities of Islam and to bind the Arabs to the Turkish cause, the Ottoman government arranged for the 'standard of the Prophet' to be brought north from Medina. It arrived in Jerusalem on 20 December and was welcomed in a ceremony on the Haram al-Sharif by Djemal

Pasha, member of the ruling Turkish triumvirate and commander of the Turkish IVth Army.[63]

As Turkey broke off relations with the enemy powers, nearly all the foreign consuls left. Most handed over maintenance of their interests to the Spanish consul, who, it was said, became 'consul for the entire planet, a very remarkable consular Pooh-Bah'.[64] Foreign influence now began to take military rather than diplomatic form. In addition to Turkish troops, a large force of Austrians was quartered in Jerusalem. Djemal, who set up his military headquarters in the city, came to rely heavily on the advice of the German military mission. At first the German role was purely advisory, but as the Turkish armies pulled back across Sinai and into southern Palestine German staff officers began to overshadow their Turkish allies.

Those consuls who remained in Jerusalem found themselves overwhelmed with requests for help from Christians and Jews. Individuals and institutions had been suddenly cut off from their sources of support in Russia, France and Britain (later also in Italy and the United States, when those countries entered the war). The Greek Orthodox Patriarchate found its revenues suddenly reduced by 60 per cent. The German consul, Edmund Schmidt, received formal instructions from his government to take Jews under his protective wing. The Austrian consul, Friedrich Kraus, also intervened on their behalf.[65] The American consul, Otis Glazebrook, took special interest in the welfare of the Jews, as did the US ambassador in Constantinople, Henry Morgenthau, himself a Jew. Morgenthau intervened repeatedly on their behalf with the Ottoman authorities. Thanks to his efforts, American warships made a series of visits to Jaffa in the first two years of the war, carrying food and medical supplies donated by American Jewish philanthropists. It was estimated that one such ship, in 1915, supplied food to 23,000 people in Jerusalem.[66] Thousands of Jews and Christians of Russian, French or British nationality fled Jerusalem and the same ships took away the refugees to Egypt whence some moved on to the United States or other countries.

On 9 November 1914 the Ottoman government abolished the Capitulations. A circular announcing the decision explained that they 'were found to be in complete opposition to the juridical rules of the century'.[67] The Allied Powers refused to accept this unilateral act, — but for the time being there was little that they could do about it. Meanwhile, they set about the hypothetical post-war carve-up of the Ottoman Empire in the various secret treaties that later became the subject of endless controversy and criticism.

So far as Jerusalem was concerned, the most directly relevant was the Anglo-French pact of May 1916 known as the Sykes-Picot agreement. This came about as a result of negotiations, initiated by Britain, with a view to fixing the border between a projected British-protected Arab state and prospective French rule in Syria. In instructions issued at the start of the discussions by the French Foreign Minister, Aristide Briand, to the French negotiator, the former consul-general in Beirut, François Georges-Picot, great stress was laid on France's long-standing role as protector of the 'Christians of the Orient'. Picot was to press for French control of the holy places. He was authorized, however, in the event of British resistance, to consider the 'neutralization' of Jerusalem and Bethlehem 'with the proviso that this shall remain limited to the territories strictly necessary around the two cities'.[68] At first the British sought control of Palestine for themselves, seeing it as a vital bulwark for the defence of Egypt. The French responded by proposing the division of Palestine into three zones: the northern area would be under French rule; the Jerusalem *mutasarriflik* (district) would be 'international'; and southern Palestine up to the Egyptian frontier would be British.[69]

In the end a compromise was reached. The agreement provided for the partition of the Fertile Crescent into zones under direct or indirect French and British influence (see Map 2, page 73). In the central area of Palestine west of the Jordan, including Jerusalem, it was agreed that 'there shall be established an international administration, the form of which is to be decided upon after consultation

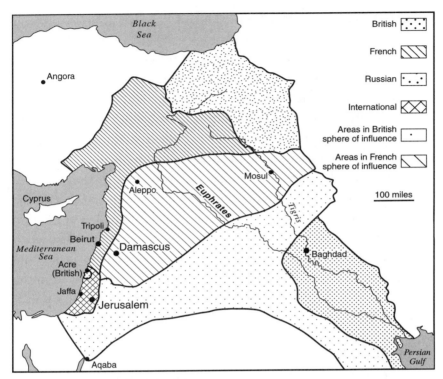

Map 2: The Sykes-Picot plan (1916)

with Russia, and subsequently in consultation with the other Allies, and the representatives of the Sherif of Mecca'.[70] The area of the proposed international zone was much wider than the municipal boundary or even the district of Jerusalem. It extended as far north as Nazareth and the Sea of Galilee. The main reason for this was the Russian insistence that none of the Christian holy places, anywhere in Palestine, should fall under exclusively French, that is Roman Catholic, control.

As we have seen, the idea of the internationalization of Jerusalem had been broached as far back as 1841 (see page 29). Its revival during the First World War seems to have been a device to avoid the dissension among the Allies that would undoubtedly have arisen if any one among them had sought to exercise power alone over the city and

73

the Christian holy places. Like the king of Prussia's abortive project, the Sykes-Picot pact emanated from a state of weakness – in this case, the fact that none of the powers involved had at the moment of the pact's signature even the slightest toehold in the holy city.

This fact was privately registered by diplomats at the time – as was its corollary, that the power that ultimately occupied the city would be best able to define the nature and form of the international regime. The Director of Military Intelligence at the British War Office remarked, while negotiations were still proceeding, that 'we are rather in the position of the hunters who divided up the skin of the bear before they had killed it'.[71] The French ambassador in London warned the French Foreign Ministry in December 1916 that, when the British advance into Palestine took place, the Union Jack could not be permitted to fly there alone.[72] His view was supported in the Quai d'Orsay and a note was prepared for the Prime Minister pointing out that, given the French 'establishments of all sorts' in Jerusalem, 'our eventual absence would be a veritable desertion'.[73] The British seemed, for the time being, ready to humour these French concerns and at the end of the month it was agreed that the administration in Jerusalem would be headed jointly by Picot and Sir Mark Sykes as French and British High Commissioners.

Realizing that British undertakings might be worth little in the absence of French forces, the Quai repeatedly pressed for the dispatch of French troops to the Levant, but the army high command could not spare men from the western front. Only a token French contingent was sent to join British forces moving slowly towards Palestine from Egypt. French diplomats were therefore compelled to rely on their ally's pledged word. In November 1917, as the Egyptian Expeditionary Force, under General Allenby, neared Jerusalem, the French Foreign Minister instructed his ambassador in London to stress the importance France attached to the presence of a French representative at Allenby's side when he entered the city. 'It would be only natural to make us part of the administration of Jerusalem, since

England has always asked that the holy cities should be international-ized and we count on England not to refuse us this necessary satisfac-tion.'[74] In order to register the French claim, Picot was sent hurriedly to join Allenby's staff.

The British have been pilloried for 'promising' Palestine twice over – to Sherif Hussein of Mecca in the famous McMahon-Hussein Cor-respondence of 1915–16, in which they promised to help establish an Arab state, and to the Zionists in the Balfour Declaration of No-vember 1917, in which they undertook to 'facilitate the establish-ment of a Jewish National Home in Palestine'. The French later complained that they too had been cheated by the British. Nor were these the only contenders for suzerainty in the holy city. In 1916 it was suggested that the Pope might become temporal ruler of Jerusalem. The Kaiser was said to favour the idea and to have pro-posed it to the Sultan. The idea was probably no more than a rumour, perhaps a product of war propaganda; yet according to one authority the Vatican may have been attracted to the idea 'either as a substitute for the rule it had lost in Rome or as a means to strengthen its claim regarding Rome'.[75] A more far-fetched proposal was made in Febru-ary 1918 by the Vatican Secretary of State, Cardinal Gasparri. He suggested the appointment of a Belgian governor for the city on the impeccable grounds that 'politically Belgium is unable to overshadow anybody' while 'its Christian vitality is expressed religiously in a thou-sand flourishing institutions'.[76]

If the British deserve to be upbraided for duplicity, the actions of other parties merit no less rigorous appraisal – in particular those of the Arabs and the Zionists. The Arabs, headed by Sherif Hussein of Mecca, self-appointed (or rather British-appointed) leader of the na-tional cause, were far from untutored in the Machiavellian art. In 1915 Hussein's son Emir Faisal visited Constantinople, where he met leaders of the secret Arab nationalist societies, al-Fatat and al-Ahd, and discussed with them the exact terms to be demanded from the British in return for an Arab rising against the Turks. On his way home to the Hejaz, Faisal stopped in Damascus, where he held further meetings with nationalist conspirators and agreed to present the project to his father and then return to Syria to raise the standard of revolt. Continuing his journey, he paid a courtesy call on Djemal Pasha in Jerusalem. There he promised Djemal that he would raise a force of 1,500 camels for the Turkish army. He also delivered an address to headquarters staff in which he swore by the soul of the Prophet that he would return 'to fight the foes of the Faith to their death'.[77] Back in the Hejaz, the young emir persuaded his father to launch the Arab revolt against the Turks – by which Faisal and his brothers, together with T. E. Lawrence, won their place in history. In his memoirs, published after the war, Djemal, with perhaps understandable bitterness, denounced Hussein and promised that 'the whole world of Islam will see well enough what a double-faced role that gentleman played'. He called down the 'curse of Heaven on Sherif Hussein and his sons' for their deceit.[78]

As for the Zionists, they too hedged their bets. Chaim Weizmann, who led their negotiating efforts with the British, was a sincere and committed advocate of the Allied cause and of an Anglo-Zionist partnership. He worked his diplomatic magic tirelessly in Lloyd-George's 'garden suburb' at the back of 10 Downing Street and in the drawing rooms of the titled classes of England. At the same time other, equally patriotic Zionists were hard at work in Berlin, persuading German officials that their movement could be a boon and a blessing to the Central Powers if given tangible recompense in Palestine. The parallel approaches to the British and the Germans were coordinated in July 1917 at a meeting of Russian and German Zionists in neutral Copenhagen.[79] As Isaiah Friedman has shown, the German government evinced serious interest – if only because of the propaganda advantages that they, like the British, discerned in a pro-Zionist declaration.[80] Probably it was only their alliance with Turkey that constrained them from joining in this universal ripping apart of the 'bear-skin'.

The truth of the matter is that there were no innocents at this feast of diplomatic double-dealing. As for promises, the one that really counted was the one the British made to their only trustworthy ally – themselves. Lloyd George put it bluntly in April 1917: 'The French will have to accept our protectorate; we shall be there by conquest and shall remain, we being of no particular faith and the only power fit to rule Mohammedans, Jews, Roman Catholics and all religions.'[81] This remarkable declaration of disinterested ecumenism by the adherent of the little Baptist sect the Disciples of Christ presaged the later effort by British rulers in Jerusalem to balance their own interests with those of all faiths – without, alas, satisfying any.

As the British advanced from Sinai, capturing first Beersheba (31 October 1917), then Gaza (7 November) and Jaffa (16 November), relations between the Turks and their allies became strained. Already on 29 September, General Kress von Kressenstein, the most perceptive member of the German Military Mission, reported, 'Civil administration and the gendarmerie fail entirely; they often have a secret understanding with the population and are open to bribery.'[82] Desertions, he said, were increasing and the Turkish authorities were failing to deliver promised food supplies.

The last months of Turkish rule in Jerusalem were marked by repression, terror and famine. Supporters of the Sherifian cause were hunted down. The Latin and Greek Patriarchs were removed to Damascus by the Turkish authorities. The food supply collapsed. Djemal, who had already expelled 9,000 Jews from Jaffa, summoned all the consuls in Jerusalem and told them he planned to evacuate the entire civilian population. Kress thought the idea 'insane' and pointed out that 'the evacuation of a town in Turkey is tantamount to its complete annihilation ... that of Jerusalem is aimed at the total ruin of its populace and of all Jewish and Christian institutions ... I consider it our inescapable duty to resist it energetically and reject Djemal's assurances as worthless.'[83] The German Foreign Ministry intervened and Djemal received an explicit order from Constantinople to desist from his plan. Soon afterwards he was ousted from power. On 5 November 1917 General Erich von Falkenhayn, the former German Minister of War, arrived in Jerusalem, installed himself in the Kaiserin Augusta Victoria building and displaced Djemal as commander of the Central Powers' armies in the Palestine theatre. The Germans were now, in effect, rulers of Jerusalem.

Turkish leaders wanted to fight to the last in Jerusalem but their ally overruled them. On 21 November Franz von Papen, Chief of Staff of the Ottoman IVth Army (later Hitler's Vice-Chancellor), wrote that further efforts to hold on to the city in the face of the advancing British army would be militarily futile. On the same day a special communiqué was issued in Berlin promising that the holy city would not be turned into a battleground.[84] On German orders, Ottoman troops began to withdraw from Jerusalem.

On 4 December 1917, in a deployment that no doubt warmed the cockles of his Prime Minister's heart, General Allenby ordered Welsh troops into the van on the Hebron–Jerusalem road. Heavy rain delayed their advance and many vehicles and camels got bogged down in mud. On 8 December the leading elements approached Jerusalem. In the evening the Turkish governor, Izzet Bey, discharged the telegraph office personnel, one of whom smashed up the instruments and then went home to change from his uniform into civvies (religious-style robes). The rearguard of the Turkish army withdrew and the governor left for Jericho on a horse-drawn cart.

The next morning two British privates, out looking for water, met the mayor of Jerusalem, Husayn al-Husayni, accompanied by a crowd and two gendarmes carrying white flags. They did not know what to do. Two sergeants wandered up to take a look. They were equally nonplussed. These were followed by two colonels. Neither of these felt able to take responsibility for accepting the surrender of the holy city. Eventually a brigadier-general rode up and 'reassured the mayor'. He communicated with a major-general who (after taking instructions from a lieutenant-general) arrived in a motorcar to accept the surrender. By this time the mayor had gone away. The conquerors eventually caught up with him at the post office and were handed the keys of the city and a letter of surrender written by Izzet Bey before his flight.[85] The mayor died of pneumonia a few weeks later, it was said 'from a chill caught by too many ceremonies of surrender in the driving rain'.[86]

The allied army that conquered Palestine was not exclusively British. It included French and Italian detachments, Australian and New Zealand mounted divisions, two Indian divisions, West Indian, Algerian, Armenian, Jewish and Arab units, Egyptian camel and labour service corps, as well as a 'miscellaneous corps of guides and interpreters'. Allenby at first showed exemplary solicitude for the feelings of all his allies. A British military correspondent recalled:

> Incidentally I may remark that, with the solitary
> exception of a dirty little piece of Red Ensign I saw flying
> in the native quarter [sic] of Jerusalem, the only British
> flag the people saw in Palestine and Syria was a miniature
> Union Jack carried on the Commander-in-Chief's
> motor-car and by his standard-bearer when riding. Thus
> did the British Army play the game, for some of the
> Allied susceptibilities might have been wounded if the
> people had been told (though indeed they knew it) that
> they were under the protection of the British flag.[87]

But for all the window-dressing, there could be little doubt after December 1917 that the British were in charge of Jerusalem and intended to stay.

Allenby's formal entry to the city took place at the Jaffa Gate at noon on 11 December 1917. On orders from London he entered on foot – to point a contrast with the Kaiser's entry on horseback nineteen years earlier. He was accompanied on his right by Colonel de Piépape of the Détachement Français and on his left by Colonel

Dagostino of the Distaccamento Italiano. Among those in the procession was François Georges-Picot, head of the French mission, no doubt pondering whether his agreement with Sykes on the internationalization of Jerusalem might yet be implemented. Sadly for the French, all such thoughts now fell by the wayside before the great fact of British conquest.

In a proclamation that he read out from the steps of the Citadel, Allenby declared the establishment of a military administration and promised 'that every sacred building, monument, holy spot, shrine, traditional site, endowment, pious bequest, or customary place of prayer, of whatever form of the three religions, will be maintained and protected according to the existing customs and beliefs of those to whose faiths they are sacred'.[88] As if to emphasize the disinterested internationalist intentions of the British, Allenby's address was published in seven languages: English, Arabic, Hebrew, French, Russian, Italian and Greek.

An unidentified wit called the capture of Jerusalem 'Lloyd George's Christmas present to the British nation' and British propaganda made the most of Allenby's triumph. The task of preparing a press release on the capture of the holy city was deputed to the military governor, Colonel Ronald Storrs. But Sykes was not happy with the result and cabled back to Jerusalem:

> Press communiqué not satisfactory. Tell Storrs ring off highbrow line. What is wanted is popular reading for English church and chapel folk; for New York Irish; Orthodox Balkan peasants and mujiks; French and Italian Catholics; and Jews throughout world; Indian and Algerian Moslems.
>
> Article should give striking actualities and description of scenes; picturesque details. Rivet Britain onto Holy Land, Bible and New Testament.
>
> Jam Catholics on Holy Places, Sepulchre, Via Dolorosa

and Bethlehem, dim religious lights, chant ...

Fix Orthodox on ditto ...

Concentrate Jews on full details of colonies and
institutes and wailing places. Vox humana this part.

Rally Moslems on absolute Moslem control of Mosque
of Omar ...

Perorate all races (not religions) acclaim justice,
humanity, nobility of conquerors.[89]

Revised versions were dispatched but Sykes was dissatisfied with
the lot: 'This is vile barren stuff. He has no idea of propaganda and
goes wrong at every turn ... I will fudge up something myself out of
this rubbish on Sunday if nothing better comes to hand.'[90] In the end
the task was handed over to Harry Pirie-Gordon and Philip Graves,
both experienced *Times* journalists. W. T. Massey meanwhile reported
that Jerusalem 'became supremely happy': a Jewish woman stopped
him in the street to sing 'God Save the King'; a wounded Arab officer
told him 'I can shout hip-hip-hurrah for England now.'[91] Massey
went on to describe how the conquerors applied 'the touch of the
civilising hand' to the holy city – with special emphasis on the installation of a British standard of plumbing.[92] A particular effort was
made to exploit the victory among the Jews throughout the world.
But Lloyd George expressed irritation that whereas the War Office
had 'ordered all the bells of London to ring out chimes of joy over the
muddled tank-attack of Cambrai, not a flag was hoisted to call attention to the capture by British troops of the most famous city in the
world which had for centuries baffled the efforts of Christendom to
regain possession of its sacred shrines'.[93] After all, said the Prime
Minister, even in San Francisco they had heard of Jerusalem.[94]

3   Jerusalem under the Mandate

B ritish rule in Jerusalem lasted only three decades. Yet it transformed the city and paved the way for Jerusalem's subsequent partition. From the outset the British swept aside their earlier commitments to an international administration and imposed their own government, a military administration until June 1920, then a colonial regime masquerading as a League of Nations mandate. This was Jerusalem's first Christian administration since the Crusades; yet it facilitated the establishment of a Jewish National Home and granted unprecedented privileges to a newly created Supreme Moslem Council. Under the British mandate the relationship of Jerusalem to Palestine changed. For the first time in its modern history, Jerusalem was a capital city. As a result, its élites, particularly Muslim notables, found that their status was enhanced. But status did not equal power and as they discovered this they became progressively more alienated from the mandatory regime. Over the next thirty years Arabs and Jews alike became disgruntled and antagonized, and each successively rose in rebellion against British rule, which was to terminate amid bloodshed, chaos, recrimination and ignominy.

From military government to mandate

The French initially laboured under the misapprehension that Allenby's diplomatic public announcements indicated a British readiness to share power in Jerusalem, thus paving the way towards internationalization of central Palestine in accordance with the Sykes-Picot agreement. But the British would have none of it. The most they would agree to was the assignment of fifty French gendarmes to the city's police force.[1] When the French ambassador in London took the matter up on 21 December with Lord Hardinge, Under-Secretary at the Foreign Office, he was told that fighting was still going on near Jerusalem and this was not the time to be organizing an administration. Besides, the British were being assailed with demands from all sides for a share in the government of Palestine. The Italian and Spanish ambassadors, the Greek minister, and even the Russian chargé d'affaires, who represented a government that no longer existed, had all raised the issue. Hardinge promised that Britain would honour all its promises but time was needed to take stock of the position.[2] Lest this sound evasive, the British ambassador in Paris gave a formal assurance to the French Foreign Minister that it was the 'firm intention' of the British government to adhere to the agreement providing for a 'mixed administrative system' at Jerusalem, but said that this must await the end of military operations there.[3]

Allenby's Chief Political Officer, Gilbert Clayton, wrote privately to Sykes in January 1918 that Picot's position in Jerusalem was 'not very satisfactory either to himself or to us'. Picot was claiming that the two governments had agreed on Anglo-French provisional administration of occupied territory, but Clayton wrote, 'I know of no such agreement, which would in any case be quite impracticable and most mischievous in existing circumstances.'[4]

Picot attempted to strengthen his position by reasserting the traditional French protective role over the Latins – which the Italians were now disputing. This resulted in an extraordinary altercation:

> ALLENBY: I have received a report from the Governor of Jerusalem who has related to me the incident at the Custody [i.e. the Franciscans' Custody of the Holy Land] and your approaches to it. The attitude that you adopted was not correct in my view. You are not to enter into contact with anybody here apart from General Clayton and you may not give out orders. I have not permitted

the presence of any consul, neither French nor Italian ...
You are no more than my adviser for Arab and Syrian
affairs.

PICOT: If that were the case, I wouldn't stay here another
hour. Already all the promises that were the origin of my
mission have not been kept ... Whatever you may think
of it, I am the sole representative of France here, and in
that capacity, as long as I remain in Palestine, I hold, and
I shall hold, I guarantee you that, the rank that both
international custom and agreements grant me.

ALLENBY: But there is no French representative in
Jerusalem. I thought you had been given to understand
that upon your arrival. I must ask you to abstain from
attending the Saint Saviour's on Sunday and I also ask
that you leave for Jaffa.

PICOT: I shall do no such thing because on that point I
take orders only from my government ... I give you fair
notice, therefore, that I shall attend the usual mass on
Sunday in my capacity as French representative and the
honours will be accorded me.

ALLENBY: Then I shall send the police with orders to watch
you and intervene at the first incident ...

After further wrangling, Picot said that if he were to follow Allenby's
instructions he didn't see what there would be left for him to do.
'Neither do I!' was Allenby's terse response.[5] Picot sent an indignant
account of this conversation to the Quai d'Orsay, but it was intercepted by the British and a copy relayed to London.

Both London and Paris were taken aback by this shocking display
of inter-Allied discord. Sykes contacted Jean Goût of the *sous-direction
d'Asie* at the French Foreign Ministry by teleprinter link to try and
smooth ruffled Gallic feathers. But Goût launched into a lengthy ex-
position of Picot's grievances, dwelling on the 'intrigues' of the Ital-

ians and Allenby's failure to accord proper recognition to the French representative. Sykes could hardly get a word in and the exchange ended with a battle of quotations:

> SYKES: Remember the Hebrew proverb: Thou shalt not nuzzle [sic] the ox that treadeth the corn.
> GOÛT: Understood. But don't forget the Persian proverb: There is only one building in the world that is without cracks — this is one built by friendship and frankness.[6]

Such literary exchanges could not disguise the severe tension between the two allies. More diplomacy was evidently required.

Sykes went over to Paris a few days later to try to secure an agreement regulating Picot's position. He prepared a handwritten draft on the back of a piece of headed notepaper from the Hôtel Meurice. This promised that the status quo at the holy places would be maintained and the 'traditional honours rendered by ecclesiastical authorities acknowledging Papal Supremacy to French officials will be regarded as part of the status quo'. The draft upheld the French Commissioner's right to advise the provisional military administration on any matters involving French institutions and citizens, but not any 'supra-national religious body'.[7] Picot was told to abide by this arrangement — advice that he accepted with bad grace.[8] The French were thus soundly beaten. They were given no share in the administration either during or after the war. Their protectorate over the Latins was reduced to a mere honorific vestige. Sykes noted (not for French consumption) that the earlier Anglo-French agreements were 'completely worn out and ... should be scrapped'.[9] Shortly afterwards Allenby was instructed from London that no French protectorate over the Latins in Palestine was to be recognized and that Picot had 'no status such as would entitle him to represent his Government in a Diplomatic or Consular capacity'.[10]

The French were not alone in being thus disabused of pretensions to a share in the government. The proposal for a Belgian mandate was renewed with some urgency by the Catholic press in Belgium. When the Belgian government refused to pursue the matter, Cardinal Mercier, the Belgian Primate, with the approval of King Albert, went over the government's head and sought French support. But having been outfoxed themselves, the French were unable to foster the claims of their exigent little neighbour.[11]

Next in line were the Italians. More realistic than the Belgians, they realized that they could not themselves aspire to rule Palestine. Their agents in Jerusalem therefore worked assiduously in 1918 and 1919 trying to drum up support for internationalization.[12] When the prospect of that receded, the Italian consul-general in Jerusalem, Alberto Tuozzi, urged instead the merits of an independent Arab state, headed by Faisal, which would include Palestine and to which Italy would provide government officials, given that Italians 'would be particularly well received'.[13] This prospect too dissipated and the Italians were reduced to competing with the French for protection over Latin rights at the holy places. In 1919 they demanded recognition of their ownership of the Coenaculum (the traditional site of the Last Supper and the Descent of the Holy Ghost at Pentecost). In 1928 the Italian ambassador in London raised questions regarding the holy places but (as a Foreign Office memorandum later noted) was 'left in no doubt that His Majesty's Government did not regard his government as having any *locus standi* in the matter'.[14] In the end, the Italians, like the French, found all that was left to them was the defence of their own religious institutions and nationals in Palestine. The greater part of the Italian troop detachment of 660 men was withdrawn from Palestine in August 1919. The last fifty carabinieri of the Legion of Naples remained for a time at the disposal of the consul in Jerusalem, but in February 1921 they too were withdrawn.

The British military governor of Jerusalem was Ronald Storrs, former Oriental Secretary to the British Residency in Cairo. After the establishment of a civil administration in 1920, he remained in office until his departure from Palestine in 1926. His colleague Norman Bentwich called him 'a diplomat, seeking to understand and interpret diverse peoples, and skilful in making contact with them'. But he added, 'His great desire as an administrator was to please everybody, and that quality tended to his undoing ... he was not trusted by either side. At a time of grave trouble he was unable to take strong and firm action.'[15] In 1918 Storrs founded the Pro-Jerusalem Society with support from British officials, Muslim notables, Christian dignitaries and Zionist leaders. Its object was to protect and restore the old city. The distinguished architect and designer C. R. Ashbee was appointed 'civic adviser' and it was largely due to his influence that an ordinance was promulgated, still enforced to this day, that all buildings in the city must be faced in stone.

On 13 April 1918 a Zionist Commission, led by Chaim Weizmann and sponsored by the British, arrived in Jerusalem. Weizmann was disgusted by what he saw of the Jewish quarter in Jerusalem: 'nothing but filth and infection. The indescribable poverty, stubborn ignorance and fanaticism – the heart aches when one looks at it all!'[16] This was a typical Zionist reaction to the 'old yishuv' of Jerusalem. Initially Weizmann's diplomatic attitude seemed to win friends among Christians and Muslims. Bishop Porphyrios, speaking for the Greek Orthodox community, sent him a friendly message.[17] Weizmann met Arab notables, including the mufti, Kamil Bey al-Husayni, and tried to reassure them that the Zionists did not plan to harm Arab interests or interfere in the holy places. Afterwards the mufti told Storrs that if the 'Jews acted up to Dr Weizmann's words, all would be well'.[18] Later the Zionist presented the mufti with 'the historic Adrianople copy of the Koran'.[19] The mufti attended the stone-laying ceremony of the Hebrew University building on Mount Scopus as well as the formal opening of the Rothschild Hospital.

Superficial courtesies could not conceal an undercurrent of mutual suspicion. In June 1918 the Political Intelligence Officer in

Jerusalem, a local Latin, warned the government that 'to the outsider the political situation may seem fairly smooth on the surface, but in my opinion it is still troubled and complicated.' The Muslim population could not yet reconcile itself to Christian domination and 'the bugbear of Zionism ... is a nightmare to Moslems and Christians alike'.[20]

Almost from the start of the British occupation, officials noticed and reported to London the growing strength of Arab nationalist and anti-Zionist feeling. In August 1919 the Assistant Political Officer in Jerusalem, J. N. Camp, prepared a detailed report on Arab political activity in the city and Arab attitudes to Zionism. The movement, he said, was organized in a number of societies. The Cultural Club was 'in direct and constant touch with the centre of the propaganda at Damascus' and aimed at 'Arab independence, prevention of any and every sort of Zionism and Jewish immigration, union of Palestine with Syria, and abolition of foreign capitulations'. The Arab Club had similar aims; its members, mainly belonging to the Husayni family, were 'not so strong on Arab independence but are just as much opposed to Zionism and Jewish immigration'. Among its leaders were the mufti's brother, Hajj Amin al-Husayni (a 'very ardent Arab propagandist'). An organization called Brotherhood and Purity was said to be composed of 'violent propagandists and ... leaders of a host of ruffians and cut-throats' who were 'expected to do the dirty work' for the Cultural Club. Its leading spirits were said to include the Arab Assistant Commissioner of Police as well as many other policemen. As for the Muslim-Christian Society, 'the Latins in it are pro-French; the Greek Orthodox are nearly all pro-British; the Moslems are out for independence, though if they cannot have it some prefer Britain and others America as Mandatory Power'. Camp warned that several of the more radical groups were supplying their members with small arms.[21] A week later a protest letter from the Muslim-Christian Society to the Military Governor of Jerusalem asserted that the whole population of the country stood 'ready to sacrifice themselves' in the struggle against Zionism.[22]

At the Paris Peace Conference in 1919 Weizmann appeared at the head of a Zionist delegation to press the case for a Jewish National Home in a British-protected Palestine. The Emir Faisal headed a delegation representing the government of Hejaz and demanded confirmation as ruler of Syria. The British made it clear to him that if he expected British support in his troubled relations with the French he had better reach an accommodation with Weizmann. Faisal complied.

Meanwhile, the French pressed their claim to the whole of Syria and continued to vent their jealousy of British control over Jerusalem and the holy places. They were rudely rebuffed by Lloyd George. In February 1920, at a conference in London on Asia Minor, a 'heated discussion' erupted over a French demand to be allowed the guardianship of the Church of the Holy Sepulchre. Lloyd George's secretary-mistress, Frances Stevenson, recorded that the Prime Minister:

> was furious, & asked whether the British were not good
> enough to guard it. They were good enough, he said, to
> protect travellers on their way to it, & to see that the
> streets leading up to it were kept clean. But when it
> came to entering the place & guarding it − no! the
> French must do that. 'What claim has France to do it,
> even from a religious point of view? Is France a Catholic
> power?' The French dared not answer yes. D. got his
> way as usual.[23]

The issue was not finally resolved until April 1920, when the San Remo Conference approved the establishment of a British mandate over Palestine and Sir Herbert Samuel was appointed the first High Commissioner. With the establishment of a British civil administration, it was clear that the French had lost the battle for Jerusalem. They decided to cut their losses. In July 1920 the French army unceremoniously booted Faisal out of Damascus. He fled to Palestine and was eventually compensated by the British with the throne of Iraq. In December France signed a convention with Britain by which the border between Palestine and French-ruled Syria was established (see Map 3, page 91).

Christian triumphalism

The mandate was, in a theoretical sense, an international form of government and Britain, as mandatory power, was nominally responsible to the Permanent Mandates Commission of the League. Yet the reality was that Palestine was governed from 1920 to 1948 as if it were a British crown colony. From the outset the British took extraordinary care to try to assuage the anxieties of other religions. In his first statement upon entering the city, Allenby had promised to respect and protect the interests of all religions. In a dispatch to London he reported:

> The Mosque of Omar and the area round it has been placed under Moslem control and a military cordon composed of Indian Mohammedan officers and soldiers has been established round the Mosque. Orders have been issued that without permission of the Military Governor and the Moslem in charge of the Mosque no non-Moslem is to pass the cordon. [24]

Yet in spite of the most conscientious efforts, the British found themselves accused from all sides of partiality.

Although the British were scrupulous not to favour Christianity, or any particular sect thereof, the fact remained that British rule between 1917 and 1948 was government by a Christian power. There is a general tendency to ignore the Christian aspect of the mandate, partly because of the British commitment in the Balfour Declaration

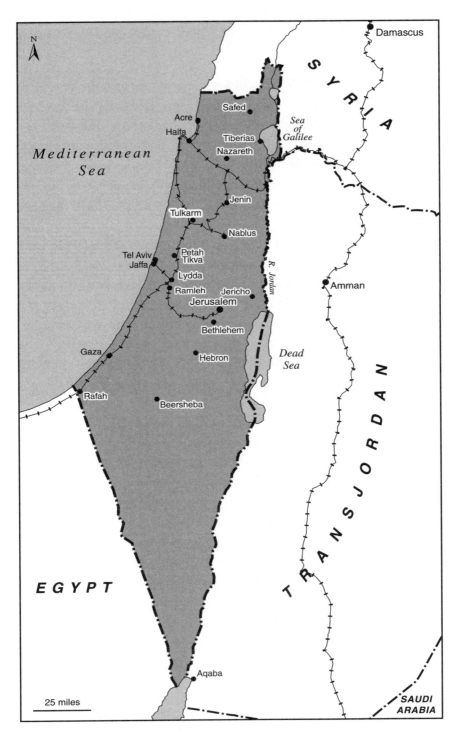

Map 3: Palestine under the British mandate

to establish the Jewish National Home, partly because the first High Commissioner was not a Christian but a Jew, and partly because the mandatory government did not appear to pursue specifically Christian interests or objectives. But this was not the way it was seen at the time – either by Muslims, who were fearful of dispossession by Jews, or by Christians, who expected something more in the nature of Crusader militancy from the first Christian rulers in the holy city since 1244.

With the resumption of Christian control over the holy places, a tidal wave of Christian triumphalism burst forth, particularly in France and Italy. A *Te Deum* was sung in Notre-Dame in the presence of the French President; the Cardinal Archbishop of Paris delivered a sermon evoking the Crusades and affirming 'the ancient rights of protection possessed by the eldest Daughter of the Church'.[25] The mood was reflected in Pope Benedict XV's speech to the College of Cardinals in early 1919:

> Who can ever tell the full story of all the efforts of Our Predecessors to free [the holy places] from the dominion of infidels, the heroic deeds and the bloodshed by the Christians of the West through the centuries? And now that, amid the rejoicing of all good men, they have finally returned into the hands of the Christians, Our anxiety is most keen as to the decisions which the Peace Congress at Paris is soon to take concerning them. For surely it would be a terrible grief for Us and for all the Christian faithful if infidels were placed in a privileged and prominent position; much more if those most holy sanctuaries of the Christian religion were given to the charge of non-Christians.[26]

Both the Roman Catholic and the Greek Orthodox Churches presented anew at the Paris Peace Conference their rival claims to the holy places. Each recapitulated the tangled history of rights, claims and counter-claims.[27] Neither persuaded the conference to dare to ensnare itself in the issue.

The Latins, however, maintained the offensive. In December 1922 Pope Pius XI declared in a consistorial allocution, *Vehementer Gratum*, that the 'rights there [in Jerusalem] of the Catholic Church, in view of their obvious superiority over those of other interested parties, must be respected and given priority, not only in relation to Jews [and] Infidels but also to members of non-Catholic confessions …'[28] It was left to the mandatory government to find some solution. In 1923 it informed the League that it had itself 'assumed responsibility for the Holy Places … as successor to the Turkish Government', pending recommendations to be made by an international commission on the holy places. The British proposed three sub-commissions to deal with the problem, one Christian, one Muslim, one Jewish. None was ever appointed. In the case of the Christians, this was because of the insistence of France that it should have a Catholic majority and a French president – and the predictable unacceptability of this to non-Catholics.

In the absence of such an authoritative international body, the British fell back on Ottoman precedent: the status quo of 1852. The difficult question of defining exactly what this meant was thrown on mandatory officials. In order to help them in their task, the government took the daring step of attempting to codify existing practice. The official assigned this duty, L. G. A. Cust, faced as his first problem determining which holy places were regulated by the status quo principle. He identified just five: the Holy Sepulchre, the Deir al-Sultan, the Sanctuary of the Ascension, the Tomb of the Virgin (near Gethsemane) and the Church of the Nativity in Bethlehem. For each of these Cust itemized in minute detail the prevailing customs and usages, including hours of opening, keyholders, rights of cleaning, processions (small, medium and large, their dates, routes and composition, the exact positions to be taken by dragomans, sextons and candle-carriers, incense-bearers and fan-wavers), vestments, bell-ringing, lamp-lighting, candlesticks, tapestries, icons and so on. The document was published by the government but with the proviso that 'the accounts of practice given in this Print are not to be taken as having official authority'.[29] Far from resolving the contentious issues surrounding the holy places, codification merely froze all the existing controversies in place without settling them. Moreover, since the status quo was formally acknowledged to apply to only a small fraction of the holy places (and of these to the Christian ones), the floodgates were opened to a torrent of new quarrels relating to other places competitively claimed as holy.

In these and other disputes the Latins strongly suspected the mandatory government of partiality towards the Orthodox, whom the British, like their Turkish predecessors, did indeed regard as 'the Church of the country'.[30] Relations between the government and the Latins, already difficult, became inflamed after 1920. The British attributed the trouble to the obstreperous personality of the Latin Patriarch, Monsignor Louis Barlassina, an Italian citizen. Harry Luke, a British official who knew him well, characterized Barlassina as 'narrow-minded to the point of bigotry. He had the temperament of an Inquisitor, something of the fanatical zeal of a Savonarola.' Barlassina's 'three bugbears', according to Luke, were 'Protestantism, Zionism and Freemasonry'.[31] The Italian consul-general in Jerusalem noted that 'tact' was a quality 'that the Patriarch wholly lacks'.[32] He owed his appointment to the British, who had protested successfully against a proposal by the Vatican to appoint an Austrian. 'Mons. Barlassina ought to be an Anglophil for ever,' Sykes had commented in 1918.[33] Never was less gratitude shown. Barlassina had hardly been installed in office in 1920 than he provoked a confrontation with the government by deciding to accord primacy of liturgical honours at the Christmas service in Bethlehem to the French consul. To avoid an awkward scene, the High Commissioner boycotted the occasion.

Barlassina's relations with Storrs were particularly difficult. The

Patriarch complained that Storrs was prone to 'smiling' at him and treating him like a schoolboy. Barlassina condemned the Girl Guide movement and protested against the holding of a fancy-dress ball at the Evelina de Rothschild School. For his part, the governor said the prelate adopted a 'somewhat querulous attitude'. Behind such squabbles lay deep-seated British suspicion that the Latins were, as in days of yore, instruments of French diplomacy.[34] In September 1921 the US consul-general in Jerusalem reported that Barlassina and Storrs had 'had some bitter controversies and the latter has recently gone to Rome, by order of the Palestine Government, to interview the Pope and discredit or minimise to such extent as may be possible the reports which have gone forward to him from the Patriarch here'.[35] Briefed by Barlassina, the Pope told Storrs that the British had defiled the holy city by introducing cinemas and 500 prostitutes. Storrs tried to mollify the pontiff by explaining that cinemas had been there before and the whores had been removed. Barlassina continued to be such a nuisance that the British tried to have him replaced by a British subject, but without success.[36] Because of his intransigence, especially over matters of precedence, he embarrassed even his own superiors to such an extent that in 1929 the Vatican appointed an Englishman, Father Pascal Robinson, Apostolic Delegate to Palestine to handle relations with the government. Barlassina, however, remained a thorn in the side of the British in Jerusalem until his death in office in 1947.

Under British rule, most of the consuls, though not the Russian, returned to Jerusalem, but they found that their former prerogatives were much diminished. The definitive abolition of the Capitulations by the League of Nations in article 8 of the Palestine mandate, definitively approved in 1922, reduced the consuls to shadows of their former power – correspondingly increasing their frustration and resentment. This was particularly the case with the French, who, deprived of the physical expression of power, sought to console themselves with its spiritual equivalent – their traditional protectorate over Latins and Latin rights at the holy places. They persisted in this quest notwithstanding their formal acceptance of the decision at the San Remo Conference in April 1920 that the protectorate was at an end.

The establishment of the British mandate diminished, but did not end, competition, controversy and occasional contretemps at the holy places. In 1922 the Italian and Spanish consuls were reported by their French colleague to have sought, with the assistance of clerics of their own nationalities, to usurp the Frenchman's traditional place of priority in the Christmas service at the Church of the Nativity and in other ceremonies. 'These incidents show with what jealousy neighbouring nations view our preponderant position in the Holy Land, and with what impatience the abolition of our privileges is awaited,' wrote the consul-general.[37] In 1925 a fracas took place outside the Holy Sepulchre, when, contrary to the rules, national flags were paraded there. Storrs wrote to the French consul-general to complain 'that a British corporal was wounded in the mouth by a gentleman who stated that he was a French general'.[38] He received scant satisfaction.

Nor were British relations with the eastern Churches happier. The Orthodox Church felt very much on the defensive in this period. In Jerusalem, where 90 per cent of the Christian population had been Orthodox a century earlier, they had lost ground steadily to the Latins. The Greek Patriarchate had been gravely weakened by debt during the war and by 1918 was virtually bankrupt. There were fears that it might suffer the same fate as the Armenian Patriarchate, which had almost collapsed under the burden of debt in the early eighteenth century. The Arab parish clergy and laity, long restive under rule of the exclusively Greek Brotherhood of the Holy Sepulchre, now revolted. Nationalist feeling was in the ascendant in the community and demands were voiced for the appointment of Arab priests to the episcopate and even to the Patriarchate. The Greeks, however, guarded their dominance over the Church jealously as a matter of their own national pride, acting as 'mandatory' of the Greek nation.[39] The Brotherhood, indeed, had come to see itself not merely as custodian of the Church but as its living embodiment.[40]

Intelligence reports at the start of the British occupation had indicated that the 133rd Greek Orthodox Patriarch, Damianos, was pro-Turkish and 'a great rogue'.[41] He was undoubtedly a skilled politician who had already survived one attempt, in 1908, to oust him from his throne. The Greek consul-general in Cairo, on a visit to Jerusalem in August 1918, drew up a long memorandum for Allenby, accusing Damianos of Turkish sympathies and calling for his deposition. The commander-in-chief was not persuaded and gave permission for the Patriarch to return from exile. He arrived on 5 January 1919, just in time to celebrate the Orthodox Christmas at Bethlehem. The National Bank of Greece offered a loan to clear the Patriarchate's debts. But stringent conditions were attached that would in effect have subjected the entire Greek Orthodox Church in Palestine to control by the Greek government. The British authorities refused to permit this and suggested instead that a loan be sought from a British bank. Unfortunately no reputable financial institution was prepared to take on this risky venture.

The Greek consul in Jerusalem, Dr Tzorbatzoglou, now tried to stimulate a coup d'état within the Patriarchate. He gathered together a party of opponents of the Patriarch in the Brotherhood and proposed a new constitution that would have destroyed the independence of the Jerusalem Patriarchate and subjected it to control by the Patriarchs of Constantinople, Alexandria, Antioch, Greece and Cyprus – and in the last resort by the government of Greece. As the Patriarchate sank ever deeper into ruin, the synod of bishops turned against Damianos. They drew up a bill of indictment, charging that he was

> arbitrary and despotic in his administration, that he
> refused to respect the decisions of the majority of his
> Synod, that he discouraged intellectual development, did
> not restrain slackness of life, squandered the resources

of the Patriarchate, had accumulated enormous debt, did not give a strenuous defence to the rights of the Orthodox Church in the Holy Shrines, tolerated the establishment of institutions of other Orthodox Churches in Palestine, did not make proper pastoral provision for the flock, oppressed the Brotherhood, did not provide for proper administration during his absence in Damascus, sought to estrange the Fraternity from the Greek nation and strove to give it a local or pan-Orthodox character.[42]

As well as much more in similar vein.

Plainly the Patriarchate had collapsed politically as well as financially. The government of Palestine was compelled to set up a commission of inquiry. It produced a 336-page report remarkable for its scholarship, precision and overriding concern to prevent the Greek government from assuming any 'mandatory' overlordship of Orthodox Christianity in Palestine. Damianos was therefore confirmed in office. The proposed new constitution of the Patriarchate was ruled out of order. The rebels in the synod were deprived of their membership, and a commission of liquidation and control was to be established to regulate and restore the finances of the Church. Some hope was placed in the prospect of compensation for properties belonging to the Patriarchate in Romania that had been sequestrated by the Romanian government. But when Damianos went there to pursue the matter in 1924, he returned with 500 sacks of flour rather than the £500,000 that was claimed in respect of the lost real estate.[43] The Patriarchate's debts, amounting to £559,000, were eventually settled by the commission – in part by the disposal to Jews of suddenly valuable building land in the expanding new city of Jerusalem. Damianos died triumphant in office in 1931 after a turbulent reign of thirty-four years.

The Patriarch's death renewed the bitter Greek-Arab conflict in a struggle over the succession. Glimpsing an opening for his own national interests, the Russian Metropolitan Antonii Khrapovitskii proposed a compromise: the election of a 'neutral' – that is, a Russian. The Greeks rejected this as an 'insult'.[44] Only in 1935 was a new Patriarch elected, Timotheos, Archbishop of Jordan, who had the supreme merit, in British eyes, of having been educated at Magdalen College, Oxford.

It must be said that the British records reveal a consistent and conscientious effort by the mandatory government to maintain the status quo and to deal fairly with the conflicting claims of the Christian sects. A generation later, after the end of the mandate, the last British District Commissioner of Jerusalem, J. H. H. Pollock, summarized the religious disputes among Christians that remained unsettled at the conclusion of thirty years of rule by a Christian power:

- Dispute between the Armenians and Greek Orthodox over the replacement of Armenian pictures in the Church of the Tomb of the Virgin Mary at Gethsemane [Mr Pollock opined optimistically that 'this dispute may have been somewhat modified by the disastrous flood which occurred at this ancient church in the Spring of 1948'].
- Dispute between the Armenians and Syrian Orthodox (Jacobites), Copts and Abyssinians regarding the right of burial in the Armenian cemetery on Mount Zion.
- Dispute between the Armenians and the Syrian Orthodox (Jacobites) regarding the ownership of the Chapel of Saint Nicodemus in the Holy Sepulchre.
- Dispute between the Orthodox and the Latins on the whole question of the administration of services and rights within the Church of the Holy Sepulchre, but more particularly a claim by the Latins to have the right of using, at certain services, the northern stairway at Calvary ...
- Dispute between the Orthodox and the Latins regarding the

ownership of a strip of flooring at the eastern arch between the Orthodox and Latin Chapels on Calvary ...

- Dispute between the Armenians and the Orthodox regarding the ownership and right to sweep the lowest step of the staircase leading from the Parvis on the east side of the main door of the Holy Sepulchre.
- The ever recurring and very bitter dispute between the Copts and the Abyssinians regarding rights claimed by the Abyssinians to own and maintain accommodation for monks round the compound on the roof of the Chapel of Saint Helena, which is part of the Church of the Holy Sepulchre.
- The annual dispute which occurs at Bethlehem in the Church of the Nativity between all the Christian communities during the ceremonial cleaning and sweeping of the floor of the Basilica.

Nor was even this the end of the lamentable catalogue of contention, for as Mr Pollock pointed out, 'Other matters which were the constant concern of the Administration as being "danger points" included the preservation of the Star marking the place of the Nativity in the Grotto of the Church of the Nativity at Bethlehem, over which it is sometimes alleged the Crimean War was fought.'[45]

It was not, however, these ancient disputations that proved most disturbing to the mandatory government but rather a new set of conflicts revolving around holy places, not between the Christian sects but between Muslims and Jews. The leading figure on the Muslim side in this new religious contest, Hajj Amin al-Husayni, succeeded in exploiting it in order to elevate himself into dominance over the Arabs of not only Jerusalem but also Palestine as a whole.

The rise of the mufti

In November 1918 a committee of Christians and Muslims, including many notable figures, was formed in Jerusalem and planned to petition the French for the inclusion of Palestine in Syria. Storrs sent for the mufti (or 'Grand Mufti' as, following Egyptian practice, he styled him) and issued a friendly warning. He also sent for the mayor of the city, Musa Kazem Pasha al-Husayni, and explained to him that, so long as he held office under the military administration, he could not 'stand on a political platform'. 'The mayor seemed grateful for this warning,' Storrs reported, 'which enabled him to say that he thought he would be more useful to his country as President of the Municipality.' Storrs next gave the Latin Patriarch the names of Latins who were on the committee. 'Discovering later that the remaining few still had thoughts of going through with the matter', Storrs sent for Sheikh Musa Budeiri 'and warned him that he was playing with fire and that the British Government and Allies were not in the mood for receiving sensational petitions on political matters at such a time as this'.[46]

Notwithstanding the efforts of the government to damp down Arab political activity, unrest continued. Until July 1920 the existence of Faisal's Arab regime in Damascus encouraged the growth in Palestine of nationalist activity that sought the country's inclusion in an Arab Greater Syria. The activities of the Zionists provoked ever greater hostility. This coalesced with an undercurrent of traditional Muslim contempt for Jews and erupted in 1920 in an explosion of communal violence in Jerusalem – the first of several that were to punctuate the history of the mandate.

The riots of April 1920 took place during the Muslim pilgrim festivity of Nebi Musa. Notwithstanding the statement in Deuteronomy (34: 5–6) that Moses had died and been buried in the 'Land of Moab', where 'no man knoweth of his sepulchre to this day', a tradition had developed among Palestinian Muslims locating Moses' tomb west, rather than east, of the River Jordan. A shrine marking the spot had been built near the Jerusalem–Jericho road, about four miles SSW of Jericho, and this became the object of an annual pilgrimage.

The origin of the festival is obscure. One authority suggests that its roots are 'older than Islam'.[47] Another has placed the growth of veneration for the tomb within the context of regional rivalry between rulers in Damascus and Jerusalem and has shown how, by the seventeenth century, the shrine had acquired general recognition among Muslims. This was in spite of the rival pretensions of no fewer than seven other alleged burial places of Moses, including one near Damascus. The shrine near Jericho was built by the Mamluk Sultan Baybars in 1269. Its construction reflected his general policy of enhancing the religious significance of Jerusalem and its environs for Muslims during a period of conflict not only with the Crusaders but also with Mongols, Armenians and others. The development of an annual mass pilgrimage to this tomb appears from a number of Muslim sources to have become firmly established by the reign of Sulayman the Magnificent. In the late Ottoman period it was revived by provincial governors with the result that, by the late nineteenth century, this was the largest pilgrim festival of Muslims in the Levant, drawing participants from Nablus and Hebron as well as from Transjordan.[48]

A striking indication of the festival's competitive character *vis-à-vis* Christianity was its timing: remarkably for a Muslim festival, its date was determined not by the Islamic calendar but by the eastern Christian one. The pilgrimage coincided each year with the Orthodox Easter, which attracted large numbers of Christian pilgrims to Jerusalem. As the mufti of Jerusalem explained in 1920, it was so fixed 'that the Muslims at that time should have a feast as those of other communities'.[49] Some historians have suggested that it may have originated after the Muslim reconquest of Jerusalem from the Crusaders as a way of asserting Islamic dominance in the face of Christian pilgrims at Eastertide. Muslim festivals that combined elements of competition and syncretism were common in many parts of the Muslim world where Muslims lived cheek by jowl with non-Muslims – for example, medieval Spain.[50] In the case of Nebi Musa, the Christian connection is suggested not only by the method of dating but also by the facts that the celebrations continued for a whole week (identical with Holy Week), that they included, in particular, processions through the streets of Jerusalem and that their primary focus was on a tomb.

By the late Ottoman period the festival had settled into an established and unchanging pattern. Each year two processions of pilgrims set out for Jerusalem, one from Nablus in the north, the other from Hebron in the south. They converged on the Haram al-Sharif where they would encamp briefly before proceeding down the Jericho road to the tomb. There the pilgrims would spend three nights, the masses in tents, some notables in buildings attached to the shrine. Finally they would all return to Jerusalem, where they would gather for prayers on the Haram on the morning of Good Friday, after which they would disperse. The processions were accompanied by feasting, banners, games, circumcisions of boys, and music – songs and percussive instrumental performances by a government band. Certain notable families in Jerusalem were by tradition accorded a central role: the most important was the part played by the Husayni family, who were recognized as patrons of the festival. Nebi Musa also had another, less convivial aspect: it was well known as a traditional season for inter-communal brawls and for fighting between rival Muslim groups. For this reason, the pilgrims from Nablus and Hebron were generally kept as separate from each other as possible.

With the British occupation, Nebi Musa entered a new phase. For the first time in its history it now took place under Christian rule. Although the principle of the status quo had originally applied purely to Christian holy places, it was extended by the British to those of all religions in Palestine. One reason was that, in the initial phase of military government between 1917 and 1920, the occupiers were required by the laws of war to maintain the status quo in all matters of civil administration. Thus the British, like their Ottoman predecessors, provided ceremonial gun salutes and a military band to accompany the pilgrims. Storrs, like the Turkish *mutasarrif*, attended a ceremony at the start of the festivities at which the Muslim religious authorities proclaimed the inauguration of the pilgrimage. Yet, however much the British might try to stick to business as usual, Nebi Musa was always a time of great anxiety. As Storrs later wrote, 'Both for them [the Muslims] and for us the transition between the Ottoman and the British control of this festival was a delicate matter, for it marked too sharply, unless the Administration was prepared for a little give and take, that passing of thirteen hundred years' Islamic theocracy.'[51] Under British rule the pilgrimage became a rallying point against Christian domination in Jerusalem, a battleground for internal Muslim rivalries and an occasion for heightened anti-Jewish feeling. As the nearest to an all-Palestine festival of Muslims, it was natural that it should also take on a nationalist and anti-Zionist hue.

In April 1920 the pilgrimage turned from a religious festival into a political demonstration, then into a riot. As the crowds gathered in Jerusalem to begin the descent to the tomb, speeches were made and banners flown urging union with Syria. Among the speakers was the young nationalist firebrand Hajj Amin al-Husayni, who exhibited a portrait of the Emir Faisal from a balcony and cried, 'This is your king!'[52] Amid ever-growing excitement, rioting broke out, in the course of which nine people died (five of them Jews) and 244 were injured (211 Jews).[53] This was the first major outbreak of Arab-Jewish violence in Jerusalem under British rule. It had two immediate consequences of far-reaching significance.

The first was the decision of Storrs, immediately following the riots, to dismiss the mayor of Jerusalem, Musa Kazem Pasha al-Husayni, whose nationalist fervour was held to have excited the crowd. He was replaced by the former Ottoman deputy for Jerusalem Ragheb Bey Nashashibi, who held the office for the next fourteen years. The Attorney-General, Norman Bentwich, described Ragheb fairly as 'a man of the world, genial, cynical and without any fanaticism ... He retained some of the Ottoman official tradition of Baksheesh and nepotism, but within limits.'[54] Here was the germ of a

bitter conflict between the Husayni and Nashashibi families that extended to their rival networks of clans throughout Palestine and that
disturbed Arab politics throughout the mandatory period.

The second decision was no less portentous. Musa Kazem Pasha's
young kinsman Hajj Amin al-Husayni had, as we have seen, also made
nationalist speeches to the pilgrims. He fled to Arab-controlled Syria
but was sentenced in his absence to ten years' imprisonment on a
charge of incitement to violence. A year later, however, in April 1921,
he was amnestied by the High Commissioner and allowed to return
to Jerusalem. An implicit bargain was reached between Sir Herbert
Samuel and Hajj Amin. In return for the latter's promise to see to it
that no trouble took place at future Nebi Musa celebrations, Samuel
arranged his appointment as Grand Mufti of Jerusalem (the position
had recently been vacated by the death of the incumbent). Hajj Amin
secured the position in spite of the fact that another candidate,
Sheikh Husam al-Din Jarallah, had received a higher number of votes
in the election that was conducted according to Ottoman procedures.[55] The rivalry between the Jarallah and Husayni families over
the office of mufti stretched back into the nineteenth century, and
was to continue in the future.[56]

Hajj Amin's appointment as mufti of Jerusalem was the first step
in the career of an ambitious and ruthless leader. Bentwich, who had
played a large part in engineering it, described him as 'foxy and cunning'.[57] But in his early years of office Hajj Amin conducted himself
with circumspection and in 1921 secured election by a large majority
to the additional post of President of the newly established Supreme
Moslem Council. These two offices, which he held concurrently, gave
him ultimate control over the system of *awqaf*, the proceeds of which
were in many cases misappropriated for purposes designated by the
mufti.[58] Hajj Amin further supervised the entire panoply of Muslim
religious, educational and judicial institutions, as well as an orphanage, newspaper, libraries, clinics and scout troops, not merely in
Jerusalem but throughout Palestine. He appointed at least twenty-

eight of his kinsmen to lucrative positions connected with the Council.[59] He thus built up an inner core of supporters who, for the most part, served him devotedly in subsequent political struggles. The immense authority that he thus wielded was unprecedented for any mufti and transformed the nature of the office. It became the power base from which he launched his career as leader of the Palestinian Arab nationalist movement.

The mufti exploited the sanctity of Jerusalem to Muslims with great effectiveness in his rise to power. He pushed the city to the fore of his political activity by collecting funds from all parts of the Muslim world for the restoration of the shrines on the Haram al-Sharif and by complaining of Jewish encroachment on the sacred compound. Above all, he became the leading exponent of Muslim claims in a simmering dispute over rights at the most important Jewish holy place in Jerusalem, indeed anywhere, the Western Wall.

In 1931 the mufti summoned an international Muslim congress to meet in Jerusalem. He secured the support for this enterprise of Muslim leaders from India, Tunisia and elsewhere. This was not the first such congress ever convened: earlier ones had met in Mecca and Cairo in the 1920s. But it was the largest up to that date and attracted widespread attention. The idea for the congress arose at the funeral on the Haram in January 1931 of the Indian Pan-Islamic leader Muhammad Ali. In discussions after the burial, his brother, Shawkat Ali, appears to have agreed with Hajj Amin on the convening of the congress.[60] Shawkat Ali was on bad terms with Ibn Saud, who had ousted Sherif Hussein from the Hejaz and from his position as guardian of Mecca and Medina – hence, perhaps, the Indian leader's focus on Jerusalem. In London, officials at the Colonial and India Offices became concerned at the potentially disturbing effects in India of the congress. They even gave thought to banning it. In the end the High Commissioner, Sir Arthur Wauchope, received an assurance from Hajj Amin that it would be entirely non-political and advised allowing it to proceed.[61]

Although it encountered opposition from some Arab countries, particularly Egypt, as well as from the mufti's local opponents in Jerusalem, the congress was attended by 130 delegates from twenty-two countries. Among the participants was the mufti's former teacher, Muhammad Rashid Rida, one of the leading Islamic thinkers in Egypt. In spite of Hajj Amin's promise, it proved impossible to exclude politics altogether from the proceedings. Several speeches were delivered against Zionism and on the alleged threat to the Muslim holy places arising from Jewish plans to rebuild the temple.[62] The congress resolved to establish a Muslim university in Jerusalem – explicitly intended by the mufti as a challenge to the Hebrew University.[63] An illustrated brochure for the project was published and some funds were collected, including £7,543 from the Maharajah of Hyderabad, but the university was never built. If the congress yielded few tangible results, it nevertheless puffed up the mufti's prestige and implanted the defence of Jerusalem and of Palestine on the agenda of pan-Islamic concerns. Henceforth Hajj Amin bore three titles: Grand Mufti, President of the Supreme Moslem Council and President of the General Islamic Congress. He could now legitimately claim to be a figure of international importance in the Muslim world.

On the local level, the mufti could also rejoice in the defeat of the Husaynis' enemy, the mayor of Jerusalem, Ragheb Nashashibi. The conflict between the two families, and their extended coalition of clans, was so bitter that in the 1927 municipal elections the Husaynis had even approached the Zionists suggesting they make common cause against Ragheb.[64] The Jewish vote, on this occasion, went to Ragheb. But by 1934 the Jews had had enough of his administration, which they judged corrupt and inefficient. Some Jewish votes swung to Ragheb's opponent in the first ward, Dr Husayn Fakhri al-Khalidi. A member of another illustrious Jerusalem family, who claimed descent from Khaled ibn Walid, the Arab conqueror of Palestine in the seventh century, Khalidi had an important support base of his own and also enjoyed the backing of the Husaynis. He won the seat. When Ragheb nevertheless tried to retain the mayoralty, Moshe Shertok of the Jewish Agency (quasi-government of the *yishuv*) urged the British authorities to appoint Khalidi.[65] Ragheb's appeal failed and Khalidi became mayor. Ragheb never recovered his former influence – and never forgave those responsible.

Towards partition

As the Arab-Jewish conflict in Palestine intensified, the concept of territorial partition was introduced into political discourse. Significantly, one of the earliest instances on which it appeared was in relation to Jerusalem. In 1932 the head of the Political Department of the Jewish Agency (in effect the Zionist movement's foreign minister), Chaim Arlosoroff, in a letter to the former High Commissioner, Sir Herbert Samuel, proposed the division of Jerusalem into two boroughs, one Arab, the other Jewish, each with its own council. In his reply Samuel expressed his personal opposition to the idea, arguing that to have two municipal authorities 'in immediate proximity to each other would almost be to invite friction', although he conceded that this might be 'the only means of avoiding greater evils'.[66]

In April 1936 a countrywide Arab general strike and rebellion broke out in Palestine. Although the mufti did not initiate or organize the revolt, by the summer he was providing money and moral inspiration to the rebels. The British were concerned not only by the scale of the rebellion but also by the changed regional context. With the Italian invasion of Ethiopia in 1935, Mussolini signalled his ambition to turn the Mediterranean into an Italian sea. For the first time since the end of the Great War British predominance in the Near East was seriously challenged by another European power. British intelligence learned that the Italian consul in Jerusalem was supplying financial support to the rebels.[67]

Fascist mischief-making was not limited to the Arabs, as can be seen from the following extract from a conversation in Rome in 1934:

MUSSOLINI: But what do you think of Jerusalem?

WEIZMANN: One thing is absolutely clear. If Jerusalem does not become a Jewish capital, it could not in any event become an Arab capital, because there is the Christian world. Jerusalem is the confluence of three religions. But it should be noted that the sanctity of Jerusalem is a somewhat recent invention for the Mussulmans, whereas Jerusalem is the City of David for the Jews, and for the Christians it is the centre of their Holy Places.

MUSSOLINI: You are right. An arrangement satisfactory to all must be found.

WEIZMANN: On the question of Jerusalem I have always been very discreet. We are today the majority in Jerusalem.

MUSSOLINI: Is this possible?

WEIZMANN: Certainly, and yet I have always counselled my friends not to make use of this fact, precisely because it is a question of Jerusalem.

MUSSOLINI: You are very wise.

WEIZMANN: When we reach the stage of practicalities, can I count on your support?

MUSSOLINI: Certainly.[68]

The danger that an outside power such as Italy might exploit the growing nationalist antagonisms in Palestine greatly concerned the British government and led it to seek a new policy that would maintain Britain's strategic interests while disentangling them from Arab-Jewish conflict.

In the hope of finding such a policy, the government appointed a

Royal Commission to inquire into the Palestine problem. Its chairman was Lord Peel, a descendant of the nineteenth-century Prime Minister; its chief intellectual force was Sir Reginald Coupland, Professor of Imperial History at Oxford. The commission's report, issued in July 1937, called for the partition of Palestine into an Arab state (to be joined to Transjordan) and a smaller Jewish state, as well as a British mandatory enclave around Jerusalem (see Map 4, page 111). The proposed enclave was much larger than the municipal area of the city. It included Bethlehem and a corridor that would stretch as far as the coast at Jaffa – wits called this the 'Promenade des Anglais' – as well as the towns of Nazareth, Tiberias, Safed, Acre and (vital to the British because of its port) Haifa.

Both Arabs and Jews were divided in their reactions to the report. Among the Arabs, the Nashashibi party, closely linked to Emir Abdullah of Transjordan (another son of Sherif Hussein), were attracted to partition, but cowed into silence by the mufti's supporters. The Arab Higher Committee, the main Palestinian nationalist body, dominated by the mufti, rejected the report *in toto*. They declined to discuss any form of partition and resumed the revolt with renewed vigour. The Zionists engaged in acrimonious internal debate but eventually came round to accepting the idea of partition in principle, though demanding more advantageous borders than those proposed by the Royal Commission.

Indeed, the Zionist response to the idea of a Zionist state without Zion was curiously complaisant. Their general view of the holy city had always had an undercurrent of hostility – particularly strong in the case of the dominant, secularizing socialist-Zionist movement. They saw Jerusalem as the fortress of the 'old *yishuv*', symbol of all that it stood for by way of conservatism, unproductiveness and anti-Zionism. Tel Aviv was the real capital of Zionism until the foundation of the state of Israel – and, in all but name, for some time thereafter.[69] In the 1930s the Jewish Agency built impressive headquarters on King George V Avenue in western Jerusalem, designed to serve as

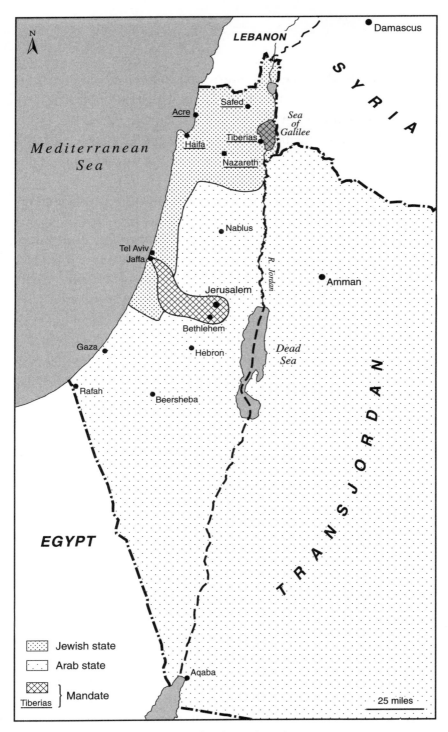

Map 4: *Royal Commission partition plan for Palestine (1937)*

the home of the Zionist quasi-government. But most political parties were based in Tel Aviv and the homes of nearly all the political leaders of the movement were in the dynamic coastal city. By the late 1930s Tel Aviv's Jewish population was double that of the capital: 177,000 to 82,000.[70] The Jewish centre of gravity in Palestine had moved decisively to Tel Aviv.

The Zionist leadership realized that, given international religious interests of Christians and Muslims in the old city of Jerusalem, there was no hope of its inclusion in a Jewish state. They therefore came reluctantly to the conclusion that the only way to gain any foothold in Jerusalem was to urge that the city, like the country as a whole, be partitioned. Moshe Shertok, head of the Political Department of the Jewish Agency, wrote to a colleague in December 1937, 'The only way to be extricated from the tangle of the demands of the various religions is to keep the entire old city as a single unit under one jurisdiction with international authority.'[71] The idea of partition was rendered more palatable to the Zionists by the semi-voluntary segregation of Arabs and Jews that had been accentuated as a result of the revolt and the Arab commercial boycott of Jewish stores. Many Jews moved out of Arab or mixed areas of the city, a process that, as the historian Yehoshua Porath has remarked, 'suited perfectly the Zionist movement's endeavour to build a self-contained Jewish national community in Palestine'.[72]

A Jerusalem Committee, established by the Zionist Executive, prepared a detailed plan for the partition of Jerusalem. It sought to retain the maximum possible Jewish population and landed property within the Jewish state. It therefore proposed that the Jewish-inhabited western and northern districts of the new city, together with Mount Scopus, be included in the Jewish state. The whole of the old city, including the Jewish quarter, as well as other areas of traditional Jewish interest, such as the burial ground on the Mount of Olives, were assigned under the plan to the residual mandatory area (see Map 5, page 113). This would leave several thousand Jews, mainly in the old city, outside the area of the projected Jewish state; it

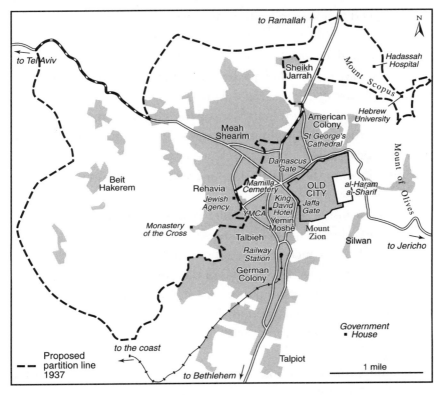

Map 5: Jewish Agency partition plan for Jerusalem (1937)

was proposed that these should nevertheless be permitted to become citizens of the Jewish state.[73]

Neither the Peel Commission's plan nor the Zionists' counter-proposal was implemented. Instead a further commission, chaired by Sir John Woodhead, was appointed by the British government to draw up a new partition plan. The Woodhead Commission's report, published in November 1938, rejected the idea of partitioning Jerusalem. In fact, it rejected the idea of partition altogether, arguing that it was impracticable to divide up such a small country as Palestine. It nevertheless felt obliged to comply with its instructions and considered various potential schemes for partition, including the proposal for a Jerusalem enclave. Its report, submitted in the autumn of

1938, argued that if such a city-state were to be created, it should be enlarged to include the Palestine Broadcasting Service transmitter, north of Jerusalem, as well as a wider corridor to the sea. Under these proposals, the Jews would have been a minority of about 80,000 in a total population of 211,000 in the enclave.

In arguing against the partition of the city, as demanded by the Jews, the Woodhead Commission pointed to several difficulties that would appear again in reactions to later Jerusalem government schemes down to the present day. One was the problem of security:

> To our mind, the chief problem would be the prevention
> of breaches of the peace along the boundary between a
> population which, on one side, would be composed
> almost entirely of Jews, and on the other, very largely of
> Arabs ... We are of opinion that it would have to be
> solved by the construction along the boundary of a road
> with a railing down the middle.[74]

The Zionist submission had anticipated this objection by citing the examples of cities such as Shanghai that were divided into different jurisdictions but without physical barriers between them. Alas, the example of Shanghai was ill-chosen: that city was notorious in the 1930s for its lawlessness and for the ease with which criminals and political terrorists would avoid arrest by crossing freely over the boundaries of its three different jurisdictions, Chinese, International and French.[75] In addition, the commission argued that there would be problems in controlling the flow of casual labour, in the organiza-tion of customs and in managing the city's water supply.

While the commission acknowledged that all these practical diffi-culties might, given goodwill, be overcome, it argued that there were overriding political and religious objections to division of the city. Muslims would be vehemently opposed because, 'in spite of all the denials issued by the Jews, the Arabs still believe that the Jews have designs on the Old City'. Also 'Christian opinion throughout the world, realizing that such a step would provoke resentment and disorder, would be deeply grieved by a proposal to entrust part of the city precincts to the control of the Jewish community.'[76] In the event, both the Peel and the Woodhead reports were shelved. The government, foreseeing the likelihood of war in Europe, had lost its enthusiasm for partition, opting instead to maintain a unitary Palestine for the duration.

Meanwhile, the British succeeded, at great cost, in putting down the Arab revolt. In July 1937 an order was issued for the mufti's arrest. He took refuge on the Haram al-Sharif, which the British dared not enter for fear of offending Muslim religious susceptibilities. A *Daily Telegraph* correspondent who interviewed the besieged cleric reported that 'his only distraction is to promenade within the walls of the area or to watch the world from his private rooms overlooking the Wailing Wall'.[77] All the gates to the sanctuary were guarded by British troops. In October, following the assassination of a senior official, the government dissolved the Arab Higher Committee. Several of its members were arrested and some deported to the Seychelles. The mufti, however, succeeded in escaping, disguised as a bedouin (according to other reports disguised as a woman), and made his way to Lebanon, from where he continued to inspire resistance to the British. Before leaving Jerusalem he had made contact with the German consul-general, seeking support for Arab resistance to Zionism.[78] It was the start of a beautiful friendship.

In October 1938 the revolt reached its highest point when rebels occupied the old city of Jerusalem. But with the four-power Munich Agreement of 29–30 September in hand, the British were free to release troops from the European theatre. Reinforcements were brought in from England and the army launched a determined counter-attack. The commander of the Jerusalem District, Major-General Richard O'Connor, ordered a reoccupation of the old city on 19 October. In the assault, the British used local Arabs as human shields.[79] The rebels capitulated. Although sporadic violence continued, this was the end of the rebellion as a military threat.

By repressing the revolt, the British decapitated the Arab leadership of Jerusalem. The mufti remained in exile until after the end of the mandate. During the war he fled to Iraq, where he helped organize an abortive anti-British coup in 1941. When that failed, he moved on to Berlin, where he broadcast for the Nazis. The mayor of Jerusalem, Dr Husayn al-Khalidi, was one of those deported to the Seychelles 'because of his moral responsibility, as a member of the Arab Higher Committee ... for the campaign of murder and terrorism in Palestine'.[80] The former mayor, Ragheb Nashashibi, who favoured a more accommodating stance towards the British, was threatened with assassination by supporters of the mufti and spent much of his time over the next few years in Cairo.

In the absence of Khalidi, his Jewish deputy, Daniel Auster, took his place in an acting capacity. Relations between Arab and Jewish councillors deteriorated and, fearing that elections would produce more violence, the government considered the appointment of a British official as acting mayor.[81] On the recommendation of a committee of inquiry, a former judge, Mustafa Bey Khalidi, was appointed mayor. The Jews protested on the ground that they constituted a majority of the city's population; but as Axis forces moved closer to Palestine, the High Commissioner, Sir Harold MacMichael, reported that the Jews 'had allowed political manoeuvring on this issue to become submerged in their general alarm'.[82]

'A glorified cockpit'

The Jerusalem question, like that of Palestine as a whole, remained politically suspended until the later part of the war. In September 1943 MacMichael proposed yet another partition scheme for Palestine under which, in addition to Jewish and Arab states, a 'State of Jerusalem' would be created, to be ruled by Great Britain.[83] The proposed borders of the state were debated between London and Jerusalem and eventually enlarged to include not only the city of Jerusalem but also Bethlehem, Ramallah, Lydda, Ramleh and the Yarkon springs. One reason for this was to ensure that there would be no Arab corridor separating the Jewish state from the Jerusalem state.

In a memorandum in February 1944, setting out the arguments in favour of his scheme, MacMichael quoted Pindar: 'As our work is beginning, we must set on it a front that shines from afar.'[84] In this spirit, he maintained that 'the creation of a new State [of Jerusalem], which will safeguard for ever the Holy City, preserve its associations and guarantee freedom of access to the adherents of all those creeds which hold it sacred, should be given pride of place in what is otherwise a project of expediency'. The state would have a population of about 300,000, of whom about 90,000 would be Jews. The form of government of the state, MacMichael wrote, 'must clearly be different from a Crown Colony and transcending it. On the other hand, it must enjoy the normal forms of democracy and representative government.' The constitution, he suggested, 'must necessarily embody some form of diarchy'. Therefore, while there would be a legislature in which twenty-six of the twenty-eight members would be elected, the High Commissioner would retain 'responsibility for the administration of certain reserved subjects ... [including] the Holy Places ... the defence and foreign relations of the State, the acquisition of citizenship, and the control of legislation'. MacMichael expected that the twenty-six elected members of the legislature would include eleven Muslims, eight Jews and seven Christians – 'with the result that no community will have an absolute majority in the Legislature'. He rejected the idea that residents of the state might be citizens of the neighbouring Arab or Jewish states. That, he pointed out, would give those states 'almost unlimited powers of interference under the guise of protection of their nationals ... Jerusalem would be no more than a glorified cockpit'.[85]

MacMichael's plan was approved by the Colonial Office, though officials there saw 'some difficulty' with the constitutional scheme. It was pointed out that 'the diarchical principle' had been tried in the Indian provinces and in Malta and had ended in failure.[86] In April 1944 MacMichael went to Cairo to meet the British Minister Resident and senior British officials in the Middle East. Some of the conferees doubted the practicability of establishing the Jerusalem state as a purely British venture. The fear was expressed that 'France and Russia in particular would be likely to put forward their claims, as protectors of the Catholic and Orthodox Churches respectively'.[87]

Meanwhile, a Cabinet committee had been set up to review the whole Palestine problem. It considered various objections and amendments to MacMichael's proposals, including the Prime Minister's view that 'the Jerusalem State was perhaps needlessly large'.[88] The Foreign Office strongly opposed the whole concept of partition and the Foreign Secretary, Anthony Eden, circulated a powerful Cabinet memorandum attacking as 'pure illusion' the view that it would at least provide 'finality'.[89] On the proposed Jerusalem state, the Foreign Office doubted whether the legislature would 'work satisfactorily, in practice':

> It seems probable that the relations between the Arab and Jewish sections of the population will reflect the state of relations existing between Southern Syria and the Jewish State. If Arab-Jewish relations are bad, and especially if outbreaks of violence occur, it is unlikely that Arabs and Jews in the Jerusalem State will co-operate. There may be periods of unrest and confusion. Jerusalem may well become one of the main battle grounds between the contending forces. In short, it is unlikely that the Jerusalem State, as a permanent member of the family of nations, will turn out to be a credit to its founders.[90]

The Cabinet committee nevertheless approved partition in October 1944. The Jerusalem state was to be 'autonomous' but 'under the protection of Great Britain or of the United Nations'. It was proposed that the state would have open boundaries but that 'neither Arab nor Jew should be permitted to take up permanent residence in it without approval previously obtained'.[91] Churchill, who had opposed partition in the 1930s, now looked with greater favour on the idea. But it continued to be opposed by the Foreign Office and was shelved following the assassination by Jewish terrorists, in November 1944, of the British Minister in the Middle East, Lord Moyne.

While British long-term policy-making on Palestine stalled in late 1944, the Zionists were laying their own plans for their future. A committee was formed to plan settlement activity in Palestine and it set up a sub-committee whose task, according to David Ben Gurion, head of the Jewish Agency Executive in Palestine, would 'include preparation of a plan to increase Jewish settlement in Jerusalem and its environs ... and to ensure that the capital of our country will have a Jewish majority'.[92] The sub-committee, however, met only twice, produced no recommendations and had no discernible effect on Zionist political planning. In fact, Jerusalem still had a low priority in Zionist thinking.

The problem was thrown back on to the political agenda in August 1944 by a crisis in municipal government arising from the sudden death of the mayor, Mustafa Bey al-Khalidi. As in 1937, the Jewish deputy mayor, Daniel Auster, took over temporarily as acting mayor. But Arab councillors threatened to boycott the work of the municipality unless an Arab mayor were immediately appointed. Members of the Khalidi family visited the High Commissioner to ask him to assuage their grief by appointing another of their number mayor in place of their dead kinsman.[93] Hebrew newspapers countered with demands for a Jewish mayor or, failing that, rotation of Muslim, Christian and Jewish mayors. Jews, they pointed out, were now estimated to constitute 61 per cent of the population of the city. Some suggested a third solution: the city should be divided into separate and independently administered Jewish and Arab sections.[94] The Arab councillors' boycott took effect from 21 March 1945. In an effort to break the impasse, the High Commissioner, Viscount Gort, proposed an annual rotating mayoralty among Muslims, Jews and Christians (the latter not necessarily to be Palestinian). The Jews accepted the idea in principle but argued about the length of the term and demanded that the first incumbent under the arrangement should be a Jew. The main (Husayni-dominated) Arab party called a general strike in protest against the plan.[95]

On 20 April Gort reported that 'Arab councillors, with some political associates' had come forward with 'extremely tentative' proposals 'that the old city and certain predominant Arab areas might be separated from the modern city of Jerusalem'. 'The Jews,' he said, 'also appear interested.'[96] The way seemed open to some agreed form of municipal partition.

By the end of the war in Europe and the Middle East in May 1945, continued bickering among Arab and Jewish council members had rendered the municipality virtually inoperable. The government therefore announced on 11 July that, 'owing to the failure of the Jerusalem Municipal Council to demonstrate its political maturity and resolve its difficulties', administration of the city would be handed over temporarily to a commission of five British officials. At the same time the Chief Justice of Palestine, Sir William Fitzgerald, was invited to conduct an inquiry into the future municipal government of Jerusalem.[97] The terms of the government communiqué, considered insulting by some, evoked complaints and the Jews refused to cooperate with Fitzgerald's inquiry.

The Chief Justice, a genial Irishman, submitted his recommendations in August 1945. He accepted that the existing municipal government, based on 'the fundamental principle of democracy that the opinion of the majority shall prevail', had failed:

The Arabs are unable to concede that principle to the city

of Jerusalem that has taken shape since the advent of British administration. In the light of history I am constrained to admit that this point of view, although not to the extent to which it has been pressed by the Arabs, is not without substance. Indeed, politically responsible Jews have repeatedly stressed that they fully appreciate that the unique position of the city of Jerusalem calls for a specialized form of administration.

The Muslims continued to demand the mayoralty on ground of tradition, the Jews on ground of majority. The latest figures available to Fitzgerald showed a Jewish population of 92,000, as against 32,000 Muslims and 27,000 others.

Fitzgerald's recommendations regarding Jerusalem echoed those of Lord Peel for Palestine as a whole. In 1937 the Royal Commission had argued that, an irrepressible conflict having broken out in Palestine, normal majoritarian democratic solutions would not work and 'the only hope of a cure lies in a surgical operation'.[98] Peel's solution was a partitioned country, Fitzgerald's a partitioned city. The difference, of course, was that Fitzgerald was dealing with a Jewish rather than an Arab majority:

> I am forced to the regrettable but irresistible conclusion
> that there is no possibility of the Arabs and Jews co-
> operating to make the Municipal Corporations Ordinance
> of 1934 effective in Jerusalem. Without that co-
> operation, municipal administration within the ambit of
> the present Ordinance must break down ... It so
> happens that geographically the present Jerusalem
> Municipal Area lends itself to being divided into two
> boroughs with clearly defined boundaries, each with a
> different outlook on life, with different aspirations and
> interests. I see no reason to shrink from the reality of the

situation, which in fact I regard as fortunate: one borough will be predominantly Jewish, and the other will be predominantly Arab.

Above the two boroughs, Fitzgerald proposed an umbrella Administrative Council, akin to the London County Council. The two boroughs would conform as far as possible to existing residential patterns (see Map 6, page 123). But Fitzgerald's plan did not find sufficient favour for the government to try to implement it.

The municipal government of Jerusalem remained, until the end of the mandate, under the direction of an unelected commission. In December 1945 George Webster, former Postmaster-General of Palestine, was appointed its chairman. He was joined by six other officials, four English, two Palestinian. A year later Webster retired and was replaced by another official, John Hilton, who was himself succeeded by Richard Graves in June 1947.

Meanwhile, Palestine as a whole descended into civil war. The Labour government, elected in Britain in July 1945, decided not to proceed with the tentative wartime partition plan. Instead, seeking to draw the United States into shared responsibility, it persuaded the Truman administration to join in appointing an Anglo-American Committee of Inquiry into the problems of Palestine and of the Jewish survivors of the death camps in Europe. The committee opposed partition. Its main recommendation was for the immediate admission to Palestine of 100,000 Jewish refugees from Europe. But the British government made their admission conditional on the disarming and disbandment of Jewish paramilitary organizations that had grown in membership and armaments over the previous few years. The Zionists would not contemplate that.

As the political argument dragged on without a resolution, the Zionists resorted to direct action. The large-scale influx of Jewish immigrants from Europe, beyond the legal limits set by the government, turned into a battle of wills and propaganda between the British and

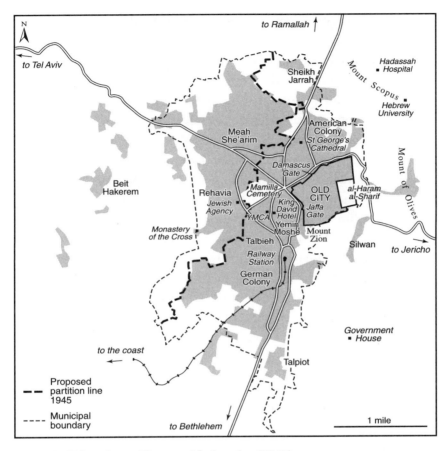

Map 6: Sir William Fitzgerald's proposal for Jerusalem (1945)

the Zionists. In Jerusalem terrorist acts multiplied. On 22 July 1946 the King David Hotel, where the Palestine government and British Army headquarters were temporarily situated, was blown up by members of the Jewish underground group Irgun Zvai Leumi; ninety-one people were killed.

The government retreated into a physical and mental fortress. Part of the central area of the city, containing government offices, and the Russian compound, which housed police headquarters, law courts and the central prison, were cordoned off. An inner security zone was surrounded by barbed wire and was dubbed by the Jews 'Bevingrad' after the hated British Foreign Secretary.

On 1 August 1946 the Jewish Agency Executive, meeting in Paris (since its members feared arrest if they went to Palestine), agreed again on the principle of partition of Palestine into Jewish and Arab states. The proposal was vague on the fate of Jerusalem, reflecting the Zionist leaders' hesitation on the issue. While they did not abjure all right to the city, neither did they lay claim to it.

The Palestinian Arab leadership remained fragmented and disoriented. The mufti was still the most influential figure, but his effectiveness was diminished by continuing enforced exile, first in France, then, from June 1946, in Egypt, and finally, from October 1947, in Lebanon. The re-formed Arab Higher Committee once again included representatives of all the main parties. It sought and gained support from the Arab League, formed in 1944, but was unable to formulate a coherent policy. Unlike the Zionists, the Palestinian Arabs did not succeed in establishing, training and supplying a disciplined armed force.

As further schemes for the future of the country were advanced and discarded, Jerusalem too was the subject of much ingenious constitutional carpentry. In the 'provincial autonomy' plan, advanced jointly in July 1946 by the British Cabinet minister Herbert Morrison and the former US Assistant Secretary of State Henry F. Grady, the mandate was to be converted into a United Nations trusteeship and the country divided into autonomous provinces; the Jerusalem area, including Bethlehem, and the Negev desert in the south of Palestine were to be ruled directly by a British High Commissioner. President Truman, under domestic pressure, rejected the plan (though the administration liked the provisions for Jerusalem) and it faded away after a few weeks.[99] In September a conference on Palestine was convened in London, but it too failed.

So far as Zionist diplomacy was concerned, Jerusalem still did not feature at this period as a leading priority. Over the next year the Jewish Agency Executive failed to reach a clear view of the question. Above all, they did not wish, by vainly demanding sovereignty over west Jerusalem, to risk losing international support for the creation of a Jewish state. Their diplomatic strategy was based on a resigned acceptance of the likelihood of internationalization of the city. With that in mind, they focused their attention on the proposed borders for such an international zone in order to secure two objectives: a Jewish majority in the area and territorial connection to the Jewish state, if necessary in the form of a corridor.[100] Why were the Zionists ready to sacrifice Jerusalem? David Ben Gurion summed the matter up with stark simplicity. This, he said, was 'the price to be paid for statehood'.[101]

Casualties, both civilian and military, were much lower during the Jewish revolt than during the Arab revolt a decade earlier: 4,000 lives were lost in the insurrection between 1936 and 1939; the Jewish revolt, up to April 1947, claimed 270.[102] Nevertheless, the British found the Zionists' rebellion even more difficult to cope with: partly this was because the British were much weaker and even more overstretched than they had been in the 1930s; partly also because the Zionist paramilitaries were better organized and coordinated and often hit much more effectively at military and official points of weakness.

By 14 February 1947 the British had had enough. The Foreign Secretary, Ernest Bevin, wound up the London Palestine conference and confessed that the British government had to 'admit failure for the first time in British history to solve a problem of this kind'.[103] That day the Cabinet resolved to turn the problem over to the United Nations. As residual legatee of the League of Nations mandate over Palestine, the world body was invited to turn its hand to solving the problem.

On 28 April 1947 a special session of the United Nations General Assembly opened to discuss the Palestine problem. It decided to dispatch yet another inquiry commission, the UN Special Committee on Palestine (UNSCOP), to elicit proposals for the future of the country. Headed by Justice Emil Sandström of Sweden, UNSCOP's eleven members were all drawn from countries presumed to be neutral on the issue. In the course of their visit to Palestine, the committee spent two workdays, 18 and 27 June, in Jerusalem, during which they visited the Haram al-Sharif, four synagogues, the Church of the Holy Sepulchre, the offices of the Supreme Moslem Council, the Hebrew University and the Hadassah Hospital. Among the documents they had before them was Sir William Fitzgerald's report on the local administration of Jerusalem and a three-page 'note on the place of Jerusalem in Jewish life and tradition', submitted by the Jewish Agency. The Arab Higher Committee refused to cooperate with the committee, but the major Arab states (except Transjordan) gave evidence. Several Christian bodies presented statements and the French consul-general handed in a memorandum on French religious and educational institutions in the Holy Land.

The proposals before the committee did not afford much prospect of common ground. Arabs almost unanimously demanded the creation of a unitary Arab state of Palestine with Jerusalem as its capital. Christians in general urged internationalization of Jerusalem – though the Vatican, at this stage, made no pronouncement in favour of this either publicly or privately.[104] The Franciscan Custos of the Holy Land pointedly refrained from endorsing the idea and seemed to favour resurrection of the historic rights of France as protector of the Latins. The Zionist position on Jerusalem was not fully spelled out, at least in public. When he was asked by UNSCOP about the Jewish Agency's view, Ben Gurion talked vaguely about the division of the city between a western section that would be incorporated in the Jewish state, and the old city and Arab-inhabited areas that would be internationalized.[105]

UNSCOP set up a sub-committee, under the chairmanship of a Dutch delegate, to consider the question of Jerusalem and the holy places. Of the eleven members of the sub-committee, four – those from Canada, the Netherlands, Peru and Sweden – presented a plan for internationalization of the city. Three – those from India, Iran and Yugoslavia – disagreed with this; and three others – from Czechoslovakia, Guatemala and Uruguay – entered reservations to the majority plan that were later withdrawn. The eleventh member of the sub-committee, from Australia, abstained.

The full UNSCOP committee produced majority and minority recommendations for Palestine as a whole. The majority favoured termination of the mandate and partition of Palestine into Jewish and Arab states, with an internationalized Jerusalem. The minority proposals, submitted by members from India, Iran and Yugoslavia, favoured a single, federated state. The minority recommended that Jerusalem should be the capital of the proposed federation and should be divided into two municipalities, one Arab, including the whole of the old city, the other Jewish, comprising 'the areas which are predominantly Jewish'.

Following the majority on the sub-committee, the majority of the committee as a whole recommended placing Jerusalem under an international trusteeship. Their grounds for doing so were based mainly on the importance of maintaining peace in a city containing holy places of three world faiths. The UNSCOP report argued (with great earnestness if questionable historicity):

> The history of Jerusalem, during the Ottoman regime as
> under the Mandate, shows that religious peace has been
> maintained in the City because the Government was
> anxious and had the power to prevent controversies
> involving some religious interest from developing into
> bitter strife and disorder. The Government was not
> intimately mixed in local politics and could, when
> necessary, arbitrate conflicts.

The whole Jerusalem area was to be demilitarized and neutralized. A governor was to be appointed who should be 'neither Arab nor Jew nor a citizen of the Palestine States nor, at the time of appointment, a resident of the City of Jerusalem'. The city was to be in economic union with the

Jewish and Arab states and open to entry by residents of both, 'subject only to security considerations'. The report contained no provision for the defence of Jerusalem save for the recommendation that protection of the holy places should be entrusted to 'a special police force'.[106]

The designated area of the proposed international Jerusalem was, as in most such plans since 1840, larger than the municipality. It stretched from Ein Karem in the west to Abu Dis in the east; and from Shuafat in the north to Bethlehem in the south. The belt of land surrounding the city was mainly Arab-inhabited. Although the stated purpose was to include some holy places remote from the city, another reason was probably to secure a roughly equal proportion of Arabs and Jews in the population of the city-state. At the end of the mandate the estimated population of Jerusalem was 165,000 (100,000 Jews, 34,000 Muslims, and 31,000 Christians). Only by enlarging the area of the proposed trusteeship to include surrounding Arab villages could approximate Arab-Jewish numerical equality be achieved. UNSCOP estimated the population of this enlarged Jerusalem in 1946 as approximately 205,000, of whom 100,000 were Jews and 105,000 'Arabs and others'.

UNSCOP's report was signed on 31 August 1947, but the General Assembly did not begin its consideration of it until 16 September and did not vote on it for another six weeks after that. This interim period was one of intense political activity. The Arab states strongly opposed the report and tried to mobilize opposition to secure the one-third blocking minority that, according to procedural rules, would be required. The Jewish Agency was prepared to accept the plan, albeit with reservations and the secret hope that they might enlarge the borders of the Jewish state in the war that seemed now almost inevitable. They lobbied hard to secure the two-thirds majority that would be required for formal approval of the plan.

Jerusalem was not seen as the main issue by the Zionists: the nub of the matter was the principle of partition. At the same time, they sought to improve their position in Jerusalem by broaching the idea to

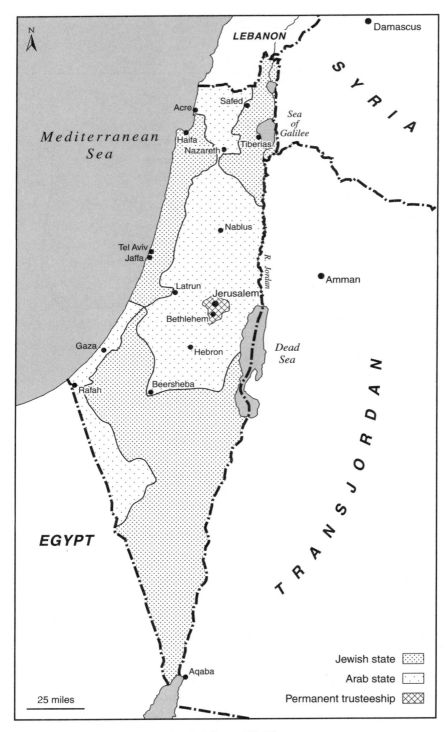

Map 7: United Nations partition plan for Palestine (1947)

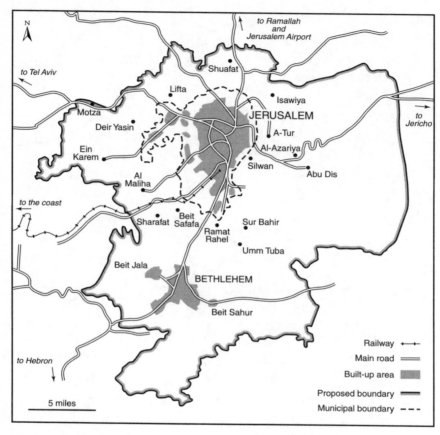

Map 8: United Nations Corpus Separatum *plan for Jerusalem (1947)*

the US State Department that only the old city be internationalized and the remainder of the proposed trusteeship area divided between the Jewish and Arab states. The State Department, however, found the suggestion 'impractical and undesirable'. It was pointed out that 'the majority of Christian establishments in Palestine are concentrated in Jerusalem but outside the Old City. Therefore [they] would fall within the area of either the Jewish or Arab sections. Christian opposition to such a move could be expected.'[107] But there was 'considerable sentiment' in favour of the Zionist proposal among members of the UN working group on Palestine. In spite of the State Department's misgivings, the US representative on the group was therefore authorized 'to go along with the majority on this question, provided that adequate safeguards for the holy places were retained'.[108]

The UNSCOP majority plan was eventually presented to the General Assembly with some changes. The most important of these was the setting of a time limit on the arrangements for Jerusalem: at the end of ten years the residents were to be 'free to express by means of a referendum their wishes as to possible modifications of the regime for the City'. This represented a considerable victory for the Zionists, who hoped to win such a referendum; but it was not quite a right of self-determination, since the resolution spoke only of the expression of a wish and referred only to modifications. A further change from the UNSCOP plan sought and gained by the Zionists was insertion of the principle of autonomous municipal government for different communities in Jerusalem. The final draft also enlarged slightly the area of the proposed *corpus separatum* to include the Jewish settlement of Motza, west of Jerusalem (see Maps 7 and 8, pages 129 and 130).

The draft General Assembly resolution called for the appointment by the UN Trusteeship Council of a governor of Jerusalem who should not be a citizen of either the Arab or the Jewish state. The city was to be demilitarized and neutralized 'and no paramilitary formations, exercises, or activities' were to be permitted. The governor was to organize 'a special police force of adequate strength, the members of which shall be recruited outside of Palestine'. The UN Trusteeship Council was instructed to prepare a statute (i.e. a constitution) for Jerusalem and given five months to complete the task.[109]

The partition resolution was approved by the General Assembly on 29 November 1947 by thirty-three votes to thirteen, with ten abstentions. Its passage was welcomed jubilantly by the Zionists; the Palestinian Arabs declared a three-day general strike. Rioting broke out in Jerusalem. Both sides prepared for war. Rather than forming a blueprint for a peaceful solution of the Palestine imbroglio, the resolution raised the conflict, of which Jerusalem was the core, to a new level.

4   Division

As the mandatory regime dissolved into chaos, the United Nations wrestled with its inability to impose its decision on Palestine in general or Jerusalem in particular. The success of the partition plan would depend in large measure on British cooperation in ensuring a smooth transition to the proposed Jewish and Arab states and the UN Trusteeship in Jerusalem. But the British government declined to have any part in enforcing partition against the wishes of the Arabs of Palestine. They refused to permit UN officials to enter Palestine until shortly before the end of the mandate, which they set at 15 May 1948. The only hope of enforcing the plan rested on the United Nations' ability to mobilize an armed force to secure its authority at least in the proposed international area around Jerusalem. But no agreement could be reached on the creation of such a force and it was never established. Even before the departure of the last High Commissioner from Jerusalem on 14 May 1948, open warfare had broken out between Jewish and Arab paramilitaries, the latter aided by regular troops from several Arab countries, including the British-commanded Transjordanian Arab Legion. By the end of the war in early 1949, the Jewish state had succeeded in enlarging the boundaries allotted to it under the UN partition plan. The greater part of the Arab population of what became Israel fled (in many instances was driven out) to surrounding Arab states. Most of the rest of Palestine was taken over by King Abdullah of Transjordan. In Jerusalem, after bitter fighting, the city was divided between an eastern half, including the old city, ruled by Abdullah, and a western half that became the capital of Israel.

Mandatory abdication

The brutishness that engulfed Jerusalem in the wake of the UN partition resolution of 29 November 1947 is portrayed, with a strange mixture of horror and English understatement, in the diary of the chairman of the Municipal Commission (in effect, the acting mayor), Richard Graves. Brother of the poet Robert Graves and of a former *Times* correspondent in Jerusalem, Philip Graves, the head of the municipality was a sensitive and fair-minded man who cared deeply for the city placed in his charge. He was not initially supplied with a car and had to make do with the municipal dog-catcher's van. The omission was a portent of the rapid loss of authority that the commission, like the Palestine government as a whole, suffered in the final months of the mandate. Graves recorded, with growing despair, the stages of descent into anarchy and his own impotence in the face of growing violence and intimidation. On 8 December he found himself attacked by mobs with stones when he ventured into the Jewish part of the city. An armoured police car nearby 'looked and behaved like a drowsy elephant, and took not the slightest interest in the proceedings'.[1] Jewish municipal officials, fearful of venturing outside the Jewish area, stopped turning up for work. When the Jews walked out, Arab officials expressed fear that the Jews might have planted a bomb. After new security measures were enforced, the absentees returned – for a time. Jewish officials pressed for the opening of a branch municipal office in the Jewish part of town; Graves resolved to resist this 'as the first step towards "partition" in the city'.[2]

But partition was already beginning as Jews in Arab areas such as the German Colony, Katamon and Baqa moved to Jewish ones such as Rehavia, and as Arabs too left mixed areas of the city. A bomb attack on 29 December led the Jewish officials to leave the municipal offices again. Graves lamented that 'there seems little hope of ever getting them back to this building'.[3] He was now compelled to set up a separate office in the Jewish part of town. But 'when we returned we found the Arab officials in a state of excitement because the Jews had been separated from them. They seemed to think that the creation of a sub-office was the first step towards partition and setting up a Jewish Municipality.' Graves's efforts to reassure them had only limited effect.

Early in the new year fighting in and around the city escalated. Further terrorist attacks claimed many victims. A bomb planted by the Haganah (the underground army of the mainstream section of the Zionist movement) at the Semiramis Hotel on 5 January killed twenty-six civilians including the Spanish consul. Another at the Jaffa Gate killed twenty and wounded forty. By 12 January Graves reported that 'hardly an hour has gone by in which it was not possible to hear the discharge of firearms'.[4] On 1 February the offices of the Zionist *Palestine Post* were blown up in a reprisal action: Zionists accused British soldiers or policemen. On 10 February a sustained Arab attack on the Jewish district of Yemin Moshe was repelled only after the interposition of a British army unit to prevent reinforcements reaching the Arabs.[5] On 12 February, after a Jewish woman was killed in the mainly Christian Arab quarter of Talbieh, a loudspeaker van belonging to the Haganah toured the area ordering all Arabs to leave. On 22 February at least fifty-two people were killed by a bomb explosion on Ben Yehuda Street in the centre of the Jewish business district. Again the Jews laid the outrage at the British door. In his memoirs, published years later, the mufti claimed that an Arab group was responsible. The truth seems to be that it was a joint operation by Arabs and British army deserters and police.[6] Nine British soldiers were killed in reprisal attacks within eighteen hours. On 11 March a car bomb, delivered in the American consul-general's car, left twelve dead at the Jewish Agency headquarters on King George V Avenue.

As mayhem enveloped the city, increasingly desperate but futile efforts continued at the United Nations to secure a means of implementing the partition resolution and establishing the international trusteeship in and around Jerusalem. There were four main reasons why the UN failed in this self-imposed mission.

The first was a matter of timing. The partition resolution provided for the mandate to terminate 'as soon as possible but in any case not later than 1 August 1948'. Jewish and Arab states and the Special International Regime for Jerusalem were to come into being 'two months after the evacuation of the armed forces of the mandatory power has been completed but in any case not later than 1 October 1948'. The British government announced in mid-December that the mandate would end on 15 May 1948. But residual British forces would remain in Haifa until 1 August.

On this schedule there would be a transition period from 15 May until 1 October during which a new UN Palestine Commission would be in charge of affairs. This commission, headed by Karel Lisicky of Czechoslovakia and consisting of four other members drawn from Bolivia, Denmark, Panama and the Philippines, began work at Lake Success, New York, on 9 January 1948. From the start it was hamstrung by the refusal of the British government, announced in a closed session of the commission on 15 January, to permit it to enter Palestine until two weeks before the end of the mandate, this on the ground that it could not accept responsibility for the commissioners' safety. Appearing before the Security Council on 24 February, Lisicky dismissed the notion that it would be possible to establish the Jerusalem state without a security force and provision for other basic needs. He uttered a 'cry from my heart. Lest we forget Jerusalem! Lest we forget Jerusalem!'[7]

In the absence of British cooperation, the UN Palestine Commission was unable to begin the transitional process towards implementation of the partition resolution. On 2 March a group of six 'forerunners' of the commission arrived in Palestine. They were headed by Dr Pablo Azcárate, former ambassador to Britain of the Spanish republic. The others were a Norwegian colonel, an Indian economist, a Greek legal adviser and two secretaries. They tried, without success, to establish a basis for the commission's authority in the country. According to Azcárate the 'chief preoccupation' of the collapsing mandatory government 'lay in impeding by every possible method the presence in Palestine of anybody or anything remotely connected with the United Nations, and particularly with the Palestine Commission'. The British, he recalled, subjected the commission to 'a policy of regular intimidation'.[8] The advance party found it difficult to move beyond Jerusalem.

A second and related reason for the UN's failure was delay in preparing the Statute for the City of Jerusalem. The Trusteeship Council had begun work on this document on 1 December 1947, just two days after passage of the General Assembly partition resolution, and appointed a committee to prepare a draft. No doubt sensing that events were spinning out of the UN's control, the council set about the task with commendable speed. The working committee was appointed on the next day and held its first meeting the day after that. It produced a report six weeks later and the council began considering it on 18 February 1948. But then all sense of urgency seemed to disappear from the proceedings.

Over the following few weeks the council put aside most of its other business and held almost daily meetings to try to produce an agreed text. They listened to the objections of the Iraqi delegate, Awni Khalidi, that Jerusalem was 'an integral part of Palestine' and that there was 'no legal basis for separation'.[9] After his statement Khalidi walked out and took little further part in proceedings. Later the committee gave the Jewish Agency an opportunity to present its views. Most of the council's time was spent arguing about the constitutional mechanisms of the prospective state. Debate continued on judicial arrangements, budgetary issues, educational, cultural and benevolent institutions, external affairs, the holy places and security arrangements. Once they had gone through a first draft, they began all over again, in parliamentary fashion, on a 'second reading'. At this point the French delegate, Roger Garreau, with some support from his Belgian colleague, pleaded for special representation to be accorded to Christians: 'he could not agree that the Council should simply ignore the numerous Christian communities which ought to be represented'.[10] Neither the Americans nor the British supported him, but Garreau threatened to vote against the statute if his views were not accommodated. In the end a form of words had to be found to satisfy him. 'It is difficult,' wrote a frustrated British delegate, 'to convey an adequate idea of the nightmare quality of these meetings.'[11] The truth of the matter was that the Trusteeship Council realized that they were treading water. A confidential British report on the proceedings noted candidly, 'It was obvious that none of the members of the Council really believed that the Statute would ever be put into effect: none of them hesitated to say so in private conversation.'[12]

Meanwhile, similarly purposeless diplomatic energy was devoted to the appointment of a governor for the projected city-state. Although ultimately futile, the exchanges on this issue are of historical interest for the underlying attitudes and prejudices that they reveal. It was generally agreed that the governor need not be a Christian, though there were obvious objections to the appointment of a Muslim or a Jew. An official in the British Commonwealth Relations Office pointed out that 'opinion in Canada, Australia and New Zealand, where there is a strong Roman Catholic element, would regard it as undesirable that the Holy Places of Christianity should be put under an infidel'.[13] A Greek Orthodox spokesman urged that the governor 'should not belong to any of the denominations which have direct interests in the keeping of the Holy Places'. Whereupon the Chinese delegate, Dr Lin Chick, said, 'I suppose he wants a philosophical atheist with a kindness for humanity.'[14]

Various nominees were considered, among them the Belgian delegate on the UN Trusteeship Council, P. Ryckmans, a Canadian, Major-General Henry Crerar, and an Australian, R. G. Casey, who had served as Minister Resident in the Middle East and as a member of the War Cabinet in 1942–3. The British considered nominating Sir William Fitzgerald, who was said to be popular in Jerusalem.[15] But the Foreign Office objected to the appointment of a British citizen. It was pointed out that Fitzgerald was Irish, but Bevin nevertheless 're-acted very badly', worried that the Russians might find him objec-tionable, and Fitzgerald's name was dropped.[16]

The US State Department was at first insistent that the governor of Jerusalem must not be an American citizen. Robert McClintock, who dealt with Palestine in the Office of Special Political Affairs, said that 'not only would an American governor be subject to immense polit-ical pressure in [the] United States, but also were he eliminated from the Governorship ... the Russians would have a plausible excuse to put forward one of their citizens for the post'. He added that 'the De-partment could not accept a Russian governor for Jerusalem and would be highly allergic to the appointment of a Governor from any country under Soviet influence'.[17] The debate over the appointment dragged on without issue until almost the end of the mandate.

A third reason for the failure to implement internationalization was the policy of the British. As early as 20 September 1947 – that is, before passage of the UN partition resolution – the British Cabinet had decided that they would not cooperate in any way with partition and would simply withdraw from Palestine. Their chief aim was to avoid incurring the odium, in the eyes of most Arabs, of helping to implement partition. Yet at the same time their secret objective was precisely the opposite: to help facilitate a partition of Palestine be-tween the Zionists and King Abdullah of Transjordan, thus precluding the creation of a Palestinian state headed by their chief Middle East-ern bogey, the mufti. Azcárate's conclusion that the British were play-ing a double game was not far off the mark: 'Under cover of official assurances that the authorities would fulfill their obligations and re-sponsibilities until the end of the mandate, the British government lent passive, and at times active aid to the progressive transfer of pow-ers and responsibilities from its own organisms in Palestine to Arab or Jewish institutions.'[18]

The instructions given to the UK representative on the Trusteeship Council Working Committee on Jerusalem were that he should 'refrain from committing HMG ... to take any active part in the future administration of Jerusalem, or the execution of the Plan or the enforcement of the Statute'. In meetings with the Palestine Commission on 14 and 28 January, the chief British representative at the UN, Sir Alexander Cadogan, insisted that the British government regarded it

> as essential that, so long as the Mandatory régime is
> retained, they must retain undivided control over the
> whole of Palestine. On the appointed day – that is, 15
> May – their responsibility for the government of Palestine
> will be relinquished as a whole. They cannot agree to
> relinquish it piecemeal. They are, however, prepared to
> agree to the Commission's arrival in Palestine shortly
> before the Mandate is terminated in order that there may
> be an overlap of say, a fortnight, during which the
> Commission can take up its responsibilities.[19]

The High Commissioner, Sir Alan Cunningham, while recognizing that a 'Governor should be appointed and present when we leave here ... [and that] there should be some form of security force in being', felt 'it would be unwise to allow the Governor of Jerusalem in any sooner than the Commission itself'.[20]

A fourth reason for the UN's failure was a shift in United States policy away from partition. The initiative for this came from the Policy Planning Staff in the State Department, headed by George Kennan. The CIA too lent its support to the proposed change in policy.[21] This became public on 19 March when Senator Warren Austin disclosed to the United Nations Security Council that the US administration had withdrawn support from partition and now 'believe[d] that a temporary trusteeship should be established' in Palestine.[22] The most vigorous international opposition to such a trusteeship came from the Soviet Union, whose representative in the Security Council, Andrei Gromyko, insisted that the partition decision was 'a just one ... because it corresponds to the fundamental national interests of both Jews and Arabs' and charged the Americans with seeking to 'block partition'.[23]

The American about-turn also provoked indignant protest from Zionists, who at the same time began a diplomatic withdrawal of their own. There is some evidence, indeed, that their private doubts about the whole concept of internationalization long antedated this and that, far from genuinely embracing the idea of the permanent exclusion of Jerusalem from the Jewish state, their acceptance of the *corpus separatum* was more a matter of tactics. Zeev Sharef, who was to serve as Israel's first Cabinet Secretary, later recalled that commitment to internationalization among the Zionist leadership began to fade as early as January–February 1948.[24] In a speech to the UN Security Council on 1 April 1948, Moshe Shertok hinted that the Zionists would not regard themselves as eternally committed to internationalization of Jerusalem:

> In deference to an overwhelming consensus of world
> opinion, the Jewish Agency accepted the idea of an
> international regime for Jerusalem ... If the international
> régime is not promptly instituted and effectively
> enforced, it will soon become a matter of elementary
> self-preservation for the Jews to do their utmost – maybe
> their desperate utmost – even alone and unaided, to save
> Jerusalem from a monstrous tyranny.[25]

Richard Graves had expressed a similar view several months earlier in the privacy of his diary: 'If at any moment there is a vacuum (which our Government, unlike nature, does not seem to abhor), there will be civil strife with much bloodshed and general anarchy.'[26]

As the wrangling continued, last-minute efforts were made to approve the statute for the proposed city-state and to create an international force to police it. On 8 March the French delegate asked the

Trusteeship Council whether the Palestine Commission would 'take steps to accelerate the entry into force of the Statute'. The police, he pointed out, 'would have to be organized, before the Governor assumed office'. And he added prophetically that the matter had to be settled soon: 'the next session in June would be too late ... It was to be feared that the withdrawal of British troops would result in a period of chaos in Palestine.'[27] Two days later the council at last resolved that the statute was 'now in satisfactory form' and that 'the question of its formal approval, together with the appointment of a Governor of the City', would be taken up 'not later than one week before 27 April'. The further six-week postponement was a manifestation of American dominance in the proceedings of the Trusteeship Council and of the US administration's growing distaste for the whole idea of partition.[28] This renewed delay destroyed any remaining prospect of implementing the internationalization of the city.

Spontaneous partition

The city was now rapidly dividing into two armed camps. British officials in Jerusalem do not seem to have known quite what to expect. On the one hand, they prevented the UN Palestine Commission from taking effective control. On the other, until close to the end, they could not quite believe that the city would be divided. On 29 January Sir Alan Cunningham wrote that he had been told by the Jewish Agency's Political Department 'that they would make no attempt to set up an administration in Jerusalem'. At the same time, he considered that Arab plans did not provide for 'offensive action against Jews in the city'. 'It is most unlikely,' he told the Colonial Office, 'that King Abdullah would attempt to seize or control the Husseini stronghold of the city.' Yet in the final weeks of the mandate, the British took a number of steps towards facilitating partition of Jerusalem. British army security zone A, comprising the German Colony, Greek Colony and Katamon, was tacitly handed over to Arab control (although the

Jews later captured these districts); security zone D, around Schneller's Orphanage in the north-west of the city, was allowed to pass into the control of the Jews. The British retreated into the central security zone. Jewish forces set up roadblocks and British army and police vehicles entering Jewish-held areas were stopped and searched and sometimes refused admission.

On 6 March a British newspaper correspondent reported, 'Nowhere are the results of spontaneous partition more clear-cut than in Jerusalem. Here, through intimidation, through open or surreptitious fighting, and sometimes by sensible exchange of houses, Arab and Jewish residents have sorted themselves out into separate blocks with partially derelict "no-man's-lands" between.'[29]

Events on the ground were by now outpacing the capacity of diplomats or officials to control them. 'The normal life of the city, commerce, social and business communication and connections have virtually ceased to exist,' wrote the District Commissioner, J. H. H. Pollock, on 20 March. Jewish paramilitary forces had taken full control of the Jewish districts and armed Arabs controlled the Jaffa, Damascus and St Stephen's gates to the old city. Some government departments were being 'split into Jewish and Arab offices in order that the public may have easier access'.[30]

By now Jewish Jerusalem was besieged by Arab forces. Its supply routes to the coast by road and rail had been blocked since February and its water supply was threatened. On 2 April the Haganah launched Operation *Nahshon* to open the road to Tel Aviv and to reinforce the beleaguered Jewish population. That night a company of the Palmach (élite commando units of the Haganah) stormed the village of Qastal on a hillside dominating the western approach to Jerusalem. After a counter-attack, the commander of the Arab forces in the area, Abd al-Kader al-Husayni, was killed.[31] He was buried on the Haram near the grave of his father, Musa Kazem Pasha al-Husayni, the former mayor of Jerusalem. The battle swung to and fro until 9 April, when the village was finally captured by the Haganah and razed to the ground. This victory reopened the Jerusalem–Tel Aviv road to Jewish traffic. Between 15 and 17 April two convoys of trucks carried a total of 1,500 tons of food to Jewish Jerusalem. But a third convoy on 20 April was ambushed and suffered heavy casualties. After that the road was rarely passable by Jews again until June.

Administrative partition moved ahead, together with the staking out of military lines. For several weeks Graves tried to effect a semi-formal separation of municipal assets and functions, seeking the co-operation of local Jewish and Arab politicians. On 25 April he recorded:

> Government have instructed me to recognise –
> unofficially, so to speak – the new Jewish municipal
> committee appointed to look after the Jewish area, with
> Auster as chairman. Arrangements proposed at present
> and likely to be put into effect are: (1) to get the
> Commission to pass a resolution giving the power of
> signature at our end to the Treasurer and the acting head
> of department concerned and at the branch office to
> Auster and Boury; (2) to place all important archives,
> title-deeds, town-planning files etc., in safe custody,
> preferably in a convent; (3) to divide between the two
> offices whatever cash remains after paying salaries for
> May and June … (4) to leave water arrangements as they
> are, and to hope that the supply will not be interfered
> with.[32]

Municipal funds were divided in half. In early May a cheque for 30,000 Palestine pounds was issued to Daniel Auster for the Jewish section of the municipality; he immediately deposited it in the Anglo-Palestine Bank. A little later a cheque for 27,500 pounds (the reason for the difference in amount is unknown) was handed over to Anton Safieh, representing the Arab section. Unfortunately, by the time this cheque was issued, no bank was open to cash it and Safieh therefore left it in a safe in the municipality. The building was later damaged in the fighting and when Safieh returned at the end of June, under UN safe conduct, both safe and cheque were gone.[33] Some of the money seems subsequently to have reached the Arab municipality via Barclays Bank in Cyprus.[34]

After narrowly surviving a shooting, Richard Graves left the country on 28 April. As he drove north towards Ramallah, he met Brigadier John Glubb with a unit of Arab Legion troops. 'I could not help thinking that his position as a British officer commanding an Arab force at the moment engaged in a war, which could neither be called cold nor hot, with the Jews was rather ambiguous.'[35] By now the municipal administration had disintegrated and the city was in a state of open warfare. Iraqi troops had occupied the Jerusalem water-supply station at Ras al-Ain. Air mail out of Jerusalem had stopped functioning and telephone trunk lines worked only intermittently.

Two bloody incidents marked a savage escalation in the level of violence and permanently affected the attitudes of Arabs and Jews. On 9 April a unit of the Irgun Zvai Leumi entered the village of Deir Yassin, a little to the west of Jerusalem, and massacred at least 100 Arabs (reports at the time said as many as 250), including many civilians, among them women and children. The incident was widely publicized and caused a wave of panic and demoralization to spread through Arab Palestine. Many of the remaining Arabs in mixed areas of Jerusalem fled. Four days later Arabs took vengeance: they ambushed a convoy of doctors and nurses driving to the Hadassah Hospital on Mount Scopus. Seventy-seven people were killed. The incident was followed by bitter Jewish complaints that British military units nearby had failed to intervene effectively. The High Commissioner and the army rejected the complaints, attributing the deaths to the 'suicidal attitude of the occupants of the Jewish vehicles', who were urged by a British officer to transfer to a British armoured truck that had pulled up nearby but 'could not be persuaded to jump the few yards between the vehicles.'[36] A British official later commented, 'The Military Authorities in Palestine much resented the febrile outbursts of Jewish self-pity occasioned by this disaster. Many more would have been saved if they had had the minimum resolution required to take advantage of Major Churchill's gallant action.'[37]

These shocking events demonstrated that British authority in Palestine had totally collapsed. Both Jews and Arabs now looked to their own resources for security. There was, however, a distinct difference between the preparedness of the two sides. By the last week of April the Jews were estimated by the British to have mobilized 7,000 men in Jerusalem. By contrast, Arab military organization in Jerusalem, as elsewhere in Palestine, was in disarray. The High Commissioner reported that 'Arabs in Jerusalem are either under no control or are acting under orders of a number of Iraqi and Syrian military leaders. Activities of these leaders are quite uncoordinated by either Arab Higher Committee, of which only one effective member is here, or local Arab National Committee.'[38]

The bloodshed also galvanized the United Nations into action. On 16 April the United Nations General Assembly met in special session to reconsider the Palestine problem. It agreed to appoint a Truce Commission consisting of 'the consular officers of those members of the Security Council who have representatives in Jerusalem'. The four states in that category were Belgium, France, Syria and the United States, but the Syrian representative in the council indicated that his country would not insist on participation.[39] The three remaining consuls, Jean Nieuwenhuys (Belgium), René Neuville (France) and Thomas Wasson (USA), were deputed to try to bring about a cease-fire in Jerusalem. Azcárate, whose role as head of the UN commission's 'forerunners' was clearly pointless, was appointed secretary of the Truce Commission. The consuls set about the task with courage and public spirit. They were constantly shot at from all sides and the commission's chairman, Nieuwenhuys, sacrificed both his private cars to the cause of peacemaking as he drove to and from his palatial residence in Talbieh. This last reminder of the great days of consular authority in the city failed to secure an end to the fighting and was to close in tragedy.

Also on 16 April, the Palestine Commission decided to proceed immediately to form a police force for Jerusalem, using as a nucleus 'about two hundred British members of the existing Palestine Police Force who have said they are willing to serve'.[40] But this was too little too late. The scale of fighting in Jerusalem by now was such that a force of this size would be ineffectual in restoring peace. The High Commissioner reported that the number of volunteers was not 200 but fifty – and these were mostly 'young and inexperienced'. Most of the existing British police force had in any case by now made 'other plans'.[41] Shortly afterwards, amid growing confusion at UN headquarters, the commission was instructed to suspend action to recruit a police force.[42]

On 21 April, just eight days before the five-month deadline set by the General Assembly the previous November, the Trusteeship Council finally approved the Statute of Jerusalem. The Arabs still refused to have anything to do with it. Nor was it at all to the Zionists' liking. The statute's most significant defect, from their point of view, was its proposal for a Legislative Council consisting of eighteen Jews, eighteen Arabs and four 'others'. These would almost certainly be Christians and the special provision for them was the result of the French delegate's insistence. The Jews would thus be in a permanent minority on the council. Any lingering Zionist commitment to the principle of internationalization now diminished further.

Five days later the General Assembly instructed the Trusteeship Council to prepare a plan for the protection of Jerusalem and its inhabitants. But it was plain that no international will existed to furnish the necessary troops. A secret appreciation the same day by General Silverthorn of the US Marine Corps estimated that no fewer than 33,000 men would be necessary to guarantee security.[43] On 27 April, in another eloquent speech, Garreau warned that Jerusalem 'was in a state of chaos'. Its population 'was threatened with partial extermination'. He proposed the immediate dispatch of a UN official with power to raise at least 'a symbolic force of, say, a thousand men'.[44] Palestinian Arab and Zionist representatives were invited to present their views. Jamal al-Husayni, a nephew of the mufti, spoke for the Arab Higher Committee. The Arabs, he said, objected to the sending of any foreign troops or police to Palestine. If such a force were sent against their wishes, they would not resist it but would not cooperate in any way since they believed it would ultimately be used to impose partition on the country. Speaking for the Zionists, Shertok agreed to the proposal but on condition that the force would not only maintain security in the city but also safeguard the approaches to it. He added that several thousand troops would be required rather than a small police force. By 29 April the British delegate announced that the situation in Jerusalem 'had deteriorated very rapidly in the past few days. The effective power of the Administration had practically come to an end.' After further discussion the council took no action.[45]

On 30 April the United States proposed a 'provisional' trusteeship for the Jerusalem area only. The US representative in the UN Trusteeship Council explained that the arrangement 'would naturally be incorporated in the trusteeship plan for Palestine as a whole, if the Assembly adopted such a plan'.[46] Jamal al-Husayni opposed the American suggestion as 'bound to bring Palestine nearer to the partition scheme'. Shertok said that the Jewish Agency 'accepted the principle of an international arrangement for Jerusalem but objected to trusteeship for any part of Palestine where the Jewish people had important interests'. The Soviet Union vehemently opposed trusteeship whether for Jerusalem or the whole of Palestine.[47] American diplomats continued to press trusteeship schemes at the UN until 14 May but failed to muster the necessary support.

On 6 May the General Assembly, with the agreement of Arab and Zionist representatives, approved the appointment of a Special Municipal Commissioner to take over the functions of acting mayor, earlier exercised by Richard Graves. This, however, was seen as a purely municipal appointment, not that of the governor envisaged under the Statute of Jerusalem. A Municipal Government Order on 11 May gave the High Commissioner powers to appoint such a commissioner 'to carry on Municipal Government in Jerusalem'.[48] The order gave the appointee 'absolute discretion' and almost unlimited powers, though his authority was to apply only within the municipal boundary and not in the larger area of the *corpus separatum* envisaged for the Jerusalem state.

The agreed nominee was Percy C. Clarke, general manager of Barclays Bank in Jerusalem. But he had no stomach for the job. The mantle then fell on a Philadelphia attorney, Harold Evans. In the rush of the government's dissolution, the High Commissioner did not issue the necessary formal proclamation before his departure from Jerusalem.[49] Technically, therefore, the appointment was of dubious validity, but a statement to the contrary was issued.[50] But in any case, Evans said that, as a Quaker, he could not accept a military escort and would take up the position only once peace reigned. Optimistically, he went to Cairo on 23 May to await that happy state of affairs. Evans did swallow his scruples and visit Jerusalem briefly in June. Unpersuaded by what he saw that peace was in the offing, he announced his resignation, though he remained on the UN payroll until February 1949, 'a transient, embarrassed phantom', as Cadogan called him.[51]

Repeated efforts by the United Nations and by the High Commissioner to secure a cease-fire in Jerusalem were unavailing. Another last-minute effort to halt the fighting was undertaken by the International Red Cross, whose delegate, Jacques de Reynier, called for Jerusalem to be turned into a 'Red Cross city'. The consular Truce Commission considered the idea 'too vague' but nevertheless discussed it in a meeting with the High Commissioner on 9 May. The French consul-general, Neuville, 'pointed out that if the Red Cross proposal were adopted and if it did not prove efficient in a few days' time, as he thought would be the case, the English would not be there any longer [and] the fighting would again start'. He 'strongly emphasized the importance of the loss of time six days before the mandate would end'. But the High Commissioner, in an absurd final burst of blimpish unrealism, simply responded 'that he would, until 15 May, have authority and the power to take the decision that seemed best to him'.[52] When the Red Cross plan was reported to the Security Council three days later, Gromyko dismissed it with scorn:

> Who has ever entrusted the administration of any city or country to the Red Cross? No one could ever have conceived such an idea. And yet we have before us a proposal to make the Red Cross master of Jerusalem. Needless to say that this would obviously be tantamount to making two or three countries [Gromyko was obviously referring to the western powers] the masters, who would use the Red Cross as their instrument to establish in Jerusalem the regime which they considered necessary.[53]

Reynier continued his well-meaning activities in Jerusalem but to little effect.

At 8.00 a.m. on 14 May Sir Alan Cunningham left Government House for the last time. His departure presented a sorry contrast with the dignity of the arrival of the first High Commissioner, Sir Herbert Samuel, in 1920. Cunningham inspected a guard of honour and the Union Jack was lowered from the building, to be replaced by the flag of the Red Cross. A few days later, taking advantage of the withdrawal of guards from the compound, a group of bedouin encamped there with their camels.

One peculiarity of Britain's position at the termination of the mandate was that, unlike most of the other powers, she had no consul in Jerusalem, since, of course, none had been required during the mandate. With the end of the mandate it was felt that it would be untoward to leave Britain without a representative in the city. Sir Hugh Dow had been chosen as consul-general designate but had not been formally appointed 'so as not to prejudice whatever de facto or de jure situation'.[54] At the last moment the High Commissioner was authorized to announce the creation of a consulate and to style himself consul.[55] An additional reason for this strange diplomatic Parthian shot may be surmised: the creation of a consulate provided a cover for continued British intelligence observation in Jerusalem.

It was appropriate, therefore, that Cunningham's last moments in Jerusalem should have been recorded by the newly minted vice-consul, Nigel Clive. He climbed to the roof of the consulate to observe the High Commissioner's

> forlorn little procession creep down St Louis's Way and turn left at the Damascus Gate along the road to Ramalla and on to Haifa ... His car, preceded by a little armour, passed at about 8.30 a.m. I think the early start must have been kept a comparative secret because there could not have been more than twenty Arabs outside the Damascus Gate, a handful of whom clapped childishly and one saluted. The salute was returned. This was how the seventh and last High Commissioner left Jerusalem ... I felt that departure in some sort of blaze, of fire more probably than glory, would have been a more fitting end. As it was, he left, waved away by three or four handclappings. Not with a bang but a whimper.[56]

The departed High Commissioner remained a kind of absentee consul *in partibus* until 24 May, when Dow's position was formalized.

Pantomime across the Jordan

Even before the High Commissioner left Palestinian soil, the Zionists seized the initiative by declaring the establishment of the state of Israel in a ceremony in Tel Aviv on the afternoon of 14 May. David

Ben Gurion was sworn in as Prime Minister of the provisional government and Moshe Shertok became Foreign Minister. The declaration of independence did not mention Jerusalem and designated no capital for the new state. A later announcement by the Jewish Agency representative at the United Nations indicated that Tel Aviv was the seat of government.

The policy of the Israeli government towards Jerusalem was determined in part by fear of the 'seed of secession' by Jews in Jerusalem opposed to the authority of the mainstream Zionist leadership.[57] The city was a stronghold of the Jewish paramilitary organizations Irgun Zvai Leumi and Lehi (known by the British as the Stern Gang). In addition, the anti-Zionist Agudist movement, representing the bulk of the ultra-orthodox population, had a large following in the city. Any attempt by minority Jewish groups to seize power at the local level would have represented a tremendous propaganda coup and severely damaged the authority of the mainstream Zionists. They therefore set about consolidating their political and military hold on the Jewish-inhabited parts of the new city.

The Palestinian Arabs, divided and disoriented, proved unable to take parallel action in the area of Palestine assigned by the UN for an Arab state. Only on 30 September did the mufti (or 'ex-mufti' as the British insisted on calling him) declare the creation of an 'All-Palestinian Government' in the Egyptian-occupied Gaza strip. It was a pathetic affair, totally dependent on the Egyptians and unable to exercise authority beyond the teeming tent-cities of refugees in the strip. Jerusalem was declared the capital of Palestine although the mufti could not set foot there. Even in Gaza, political control remained firmly in the hands of the Egyptian military government; and administration of services such as schools and health devolved on the United Nations Relief and Works Administration. Two weeks after this first declaration of Palestinian independence, the mufti was removed to Cairo under armed escort by the Egyptians.

Meanwhile, Israeli and Arab forces battled for the country — and for Jerusalem. An estimated 10,000 shells were fired in Jerusalem during the three weeks after 14 May. During the first four weeks Israeli Jerusalem suffered 1,738 casualties (316 dead and 1,422 injured, the majority civilians); Arab casualties were almost certainly even higher. The French, Greek and Spanish consulates were among the many buildings hit. By mid-May the Haganah controlled most Jewish areas of the new city and was holding out precariously in the Jewish quarter of the old city. In several cases, such as 'Bevingrad', local British commanders handed over buildings to Jewish forces.[58] On 18 May the Palmach took Mount Zion. Arab forces controlled most of the old city and some Arab districts of the new city. But fierce house-by-house combat proceeded in several areas.

Although the general contours of a divided Jerusalem had already taken shape as a result of 'spontaneous partition', engagements between regular armed forces now determined the exact lines of division. Given that both the Zionists and King Abdullah had originally been ready to abide by the UN internationalization plan and that they also had a general understanding about the partition between them of the rest of the country, why did serious fighting nevertheless continue in Jerusalem?

One reason was the impulsive and contradictory character of the ruler of Transjordan. His lifelong ambition was to occupy the throne of Greater Syria, from which his brother Faisal had been rudely ousted by the French in 1921. Rule over Palestine would be a stepping stone in this direction. He had approached the Zionists in the 1920s with proposals whereby he would cooperate with them in return for their support for his kingship. As the mandate disintegrated, he saw his opportunity to steal a march on his hated enemy the mufti. On two visits to Jerusalem in 1945 and 1946 Abdullah sought to consolidate his support among local politicians opposed to the Husaynis. The British, who shared his hatred for the mufti, gave Abdullah diplomatic support and military and intelligence assistance. In March 1946 they signed a treaty with him recognizing Transjordanian independence, though in reality British influence in the country remained paramount until 1956. In January 1948, at a meeting in London with the Transjordanian Prime Minister, Tawfiq Abul Huda, Bevin approved the movement of the Arab Legion into the portion of Palestine allocated by the UN to an Arab state.[59] At the same time Britain and Transjordan signed a further treaty: under this Britain continued to subsidize the cost of the Arab Legion at £2 million a year plus £500,000 for military equipment.[60]

The one area about which Abdullah had reached no agreement of any kind, with either the British or the Zionists, was Jerusalem. Here, as elsewhere, were already stationed some Arab Legion units under British command. This was the most disciplined of the Arab forces and, by and large, did not join in the fighting in the city until after the end of the mandate. Shertok complained vigorously to the UN Security Council on 16 April that the Legion, 'which today forms an integral part of the British forces in Palestine', was 'in occupation of important Jewish centres'. The British representative repeated an earlier assurance 'that the units of the Arab Legion in Palestine will be withdrawn before the mandate comes to an end'.[61] But a week later the Ukrainian representative issued a biting challenge. Noting that a statement had been issued that additional Legion forces would be moved into Palestine, he asked Sir Alexander Cadogan, 'what are we to believe: his official statement, made on behalf of the United Kingdom Government, or the contradictory statement and actions of the King of Transjordan who is in the pay of the British, and who cannot take a step or make a political move without their permission?'[62] Cadogan disdained to respond, but the Legion was to play a critical role in the partition of Jerusalem over the next few weeks.

Abdullah, meanwhile, swung to and fro between public bellicosity and private attempts to consolidate his understanding with the Zionists. Two weeks before the end of the mandate he proposed to lead a force to Jerusalem immediately to protect the holy places; he withdrew the threat on the advice of the British Minister in Amman.[63] On

13 May Brigadier Glubb ('Glubb Pasha'), the British commander of the Arab Legion, withdrew all his forces from the city, in accordance with the commitment that had been given at the United Nations by Cadogan. At that stage Glubb gave the appearance of hoping to achieve a cease-fire between the Jews and irregular Arab forces in the city. The same day the senior British staff officer in Jerusalem informed the Haganah liaison officer officially that the Arab Legion was no longer under British command.[64] In the UN Security Council on 15 May, Cadogan studiously read out a cable that had been dispatched from the War Office at 6.43 p.m. London time the previous day. This stated that 'all companies of [the] Arab Legion except two companies have already left Palestine for Transjordan. The General Officer Commanding Palestine telegraphed this morning that the last two companies were leaving today.'[65]

These British statements were technically correct but the Legion's withdrawal amounted to little more than military-diplomatic pantomime. Glubb's service as a British officer terminated at the end of the mandate. He and his thirty-six fellow British officers in the Legion were now said to be mercenaries who did not take orders from the British government. In some formal sense there was a modicum of truth in this: technically, sixteen were directly employed by the Transjordanians; the remainder were on secondment from the British forces.[66] But Glubb undoubtedly continued to follow basic policy lines formulated in London, not Amman, and he continued to supply reports for the War Office. His real position as a faithful executor of British interests remained for all practical purposes unchanged. The withdrawal of the Legion forces across the Jordan was more in the nature of a diplomatic feint than a military retreat. As soon as the mandate ended, the Arab Legion, now legally a Transjordanian rather than a British entity, recrossed the Jordan.

In a telegram to the UN Secretary-General on 16 May, Abdullah, using the royal plural, explained:

We were compelled to enter Palestine to protect
unarmed Arabs against massacres similar to those of Deir
Yasin. We are aware of our national duty towards
Palestine in general and Jerusalem in particular and also
Nazareth and Bethlehem. Be sure that we shall be very
considerate in connection with Jews in Palestine while
maintaining at the same time the full right of the Arabs in
Palestine. Zionism did not react to our offers made
before the entry of armed forces.[67]

The last sentence was an allusion to the inconclusive results of his last
contacts with the Zionists.

The next day Abdullah, for once overruling Glubb, ordered the Legion back into Jerusalem. The decision was said to have been taken in
response to desperate messages from Arabs in the city. Such pleas
were indeed sent: 'Unless you rescue us immediately, Jerusalem will
fall finally into the hands of the Jews,' read one such cable.[68] It is
doubtful, however, that the British really opposed the Legion's reentry to the city. Once again, the British wished to avoid public responsibility for what they privately desired. An order by Glubb for the
Legion to re-enter Jerusalem might be seen as implicating the British
in aggression against the UN-designated area. Abdullah was therefore
given the opportunity to shine in Arab nationalist eyes by issuing the
order himself. At 11.30 a.m. on 17 May Glubb received a royal command to 'advance towards Jerusalem from the direction of Ramallah'.[69] He later claimed to have had serious doubts, on military
grounds, about the practicability of the order. But he lost little time in
obeying it. Arab Legion troops entered Jerusalem the next day and
serious hostilities developed. The Legion eventually succeeded in
holding most of the eastern half of Jerusalem, including the old city.
The British were embarrassed but not unduly upset by this development. The British Minister in Amman, Sir Alec Kirkbride, was told to
warn Abdullah against an onslaught on Jerusalem. But whether by

design or good fortune, the instructions arrived too late and thereafter Kirkbride happily defended the king's order and Glubb's obedience.

The participation of British officers in the warfare in Jerusalem remained, for the British government, an awkward point. On 25 May the USA made a formal request to London for the withdrawal of British officers 'from all participation in Jerusalem fighting'. The message was accompanied by worrying noises in the Senate Appropriations Committee, then considering the terms of a loan to Britain. Formal instructions were issued to Kirkbride, to 'make every effort to ensure Abdullah will withdraw all British officers'.[70] Cadogan claimed on 27 May that no British officers were taking part in the fighting in Jerusalem.[71] But this was a another case of diplomatic *suggestio falsi*. In a small-scale reprise of the earlier pantomime, the British officers were withdrawn for forty-eight hours in order that the public denial of their presence could be issued; the speech over, they returned to normal duties.[72] The twenty British officers who were seconded from the British army were ordered to cease participation in the fighting on 30 May, but the rest carried on leading their units.

Glubb remained throughout in overall control of the Legion and his deputy, Brigadier Norman Lash, continued to command the Jerusalem front. Their basic objective, in accord with the British government's policy, was to facilitate a Transjordanian take-over of the area of Palestine assigned by the UN to the Arab state, as well as, after 17 May, of the old city and Arab sections of new Jerusalem.

Collapse of *corpus separatum*

The siege by Arab forces of the Jewish quarter of the old city and the predominantly Jewish western districts of the new city continued throughout May and into June. An assault on the Hebrew University and Hadassah Hospital area on Mount Scopus, however, was countermanded by Abdullah on 24 May, after an appeal by President Truman to the British to ensure the safeguarding of these Jewish cultural institutions.[73] On 27/8 May the remaining inhabitants of the Jewish quarter in the old city left and the area was surrendered to Arab control. In the Jewish new city food and water ran short and by the end of May the Israeli military governor reported that no more than a week's supplies remained. In spite of brave talk of 'another Stalingrad', there were real fears that the city would not hold out if the route to the coast were not reopened.

Pending the arrival of the Municipal Commissioner, Evans, Azcárate was nominated as his deputy. Azcárate, whose office was in the Israeli-controlled sector of the city, secured a promise of cooperation from the emerging Jewish municipality. He had more difficulty locating any responsible authority on the Arab side. With the Belgian consul-general he went to see Abdullah in Amman. The king received them clad in breeches and a lumber jacket. When Azcárate raised the question of Jerusalem's water supply, the king flared up and said that so long as the Jews continued to fight the Arabs not a single drop of water would reach Jerusalem.[74] A few days later Azcárate set out with two guides and a donkey to make a hazardous crossing from Jewish- to Arab-controlled Jerusalem. When he arrived at the Arab Legion headquarters, he was told that the decision had been taken not to cooperate with the UN Municipal Commission. Unable to assert his theoretical authority, he went to report to Evans, still biding his time in Cairo. As Vivian (later Chaim) Herzog, at that time an Israeli army liaison officer to the UN Truce Commission, noted on 21 May: 'Up to now [Azcárate] had behaved in an apathetic and lethargic manner, not even informing the citizens of Jerusalem that he was the UN Municipal Commissioner. In fact the ordinary man in the street was not aware that such a UN Commissioner existed for Jerusalem.'[75]

Nor was the consular Truce Commission able to accomplish much more. In the Security Council Gromyko described the latter accurately, if ungenerously, as 'powerless, impotent, absolutely toothless'.[76] On 22 May it suffered a tragic blow when the American consul, Thomas Wasson, was mortally wounded by a sniper on his way home from a commission meeting at the French consulate.

Meanwhile, on 14 May the General Assembly had dissolved the ineffective Palestine Commission, headed by Lisicky, and recommended the appointment of a mediator. Count Folke Bernadotte, President of the Swedish Red Cross, was chosen for the position. A Swede who had negotiated with Himmler during the war for the release of concentration camp prisoners, he took up his responsibilities on 21 May and set as his first task negotiation of a cease-fire. At first the auguries seemed mildly promising. On 11 June a four-week truce, first ordered by the Security Council on 29 May, came into force. In Jerusalem it was generally observed by both sides: there were 197 complaints (thirty-nine by Arabs, 131 by Jews and twenty-seven by UN observers); most were 'cases of sporadic and individual sniping and firing', though there were also 'attempts by each side to improve its position by fortifying houses and strategic points, digging trenches and erecting barriers'.[77] At the start of the truce the Israelis held most of the new city, the Arab Legion the whole of the old city as well as some eastern parts of the city outside the walls. Arabs also controlled the Jerusalem water source at Ras al-Ain and the pumping station at Latrun. Along the front line in the city the opposing forces were often very close, sometimes on opposite sides of the street. The truce saved the Israeli-held new city from being starved out. The opening in June of the hastily built 'Burma road' to the coastal plain enabled them to bring in supplies and eventually to break the siege.

During the truce, on 16 June, Jean Nieuwenhuys, the Belgian consul-general who was chairman of the Truce Commission, and Colonel Nils Brunsson, a truce observer, succeeded in negotiating a 'no-man's land agreement' for Jerusalem with the two sides. Under this, 'each of the opposing parties withdrew its forces to an agreed line, and a no-man's land was established between the two lines, the houses and buildings in the no-man's land being evacuated'. The agreement was to have long-term implications: it more or less crystallized the lines of division of Jerusalem between Israel and Jordan for the next nineteen years.

A second agreement was brokered by Colonel Brunsson just before the end of the truce. On 7 July Israeli and Arab commanders in Jerusalem agreed on the demilitarization of Mount Scopus. The area was divided into three sections: a Jewish zone, which included the Hebrew University and the Hadassah Hospital; an Arab zone; and a thin strip of no-man's land. The Augusta Victoria building at last found its vocation as a hospital for Arab refugees, administered by the United Nations Relief and Works Administration. Arab and Israeli 'armed police' were to be placed on duty in their respective areas under UN command.[78] Bernadotte tried, but failed, to persuade the United States to send a token force of 333 soldiers to supervise the demilitarization of the area.[79] On behalf of the UN he nevertheless accepted responsibility for security in the demilitarized area, 'despite [as he put it] the shortage of UN personnel to enforce it'. The UN also undertook to provide food and water supplies to the area.

Meanwhile, on 28 June Bernadotte put forward his own proposals for a long-term settlement of the Palestine problem. He proposed a number of changes in the UN partition map of Palestine and recommended that internationalization of Jerusalem be abandoned. Instead he suggested 'inclusion of the City of Jerusalem in Arab territory, with municipal autonomy for the Jewish community and special arrangements for the protection of the Holy Places'.

Bernadotte's proposals on Jerusalem led to fierce attacks on him in the Israeli press, where he was accused of anti-Israeli bias. Supporters of the extremist Lehi group denounced him without restraint. In the UN Security Council Gromyko accused him of having taken his cue from the British Foreign Office. Some of this criticism was misdirected. Bernadotte was not, in fact, the originator of the proposal for Jerusalem. At least initially, in discussions with his advisers, he had favoured internationalization. The authors of the plan for Jerusalem were, in fact, Bernadotte's assistants Ralph Bunche, John Reedman and Constantin Stavropoulos, though of course the mediator took ultimate responsibility for his 'suggestions'.[80]

Both the Arabs and the Israelis rejected the mediator's proposals, though the tiny anti-Zionist, ultra-orthodox Jewish Neturei Karta (Guardians of the City) in Jerusalem voiced approval. The Arab League refused to consider anything other than a unitary state of Palestine. Israel stood its ground for the time being on the General Assembly resolution of 29 November 1947, objecting in particular to the mediator's suggestions that immigration be restricted and Jerusalem transferred to the Arab state. The Israelis were emboldened on 30 June by the final withdrawal from Haifa, ahead of schedule, of the residual British forces in Palestine, thus reducing the likelihood of British intervention in the conflict. In a letter he handed to Bernadotte on 5 July, Shertok wrote bluntly that Israel would 'never acquiesce in the imposition of Arab domination over Jerusalem' and would 'resist any such imposition with all the force at their command'.[81] In a response the next day, Bernadotte attempted to justify his departure from the original UN partition plan: 'Jerusalem stands at the heart of what must be Arab territory in any partition of Palestine. To attempt to isolate this area politically and otherwise from surrounding territory presents enormous difficulties … Arab domination of legitimate Jewish and other non-Arab interests in Jerusalem was never intended or implied in the Suggestions.'

In spite of rebuffs by both sides, Bernadotte was encouraged by the two local agreements that had been reached in Jerusalem. Pending a broader settlement, he submitted proposals for demilitarization of the city. The Israelis indicated guarded interest. The Arab Higher Committee, from its office in Damascus, rejected the idea on the ground that it 'tends to obliterate [Jerusalem's] Arab and Islamic character, detach it from Palestine, and establish an international administration therein, thus implementing the partition scheme. Furthermore, it is impossible actually to disarm the Jews, thus exposing the Holy City to their occupation'.

The truce came to an end prematurely on 8 July and bitter fighting resumed. Israel captured Lydda, Ramleh and Nazareth. Israeli forces also gained the Jerusalem water source at Ras al-Ain but in a critical battle failed to capture Latrun with its pumping station – it was destroyed by Arabs on 12 August. In Operation *Kedem* in Jerusalem the Israelis tried but failed to advance into Sheikh Jarrah and the old city. A cease-fire was ordered by the UN Security Council on 15 July and formally came into force in Jerusalem at 5.45 a.m. on 17 July – thirty-seven hours before it did so elsewhere. This was critical. Just as the first truce had saved Jewish control of the new city, so the second probably saved Arab control of the old city. Hostilities concluded with only slight changes to the battle lines in the city. The 'no-man's land agreement' came to an end, but the Mount Scopus agreement remained in force. During August and early September an uneasy quiet reigned in the city, broken, wrote Bernadotte, by 'heavy firing ... almost every night'.

Although the UN failed to send any troops to enforce its decisions on Palestine or to guard the proposed Jerusalem state, it did eventually send some military observers to support the mediator and the consular Truce Commission. On 1 August ten observers were stationed in Jerusalem and by 8 September the number there had increased to seventy-nine.[82] They were mainly Americans, French and Belgians – that is, the same nationalities as the three consuls who were supposed to help enforce the truce. Their first commander was Major-General Age Lundström of the Swedish Air Force. He lasted only seven weeks in the job and was replaced in September by General William Riley of the US Marine Corps. On 30 September the UN took over the 'Red Cross zone' that Reynier had established in and around Government House. The area had been partly occupied by Egyptian troops and was attacked unsuccessfully by the Israelis on 17 August in breach of the truce. Arab and Israeli forces both agreed to withdraw on 4 September. The High Commissioner's former residence became a United Nations zone outside the jurisdiction of any state. Initially it was guarded by two detachments of Arab Legion and

Israeli soldiers, who operated harmoniously together until the arrival of UN guards. Government House remained under UN control, except for a short break in 1967, when it was occupied successively by Jordanian and Israeli troops, until the present. It thus became the only morsel of Jerusalem that was, in some sense, internationalized.

On 16 September, on the island of Rhodes, the mediator signed a report offering revised proposals. He had withdrawn from his earlier position towards the UN partition plan; he now recommended that Jerusalem, as defined in that plan, 'should be placed under effective United Nations control with maximum feasible local autonomy for its Arab and Jewish communities, with full safeguards for the protection of the Holy Places and free access to them, and for religious freedom'. The changes were probably the result of discussions that he had had with American and British representatives a few days earlier.[83]

Bernadotte's report was distributed to the General Assembly two days later. But by then its author was dead. On 17 September the mediator was assassinated by a squad of Lehi hit men in Jerusalem, acting on orders from the three-man leadership of the organization, among them Yitzhak Shamir, later Prime Minister of Israel. Yehoshua Cohen, who probably fired the fatal shot, later served as bodyguard for Ben Gurion after his retirement in 1963; he was never brought to justice. Ralph Bunche became acting mediator in Bernadotte's place.

The murder of the mediator greatly strengthened the moral force of his final recommendations and the UN Secretary-General, Trygve Lie, ensured that they were placed on the agenda of the General Assembly. US Secretary of State George C. Marshall and the British Foreign Secretary, Ernest Bevin, both endorsed Bernadotte's recommendations. But Israel and the Arab states rejected them and they soon fell by the diplomatic wayside like so many earlier plans for Palestine and Jerusalem.

Instead, Israel resumed fighting in mid-October, pushing back the Egyptians in the Negev and widening her area of control in Galilee.

An Israeli army request, towards the end of this phase of hostilities, for permission to launch a renewed attack in Jerusalem was rejected by Ben Gurion. He feared international complications if Israel were to move into the old city. After a fourth and final phase of warfare between 22 December 1948 and 7 January 1949, the Arabs recognized defeat. Egypt signed an armistice agreement with Israel on 24 February. Meanwhile, on 30 November 1948 Israel and Transjordan agreed on 'an absolute and sincere cease-fire' in Jerusalem. The lines of division in the city at that time were sealed into semi-permanence. The battle for the city had cost 1,976 Israeli lives (out of a total of about 6,000 Israeli dead in the war). Casualties on the Arab side are less precisely enumerated but it is known that 40 per cent of the Arab Legion's losses in the war were in Jerusalem.

By the end of the war seven mixed or mainly Arab neighbourhoods in west Jerusalem (Baqa, Katamon, Talbieh, Musrara, Mamilla and the German and Greek colonies) had been emptied of Arab inhabitants. So were nearly all Arab villages to the west of the city, including Ein Karem, Romema, Lifta, Malha and Deir Yassin. In some cases the Arabs were expelled or intimidated into leaving; in others they fled for fear of massacre. In no case were any of these populations permitted to return. On the Jordanian side of the line, a similar fate befell the Jews of the old city and those of settlements near the Dead Sea that were occupied by the Arab Legion.

A king for Jerusalem

As Jerusalem was cut in two, American and (more slowly) British enthusiasm for its internationalization began to cool. In August 1948 Marshall considered the possibility of a 'modified condominium principle under which Israel, [the] future Arab state [of Palestine], and [the] UN would share administrative responsibility for Jerusalem'.[84] In September he declared a willingness to accept 'any other arrangement satisfactory to both Jews and Arabs ... provided guarantees were given for access to and safety of the holy places'.[85] By the end of September Britain too was moving towards formal acceptance of the division of Jerusalem. Sir Hugh Dow said that 'personally [he] saw no objection to placing these separate areas under the respective sovereignty of the Jewish State and the [Arab] State'.[86] Dean Rusk of the US State Department was impressed by this idea and suggested that the Arab and Jewish states might each administer their respective parts of Jerusalem under a UN trusteeship.[87]

The Israeli position too had changed. Heartened by her military victories, Israel was no longer interested in internationalization. The first stage towards the assertion of Israeli authority in the city was the imposition of Israeli military law on 25 July 1948. On 2 August Bernard Joseph (later Dov Yosef), who had headed the Jerusalem Emergency Committee of the Jewish Agency since the previous December, was appointed military governor. The same day the Israeli army issued 'proclamation no. 1' in Jerusalem. Signed by Ben Gurion in his capacity as Defence Minister, this declared that the area of Jerusalem under Israeli military control was an 'administered area' in which 'the law of the State of Israel prevails'.[88] This was understood by the Israelis to constitute a declaration that they were in military occupation; it thus fell short of annexation.

By now the Israeli government had, in effect, concluded that, in a choice between an unenforceable and unattractive internationalization and an enforced partition of the city, it preferred partition. As Dov Yosef put it, 'I find it difficult to understand the political logic that holds that instead of the Arabs having something it is preferable that both they and we have nothing. We will pluck out one of our eyes so that we can pluck out both of theirs.'[89] In line with such thinking, Israeli diplomacy glided with some skill from the original Zionist acceptance of internationalization towards an effort to secure international recognition of the status quo of partition. By 20 September the Israeli Cabinet was so anxious to obtain acceptance of the division of the city that it even approved Shertok's proposal that Israel should be prepared to give up a small part of the new city if that were the price of avoiding internationalization.[90] In a report to his party's central committee on 30 November, Ben Gurion indicated clearly that his objective now was partition of Jerusalem.[91]

Meanwhile, the other major actor too had adjusted to the new realities. Abdullah's response to the declaration of independence by the mufti (that 'devil from hell' as he called him [92]) was immediate. On 1 October a meeting of notables styling themselves the 'National Palestine Congress' met at Amman and called on Abdullah to take Palestine under his protection. Six weeks later, Abdullah had himself crowned 'king of Jerusalem' – rather strangely, by the Coptic bishop of the city.[93] This was the first crowning of a monarch in Jerusalem since the coronation there of Emperor Frederick II in 1229. (Since the emperor was at the time under a papal ban, he had placed the crown on his head himself.) On 1 December a conference of 2,000 Palestinian Arab notables at Jericho declared Abdullah 'king of all Palestine' and called for unification of the two banks of the Jordan in a single state. The country's parliament adopted a resolution to this effect on 13 December. A week later Abdullah appointed a candidate of his own as mufti of Jerusalem, Sheikh Husam al-Din Jarallah. He had been the unsuccessful candidate in 1921, when the British mandatory government appointed Hajj Amin al-Husayni. This was a sweet, albeit long-delayed, revenge for both Jarallah and Abdullah. Henceforth a cardinal objective of Abdullah's policy would be to maintain his hold over the West Bank and the old city of Jerusalem. The inevitable consequence was the diplomatic alignment of Jordan and Israel in favour of the city's partition, as against much of the rest of the world, which still advocated internationalization.

Following their cease-fire, Israeli and Jordanian representatives held a series of meetings to discuss not only the truce but also wider issues relating to a possible peace agreement. At one such meeting, on 30 December, the Jordanian military governor of Jerusalem, Abdullah al-Tall, told the Israeli intelligence chief, Reuven Shiloah, that

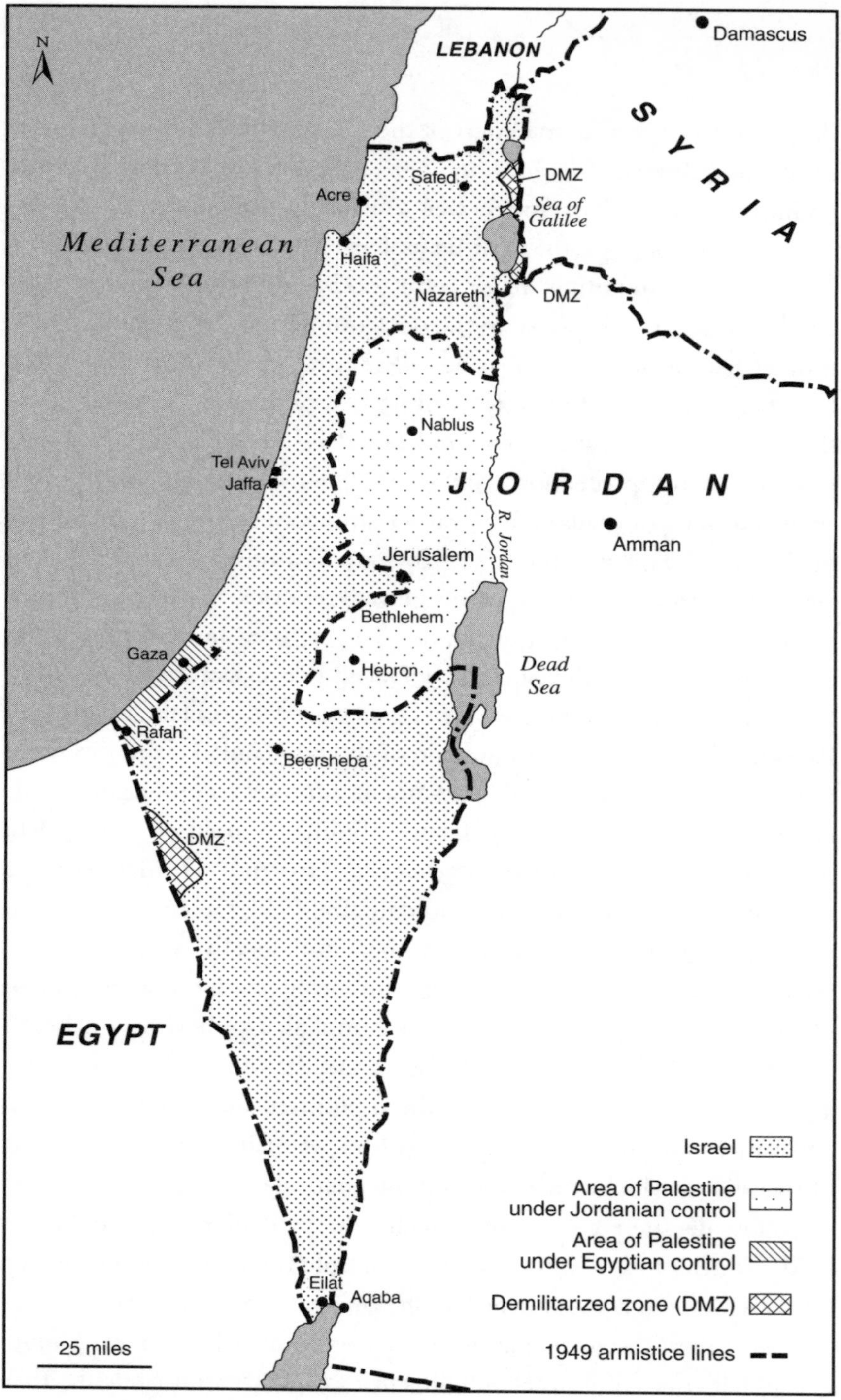
N
LEBANON
Damascus
SYRIA
DMZ
Sea of Galilee
Safed
Acre
Mediterranean Sea
Haifa
Nazareth
DMZ
Nablus
Tel Aviv
Jaffa
JORDAN
R. Jordan
Amman
Jerusalem
Bethlehem
Gaza
Hebron
Dead Sea
Rafah
Beersheba
DMZ
EGYPT
Israel
Area of Palestine under Jordanian control
Area of Palestine under Egyptian control
Demilitarized zone (DMZ)
1949 armistice lines
Eilat
Aqaba
25 miles

Map 9: Israel (1949–67)

Abdullah too was thinking of an agreed division of Jerusalem – 'Arab areas would go to him and Jewish areas to us' (this according to Shiloah's report on the meeting).[94] At the next meeting, on 5 January, Tall spelled out the proposal in more detail: the old city, Katamon and the German Colony as well as Talpiot and Kibbutz Ramat Rahel would be ruled by Jordan; Israel could have the rest of the Jewish new city. Plainly this was an opening gambit. The Israeli military commander in the Jerusalem area, Colonel Moshe Dayan, proposed instead that Sheikh Jarrah should be handed over to the Israelis in exchange for territory elsewhere, in order to give Israel a passage to Mount Scopus. But Tall pointed out that this would separate Arab Jerusalem from Ramallah which was unacceptable. No agreement was reached and the discussions were not resumed until a few months later.[95]

When the first Israeli general election took place in January 1949, residents in Israeli-held Jerusalem participated in the voting. On 4 February the Israeli government took another step towards annexation of west Jerusalem when it published its decision 'to abolish the military government in Jerusalem and to institute there civil administration which is in force in other parts of Israel'.[96] Ten days later the first Knesset (parliament) was opened in Jerusalem by President Weizmann. Representatives of the Soviet bloc, Latin American countries and the churches attended. But by prior agreement among themselves, the envoys of the United States, Britain and France declined invitations to attend.[97] The boycott marked the beginning of a long diplomatic impasse between Israel and the western powers over the status of Jerusalem.

On 3 April 1949, after talks on Rhodes under the chairmanship of Bunche, Israel and Jordan signed an armistice agreement (see Map 9, page 166). In Jerusalem the armistice demarcation line corresponded to the cease-fire line of 30 November 1948 (see Map 10, page 168).[98] With this agreement the division of Jerusalem froze into semi-permanence.

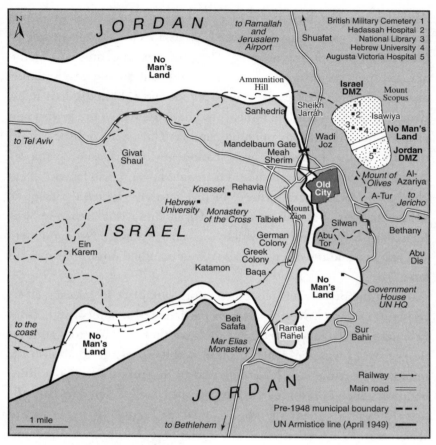

Map 10: Divided Jerusalem (1949–67)

'Will the Vatican send an army here?'

While Israel and Jordan strengthened their grips on their respective parts of divided Jerusalem, discussion of the subject at the United Nations became ever more abstract and unrealistic. On 11 December 1948 the UN General Assembly decided, under strong pressure from the United States, to establish a Palestine Conciliation Commission. All the functions of the mediator were transferred to this new body and it was also called upon to devise 'detailed proposals for a permanent international regime for the Jerusalem area'.[99] The commission had three members: an American, Mark Etheridge, a journalist from Louisville, Kentucky; a Frenchman, Claude de Boissanger, a quick-witted diplomat; and a Turk, H. C. Yalçin, a literary figure of distinction, aged nearly eighty. The ubiquitous Azcárate served as secretary. They set up initial headquarters in Jerusalem and installed themselves in the King David Hotel (no running water, no telephone, no working lifts). The Israeli military governor, Dov Yosef, told them 'angrily, almost violently' that there was no way of guaranteeing their safety and that they would be better advised to move to the Arab sector of the city.[100] Making little progress in Jerusalem, they moved to Lausanne in April 1949. On 1 September they completed a draft Instrument on Jerusalem. This was a watered-down version of internationalization. Instead of a *corpus separatum*, the division of the city was half recognized: Jordan and Israel would each administer their own zone under powers delegated to them by the UN; the city would be demilitarized and a UN governor would be appointed. The plan stipulated that the 'present demographic equilibrium' of the two zones was not to be upset by immigration. The proposals reflected American State Department views – though the strongly pro-Zionist US ambassador to Israel, James G. McDonald, wrote privately to Clark Clifford, Truman's Special Counsel, 'I dread what might happen if an effort were made under United Nations auspices to force Israel to accept immediately a United Nations Administrator in Jerusalem. A repetition of the Bernadotte tragedy would not be improbable ...'[101]

The Conciliation Commission's scheme was considered at the General Assembly session that opened the following month. Jordan, not yet a member of the UN, rejected it: 'Nobody will take over Jerusalem from me unless I am killed,' Abdullah declared.[102] Israel, which had been admitted to membership in May, was no less firm: Sharett (as Shertok henceforth called himself) called the plan 'anachronistic and incongruous'.[103] In the absence of assent by either of the two parties in possession, the Conciliation Commission's proposal was set aside. Sentiment in the United Nations now returned to the *corpus separatum* plan. The main reason was vigorous diplomatic advocacy by an influential, if sometimes discounted, power, the Holy See.

The Vatican became, indeed, the most vociferous champion of internationalization in this period – a further illustration of the rule that internationalization of the city was generally the favoured policy of those who were weak on the ground in Jerusalem itself. The policy was a decided change from the Vatican's earlier position. In March 1948 the Latin Patriarchate and the Franciscan Custody of the Holy Land had issued a joint statement opposing 'the erroneous policy which has been imposed in the country and which has culminated in the partition of Palestine'.[104] Until May the Vatican Secretariat of State had tried, as far as possible, to avoid commitment on the issue. On 24 October, however, Pope Pius XII, in his encyclical *In multiplicibus curis*, announced Vatican support for giving 'an international character to Jerusalem and its vicinity'. A further encyclical, *Redemptoris nostri cruciatus*, in April 1949, repeated the call for internationalization and issued a summons for international Catholic mobilization on the issue. It called on Catholics

> wherever they are living to use every legitimate means to
> persuade the rulers of nations, and those whose duty it is
> to settle this important question, to accord to Jerusalem
> and its surroundings a judicial status whose stability
> under the present circumstances can only be adequately
> assured by a united effort of nations that love peace and
> respect the right of others.[105]

In taking up this position, the Vatican was influenced by allegations of damage caused to Christian institutions in Israeli-ruled Jerusalem, by concern for the fate of Christian Arabs among the Palestinian refugees and, in particular, by pressure from France. The fact that the former fascist states of Italy and Spain were not members of the

United Nations gave France added weight in its effort to revive its old protectorate of Latin Christianity.[106] The Vatican's clear-cut position had ripple effects throughout the Catholic world and helped to shore up diplomatic support for internationalization at the United Nations.

Concerned at the threat of a revival of the *corpus separatum* plan, Israel took a number of diplomatic counter-measures. Weizmann, in a speech at his old university of Fribourg in Switzerland, tried to reassure Catholic opinion that Israel would 'welcome direct international supervision' of the holy places.[107] Although Israel had no diplomatic relations with the Holy See, an Israeli representative, Jacob Herzog, visited Rome to try to move the Vatican, but in vain.[108] In October 1949 Israeli diplomats floated the idea of an agreed internationalization of the old city (of course, now held by Jordan), coupled with an agreed partition of the rest of the city between Israel and Jordan along the existing armistice lines. Such an idea had been floated tentatively within the US State Department in June 1948 and it is possible that some echo of this reached the Israelis.[109] The Israeli proposal was based on a plan drawn up in October 1948 by Dr Avraham Biran, Assistant to the Military Governor of Jerusalem (later District Commissioner of Jerusalem). It envisaged a Christian governor of the old city, responsible to the UN Trusteeship Council. He would be assisted by three deputies, a Christian, a Muslim and a Jew, as well as by an advisory council (five members for each religion). The area would have its own police force and would

> take on the character of a Holy City, somewhat like the
> Vatican ... It will consist of institutions of all religions,
> churches, synagogues, mosques, schools of learning of all
> kinds, hotels for tourists and pilgrims. A small civil
> population will derive its livelihood from these
> institutions and from tourists by catering to their
> religious needs, for example, the sale of clerical items,
> mother of pearl and olive wood articles etc.[110]

The scheme held obvious attractions for the Israelis, notably in opening up the possibility of access from the new city to the old.

Rather than pursue this initiative directly herself, however, Israel tried to persuade Christian leaders to do so. This appears to have been part of a general effort to divide the Churches on the Jerusalem issue – most especially to build up Christian support against the Vatican's internationalization campaign. The Israelis were able to make some headway in discussions with the Armenian and Greek Orthodox Churches, exploiting their historic animosities against the Latins. The main Israeli negotiator in relations with the Christian Churches was Jacob Herzog, at that time head of the Christian Department of the Religious Affairs Ministry. In April 1949 he wrote to Ben Gurion and Sharett, setting out Israeli tactics. In meetings with the Greek Orthodox Patriarchate, the Israelis had argued that whatever form of internationalization might be adopted, in the course of time the Latins would gain the ascendancy in the city. In order to win Orthodox support, the Israelis had made some significant concessions regarding treatment of real estate owned by the Patriarchate in west Jerusalem. In return the Orthodox had indicated that they would 'fight with all means at their disposal' against internationalization. Given the position of their communities in the Arab world, they would not be able to oppose internationalization publicly. But at a suitable opportunity they would make it clear that the Orthodox did not follow the Vatican line on the issue and they promised to convey this position to Athens and Washington.[111]

About the same time, the Israeli Minister in London, Mordechai Eliash, visited the Archbishop of Canterbury and presented a memorandum arguing that:

> Christian interests cannot expect Israel to take the lead in claiming full international status for the City within the walls, seeing that Israel's main efforts are now concentrated on securing its own population and its

future. But coming generations would, one feels, judge it
an appalling political and religious blunder were the
Christian world willingly to surrender the Walled City to
Arab sovereignty merely on the flimsy argument that it
might be a matter of discomfiture for King Abdullah to
give up the only prize that he secured in a war which he
ought never to have begun.[112]

The Anglican Primate expressed polite interest but no more. In a
'private memorandum' he submitted to the UN Trusteeship Council
shortly afterwards, he suggested that the greater part of the Jewish-
inhabited areas of the new city should be incorporated into Israel,
while the whole of the remainder of the projected *corpus separatum*
should be internationalized.[113] The idea of an international regime
limited to the old city evoked little interest in the Christian world and
was soon dropped by Israel in favour of a proposal that restricted internationalization even more narrowly.

This was the concept of 'functional' as distinct from 'territorial' internationalization, limited to the holy places. A draft scheme was
drawn up in the Foreign Ministry for a treaty between Israel and the
United Nations under which the holy places would be placed 'under
the control and authority of the United Nations'.[114] In an accompanying memorandum, the ministry's legal adviser, Shabtai Rosenne,
suggested that the word 'control' should be understood 'in its French
sense', apparently conveying a right to check entry rather than to administer. He stressed that the draft did not confer any extra-territorial status on the holy places, and he added that 'if the treaty was
acceptable to the United Nations, and Transjordan could be induced
to enter into a similar one, it would follow that Jews would obtain access not only to the Wailing Wall, but also to the Tomb of Rachel and
the Haram el Khalil in Hebron, and other holy places and sites (if
any) at present in Arab hands, with, as far as I am aware, little if any
real quid pro quo to the Arabs.'[115] Functional internationalization

found some significant support at the UN and such a plan was formally proposed by the Netherlands and Sweden in the autumn of 1948, only for this too to be set aside.

The opponents of internationalization, most notably and self-interestedly the two states in possession, now found themselves in some difficulty on the Jerusalem issue. The awkwardness of Israel's position was candidly acknowledged by the Director-General of the Foreign Ministry, Walter Eytan:

> It is certainly true that we are trying to have our cake and eat it too, in other words, to maintain our hold on the New City while at the same time trying to keep the Old City from falling into Abdullah's hands. The reason for this is that we are caught in a trap which presents us with only two logical choices: either we agree to the internationalization of the entire city, which we do not want, or else we agree to Arab rule in those parts of the city which are not in our possession – which we also do not want. Under these circumstances we are forced to take a stand lacking all logic ...[116]

As Israel tried to formulate a coherent policy on Jerusalem, she found that virtually her only supporter was her erstwhile enemy Jordan. But as a non-member of the UN (her membership was blocked by the USSR) and without the support of other Arab states, Jordan could achieve little in the diplomatic sphere.

In the United Nations General Assembly in November 1949 Iraq, Lebanon and Syria led the way in upholding internationalization. Those Arab states declared that 'in justice and equity Jerusalem should remain an Arab city, but since, regrettably, the Arab point of view did not prevail in international politics, they were forced to accept full and complete internationalisation as the lesser evil'.[117] The British Minister in Tel Aviv commented, 'The Arab League, with their usual marmoreal impercipience of the trend of events, are only supporting internationalisation because: (i) it is opposed by Israel, and (ii) it will be a smack in the eye for King Abdullah.'[118] The Israeli response to the renewed threat of internationalization was sharp. On 5 December Sharett, who was leading the Israeli delegation at the UN, telephoned Tel Aviv with the news that a UN reaffirmation of the *corpus separatum* scheme was imminent. At a Cabinet meeting that day Ben Gurion said the question was whether the UN could give effect to such a decision. He did not think that they had the power to enforce it. America would not permit Russia to send an army to Jerusalem to do so; nor would America send a force herself. 'Will the Vatican send an army here?' he asked. 'If the choice is between membership of the United Nations or Jerusalem, we shall choose Jerusalem.' All the ministers who spoke in the meeting supported Ben Gurion. Dov Yosef said it was essential for the government to take a stand: 'I've got the impression that the inhabitants of Tel Aviv, even if not all of them, could rest content without Jerusalem.' Yosef said government offices should move to Jerusalem but it was agreed that the time had not yet come for that.

In the course of the Cabinet discussion, Ben Gurion disclosed that, even though Israel might be in a minority of one in the United Nations, she had a potential ally in opposing internationalization. The subject of Jerusalem, he revealed, had come up in further secret discussions between Israeli representatives and King Abdullah: 'Abdullah said he agrees to the partition of Jerusalem. They [the Israeli representatives] told him that we want part of the old city, all the path to the Western Wall.' Abdullah's answer had been equivocal but he made it clear he was willing to negotiate a general peace that would include a partitioned Jerusalem. Ben Gurion told the Cabinet that if part of the old city could be regained, that would be 'a tremendous thing'. He would even be prepared to give up part of the new city in return; he mentioned Kibbutz Ramat Rahel, if that were the necessary price – rather surprisingly given the blood that had been shed the previous year in a see-saw battle to retain it under Jewish control.[119] The Cabinet approved Ben Gurion's policy. In a fiery speech to the Knesset later that day, the Prime Minister warned of the likely Israeli reaction to any attempt to internationalize Jerusalem by force: Israel, he declared, would 'not give up Jerusalem of its own free will'.[120]

Later that day the UN Ad Hoc Political Committee voted by thirty-eight to fourteen for an internationalized Jerusalem. The USA and Britain opposed the resolution but it was supported by the Arab states, the communist bloc and, under strong Vatican pressure, most Catholic countries. The General Assembly followed on 9 December with a resolution reaffirming that 'the City of Jerusalem shall be established as a *corpus separatum* under a special international regime and shall be administered by the United Nations'. The Trusteeship Council was instructed 'to complete the preparation of the Statute of Jerusalem … introducing therein amendments in the direction of its greater democratization, approve the Statute, and proceed immediately with its implementation'. The council was adjured not to 'allow any actions by any interested Government or Governments to divert it from adopting and implementing the Statute of Jerusalem'.[121] The vote was a victory for Vatican diplomacy, incongruously allied on this issue with the Soviet Union. But it was a paper triumph only: Israel and Jordan now demonstrated their capacity to thwart the expressed view of the international community on Jerusalem.

Two days later the Israeli Cabinet, again acting on the initiative of Ben Gurion, responded by announcing its decision to make Jerusalem Israel's capital. This was not a foregone conclusion. Prior to independence Zionists had been by no means clear in their minds that Jerusalem must be the capital of the future Jewish state. Among the various suggested locations for a capital before May 1948 were Ben Gurion's proposal of a Negev settlement and Golda Myerson (Meir)'s of Mount Carmel.[122] The Cabinet did not even discuss seriously the idea of making Jerusalem the capital until late 1949. With the exception of the Supreme Court, none of the main organs of government moved to Jerusalem until later. The first President of the state, Chaim Weizmann, who had never had much fondness for Jerusalem, preferred to establish his official residence in Rehovot in the coastal plain and it remained there until his death in 1952. The decision to declare Jerusalem Israel's capital was not planned in advance. Ben Gurion's proposal was a characteristically headstrong reaction to the UN General Assembly resolution of 9 December.

The Prime Minister was again supported by the Cabinet. But when Sharett, who was still in New York, heard about the decision, he was horrified. He had long favoured a gradualist, unassertive approach to the problem. In his view Israeli control of Jerusalem was a reality; there was no need for demonstrative gestures in reaction to the UN resolution. Sharett threatened resignation but Ben Gurion refused to accept it and it was withdrawn.[123] The Foreign Minister was not the only Israeli politician to have doubts about the wisdom of the move. In a debate among Knesset members of the governing Mapai (Labour) Party, Pinhas Lubianker (Lavon) spoke for many when he argued that Jerusalem was 'a bad place for a national capital'. 'Practically speaking,' he maintained, 'I think some of the ministries could be in Jerusalem but there are others which it would be absurd to move there. Transferring the Knesset is absurd … moving the Treasury is insane.'[124] But with help from Levi Eshkol and Golda Myerson, Ben Gurion secured a clear majority among those present. Speaking defiantly to the Knesset on 13 December, he insisted that the UN decision to place Jerusalem under an international regime was 'utterly incapable of implementation – if only because of the determination and unalterable opposition of the inhabitants of Jerusalem itself'.[125] Thereafter the Knesset always met in Jerusalem, although its permanent home, above the Valley of the Cross in the new city, was not opened until 1966.

The Israeli action was not accepted by any of the powers. The State Department informed the US embassy in Tel Aviv that the USA did 'not recognize the sovereignty of Israel in Jerusalem' and instructed

US diplomats not to conduct official business with 'Israeli Central Govt. officials' there.[126] The British and the French decided similarly.

Years after the critical decision of December 1949, Ben Gurion explained why he had taken such a risky gamble: 'I knew we had an ally – Transjordan. If they were permitted to hold on to Jerusalem, why weren't we? Transjordan would permit no one to get them out of Jerusalem; consequently no one would dare to remove us. I would have done it without this, but it was a great reinforcement. I knew nothing would happen to us.'[127]

On the same day as Ben Gurion's Knesset speech, 13 December 1949, Israel and Jordan reached agreement on a draft peace treaty.[128] Among other provisions, the document set out the details of a partitioned Jerusalem in which the Jewish quarter of the old city as well as the Western Wall would be handed over to Israeli sovereignty.[129] The agreement was never implemented, but its spirit hovered uncertainly over the divided city for the next eighteen years.

5   Two Jerusalems

From 1949 to 1967 the holy city was grotesquely divided by walls and barbed wire between two sovereignties. The division of populations was almost total. Hardly any Arabs remained in west Jerusalem (1,930 non-Jews were counted there in 1950, but many of these were foreign Christians).[1] No Jews remained in east Jerusalem save for one or two Jewish women married to Arab husbands. During this period the diplomacy of the Jerusalem question changed radically. The key questions were no longer to do with religion or holy places. The issues were directly political. Should Jerusalem remain partitioned? Should the question of internationalization remain on the agenda? If so, in what form? Should Israel establish her capital in Jerusalem? The answers to these questions were not self-evident. External forces – the great powers, the United Nations, the Vatican – all offered their own answers. But they found themselves unable to determine the course of events. The effective decisions were now taken mainly by the two powers in possession, Israel and Jordan. They remained technically in a state of war with each other throughout this period. Yet a strange diplomatic symbiosis grew up between them. Although they failed to agree on a permanent peace, a modus vivendi was achieved in Jerusalem. In defiance of much of the rest of the world, both refused to budge from the positions that, at enormous cost, they had won in Jerusalem.

Divide and rule

While the armistice agreement with Israel was generally observed in Jerusalem, sniper fire across the dividing line remained a perpetual hazard. The front line running through the city was often tense and in July 1954 nine people were killed and fifty-five wounded by sniper fire. Israeli communications to its enclave on Mount Scopus remained precarious. Traffic between the city's Arab and Jewish sectors, mainly of diplomats, Christian clergy and pilgrims, was confined to the single crossing point at what became known as the Mandelbaum Gate – although there was no gate and the Jewish merchant who had once owned a house at the site had long since departed.

As the partition of Jerusalem settled into everyday reality, public opinion in the west began to lose interest in internationalization. In May 1950 the *New York Times* pronounced in favour of an Israeli proposal to maintain the territorial status quo in Jerusalem, while placing the religious shrines in the city under UN authority.[2] *Le Monde* and *The Times* also endorsed this position.[3]

In spite of the draft treaty agreed on 13 December 1949, no permanent peace was signed between Abdullah and the Israelis. But negotiations continued and a large measure of understanding was reached about Jerusalem. In January 1950 the Israeli representative to the United Nations, Abba Eban, told his British colleague that 'Israel and Jordan were practically in agreement as regards Jerusalem (simple territorial partition with guarantees for the holy places) but that agreement on Jerusalem must be part of a general agreement. Latter was stalled on question of access to the sea for Jordan.'[4] Eban's optimism was a little premature, and was dismissed in the Foreign Office as 'a manoeuvre'.[5]

The Jerusalem question was discussed again a few days later at a secret meeting between Israeli and Jordanian representatives at the Jordanian monarch's desert palace at Shuneh. Israel was again represented by Reuven Shiloah and Moshe Dayan, the Jordanian delegation was headed by Samir Rifai, the Jordanian Minister of Court. On this occasion the exact lines of a proposed partition of the city were discussed. Again the Jordanians indicated their readiness to hand over certain areas to the Israelis, including the Jewish quarter of the old city and the Western Wall, and offered to guarantee access to Mount Scopus. In return the Israelis should transfer to Jordan certain Arab quarters in west Jerusalem that had been abandoned in the war, among them Talbieh, the Greek Colony and Baqa.[6] A series of further meetings on the subject over the next few weeks hammered out details of the arrangement. Abdullah seemed ready to approve it but he faced opposition from his government to the proposed concession of the Jewish quarter and the Western Wall: the Prime Minister and Cabinet threatened their resignations.[7] Jordan was far from being a parliamentary democracy and Abdullah might have had the capacity to overrule his ministers. On 24 February Rifai and the Jordanian Defence Minister Fawzi al-Mulqi met Shiloah and Dayan again and the two sides initialled an outline agreement to serve as a basis for formal negotiations between the two countries. But leaks appeared in the press and in Jordan political opposition to the agreement stiffened. By April the talks again appeared to have broken down.

Abdullah remained anxious to secure an agreement with Israel – if only to put an end to the danger that he might yet lose the jewel of his kingdom to the international regime that his Arab allies had now joined in demanding. That month he visited Jerusalem and, pointing across a window overlooking the Haram al-Sharif, he said emotionally, 'This is Al Aksa mosque which God has blessed. The mosque is an Islamic legacy embodying the holiness and grandeur of Islam. Am I to surrender it, whilst it is a pledge binding my neck and a point I defended with the blood of my soldiers, to a foreign administration called internationalization? No – No – I shall not do so and if I did I should not be Abdullah ibn Hussein.'[8] On several occasions, indeed, Abdullah declared that Jerusalem would be internationalized 'only over his dead body'.

A momentary public manifestation of Israeli-Jordanian cooperation in the division of Jerusalem's assets was recorded in October 1950 when the UN Public Information Officer in the city issued the following communiqué:

United Nations observers today supervised – with the cooperation of Jordan and Israeli authorities – the transfer of the 'Biblical Zoo' from Israeli-controlled Mount Scopus through Jordan-held Jerusalem to new quarters in the Israeli part of the city.

Involved in the transfer were the following: one lion, one tiger, two bears, one hyena, three kangaroos, one monkey and innumerable birds.

International action was required for the following reason: the question of feeding the animals while at Mount Scopus had presented unique problems to the United Nations, to Israel and to Jordan. Decisions had to be taken whether

(a) Israeli money should be used to buy Arab donkeys to feed the Israeli lion or

(b) whether an Israeli donkey should pass through Jordan-held territory to be eaten by the lion in question.

Since no other satisfactory solution could be reached, the Israeli and Jordan authorities agreed to transfer the zoo.[9]

If this was a reductio ad absurdum of partition, it was also evidence of the desire of both sides to consolidate the division of the city.

Why, then, did formal agreement continue to elude the two sides? Jerusalem itself was not the main stumbling block – Abdullah could probably have overcome Palestinian opposition to his proposed carve-up of the city. But the city was part of the larger context of Israeli-Jordanian and Israeli-Arab relations. Neither side, it seemed, was yet fully prepared to make the dangerous leap towards a contractual peace agreement. Sporadic discussions between Abdullah and the Israelis continued over the next few months, but relations were disturbed by several border incidents and public opinion on both sides remained mutually hostile.

The matter in any case became academic when, on 20 July 1951, Abdullah was assassinated in Jerusalem. He was killed by a single shot at close range as, together with his grandson Hussein, he entered al-Aqsa mosque for Friday prayers. The assassin, Mustafa Ashu, a Jerusalem tailor's apprentice, was killed on the spot by bodyguards. Following the assassination, soldiers of the Arab Legion went on a vengeful rampage through the city, smashing up shops and stall-keepers, looting and causing severe damage to businesses.[10]

Abdullah's assassination was widely held to be the result of a conspiracy. The hand of the mufti was generally suspected although no evidence directly implicating him was ever produced. Several of the mufti's supporters were arrested. Investigators concluded that a key figure in the conspiracy had been the former Jordanian governor of Jerusalem, Abdullah al-Tall. An east-banker, he was a supporter of Palestinian nationalism and, as an officer in the 1948 war, had played a central role in the fighting in Jerusalem. He also accepted at least one cash bribe directly from the Israelis.[11] Tall accused Abdullah of betraying the Arab cause by holding back Arab forces from the city in May 1948. He quarrelled with the government and went into exile in Egypt in 1949. From Cairo Tall appears to have played a significant role in the assassination plot, receiving a large sum of money from an unknown source to oil the wheels of the conspiracy.[12]

Some contacts between Israelis and Jordanians continued even after Abdullah's death. For example, in October 1951 the Israeli District Commissioner for Jerusalem, Avraham Biran, met Ragheb Bey Nashashibi for a talk about Jerusalem. Nashashibi said that Jordanian opinion was swinging back towards internationalization, though that may have been as much a tactical ploy as a reflection of the absence of a clear political line in Jordan in the aftermath of the assassination.[13] But soon after that contacts were broken off altogether and by the following summer the Israelis were reduced to asking the British whether they could find out the current attitude of Jordan towards the internationalization of Jerusalem.[14]

While these direct Israeli-Jordanian discussions proceeded, the Palestine Conciliation Commission and the UN Trusteeship Council returned wearily to the task of perfecting the Statute of Jerusalem. This was one of the most elaborately conceived, lengthily debated and carefully formulated constitutional acts ever framed by man. In some respects it was a masterpiece of public law. Yet in spite of the elephantine efforts involved in its gestation, it never came into force. On 30 January 1950 the French representative on the Council, Roger Garreau, had presented yet another plan: this provided for Jerusalem to be divided (like Gaul) into three parts: an Israeli zone, a Jordanian zone and an 'International City' under UN sovereignty. Arab spokesmen objected that the plan cut Jerusalem up into pieces. The Israeli representative at the UN, Abba Eban, told the US State Department that the statute was a 'completely unrepresentative and unrealistic document'.[15] On 4 April the new statute was approved by the council by nine votes to none, the USA and USSR both abstaining. Opposed by both Arabs and Jews, the statute was never even presented to the UN General Assembly. The council turned to other problems and the Conciliation Commission settled down to a ghostly afterlife in New York. From 1951 to 1967 the United Nations passed no further resolutions on Jerusalem and the international body's incapacity to give effect to its supposed authority in the city inevitably eroded respect for the idea of a *corpus separatum*. The evident satisfaction of Israel and Jordan with partition, *faute de mieux*, and their capacity to enforce their views on the ground led eventually to reluctant acquiescence in the status quo by the powers.

They, like the United Nations, lost interest in the Jerusalem question in these years. Only Britain and the United States, among the great powers, took any significant diplomatic initiatives on the subject between 1950 and 1967. The British, anxious to regularize the position of their client Abdullah, were most interested in an agreed solution. But the Americans regarded the matter with less urgency. In

August 1950 the US Secretary of State, Dean Acheson, told the British that while he considered internationalization 'just and workable', the 'primary US concern' was 'an agreed solution'. The Americans, therefore, would support a new initiative on Jerusalem only if there was a 'good chance [of] acceptance by [the] two states controlling Jerusalem and [by a] large proportion [of the] international community'.[16]

In July 1952 the Foreign Office set out 'tentative conditions for an Arab-Israeli Settlement' that were conveyed to the Americans. These proposed, within the framework of a general settlement, 'recognition by all Arab States of Israel's and Jordan's sovereignty over their respective sectors of Jerusalem and a promise of support in the United Nations for a resolution giving such recognition, against guarantees to preserve international rights and interests there'. The document also suggested 'adjustments to the line of demarcation in Jerusalem to establish a logical common frontier'. Least likely to find favour with the Israelis was the provision that Israel should 'surrender (against compensation) all claims to Mount Scopus which will be handed over to Jordan'.[17] While the author of the document, Archie Ross, confessed that he had 'no illusions' about its acceptability to either side, it seemed to demonstrate that Britain was no longer wedded to internationalization.[18] A memorandum by Evelyn Shuckburgh in December 1954, however, indicated some backsliding in the Foreign Office: 'Jerusalem: a very complicated issue for which there are many conflicting solutions, all of them beset with difficulty. Internationalisation or neutralisation should still be our aim.'[19] But by the mid-1950s this was becoming a minority view.

While neither the British nor the Americans changed their formal diplomatic position, both recognized privately that internationalization was no longer practical politics. In 1955 a joint Anglo-American effort to bring about an Arab-Israeli settlement, known as Operation Alpha, yielded a joint US-UK memorandum setting out the bases of an agreement. On Jerusalem this called for demilitarization, *de jure* recognition of Israeli and Jordanian sovereignty in their respective sectors of the city and the creation of an international authority charged with supervision of the holy places.[20] But the attempt to impose a settlement along these lines got nowhere and after Washington and London parted company over the Suez Canal crisis in 1956 the matter was dropped.

Thereafter, the general policy of the western powers on Jerusalem until 1967 may be encapsulated in the famous, if apocryphal, maxim allegedly impressed on young members of the British Foreign Service: 'All actions have consequences; consequences are unpredictable; therefore take no action.'

Jerusalem demoted

During the 1948–9 war a large part of the Arab population of Jerusalem had fled from the city. In spite of the armistice, the proximity of the border and continued sniping in both directions discouraged many from returning quickly. Significant movement of population back to east Jerusalem began only in 1950. Not only Jerusalemites but also some refugees from what had now become Israel settled in the Jordanian sector of the city. In June 1953 19,106 refugees were registered in Jerusalem. Many more settled in villages just outside the municipal boundary, such as Abu Dis (1,297 refugees reported in June 1953), Silwan (1,621) and a-Tur (800).[21] Initially most of the refugees lived in tents or caves, later in mud huts or shacks with tar-barrel roofs. As economic life slowly resumed in the 1950s, east Jerusalem began to attract immigrants, particularly from Hebron. New building appeared, mainly towards the north, especially in Wadi Joz, and to the east on and around the Mount of Olives. Between 1949 and 1967 the population of Jordanian Jerusalem grew from 42,000 to 70,000.

On 21 March 1949 Abdullah announced that the military administration in the West Bank, including east Jerusalem, would give way to a civil one. None of the powers recognized Jordanian sovereignty over east Jerusalem. But since Jordan, unlike Israel, did not claim Jerusalem as its capital, fewer diplomatic issues arose. Moreover, the British ambassador in Amman wrote in 1962, 'even if they did have an axe to grind, the Jordanians are not by nature endowed with the ingenuity, legal finesse and tenacity deployed by the Israelis in pursuit of their objectives'.[22]

Nevertheless, problems of protocol troubled foreign consuls and diplomats. When, for example, a royal reception was held for King Hussein in Jerusalem in 1956, the question arose whether the consular corps should attend. Would not such attendance constitute recognition of Jordanian sovereignty in the city? Would attendance oblige the consuls to attend receptions by the President of Israel? Should a distinction be drawn 'between, on the one hand, receptions given by the local authorities for the King, and, on the other, receptions given by the King himself to which invitations are sent out in his name?'[23] In the end the British Foreign Office (which set the tone in such matters in Jordan at that period) decided that consuls were, as the consul-general put it, 'such a low form of life that their presence at Royal functions in (Jordan) Jerusalem could not affect the question of sovereignty'. As it turned out, the consuls, except for those from Arab countries, were not invited – 'to our private delight as it was a stinkingly hot day!' the British consul-general commented. He added, in even more Pooteresque fashion, 'Nevertheless, our official feelings were hurt, and there is talk of making a protest.'[24]

During the nineteen years of Jordanian rule, Jerusalem's relative weight in the Jordanian polity was systematically reduced. The exiled Abdullah al-Tall was one of many who accused Abdullah of the deliberate downgrading of Jerusalem. Although Tall's accusations against Abdullah in general appear to have been largely motivated by personal spite, there was some substance in this one. The Arab sector of the city was a much-diminished rump. It lost its former importance as a capital, since main government offices were all in Amman. In 1950 the municipal council was disbanded and the city was run for a time by an appointed mayor, Aref al-Aref, and an official committee. In 1951 the Supreme Moslem Council was abolished. In 1956 the Muslim religious appeal court was moved to Amman. The festival of Nebi Musa, long an occasion for nationalist demonstrations and closely associated with the Husaynis, was allowed to lapse. A British resident in the early 1950s recorded that the festival had 'been abolished by adversity. There was talk of reviving it this year. The Mayor even spread his pavilion at Ras al-Amoud. But it remained empty and forlorn. The peasants were too poor, too sad to keep holiday.'[25] That was one way of explaining the demise of this uproarious and colourful tradition. A more plausible interpretation is that the Jordanian government judged the event too politically dangerous to be allowed to revive.

The British, who retained great influence in Jordan in the early 1950s, occasionally expressed irritation at the reduced role of the city: 'we would be well advised to make it clear to the Jordan Government ... that we are not prepared to allow them to treat the Old City of Jerusalem as though it were nothing more than a provincial townlet in Jordan, without history or importance,' wrote the British consul-general in April 1955.[26] The statement was eloquent testimony to the confusion that the Jerusalem issue engendered in the diplomatic mind: on the one hand, the Israelis were reprimanded for making the city their 'capital'; on the other, the Jordanians were rebuked for treating Jerusalem as if it were merely 'provincial'. The Jordanians, in any event, like the Israelis, paid little heed to outside advice on the Jerusalem issue.

At the same time, the complaints about Jordanian demotion of Jerusalem were not altogether fair. In fact, Abdullah took some steps to recognize the importance of Jerusalem and, making deft use of a spoils system, he and his successors sought to retain the support of the notable leaders in the city. In 1950 he appointed a former mayor of Jerusalem and long-time political ally, Ragheb Bey al-Nashashibi, governor of the West Bank. The following January he made Ragheb also guardian and supreme custodian over the holy places of all three religions – though the United States, the Vatican and other countries refused to recognize this appointment. After Abdullah's death, more Palestinians, including some Jerusalemites, were incorporated into the ruling élite. In 1955 Aref al-Aref, then mayor of Jerusalem, was appointed Minister of Public Works. Anwar Nusseibeh, who had served as Cabinet Secretary of the mufti's short-lived All-Palestine Government in Gaza, was appointed Jordanian Defence and Reconstruction Minister in 1953 and governor of Jerusalem in 1961. And in 1957 Dr Husayn Fakhri al-Khalidi, the former mayor of Jerusalem in the 1930s, became Prime Minister, though only for nine days. Hashemite policy towards the Palestinians was essentially one of co-option mixed with repression.

The policy was only partly successful. Throughout the period Jerusalem remained the centre of Palestinian Arab nationalism in the West Bank, and therefore an object of dangerous preoccupation for Jordanian internal security organs. A candidate in the 1962 election campaign in the Qalandiya refugee camp just north of Jerusalem declared bitterly, 'Look at the palaces which are being built in Amman and not in Jerusalem, erected after 1948 on Palestinian shoulders. They [should have been] built in Jerusalem but were removed from there so it would stay like a village!'[27] In the period of turmoil that followed Abdullah's assassination, Palestinian Arab notables were emboldened to present demands forcefully to the Jordanian government. In a memorandum to the Prime Minister in 1952 fourteen leaders from the West Bank urged a number of measures to enhance the standing of Jerusalem. These demands were rejected, though the city's administrative status was raised nominally in 1955. There were anti-government riots in Jerusalem in 1951 and again in 1955, when consulates were attacked and the French and Turkish consuls wounded. The exiled mufti retained a following and pro-Husayni elements formed the core of opposition to Hashemite rule. Undercurrents of hostility to the regime remained strong and were fanned from the mid-1950s by the winds of Nasserist nationalism blowing from Egypt. In spite of occasional rhetorical flourishes in the direction of Jerusalem, the policy of Jordanization was intensified.[28]

The Middle East crisis of 1956 heightened tension in Jerusalem both between Israel and Jordan and between Jordan and Britain. Nasserism kindled hope, for a time, among Palestinians. Until it was closed in 1957, the Egyptian consulate in Jerusalem helped fan the flame by organizing the smuggling of arms for use by *fidaiyun* (cross-border infiltrators to Israel).[29] The dismissal of Glubb Pasha as commander of the Arab Legion in March 1956 marked a dramatic terminus in the old paternalistic system of British overlordship in Jordan.

Later that year the caretaker Foreign Minister, Awni Abdul Hadi, called in the French Minister and told him that the anomalous consular system in Jerusalem was 'an outrageous state of affairs that should not be allowed to continue'.[30] A few days later the Foreign Minister withdrew all permanent passes for crossing between the old and new cities from members of the consular corps.[31] Around the same time the consuls' telephone lines between east and west Jerusalem, which, surprisingly, had continued to function since the division of the city, were cut: they remained so until 1967.[32] The governor apologized and said he found the order cancelling the passes 'stupid and discourteous'.[33] He tried but failed to persuade the Foreign Minister to change his mind. The consuls protested vehemently and retaliated for the loss of their permanent passes by lodging claims for passes for themselves and their staffs every day.[34] The western powers considered threatening to close their offices in east Jerusalem and even to recognize Jerusalem as capital of Israel if the Jordanians did not desist. But the Quai d'Orsay objected to the latter suggestion and that was dropped.[35] A more fruitful line of approach was taken instead: it had been discovered that the official responsible was Director of External Liaisons in the Foreign Ministry; he was in receipt of a British government pension paid through the Jerusalem con-

sulate; the possibility was mooted that the new consular arrangements would create difficulties in the payment of such pensions;
shortly afterwards, the passes were reissued – except to the French
consul-general, who was confined to west Jerusalem for several years
as a kind of punishment for the Suez episode (strangely, his British
colleague suffered no such sanction).[36]

At the height of the Suez crisis in early November, the French
raised with the British the possibility of putting forward again to
Israel and Jordan their old plan for the demilitarization of Jerusalem.
The Foreign Office was highly suspicious. Did this suggest that the
French had information that the Israelis were about to attack the
West Bank? Would the French be happy with that provided Jerusalem
were left alone? 'It is typical of the French,' wrote a British diplomat
on 5 November, 'that, at this time when the entire British position in
the Middle East is collapsing, their main preoccupation should be to
maintain their self-appointed rôle of protector of the Holy Places.'[37]
The crisis passed. Israel did not attack, the French plan got nowhere
and life in Jerusalem returned to its abnormal normality.

Political unrest and opposition to the Hashemites remained rife
over the next couple of years. Further disturbances broke out in
Jerusalem in 1957. The rise of Nasserism in Jordan and temporary
British military intervention in 1958 brought a new crisis. Israel facilitated the British action by permitting overflights of her territory
by the RAF. At the same time she made it clear to the British that, in
the event of a coup against the Hashemite regime, such as had occurred in Iraq, she would consider occupying the West Bank herself,
or at least east Jerusalem and other strategically important areas.

Neither the popularity of pan-Arabism nor official Jordanization
snuffed out Palestinian Arab nationalism. There were renewed riots
in the city in 1963. The following year Jordan paid tribute to the reality of such nationalist undercurrents by granting permission for the
convening in Jerusalem of a Palestinian Congress – though King Hussein had first suggested that it take place in Amman or near the Dead

Sea.[38] It was opened by King Hussein at the Intercontinental Hotel on the Mount of Olives on 29 May and marked the effective foundation of the Palestine Liberation Organization, headed initially by Ahmad Shuqayri. At first, the PLO's headquarters were in Jerusalem, but in January 1967 the Jordanian government, sensing a challenge to its authority, closed the office down and the organization was compelled to move its base to Cairo.

In March that year the mufti, now aged about seventy, returned to Jerusalem for the first time since his escape from the British thirty years earlier. Hussein received him with great honour and put him up at his house at Bet Hanina, north of Jerusalem. He was now reconciled with the Hashemites, if only because of their opposition to the PLO. After two weeks he left, never to return, though he remained politically active in his final years, spent mainly in Lebanon. In a general election the following month two of his supporters were elected to parliament to represent Jerusalem. But if the PLO had not yet realized its potential, the mufti was, in truth, a spent force.

Christians in a divided Jerusalem

One significant feature of the period of Jordanian rule in Jerusalem was the decline of the Christian Arab population. From 31,400, constituting 19 per cent of the population in 1946, it shrank to 12,900, only 4.9 per cent, in 1967.[39] These were almost all in east Jerusalem. The main factor in the decline was emigration. The cause was not so much the mildly anti-Christian policy of the government, or social tensions and occasional violence between Christians and Muslims, but rather the decline of economic opportunities, including employment in administration, commerce, crafts and tourism, on which the city's Christian population had hitherto largely depended.

The decline in numbers reflected a decline in political influence. The number of Christian public employees, always disproportionately high in mandatory Palestine, declined under Jordanian rule. Jordan was a Muslim state and Christian holy days were no longer officially recognized. Laws enacted in 1953, 1954, 1965 and 1966 placed restrictions on the purchase of property by Christian institutions in Jerusalem and curtailed their activities.[40] Christian schools, for example, were compelled to close on Fridays and adjust their curricula. Customs privileges long enjoyed by Christian institutions were abolished. The British consul-general in Jerusalem expressed repeated annoyance at the 'anti-Christian tendency'. The Jordanians, he wrote in 1955, were waging 'open warfare ... against Christian institutions in Jerusalem'. He urged that the British government use their considerable influence with the Jordanians to defend Christian interests.[41]

The struggle within the Greek Orthodox community between the Greek hierarchy and the Arab laity, which had rumbled on under Ottoman and British rule, came to a head in 1955 when the Patriarch Timotheos fell mortally ill. Even before the Patriarch's demise, the Soviet government indicated its support for Archimandrite Isidoros of Nazareth as the successor. A Russian cleric was reported to have turned up in the Middle East 'with $200,000 in his pocket which he was going to use to ensure the election of Isidoros'. The Greek government pressed the British to intervene against him. But when the head of the Jordanian Criminal Investigation Department, Sir Patrick Coghill (a British officer), investigated the case he acquitted the Archimandrite of communist sympathies and said he was favourably impressed by him. The Greek consul-general retorted that while Isidoros might not be 'an out-and-out Communist, he looked on him as a fellow-traveller'.[42] Later he suggested that Isidoros had been 'suspected of cooperating with the Nazis'.[43] The British did not take all this very seriously but were nevertheless concerned at the possibility of Soviet influence in the election. A Foreign Office appreciation warned of the danger and noted that the head of the Soviet ecclesiastical mission in Palestine, Archimandrite Polycarp, had been 'expelled by the Americans from Seoul' and recalled 'his notorious predecessor Porphyrios Uspensky of Crimean war fame'.[44]

Isidoros's real crime, in the eyes of the Greeks, however, was his popularity with the Arab laity. Following Timotheos's death, the by now ritual struggle developed between the Greeks, who sought to protect their ancient privileges, and the Arabs, who enjoyed political support from Arab nationalists. The Greek government intervened on behalf of the ruling Hellenic Brotherhood. Miraculously Patriarch Benediktos was elected with the blessing of the Jordanian, Israeli and Greek governments. The struggle against Greek dominion, however, continued. In 1956 the Jordanian government of Sulayman al-Nabulsi sided with the Arab laity and clergy and sought to impose a new constitution on the Church. After diplomatic pressure, this was eventually withdrawn and a more moderate version was enacted that encroached only marginally on Greek prerogatives.[45] In 1960, for the first time, an Arab was appointed a member of the Synod. But the war against Hellenic dominance in the Church was by no means at an end.

The Armenian Patriarchate too became embroiled in politics. The Armenian community was geographically divided, since several hundred Armenians remained in Israeli Jerusalem, separated from their brethren in Jordan. It was also ideologically divided between adherents of various Armenian political parties. In November 1950 the Israelis tried to persuade the Armenian Locum Tenens (the Patriarchate was then vacant) to cooperate by issuing a public announcement friendly to their proposals for the city. He said he would do so only after the restoration of Armenian property in Israel and the grant of what the Israeli negotiators called 'an extravagant amount [of money in] sterling'. The Israelis immediately restored all Armenian property in Jaffa 'and exchanged one thousand to sterling for transfer [to] Old City', though they held back on Armenian property in west Jerusalem. Whether this produced the desired result is, unfortunately, not recorded.[46] In the mid-1950s a fierce power struggle in the Patriarchate, amid accusations of communist and Zionist loyalties, led to the deportation of several senior clergy by the Jordanian government.[47] At the height of the controversy, in early 1958, the monastic compound in the Armenian quarter was barricaded by its residents; it took the Jordanian army several days to break open the gates.[48] Finally, in 1960 King Hussein resolved the conflict by recognizing Yeghishe Derderian, identified with the anti-Soviet Dashnak party, as Patriarch.[49]

In general, the Christian holy places receded as objects of discord in this period, although there were occasional flare-ups that gave the Jordanian government headaches (Israeli Jerusalem retained relatively few Christian holy places or institutions). At the eastern Christmas in January 1954, for example, the Coptic archbishop, 'an arch-troublemaker' as the British consul-general characterized him, 'told the Governor quite openly that since he was an Arab he expected the Jordan Government to give him increased influence in the Holy Places'. The Copts, though a tiny group in Jerusalem, could rely on the diplomatic backing of Egypt in their long-running dispute with the Ethiopians over rights near the Church of the Holy Sepulchre.[50] A dispute of a different sort arose at the Holy Sepulchre over urgently needed repairs. The Latins proposed pulling the entire building down and constructing a new one. The Greek Orthodox, fearing this would adversely affect their privileges, disagreed and tried to raise money for repair work. The Soviet-dominated Russian Orthodox Church volunteered to contribute but their offer was not accepted and money was sought instead from Orthodox Christians in North America.[51] Such matters excited local Christians and some foreign supporters. But they were no longer issues of great power concern that threatened peace among nations. Christian Jerusalem thus shrank not only demographically but also in the political consciousness of the Christian world.

New consular wars

From 1949 until 1967 most of the powers maintained an anomalous consular presence in Jerusalem. Each had one consul but two consular offices, one in Israeli west Jerusalem, the other in Jordanian east. Most lived in west Jerusalem, many in Balfour Street in Talbieh, known as Street of the Consuls, but crossed to and fro between the Jordanian and Israeli sectors of the city. Yet the consuls were instructed not to apply to either Israel or Jordan for exequaturs, thus maintaining the legal fiction of adherence to the UN internationalization plan. In the early years some refused to have any dealings with the Israeli or Jordanian central governments, even in such matters as car registration plates, saying they would deal only with the local authorities.

In this, as in so much else during the early Cold War years, most western states followed the American lead. Upon the Israeli declaration of Jerusalem as its capital in December 1949, the State Department reaffirmed that it did not recognize Israeli sovereignty in Jerusalem and that it would continue to support the principle of internationalization.[52] Thus the USA maintained a consulate-general (theoretically united, though in fact in two buildings, one in east and the other in west Jerusalem) that reported directly to the State Department and did not seek exequaturs from either Jordan or Israel. When some smaller western states evinced interest in moving their embassies to Jerusalem, the United States, under the Eisenhower and Kennedy administrations, was particularly active in pressing them not to do so. This practice evoked repeated Israeli complaints but appears to have ceased only in 1962.[53]

The smallest nuances and variations in consular behaviour towards Israel and Jordan attracted attention. In 1953, for example, it was noted that the American consul 'chargé', signed himself 'S. R. Tyler' on the Arab side and 'Samuel R. Tyler' on the Israeli. The Dutch consul combined his post with that of Minister to Israel – he was thus one of the few accredited diplomats who lived in Jerusalem; unlike the other consuls, he did not maintain an office in east Jerusalem but 'use[d] a Dutch monk in Gethsemane as a post-box'. The Polish and

Yugoslav consuls were refused a pass to enter Jordanian Jerusalem. The Lebanese consul, on the other hand, would not enter the Israeli sector.[54]

The most far-reaching effort to renew consular powers and prerogatives was made by the dean of the consular corps, the French consul-general, René Neuville. During the siege of west Jerusalem in 1948 he revived the old consular post office and issued special consular stamps. In December 1950 he told a meeting of consuls that citizens of foreign countries resident in Jerusalem were not subject to Israeli law and could not be forced to appear before Israeli courts.[55]

In January 1951 Neuville called another consular meeting at which he engaged in a bitter row with the British consul-general, Sir Hugh Dow, over the question whether consuls should attend the inauguration of Ragheb Nashashibi as Guardian of the Holy Places. Neuville, a keen student of the history of consular privileges in Jerusalem, suspected that the British had put Abdullah up to making the appointment. He argued that the post was an innovation and an interference both with the diplomatic status of Jerusalem and with the status quo in the holy places. The Frenchman (who was, in fact, half-Spanish) persuaded most of the other Catholic consuls and ecclesiastical dignitaries to join him in boycotting the ceremony.[56] In the event, Ragheb Bey's tenure in the post was short. He died later that year and not long afterwards the position was abolished. A re-enactment in miniature of the great Anglo-French encounters of the past on the same battlefield, the affair hardly registered on the diplomatic sounding board. Nevertheless, at the local level it left bad blood between the British and French. Most of Neuville's colleagues did not pursue quite such an assertive policy, but the anomalous position of the consuls in Jerusalem repeatedly vexed the powers in their relations with both Israel and Jordan.

In truth, the consuls of the powers, for all their attempts to puff up their own importance, counted by now for little – and those of the small powers for nothing at all. On one occasion the Ethiopian consul wrote to the Jordanian governor of Jerusalem four times, with great politeness, concerning the rights of the Ethiopian Church at the holy places. Receiving no reply, he pleaded at least for some sort of answer. Whereupon the governor forwarded the letter to Neuville, in his capacity as dean of the consular corps, declaring that he was not prepared to accept insulting letters from consuls, that they were not to mix themselves up in matters relating to the status quo and that he was considering revoking the Ethiopian's permit to cross between the two sides of Jerusalem.[57]

The first big power to move towards acceptance of the status quo in Jerusalem was the most militantly anti-Christian one: the Soviet Union. As early as February 1949 the Soviets had given some signs of weakening when the Russian Minister was the only great-power representative to attend the opening of the first Knesset in Jerusalem. In April 1950 the Soviet Union formally declared its withdrawal of support for internationalization, since 'it has become clear that the above-mentioned decision of the General Assembly satisfies neither the Arab nor the Jewish population, either of the city of Jerusalem or of Palestine as a whole'.[58] Given the hitherto leaden insistence of Soviet spokesmen at the UN on strict adherence to the General Assembly partition resolution, this represented a major shift – though it was consistent with the primary Soviet aim of reducing British and American influence in the region. In any case, as the British Minister in Tel Aviv, Sir Knox Helm, commented, the 'Soviet *volte face* over Jerusalem' was regarded by Israel 'as having dealt a death blow to [the] United Nations plan for internationalisation'.[59]

The Israeli view turned out to be correct. Shortly afterwards, when the British accorded *de jure* recognition to Israel, they moved towards what Helm called '*quasi de facto* acceptance ... of the partition of Jerusalem'. Meanwhile, the Anglo-Jordanian alliance of 1946 was extended to cover not only the West Bank but also east Jerusalem. This was yet another step towards consolidation of the status quo in the city.

During those years, the Israelis gradually moved government departments, though not the all-important Defence Ministry, from Tel Aviv to Jerusalem. But such moves tended to be of a symbolic character. The centre of gravity of Israeli government remained in Tel Aviv until 1967 – a fact that was recognized in the Foreign Ministry as weakening Israel's diplomatic position regarding Jerusalem.[60]

In May 1952 the Israeli Foreign Ministry itself announced that it planned to move to Jerusalem in the near future. The western powers consulted one another at great length and pressed the Israelis unsuccessfully to change their mind, though when the American Secretary of State, John Foster Dulles, visited Israel in May 1953 he raised the issue only tangentially.[61] The British were half inclined to follow the Foreign Ministry by moving their legation and even surveyed suitable properties in Jerusalem, a fact that became publicly known. The Israelis concluded that western opposition would be demonstrative for an Arab audience rather than substantive. In the summer of 1953 they went ahead with the move. In a show of mutual solidarity, nearly all western countries decided to maintain their embassies in Tel Aviv – at consequent grave inconvenience to their diplomats. Dulles pronounced himself 'displeased' over the Israeli move and suggested it would have an effect on US aid to Israel.[62] The Jordanian reaction was to convene a meeting of its Cabinet in Jerusalem – though the Prime Minister assured the British envoy that this 'was intended almost entirely for internal consumption ... There was no intention of suggesting that Jerusalem was a second capital or that the Jordan Government would be moved there.'[63] After the move the United States pressed its allies to refuse to send their representatives to call on the ministry. Most complied, and Sharett was compelled to backtrack a little and agree, for a time, to continue to meet diplomats in Tel Aviv. The Ministry's 'Tel Aviv Liaison Office' was not finally closed until 1962.

In December 1953 the Russian Minister, Alexander Abramov, was the first big-power envoy to present his credentials to the Israeli

President in Jerusalem. The Swiss Minister declared that 'the Battle of Jerusalem' had been lost.[64] Shortly afterwards the new Italian Minister paid a visit to Sharett at the Foreign Ministry, though, on orders from his government, he presented his credentials to the President at Tiberias. In January 1954, when Sharett succeeded Ben Gurion as Prime Minister, retaining at the same time the foreign affairs portfolio, the French ambassador, who was doyen of the diplomatic corps, paid a formal visit to him in Jerusalem. After that the western diplomatic front crumbled. In October 1954 the British Foreign Secretary, Anthony Eden, raised the issue over lunch with Dulles. They eventually agreed that credentials would be presented in Jerusalem 'with the proviso that this does not change the UK and US positions re Jerusalem's status'.[65]

Throughout these years, diplomats agonized over minutiae of protocol. Should new envoys present credentials in Jerusalem? Should they attend official functions there? Should they attend unofficial functions there? Should they stay overnight there? If they did visit the Foreign Ministry there, should these be merely courtesy calls or should they conduct official business? If heads of missions could not visit the Ministry, what about lower-level diplomats? And was not the position of consuls different from that of diplomatic representatives? Should official correspondence be addressed to Jerusalem? And so on and so on.

In the late 1950s international resistance to the division of Jerusalem slowly eroded. In 1955 Guatemala appointed Dr García Granados as its Minister in Israel. Granados had served as chairman of the United Nations Special Committee on Palestine in 1947; he was known to be strongly pro-Israeli and unkind diplomatic rumour had it that he had emerged 'unaccountably richer' after his period with UNSCOP.[66] When Granados arrived in Israel he decided, contrary to his instructions, to install himself in Jerusalem rather than Tel Aviv, thus breaching the taboo on the establishment of diplomatic missions there. Other diplomats were annoyed and, led by the

British, gave the Guatemalan the cold shoulder. A year later the Uruguayan Minister moved his legation to Jerusalem and in 1959 Venezuela followed suit. Israel's success in cultivating good relations with many newly independent African countries in the early 1960s led some of them too to establish missions in Jerusalem: the Ivory Coast did so in 1961 and Gabon in 1962. Of the forty-one countries maintaining representation in Israel in that year, eleven were located in Jerusalem.[67] By the mid-1960s there were twenty embassies in west Jerusalem, but no great power was among them, nor any European state except for the Netherlands.

Even Arab states, including some not friendly to the Hashemites, moved tentatively towards acceptance of the status quo of a divided Jerusalem. In August 1950 the Syrian Minister in Washington told the State Department that 'internationalization was wholly impracticable'.[68] In November 1955, in discussion of a joint Anglo-American initiative for an agreement between Israel and Egypt, the Egyptian Foreign Minister, Dr Mahmud Fawzi, indicated that on Jerusalem 'Egypt was willing to follow the UN consensus, whether on internationalization or a split system for protection of the holy places'.[69]

Gradually the western powers began to realize that they had boxed themselves into a ridiculous position. As the British consulate-general in Jerusalem commented in 1955, 'We regard it as one of the tasks for which this Consulate is responsible to support as far as possible … the theory of Jerusalem's separate status. It is a theory which it is growing ever more difficult to sustain without resorting to pompous pedantry.'[70] By 1960 the general opinion in the Foreign Office was that 'the accumulation of acts which seem to imply recognition must sooner or later reach a point at which we merely look ridiculous if we pretend that we do not recognise'.[71]

In the early 1960s the Israelis decided to embark on a consistent policy of pressure on consulates to try to induce them to recognize Israeli sovereignty in Jerusalem. A number of minor bureaucratic devices were employed: for example, in 1963 it was ordained that exemption from import duties for automobiles would be granted only to consuls who had applied to Israel for an exequatur. Foreign institutions in Jerusalem applying for such exemptions were instructed to do so through their embassies in Tel Aviv rather than their consulates.

Israel's greatest hopes in this regard were focused on France, once a standard-bearer of the cause of internationalization. In the years between Suez and 1967, the period of the Franco-Israeli 'honeymoon', a slow evolution in the French diplomatic position on Jerusalem began to be discernible. In 1965 the French ambassador appeared at a number of official occasions in Jerusalem. By 1966 the Israelis even began to hope that the French embassy might move to Jerusalem. But they found that, even in the case of a friendly power such as France, neither sticks nor carrots seemed to have much effect.[72]

Cul-de-sac capital

In several respects the position of Israeli Jerusalem from 1949 to 1967 was a mirror image of Jordanian Jerusalem. Israeli sovereignty in the west, like Jordanian in the east, was unrecognized by the international community. Israel became, with Jordan, the most determined opponent of internationalization. True, the Israeli government did not, like the Jordanian, deliberately play down the importance of Jerusalem. In contrast to Jordanian Jerusalem, which declined into provincial torpor, Israeli Jerusalem enjoyed dynamic growth. But a comparison with Israel's largest city, Tel Aviv, points to a different conclusion. Viewed from the coast, Israeli Jerusalem was a strangely remote capital city, a cul-de-sac at the end of a single-track railway line meandering through the Judean hills. Surrounded on three sides by a closed frontier, with only a narrow corridor to the sea, Jerusalem was cut off from its natural economic hinterland. Little industry moved to Jerusalem. The overwhelming financial burdens of defence and immigrant absorption prevented Israel from investing heavily in infrastructure or showpiece developments in its capital. The austere, socialist ethos of the early years of the state in any case militated against monumental architecture. Unlike Weizmann, Israel's second President did establish his residence in the capital. But he did so in a modest presidential 'hut'. All the country's Hebrew daily newspapers remained in Tel Aviv.

From 1948 to 1967 the population of west Jerusalem approximately doubled to 198,000. Large new suburbs appeared in order to house new immigrants; box-like blocks of apartments were shoddily built, often rebarbative in appearance. This was only the second period in Jerusalem's modern history when the order, first given by Ronald Storrs at the start of British rule, that all new buildings must be faced in stone, was systematically ignored (the first was in the 1930s during a stonecutters' strike).

While the general view of the Israeli establishment in these years was that they could live with a divided Jerusalem, some aspects of the partition struck them as irksome and requiring eventual rectification. Among the items on which the Israel-Jordan armistice agreement of 3 April 1949 stated that 'agreement in principle already exists' were 'resumption of the normal functioning of the cultural and humanitarian institutions on Mount Scopus and free access thereto; free access to the Holy Places and ... use of the cemetery on the Mount of Olives'.[73] Principle was not, however, translated into practice. Until 1967 the Jordanians prevented access to the Western Wall and the cemetery and communications with Mount Scopus were not fully restored.

The Israeli interest in Mount Scopus was not merely sentimental. As the commander of Israeli forces in the enclave, Baruch Neumark, pointed out in October 1948, the area dominated the northern approaches to the old city: 'I believe that he who controls this commanding ground will rule Jerusalem.'[74] In November 1948 Moshe Dayan and Abdullah al-Tall confirmed the agreement of the previous July under which fortnightly convoys would be permitted to pass between west Jerusalem and the enclave under UN protection. The arrangement did not, however, really satisfy the Israelis, both because normal civilian life could not resume in the enclave and because they saw the area as of key strategic importance. In September 1949 Dayan urged Ben Gurion to sanction an Israeli military attack to break open a corridor to Mount Scopus, but the Prime Minister was not willing to reopen the war.[75]

Although both sides continued to recognize the agreement demilitarizing Mount Scopus, each used different maps, with the result that there were frequent clashes. The Israelis were permitted by the UN to send in police and 'a limited number of artisans' to work 'as guards and maintenance crew in and about the hospital and university buildings'.[76] In fact, they stockpiled arms, built foxholes and trenches, and sent in soldiers in the guise of police and civilians. In 1953 Israeli 'police' prevented UN observers from entering the enclave.[77] In 1957 the convoy was refused admission by the Jordanians, who alleged breaches of the agreement. In 1958 Jordanian snipers killed four Israelis and a UN observer. In 1960 there were further incidents when inhabitants of the Arab village of Isawiya diverted the dust track connecting their village to the Ramallah road. The Israelis claimed that the new track trespassed on their territory.[78]

Throughout these years the Hebrew University and Hadassah Hospital buildings remained eerily empty. The books in the National Library were slowly smuggled out and restored to use in the new library building constructed on the university's replacement campus at Givat Ram in western Jerusalem. The huge investment at that site and at the Hadassah Hospital's new centre in Ein Karem, both constructed in the 1960s, signalled Israel's reluctant acquiescence in the status quo of a divided Jerusalem.

Few political voices in Israel and none in the government before June 1967 called for an irredentist policy towards east Jerusalem. The country thus found itself politically, diplomatically and psychologically unprepared when, quite unexpectedly, after nineteen years of division, Jerusalem was, almost overnight, reunited under Israeli rule.

1. German and Turkish officers on the Palestine Front, 1917. The Turkish commander, Djemal Pasha, is third from the right. General Friedrich Freiherr Kress von Kressenstein of the German Military Mission is the tall figure in the centre. He thought Djemal's plan for evacuating the civilian population of Jerusalem 'insane'.

2. General Allenby's address at the Citadel of Jerusalem on his ceremonial entry to the city after the British conquest, 11 December 1917.

3. General Allenby (front, centre) in Palestine, 1918. Colonel Ronald Storrs, Military Governor of Jerusalem, is descending stairs just behind Allenby.

4. Emir (later King) Abdullah with Sir Herbert Samuel (centre) and Winston Churchill (front right) in Jerusalem, 1921.

5. 'Foxy and cunning': Hajj Amin al-Husayni, Grand Mufti of Jerusalem and President of the Supreme Moslem Council from 1921 until his flight from Palestine in 1938.

6. Dr Husayn Fakhri al-Khalidi, who was elected Mayor of Jerusalem in 1934 with the help of Jewish votes. This photograph was taken in 1936.

7. 'A man of the world, genial, cynical and without any fanaticism ... He retained some of the Ottoman official tradition of baksheesh and nepotism, but within limits': Ragheb Bey Nashashibi, Mayor of Jerusalem, 1920–34. He is shown here greeting guests at the ceremony marking his installation as Protector of the Holy Places in Jerusalem, January 1951.

8. *'A traditional season for inter-communal brawls' — pilgrims gathering outside the walls of Jerusalem for the Nebi Musa festival, 1921.*

9. *'Bevingrad': Princess Mary Avenue (today Rehov Shlomzion Ha-Malkah) in the fortified central security zone of Jerusalem, early 1948.*

10. *Crowds in Ben Yehuda Street after the bombing of 22 February 1948.*

11. *Count Folke Bernadotte, UN Mediator in Palestine (second from right), at the YMCA building in Jerusalem, 12 June 1948.*

12. Moshe Dayan (centre) and his Jordanian opposite number, Abdullah al-Tall (right), in Jerusalem, late 1948.

13. Moshe Sharett, Foreign Minister (later Prime Minister) of Israel. He was horrified by the Israeli Cabinet's decision in December 1949 to declare Jerusalem Israel's capital.

14. Dr Chaim Weizmann (centre, wearing dark spectacles) on his first visit to Jerusalem as President of Israel, 1948. He is accompanied by his wife, Vera, and by the military governor of Jerusalem, Dov Yosef.

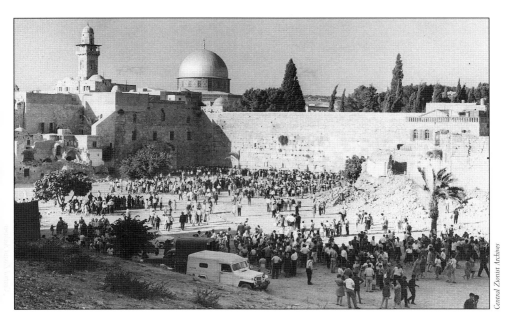

15. The Western ('Wailing') Wall in Jerusalem, in August 1967, a few weeks after the Israeli conquest of the eastern part of the city and the razing of 135 houses in front of it to create a broad plaza.

16. Teddy Kollek, Mayor of Jerusalem, 1965–93.

Flash 90

17. Palestinians evacuate a wounded protester during clashes with Israeli police at the Temple Mount in Jerusalem, October 2000.

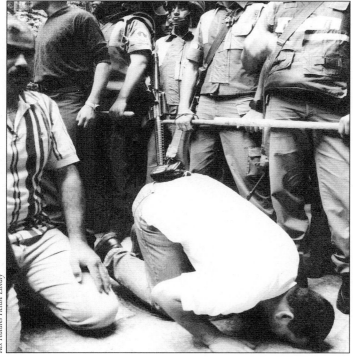

Rex Features Picture Library

18. Muslims praying as Israeli troops bar access to the Muslim holy places to men under 45 during the 'al-Aqsa intifada', *Jerusalem, October 2000.*

6   Annexation

On 7 June 1967 Israeli forces captured east Jerusalem as part of their sweep through the West Bank. At noon that day, the Israeli Defence Minister, Moshe Dayan, went to the Western Wall and declared that Jerusalem had been 'liberated': 'We have united Jerusalem, the divided capital of Israel. We have returned to the holiest of our Holy Places, never to part from it again.'[1] The event was greeted with almost apocalyptic joy in the Jewish world. This was despite the fact that Israel had not exhibited any pressing anxiety prior to June 1967 to control the old city of Jerusalem. Yet Israel eventually found that, by taking east Jerusalem, it had opened a veritable Pandora's box.

Conquest

Whether Israel would have gone to war against Jordan if King Hussein had not given her a pretext to do so remains an open question. The Israelis half expected the Jordanians to remain quiescent, as they had in 1956. Although Jordanian forces had nominally been placed under Egyptian command as a result of the Egyptian-Jordanian treaty of 30 May, King Hussein retained a large measure of control over them. Subsequent Israeli propaganda laid stress on the message, sent by the Prime Minister, Levi Eshkol, to General Odd Bull, Chief of Staff of the UN Truce Supervision Organization in Jerusalem, for delivery to Hussein.[2] The message stated that Israel would not open hostilities against Jordan but that if Jordan started fighting she would bear the consequences. Bull later defined the communication as 'a threat pure and simple'.[3] Hussein's reply to the message was, 'They started the battle. Well, they are receiving our reply by air.'[4] His decision to join the war did not represent a strategic threat to Israel once the Egyptian air force had been destroyed at dawn on Monday 5 June, since Jordan by herself had little real offensive capability. Jordanian military activity in Jerusalem that morning was largely symbolic, although the Israeli enclave on Mount Scopus was bombarded and Jordanian troops entered the UN compound at Government House. There is no evidence that Jordan was planning a major attack on the Jewish state; her forces were largely deployed in defensive formation.

Even had Hussein not opened hostilities, Israel would probably have been unable to resist the temptation to take Jerusalem in June 1967. On the afternoon of 5 June the Jordanian air force was wiped out by the Israelis from the air. Meanwhile, Israeli ground forces drove the Jordanians out of the UN compound and entered Government House. General Bull and his staff were ordered out and escorted into Israeli territory.

Israeli ministers' hesitations and divisions about launching an all-out attack on east Jerusalem were evident in a Cabinet meeting that day. The Minister of Labour, Yigal Allon, whose military experience gave his views weight with his colleagues, argued strongly for an attack on the old city. He was supported by Menahem Begin, leader of the right-wing Herut party. But Haim Moshe Shapira, the dovish Interior Minister and leader of the National Religious Party, urged caution: 'To hold the old city will be a political problem. When it is in our hands, they will call on us to turn it into an international city. If that happens, I shall support it.' This view was supported by the Education Minister, Zalman Aranne, of the Labour Party. Allon insisted that east Jerusalem could be captured without causing damage to the holy places. The old city, he pointed out, could be 'surrounded from the direction of Nebi Samuel, French Hill and Mount Scopus'.[5] The discussion was inconclusive. Eshkol summed up, 'Nonetheless there has to be a counter-attack against the shelling from Jordan.' The Prime Minister was later recorded as having said that day, 'Even if we conquer the Old City and the West Bank, in the end we will have to leave them.'[6]

In a battle on the night of 5/6 June at Ammunition Hill, commanding the road to Mount Scopus, the Israelis routed the Jordanian forces. The next day Dayan was given Cabinet approval for the old city to be surrounded by Israeli forces. The Israeli Cabinet was still divided, however, over whether to authorize an assault on the old city.

Three decades later General Motta Gur, commander of the paratroop brigade that captured the old city, recalled that at the start of the war he was looking for some pretext for a move against Jordan. He hoped it might come on 7 June if the Jordanians tried to block the fortnightly convoy to Mount Scopus.[7] Contingency plans for forcing a passage in such an eventuality had been prepared several years earlier. During the Suez crisis of October 1956 such a plan had come close to being implemented, but was abandoned when Jordan failed to provide a *casus belli*.[8] Gur's initial orders called for a limited move to protect Mount Scopus. Then these were expanded to include capture of the Mount of Olives. Early on the morning of 7 June Begin woke Eshkol up and urged an immediate assault on the old city, lest the UN order a cease-fire. Eshkol assented and the order was given for an attack.

Gur himself entered the old city by the St Stephen's Gate at 9.50 a.m. and drove towards the Temple Mount, which had already been captured by infantry. 'At this point [Gur wrote shortly afterwards] the Governor of the City came up to me together with the Kadi and informed me of the solemn decision not to defend the city. He assured me that the [Jordanian] troops had all left and there would be no further resistance.'[9] At 2.00 p.m. Dayan entered the old city, accompanied by the Chief of Staff, Yitzhak Rabin, and the OC Central Command, Uzi Narkiss. By the end of the day Israeli forces had swept through the whole of the West Bank; some units even crossed over to the east bank, but were ordered to return after United States diplomatic intervention.[10] In spite of the speed of the Israeli victory, it was by no means bloodless: 645 Arabs were killed, including 240 civilians, most of whom died as a result of Israeli shelling; the Israelis lost about 200 dead, including fifteen civilians.

Unification

Israel had long had military contingency plans for the occupation of the West Bank in the event of the collapse of the Hashemite regime – which had seemed very likely in the early years of King Hussein's reign. In 1963 an Israeli officer, Chaim Herzog, later President of Israel, had been designated as potential military governor of the West Bank. In accordance with these plans, immediately upon occupying the city Israeli agents quickly arrested several hundred people whose names had been listed in advance.[11] The ugly walls that cut grotesquely across the city at key points such as Notre-Dame de France and Mamilla Street were knocked down. Barbed-wire entanglements, fortified emplacements and minefields were removed. On 29 June most physical obstacles to free movement between east and west Jerusalem were withdrawn. Residents of east and west were free to wander in either direction. Most of the movement was from west to east: tens of thousands of Israelis walked in wonderment in a universe that they had been able to see but not enter for the previous nineteen years. There was no sign of tension. By and large, the conquerors were greeted with a courtesy and friendliness that enabled many to persuade themselves that they were welcome.

These days produced a transformation in the Israeli – and world Jewish – attitude towards Jerusalem. Suddenly, life for the Jewish state without it became difficult to imagine. As an American observer put it, 'It was only *after* the capture of East Jerusalem that the ancient city assumed retroactively the status of *terra irredenta* for Israel.'[12]

Remarkable as it may seem, while Israel activated its military plan with ease, it had no diplomatic contingency plan. The occupation of east Jerusalem caught its Foreign Ministry – and civil authorities in general – rather by surprise. The question immediately arose whether the former Jordanian sector of the city should be treated, like the rest of the newly conquered West Bank, as occupied territory, or whether it should be integrated immediately into Israel – in effect, annexed. The laws of war required that occupied territory remain subject to Jordanian law, though under Israeli military government, pending a peace treaty. Integration of east Jerusalem into Israel, on the other hand, would involve its subjection to Israeli law.

A memorandum prepared in the Foreign Ministry two days after the occupation gave the first indication of the path that was to be taken. 'The objective,' wrote Michael Comay, a senior official of the ministry, 'should clearly be "de facto integration" with Israel Jerusalem. This involves giving responsibility for public services to our national and municipal agencies, instead of to the military government for the West Bank. The latter course would only assimilate the position of the Old City to that of other occupied towns like Bethlehem or Nablus.' Comay added that 'along the same line of reasoning, the religious interests and institutions in the Old City should immediately be brought under the auspices of the Misrad Hadatot [Ministry of Religious Affairs], and not be the direct concern of the military government'.[13]

On 10 June Professor Avigdor Levontin of the Hebrew University Law Faculty submitted to the government a memorandum that affords an early insight into Israeli thinking (and lack of prior planning) for the future of a unified Jerusalem. Levontin warned that the capture of east Jerusalem presented Israel with thorny legal and political problems. He anticipated little trouble from Christendom, more from the Muslim world. Presciently he warned that a significant danger might emanate from Jews: the threat that extremists might seek to realize the dream of rebuilding the Temple.

Levontin proposed a five-point programme for Jerusalem. 1. The whole of Jerusalem should be brought within the sovereignty of Israel. 2. A distinction should be made between the 'intra-mural' old city and the 'extra-mural' portions of east Jerusalem (i.e. the Arab new city). Israel should be prepared for serious opposition to the annexation of the old city because of its wealth of religious associations. 3. For this reason Israel should announce that it would maintain the status quo in the old city. While the area should be under full Israeli sovereignty, it should be specially protected from untoward development. 4. The Ministry of Religious Affairs should establish an international Muslim council for the Muslim holy places. Non-Arab Muslims from countries such as Iran and Turkey, as well as Israeli Muslims, should be invited from the outset to participate. A similar council of Christians should also be established, though here it might be difficult at first to find willing participants. These councils, he considered, should be purely advisory. The Israeli Ministry of Religious Affairs should be the sole 'address' for all administrative questions concerning the whole area (by 'the whole area' Levontin seems to mean the Christian and Muslim quarters of the old city, though that is unclear from his form of words in Hebrew). 5. The Jewish quarter of the old city should be incorporated under the direct administration of the Jerusalem city council, though with special protection of its historic character.[14]

Levontin's memorandum was one of the first attempts to grapple with the problem of how exactly the different areas of the city were to be treated under the new dispensation. Evidently this was an issue that had not received serious attention hitherto from the Israeli policy-making élite. Just as there seems to have been little or no diplomatic contingency planning for the annexation, so legal and administrative forethought seem to have been similarly deficient.

What was clear to all concerned was that Israel was determined to retain control over the whole of Jerusalem. The exact legal form of that control, and whether it would take the same shape over the various parts of the city, remained, for the time being, uncertain. The Foreign Minister, Abba Eban, was cagey on 14 June in reply to an inquiry from the British ambassador about 'his ideas on Jerusalem'. He said that 'there were certain obvious facts'. First, 'Jerusalem was now a united city. Surely this was to the good.' Second, 'it was unrealistic to talk about the internationalisation of Jerusalem if this meant political or administrational internationalisation'. At the same time, he suggested that 'Israel would give spiritual interna[tiona]lisation to the holy places', though 'how this would be done he had not yet worked out'.[15] A week later Eban was reported to have told Latin American UN delegates that Israel was willing to see a Christian authority administer the Christian holy places and a Muslim one the Muslim shrines.[16]

On 17 June the Israeli Cabinet decided in principle on the extension of Israeli jurisdiction to east Jerusalem. The American administration urged caution on the Israelis. The British Foreign Secretary, George Brown, warned them much more robustly not to annex the old city.[17] The guidance was not, however, accompanied by any threat of sanctions – and was not taken too seriously by the Israeli government. The Jewish state was in an exultant mood and neither public opinion nor the government was much disposed to heed advice, however well meant, from friends who had, as they saw it, left Israel in the lurch during the pre-war crisis with Egypt.

Before any legal steps towards annexation could be taken, a decision had to be made about the exact area involved. The government wished to be sure that the city would have sufficient space to absorb a large inflow of Jewish immigrants. A government committee was therefore appointed to draw up new boundaries for the municipal area. It included representatives of ministries, of the army and of the Israeli municipality. The general public was not consulted or even informed of the existence of the committee. In the course of its work members divided between minimalists and maximalists. Among the most vocal of the latter was the hawkish General Rehavam Ze'evi. He and others advocated a strategic approach that would ensure the defences of the city by Israel for all time. This would require, he argued, the incorporation into the city of all the surrounding hillsides as well as the civilian airfield north of the city. But the hills included twenty-two Arab villages with a combined population before the conquest of 103,000. An estimated 8,000 of these had fled during or immediately after the war, but this still left 95,000 inhabitants. Other committee members balked at the idea of adding such a large number of Arabs to the city's population. Accordingly, the more far-reaching plans of the maximalists were rejected and Arab villages such as Abu Dis and al-Azariya remained outside the municipal boundaries. In the north the boundary was set just east of the Jerusalem–Ramallah road, thus excluding the large Arab population of ribbon development and refugee camps clustered east of the road. The committee also resolved not to recommend absorption of the municipality of Bethlehem into Jerusalem. Nor did they suggest extension of the city's borders on the west (i.e. within pre-1967 Israeli territory). The area of the city was nevertheless considerably expanded, from 13,000 acres for the combined pre-1967 Israeli and Jordanian municipalities to 28,000 acres. As a result of the changes the population of the city was increased to 267,800 (196,800 Jews and 71,000 Arabs).[18]

The new borders brought within the city a large cordon of mostly uninhabited land on the northern, eastern and southern fringes of the city. The added area stretched from the Jerusalem airport at Qalandiya (Atarot) in the north, along the crest of the central Judean ridge in the east, down to Gilo in the south. It was mainly on this newly incorporated land that Israel, over the next thirty years, built a great ring of Jewish suburbs that helped to more than double the population of the city.

On 23 June a committee of ministers, charged with making proposals on the formal status of Jerusalem, met to discuss further action. The committee was chaired by the Justice Minister, Yaakov Shimshon Shapiro, and included Dayan and Begin, as well as Mordechai Bentov of the left-wing Mapam Party, and Zerah Warhaftig, the Minister of Religious Affairs. They resolved to recommend to the Cabinet approval of the expansion of the city's boundary.[19]

The recommendation was endorsed by the Cabinet in meetings on 25 and 26 June.[20] The next day the Knesset enacted legislation providing that Israeli 'law, jurisdiction, and administration ... shall extend to any area of the Land of Israel designated by the Government by order'.[21] At the same time the Municipalities Ordinance was amended to enable 'the minister ... at his discretion and without an inquiry' to 'enlarge, by proclamation, the area of a particular municipality' and to permit the minister to 'appoint additional councillors from among the inhabitants of the newly-included area'.[22] Also that day the Knesset passed a law declaring that 'the Holy Places shall be protected from desecration and any violation and from anything likely to violate the freedom of access of the members of the different religions to the places sacred to them or their feelings with regard to those places'.[23] The next day an order was issued incorporating east Jerusalem within the municipality of Jerusalem under Israeli law (see Map 11, page 214).

During the first three weeks of the Israeli occupation, the Arab mayor of Jordanian Jerusalem, Rawhi al-Khatib, had cooperated in every way with the Israeli authorities and had held friendly meetings with several senior figures, including Teddy Kollek.[24] After reading in the newspaper about the Knesset legislation, he called an emergency meeting of his municipal council. But of the eleven members only two showed up.[25] On the evening of 29 June Khatib was summoned to Israeli military headquarters with four of his councillors and issued with a military order declaring the municipal council dissolved. Khatib and his colleagues were thanked 'for their services' and dismissed.[26]

The government deliberately avoided using the word 'annexation' and Israeli spokesmen even denied that what had occurred constituted that. At a news conference Eban insisted that the legislation 'dealt solely with the municipal and administrative aspects of this policy [of promoting the unity of Jerusalem]' and the Israeli ambassador in Washington, Abraham Harman, told Eugene Rostow of the State

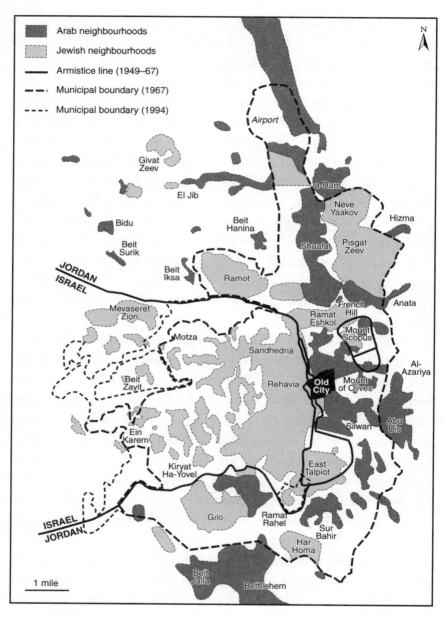

Map 11: Jerusalem since 1967

Department that what was involved was simply an extension of municipal authority so as to provide municipal services to inhabitants in sections occupied by Israeli forces.[27] Eban's statement remained the formal Israeli position, though in later years he referred to the legislation as an 'Act of Union'.[28] In some senses the limited interpretation was correct both theoretically and practically: in international law annexation cannot take place by unilateral legislation. And the municipal services of the two halves of the city were unified, with most of the employees of the Jordanian municipality continuing to work for the Israelis. The Israeli legislation was nevertheless generally regarded as annexation in all but name, and that too was its commonly understood effect.

Israel quickly registered its determination to restore the Jewish quarter in the old city. Beginning on 10 June, Arab 'squatters' were evicted from the area in what Meron Benvenisti, the municipal official responsible for east Jerusalem, called a 'voluntary evacuation'.[29] By the end of the year a total of 2,959, most of the Arab residents in the quarter, had been removed.[30] The Beth Din (Jewish religious court) of appeals held a session there on 14 August and a *yeshiva* (talmudical college) moved back there a week later, the first of several to do so. Over the next twenty years the quarter, formerly a half-ruined slum, was substantially rebuilt and repopulated with mainly orthodox Jews.

A number of cases in the Israeli Supreme Court, particularly in 1969 and 1970, tested the validity and nature of the Israeli presence in east Jerusalem. In *Hanzalis* v. *Greek Orthodox Patriarchate Religious Court,* the Deputy President of the court, Justice Silberg, stated that 'since 28 June 1967 east and west Jerusalem have been one with regard both to physical division and to the application of the law'. Justice Halevi (known for his nationalist views) agreed and went further: 'On 28 June 1967 the law, jurisdiction and legal administration of Jordan in East Jerusalem were replaced by Israeli jurisdiction and administration and from that date *united Jerusalem became an inseparable part of Israel* [emphasis in original].'[31] In *Ruidi and Maches* v. *Military*

Court of Hebron, a dealer who had imported antiquities into east Jerusalem without the Jordanian export licence required on the West Bank claimed that east Jerusalem was not foreign territory in relation to Jordan and therefore no licence was required. But the Supreme Court ruled that east Jerusalem had become part of Israel. This became the definitive ruling under Israeli law.[32]

Jerusalem under Israeli rule

The central political figure in Israeli Jerusalem over the next quarter-century was its mayor, Teddy Kollek. A large, gregarious, independent-minded and liberal-spirited man, bubbling with the stereotypical *Gemütlichkeit* of his native Vienna, he secured international acclaim for his policy of seeking practical solutions and day-to-day harmony among the city's variegated groups. He made little secret of the fact that his overriding aim after 1967 was to secure Israel's permanent hold on Jerusalem as its unified capital. But he argued that this could be more successfully attained by the determined application of goodwill than by brute force. He created an International Jerusalem Committee, well stocked with the good and the great, and a Jerusalem Foundation that funded the new Israel Museum, parks and other social and cultural projects in both halves of the city. He showed sensitivity and political courage in his successful fight to secure the erection of a memorial to Arab dead of the 1967 war. Yet Jerusalem under his administration remained a divided city, and in many ways became more so as a result of government and municipal policies.

In some technical senses unification was achieved quite quickly. Telephone and utility lines between the two parts of the city were reconnected. The number 9 bus to Mount Scopus resumed service on its pre-1948 route as if after a short holiday. New trilingual street signs began to appear. Eventually some street names in east Jerusalem were changed – for example, Sulayman the Magnificent Street became Paratroopers Street and Allenby Square became Tsahal Square (*Tsahal* is the Hebrew acronym for Israel Defence Force).

As the Israelis strengthened their hold on the city they began to devise long-term plans for its future. In September 1967 a ministerial committee headed by the Prime Minister considered a plan to create a national park around the old city. This was initially opposed by the Minister of Religious Affairs, Zerah Warhaftig, as he feared it might cut off the old city from the main centre of Jewish population in west Jerusalem.[33] Others saw it as a welcome opportunity to clear away ruins and rubbish dumps that had accumulated in no-man's land during the previous nineteen years, as a means of enhancing the beauty of the old city's walls and as a tourist attraction. It was eventually realized in a modified form.

In 1968 a master plan for the city's development was approved. The plan provoked criticism from city planners and others and was condemned by an international panel of experts in 1970. Arthur Kutcher, an architect who for a time worked as planning officer responsible for the old city, wrote a powerful critique, arguing that 'the intention which lay behind the proposal of a unified city, focused upon a single commercial centre and bound together by a grid-iron of new roads, was a political one'. This unity, he feared, 'was to be imposed ... at the expense of many aesthetic and environmental qualities'.[34] He and others drew attention to the wrecking of Jerusalem's delicate skylines by many of the new buildings constructed after 1967: the huge Omariyya skyscraper in Talbieh, erected without a building permit; the graceless tower blocks on French Hill; the Wolfson high-rise blocks overlooking the Valley of the Monastery of the Cross, completely out of proportion to their surroundings; the architectural leviathan of the new Hebrew University campus on Mount Scopus; and, most monstrous of all, the Plaza Hotel, encroaching on and overshadowing Independence Park.

Much of the new construction was on territory that had been Israeli before 1967. But in January 1968 the government announced the expropriation of 838 acres of land in east Jerusalem on which it planned to build 1,400 housing units, including 400 said to be earmarked for Arabs removed from the Jewish quarter of the old city.[35] This was the first of a series of large-scale expropriations of Arab-owned land in east Jerusalem. New Jewish neighbourhoods were built on this land, among them Ramat Eshkol, French Hill, Gilo and Pisgat Zeev. Building moved ahead at a rapid pace. Gradually it emerged that the plans had a geopolitical aim: the creation of a ring of Jewish population around the northern, north-eastern and southern periphery of the city. 'The object,' said Kollek, in a candid newspaper interview in 1968, 'is to ensure that all of Jerusalem remains forever a part of Israel. If this city is to be our capital, then we have to make it an integral part of our country and we need Jewish inhabitants to do that.'[36]

The Israeli political class endorsed these decisions with virtual unanimity. David Ben Gurion, who said in April 1969 that 'in exchange for peace I would return all the territory conquered in June 1967', added that this would 'certainly not' include east Jerusalem or the Golan Heights.[37] Almost the only Israeli complaint came from those, like the former Prime Minister, who grumbled that new construction was proceeding too slowly. Spurred on by Ben Gurion's carping from the sidelines, Eshkol established a ministerial committee for east Jerusalem in December 1967. This increased the target number of new apartments to 7,000, and doubled the projected size of the Hebrew University campus on Mount Scopus.[38]

The underlying political motivation in development policy for Jerusalem was stated explicitly in a Local Town Planning Scheme for Jerusalem, prepared by the District Planning and Building Committee in 1978, 'Every area of the city that is not settled by Jews is in danger of being detached from Israel and transferred to Arab control. Therefore the administrative principle regarding the area of the city's municipal jurisdiction must be translated into practice by building in all parts of that area, and, to begin with, in its remotest locations.'[39]

While construction of homes for Jews was encouraged in accordance with this principle, Arab residential construction in east Jerusalem was strictly limited. This was in spite of the fact that the city's Arab population grew faster than the Jewish. Whereas 64,880 housing units were built for Jews between 1967 and 1995, the number built for Arabs was 8,890.[40] None of the expropriated land was used to build housing for Arabs, contrary to public announcements by the Israeli government.[41] In general Arabs encountered difficulties in securing building permits. Most of the unexpropriated land still vacant in east Jerusalem was zoned for purposes other than construction. New construction was forbidden in the absence of a zoning plan, but between 1967 and 1994 such plans were approved for only thirteen of the city's thirty or so Arab neighbourhoods. Some unauthorized Arab building was winked at, but in a few cases houses built without permits were demolished *pour encourager les autres*. Whereas new Jewish housing generally took the form of high-rise apartment blocks, such Arab building as was permitted at all was more often low-density construction. Many Arabs found it easier to build homes outside the municipal boundaries, often in immediately adjacent areas such as a-Ram on the Ramallah road.

Housing was only one area in which the Arabs of east Jerusalem suffered from politically driven discrimination in allocation of resources. Reports commissioned by the municipality in 1994–6, as well as books by former municipal officials published in the 1990s, disclosed in detail the extent and nature of such discrimination in services of all kinds from street lighting to sewage, road paving, rubbish collection and classroom building. West Jerusalem, for example, had 1,079 public parks; east Jerusalem twenty-nine. West Jerusalem had 690 residents per kilometre of sidewalk; east Jerusalem had 2,917. And so on. Teddy Kollek strove for at least an outward appearance of decent treatment of Arab residents. But in 1992 his last municipal budget set per capita expenditure at $900 in the Jewish sector compared with $150 in the Arab. Of the total budget 6 per cent was allocated for the Arab sector, which constituted some 28 per cent of the population.[42]

Arab resistance

The Arabs of east Jerusalem had, as we have seen, developed powerful and self-conscious élites in the late Ottoman and British periods. In spite of Jordanian attempts to downgrade the status of Jerusalem between 1949 and 1967, these élites had by and large retained their standing under Jordanian rule. After 1967 they resumed their traditional role as leaders of the Arab population and were able to maintain and strengthen its institutions and help preserve its identity.

Arab resistance to Israeli measures appeared from the early days of the annexation. At first it was non-violent. One of its earliest manifestations was in relation to the municipality. Following the dismissal of Khatib as mayor, the question arose whether he would put himself forward for nomination to the enlarged council that was expected to be set up for the unified city. The Knesset legislation had provided for additional councillors to be nominated in the first instance. The Israelis hoped that co-option of former Jordanian councillors to the Israeli municipality would pave the way for a unified municipality elected by all parts of the city. Khatib was 'tentatively approached' and also 'asked to sound out the other Arab councillors'.[43] But he decided not to comply and was followed in this by the other councillors. Khatib and seven other councillors were eventually invited formally to accept nomination (the other four councillors had fled to Jordan). After meeting together, they submitted a written response declaring that their acceptance 'would be an official recognition by us in principle to accept the annexation of Arab Jerusalem to the sector occupied by Israel, a thing which cannot be accepted de facto by us, not even recognized'.[44] When Kollek was asked who might be nominated instead, he replied lamely (and not altogether exactly) that 'he did not know anyone over there'.[45]

Table 2   **Participation of east Jerusalem Palestinians in municipal elections (1969–93)**

Year	Number of Arabs voting	Percentage of eligible voters
1969	7,500	21
1973	3,150	7
1978	8,000	14
1983	11,603	18
1989	4,000	3
1993	8,000	5

Sources: Michael Romann and Alex Weingrod, *Living Together Separately: Arabs and Jews in Contemporary Jerusalem* (Princeton, 1991), p. 207; Roger Friedland and Richard Hecht, *To Rule Jerusalem* (Cambridge, 1996), pp. 332 and 519; *Daily Telegraph*, 9 November 1978; *New York Times*, 9 November 1978; *Jerusalem Post*, 6 November 1983; *New York Times*, 3 November 1993.
Note: Exact figures for Arab election participation in east Jerusalem are very hard to establish. The Ministry of the Interior apparently records such statistics and the above figures for the years to 1983 are based on those data. Figures published in the Israeli press and announced by the Jerusalem Municipality often varied widely: for example, in 1969 a municipal spokesman announced that 10,000 east Jerusalemites had participated in the election, representing a turnout rate of 80 per cent.[a] According to Teddy Kollek, 11,000 Arabs voted in 1969 but for various reasons only 8,000 votes were valid.[b]

a Gideon Weigert, *Israel's Presence in East Jerusalem* (Jerusalem, 1973), p. 17.
b Teddy Kollek, *For Jerusalem* (New York, 1978), p. 213.

Khatib's example paved the way for what was to be a highly effective Arab boycott of the Israeli political system, including the municipality. Although offered the possibility of becoming Israeli citizens, the overwhelming majority chose not to do so and remained Jordanians. Residents of east Jerusalem, unlike those of the West Bank, were, however, issued with Israeli identity cards. As a result of an amendment to the election law, approved by the Knesset in January 1969, Jordanian citizens in east Jerusalem were permitted to vote in municipal elections, and Kollek hoped that significant numbers might do so. But only a small minority exercised this right in successive municipal elections (see Table 2, above). Nor would any east Jerusalem Arab stand for election to the city council. Such resistance was effective in a negative sense in not lending legitimacy to Israeli rule in the eyes of

the Arab population. But, of course, it had the untoward consequence, from the Arab point of view, of surrendering the whole government of the city to the Israelis.

Unlike the councillors, the salaried officials of the Jordanian municipality continued to work under the Israeli municipality, but
almost invariably in a subordinate capacity. Thus the Jordanian town
clerk, Salah al-Din Jarallah, became assistant town clerk and the Jordanian city engineer became the deputy city engineer. Jordanian
policemen were integrated into the Israeli force but were deployed
mainly in the Arab areas of the city. Such employment, in technical as
distinct from political positions, was generally regarded by the Arab
population as acceptable and even the policemen were not tarred
with collaboration. Nevertheless, as time went on it became clear that
Arab political non-participation was having a severely adverse effect
on the capacity of east Jerusalem Arabs to protect or advance their
day-to-day interests in the city. To this extent Arab resistance in this
sphere must be judged only a very limited success.

The Muslim religious establishment, on the other hand, succeeded in mounting much more effective opposition to Israeli policy. On 24 July 1967 a meeting of twenty-four Muslim notables was
convened on the Haram al-Sharif. Among the religious dignitaries
present were the President of the *shari`a* court of appeal, Sheikh
Abd al-Hamid al-Sa'ih, and the mufti of Jerusalem, Saad al-Din al-
Alami. The participants also included secular figures such as Anwar
al-Khatib, the former Jordanian governor of Jerusalem, Aref al-Aref,
a former mayor and Jordanian minister, and Anwar Nusseibeh, who
was to emerge as the leading Palestinian political figure in Jerusalem
in the early years of the occupation.[46] They all declared that they did
not recognize the legitimacy of the annexation, would not cooperate
with the Ministry of Religious Affairs and would refuse to comply
with the 'request' by the ministry's Muslim department to check the
sermon to be read by the imam in al-Aqsa mosque each Friday.[47]
They went further and announced the creation of a new body, the

Muslim Council, with al-Sa'ih as its President. (The council is not to be confused with the Supreme Moslem Council of mandatory times; although it was sometimes called by the same name in English, its Arabic title, al-Haya al-Islamiyya, was different. But since it operated from the same premises on the Haram and eventually combined religious, judicial, financial and political functions, it inevitably acquired some of the aura of its predecessor, although never the same degree of power.) They further announced that they would remain in post and continue to perform their functions 'until the termination of the occupation'.

Interestingly the Muslim leaders' statement, delivered by hand to foreign consuls by Aref al-Aref, did not once mention the words 'Palestine' or 'Palestinian'. The writers, all former Jordanian officials, stated explicitly, 'Arab Jerusalem is an integral part of Jordan.' A version of the document was circulated at the United Nations by the Jordanian representative. (Strangely, this version gave only twenty signatories, the most notable absentee being Anwar Nusseibeh.[48])

The Israeli reaction was immediate and sharp. On 31 July Anwar al-Khatib and three other political figures were exiled from the city for a three-month period. Khatib was to live in Safed, the others in other towns in Israel or the West Bank.[49] On 7 August a one-day general strike was observed in east Jerusalem – the first of many over the next thirty years. On 9 August another protest statement appeared, signed by five Muslim leaders, including al-Sa'ih.[50] On 25 September he and other members of the Muslim Council were deported to the West Bank. (Nusseibeh remained unmolested.)

The deportations did not suppress Muslim opposition to Israeli rule in Jerusalem. As on some previous occasions with the Christian Churches, the Israelis initially tried to use the power of the purse to bring the Jerusalem *waqf* authorities into line. Shortly after the start of the occupation, the Israelis lent a substantial sum to the *waqf* to cover salaries and 'other obligations'.[51] But the *waqf* soon succeeded in asserting its independence of the occupying authorities.

The Israelis found it impossible to suppress the council or to deprive it of control of religious endowments, courts and other institutions in Jerusalem and to some extent also in the West Bank. The story of how the Israelis tried and failed to gain ascendancy over the Islamic establishment in Jerusalem has been told by the late Colonel David Farhi, an orientalist who served as the Israeli military government's liaison officer with the Arab leadership in east Jerusalem in 1967.[52] Farhi pointed out that one immediate effect of the war was to cut off the Muslim religious courts in the West Bank from Jordan. The schism effectively meant that the appeal court in Amman could no longer hear appeals from the West Bank. The Israeli government in 1967 did not wish to appear to be taking annexationist steps in regard to the West Bank — as distinct from Jerusalem. It therefore faced the question whether it should integrate only the Jerusalem religious court and Muslim institutions. But to have cut these off from the remainder of the West Bank would have been difficult and would have been vigorously resisted by the Arab population. The Israelis faced the further problem that if they tried to stop the council's activities they would be accused of interfering with religious liberty — this at a time when they were concerned to demonstrate to the world that they were worthy guardians of the holy places of all religions.

While the Muslim Council's initial declaration paid lip service to Jordanian authority, it was not established under Jordanian law. It was nevertheless able to enforce its authority by acting as one of the main conduits for the distribution of funds from the Jordanian government to the West Bank. The Jerusalem Muslim religious court, which operated under the council's auspices, played an important part in establishing its authority. At first its judgements were not officially noticed by Israel, marriages under its auspices were not recognized by the Israeli Ministry of Interior and decisions were not enforced by Israeli bailiffs. The Israelis found, however, that the attempt to subordinate the Jerusalem court to the Israeli Muslim religious court system would not work. Eventually a compromise was reached whereby the

Israeli Muslim court of Jaffa 'endorsed' the decisions of the Jerusalem court. In 1987 an Israeli Muslim religious court was established in west Jerusalem. While this succeeded in attracting some applicants, particularly those who wished to make use of execution proceedings which this court was said to be 'equipped to handle' (presumably since it could rely on Israeli government officials to enforce writs), it did not succeed in displacing the Muslim *shari `a* court in east Jerusalem.[53]

The modus vivendi that was achieved worked well for both sides. Muslims maintained control of their own institutions, most particularly the shrines on the Haram al-Sharif. Sheikh Hilmi al-Muhtasib, who headed the council from 1968 until his death in 1982, hewed a cautiously moderate approach, seeking to affirm Muslim rights without antagonizing the Israelis unnecessarily. Israel tacitly recognized the Jerusalem Muslim establishment – since late Ottoman times the core of the nationalist movement in Arab Palestine. Retreating in this instance gracefully, the Israelis accepted that, in this significant sphere, east Jerusalem could not be annexed nor its distinct identity suppressed.

Education was another sphere in which east Jerusalem Arabs after 1967 succeeded in resisting integration into Israel. At first Israel tried to assimilate east Jerusalem public schools into the Israeli Arab school system – unlike schools in the West Bank, which continued to operate under the Jordanian system. But teachers in east Jerusalem insisted that, like their colleagues in the West Bank, they would continue to use the Jordanian rather than the Israeli Arab curriculum. They resorted to a variety of means, including strikes by teachers and pupils, in order to resist Israeli policy. The tussle continued for several years until here too Israel had to give way. Israeli legislation in 1970 made some concessions, but these were judged inadequate and resistance continued until the Israelis saved their face by further concessions that were embodied in an agreement in 1975. This provided for a 'choice' from the seventh grade onwards in east Jerusalem Arab schools between the Israeli and West Bank curricula. The choice was invariably for the latter, which led to examinations of the Arab League, conducted in accordance with Jordanian law. The arrangement, effectively acknowledging that for these purposes Jerusalem was part of the West Bank, was approved by the Israeli Education Ministry.[54]

The Arabic press of east Jerusalem, which circulated throughout the West Bank, reinforced Palestinian identity and accentuated the role of Jerusalem as the cultural centre of the region. Newspapers were censored by the Israelis (as previously by the Jordanians) and in the early days of the occupation criticism of Israel was quite tame. But in the 1970s it became more outspoken, especially in the dailies *al-Fajr* and *al-Shaab*, reflecting and reinforcing the radicalization of Palestinian politics throughout the occupied territories. (The pro-Jordanian *al-Quds* tended to be less militant.) For a time the Israelis tried to counter the radical tendency by prohibiting the circulation of some east Jerusalem papers in the West Bank and Gaza, thus reducing their influence and harming their commercial viability. In 1975 the editor of *al-Shaab*, Ali al-Khatib, was expelled.[55]

Resistance in the area of property rights was much less successful. Efforts by east Jerusalem Arabs to reclaim property in west Jerusalem generally failed. A rare case to the contrary was in the former no man's land area that, between 1949 and 1967, had bisected Abu Tor, an Arab village within the municipal boundary. As a result of the division of the city, Jews had occupied abandoned houses in its western (Israeli) section. After 1967 they remained. But some Jews now tried to occupy houses in the no man's land that had lain empty for the previous eighteen years. The Arab owners took them to court. The case became a *cause célèbre* and eventually went to the Israeli High Court of Appeals, which decided in favour of the owners.[56] Israel made much of offers of compensation to Palestinian Arabs for property in Jerusalem that had been abandoned by its owners in 1948. But the fine print of legislation on the subject passed by the Knesset deterred most owners from invoking it.

For a short time after June 1967 Israel hoped that it might be possible to secure a peace agreement with Jordan. Israel was prepared to return some territory in the West Bank to Jordan in a partial or full peace settlement, though she was not prepared to do so in Jerusalem. But Israeli leaders privately indicated readiness to recognize King Hussein as 'Guardian of the Muslim Holy Places in Jerusalem'. Prime Minister Eshkol also raised the prospect of the Jordanian flag flying over the Haram and of extra-territorial status for it.[57] Hussein, however, did not dare be the first Arab leader to sign a peace treaty with Israel. Instead he concentrated on preserving influence on the West Bank (where he continued to pay the salaries of Jordanian officials) and on trying to mobilize support from the Islamic and western worlds. In pursuit of the former, he sanctioned the convening of a World Islamic Conference in Amman on 16 September 1967. It was headed by Hajj Amin al-Husayni, who spoke of the danger to al-Aqsa mosque and called for the return of the holy places to Hussein's rule.[58] Few now paid much attention to the former mufti.

Instead Palestinian Arab leadership was seized by the Palestine Liberation Organization and its paramilitary offshoots, Yasir Arafat's Fatah and smaller and more extreme groups such as the Popular Front for the Liberation of Palestine, led by George Habash. Soon after the 1967 war a terrorist campaign was launched against Israel. Its first results were unimpressive and Israeli security succeeded in preventing the creation of a large-scale underground military movement in the occupied territories. A small bomb attack in Jerusalem in the autumn of 1967 caused little damage. In March 1968 the Israeli army captured Kamal Namari, the Jerusalem commander of Fatah. They then blew up his home in the Wadi Joz district. The practice of blowing up houses, under emergency regulations inherited from the British mandatory period, had been applied earlier in the West Bank, but this was its first use in Jerusalem. Although not many houses were blown up in this way in Jerusalem during the early years of the occupation, this too later became a familiar, if generally futile, practice of the authorities in their effort to contain terrorism. Mayor Kollek, who had not been informed in advance of the decision to blow up the house, protested publicly. He also complained that the unification of the city was being hampered by bureaucratic obstinacy that, he said, 'took the joy out of every good idea we ever had'. He charged, for example, that Arabs evicted from their homes had still not been compensated months later.[59]

Concerned that violent Arab resistance might grow, Israeli policy gradually became more repressive. Rawhi al-Khatib, the former mayor, was deported to Jordan in March 1968. The Israelis claimed that he had 'served as a link for the illegal transmission of money, supported strikes by shopkeepers and teachers and sent to Jordan false charges of Israel[i] brutality'.[60] Another probable reason was that Khatib kept in touch with foreign diplomats and supplied them with information considered damaging to Israeli interests. In November 1968 a terrorist bomb in the Mahane Yehuda market killed ten Jews and two Arabs. This was the first major incident of its kind in Jerusalem. Others followed and in August 1969 serious rioting broke out after a deranged Australian arsonist set fire to al-Aqsa mosque.

With the elimination by King Hussein of the presence of the Palestinian guerrilla organizations in Jordan in September 1970, the number of attacks on Israel decreased for a time. But after the war of October 1973 the atmosphere changed. Terrorism now reached the heart of Israel's capital. In 1975 fifteen people were killed and sixty-five injured by a bomb planted at Zion Square in the centre of the Israeli new city. After the explosion some Jewish rowdies attacked Arab passers-by. Over the next twenty years this cycle of violence and counter-violence was to become sadly familiar in the 'unified' city.

World reaction

On 4 July 1967 the UN General Assembly passed a resolution, proposed by Pakistan, declaring the Israeli measures in Jerusalem invalid and calling on the Israeli government to rescind them.[61] The resolution was carried by ninety-nine votes to none, with twenty abstentions; among the latter was the USA. In a letter to the Secretary-General on 10 July, the Israeli Foreign Minister, Abba Eban, protested that the term 'annexation' was 'out of place'. 'The measures adopted,' Eban explained again, 'relate to the integration of Jerusalem in the administrative and municipal spheres and furnish a legal basis for the protection of the Holy Places in Jerusalem.'[62] Israel rejected the resolution as well as a similar one passed ten days later.

A few weeks later the UN Secretary-General, U Thant, sent a personal representative, Ambassador Ernest Thalmann of Switzerland, to Jerusalem. The Israelis set stringent conditions for Thalmann's visit before admitting him: it was agreed that his mandate was restricted to the 'gathering of information'. As a token gesture towards the United Nations (regarded by Israeli public opinion with extreme hostility because of the withdrawal of the UN Emergency Force from Sinai in the days before the outbreak of the Six Day War), Israel returned Government House to UN control on 23 August. The UN compound, however, was much reduced in area, comprising about forty-four *dunams* (eleven acres) or a third of its pre-war size. Thalmann stayed in Jerusalem two weeks and reported that it had been 'made clear beyond any doubt that Israel was taking every step to place [east Jerusalem] under its sovereignty'. He added that the Israeli government 'stated unequivocally that the process of integration was irreversible and not negotiable'.[63]

The matter eventually passed to the Security Council, where a resolution critical of Israeli actions in Jerusalem was carried in May 1968 by thirteen votes to none (the United States abstained but did not use its veto to kill the resolution).[64] Several more such resolutions were passed in subsequent years but to no effect.[65] Israel also came under fierce attack at the UN and in UNESCO for her archaeological excavations in and around the old city.

In addition to difficulties with international organizations, the

Israeli annexation of east Jerusalem accentuated the existing problems in her relations with foreign consuls and diplomats. On 13 June
1967 the British consul-general sent the Foreign Office a 'flash' *en
clair* (i.e. so that the Israelis could read it) reporting that

> The Consular Corps are in a rare rage about the
> treatment being meted out to them. They are being
> obstructed in their proper duties and pushed from pillar
> to post, while the Jews pour their long-haired acolytes to
> and fro and even allow private citizens to cross over
> without difficulty. My Turkish and American colleagues
> are concerned about the distinction and the Italian and
> French Consuls-General are enraged. The Spanish
> Consul-General has received disgraceful treatment.
>
> One of the weakest spots in the Israeli public relations
> work has always been their treatment of Consuls, and
> they have few friends among those who leave for other
> posts. They are keeping up this tradition.[66]

Now that the whole of Jerusalem fell under Israeli rule, those consuls
who maintained offices on both sides of the city might have been expected to unify them as a sign of their continuing adherence to the
doctrine of the *corpus separatum*. But whereas they had earlier maintained the theoretical unity of their physically divided establishments
in order to demonstrate loyalty to the *corpus separatum*, now they
maintained their separation in order to register their non-recognition
of Israeli actions in Jerusalem. The consuls' position therefore became even more anomalous than hitherto, since they were now committed to the symbolic upholding of two contradictory principles: the
unity of Jerusalem (as ordained by the United Nations) and its division (i.e. the 1949–67 status quo). Thus although the consuls no
longer had to contend with the physical problems of operating in a
divided city, the tortuous wranglings over protocol multiplied.

At first Israel seemed to make some progress in persuading foreign governments to recognize its sovereignty in Jerusalem. By 1968 twenty-two out of forty-six foreign missions in Israel were stationed there. But these included none of the great powers; most were Latin American or African states of little diplomatic consequence. In particular, the position of the great powers remained virtually unchanged: they refused to accept the legitimacy of Israeli incorporation of east Jerusalem.

The United States attitude on Jerusalem after the Six Day War was at first quite mild. A White House statement on 19 June 1967 merely urged consultation 'before any unilateral action is taken on the status of Jerusalem'.[67] Only following the installation of the Nixon administration in January 1969 did American policy undergo a subtle modification. President Nixon's appointee as ambassador to the UN, Charles A. Yost, was notably less sympathetic to Israel than his predecessor, Arthur Goldberg. In July 1969 the USA supported a Security Council resolution that censured 'in the strongest terms all measures taken to change the status of Jerusalem'.[68] Explaining the American position, Yost made it clear that the USA considered east Jerusalem occupied territory.[69] Goldberg later protested that the Nixon administration's position on Jerusalem was 'a far cry' from that of the Johnson administration.[70] In December 1969 Secretary of State William Rogers announced a peace plan for the Middle East. This proposed vaguely that Jerusalem should be 'a unified city' with 'open access' and 'roles for both Israel and Jordan in the civic, economic, and religious life of the city'.[71] The plan was welcomed, with some reservations, by Egypt and Jordan, but denounced by the more militant Arab regimes. Israel rejected it out of hand. In August 1970 Rogers succeeded in persuading the Egyptians and Israelis to agree to a cease-fire in the 'war of attrition' that had raged along the Suez Canal since March 1969, but his outline for a permanent peace joined the scrap-heap of proposals discarded over the previous two decades.

The British attitude, of course, counted for far less than of yore. Nevertheless, given the sudden cooling of Franco-Israeli (and even more of Soviet-Israeli) relations after June 1967, the Israelis had to pay some heed to the British position on Jerusalem. This turned out to be less sympathetic than the Israelis might have hoped, especially given the personal support for Israel of the British Prime Minister, Harold Wilson, and his Foreign Secretary, George Brown. The British ambassador to the United Nations, Lord Caradon, took a lead on the issue, advancing a personal plan for Jerusalem. In private discussions and later in a series of speeches and articles he called for Arab sovereignty and administration to be restored to east Jerusalem, for demilitarization, freedom of religion and access to the holy places, and for 'an international statute and an international presence, not to administer the city, but to ensure, with the civil authorities on both sides, that freedom of communication and movement and access is maintained'. Declaring that Jerusalem should be a 'gateway to peace', he urged that it should be the first, not the last item on the agenda for Arab-Israeli negotiations.[72] Caradon's views derived force from his experience as a district officer in mandatory Palestine in the 1930s and from his role as architect of UN Security Council Resolution 242 of November 1967 – the most widely agreed basis for peace between Israel and her neighbours (the resolution made no direct reference to Jerusalem). But the Israelis disagreed with Caradon's approach, maintaining, as Teddy Kollek put it in 1974, that Jerusalem 'should be left to the very end', and they were joined in this view by Rogers's successor as US Secretary of State, Dr Henry Kissinger.[73]

The October 1973 war, in which the simultaneous Egyptian-Syrian attack initially caught Israel by surprise, and during which the Arab states discovered the power of the 'oil weapon', led to a sudden deterioration in Israel's diplomatic position. One consequence was damage to Israel's efforts to secure recognition of her capital. Under pressure from oil-producing Arab states, most African and some other countries broke off diplomatic relations with Israel. Many of these had located their diplomatic missions in (west) Jerusalem. Now nearly all quit Israel altogether, leaving only the Netherlands and some Latin American states with missions in the capital.

The Arab position on Jerusalem, as on the Middle East conflict in general, became more militant, reflecting the increased power of oil-producing states. In December 1973, King Faisal of Saudi Arabia told an American journalist, 'Only Muslims and Christians have holy places and rights in Jerusalem.' The Jews, he maintained, had no rights there at all. As for the Western Wall, he said, 'Another wall can be built for them. They can pray against that.'[74]

No significant section of Israeli opinion contemplated in these years bending policy on Jerusalem, or anything else, in response to violence; if anything, terrorism stiffened Israeli determination to hold on to occupied territory, including east Jerusalem. But as world pressure intensified after 1973, a slow retreat from occupied territory began. Following Kissinger's indefatigable 'shuttle diplomacy' in 1973–5 and the resultant Egyptian and Syrian disengagement agreements with Israel, some easing of the Egyptian and Jordanian positions on Jerusalem appeared.[75] And even a Saudi spokesman conceded that 'the Jews have a right to worship at their sacred sites in Jerusalem'.[76]

In 1975 the Brookings Institution in Washington produced a report entitled *Towards Peace in the Middle East*. Prepared by a group of senior academics and policy-makers from the Democrat Party, among them Zbigniew Brzezinski (later President Carter's National Security Advisor), Najeeb Halaby, Rita Hauser, Malcolm Kerr, Philip Klutznick, Nadav Safran, Charles Yost and William Quandt, the report had an important impact on American policy formation, particularly after the installation of Jimmy Carter as President in January 1977. On Jerusalem the report set minimal criteria for a settlement, among them free access to all holy places and no physical barriers to free circulation within the city. It specified that 'each national group within the city should, if it so desires, have substantial political autonomy in those areas where it predominates. Since the issue was highly symbolic for both sides, and since no solution would 'be able to satisfy fully the demands of either side', the report advocated leaving the whole question of Jerusalem to a late stage in any negotiation.[77]

Israeli thinking on Jerusalem in these years remained generally immobile. An opinion poll in Israel in December 1973 reported 92 per cent of respondents opposed to making Jerusalem an international city and 99 per cent opposed to returning east Jerusalem to Jordan (the results probably refer only to Jewish Israelis).[78] The rise of militant nationalism in Israeli politics was reflected in Jerusalem in these years by the reappearance of extremist Jewish terrorism. In early 1974 a number of Christian institutions suffered arson attacks.[79] And far-right groups began to plot counter-terrorist attacks against Muslim targets.

Almost the only place where serious thought about the future political shape of Jerusalem was undertaken by Israelis in these years was in the municipality. Its most important fruit was the 'borough' plan adumbrated by Teddy Kollek in a number of papers and speeches after 1968. The mayor did not suggest yielding sovereignty over any part of Jerusalem. But he recognized the necessity somehow to draw the Palestinian Arab élites of east Jerusalem into the political community. Since they would not cooperate in the city-wide municipality (in which, of course, they would have been a permanent minority), he proposed instead the creation of borough councils with substantial powers, rather like those in London or New York; this, he hoped, would provide the Arab inhabitants of east Jerusalem with a measure of autonomy and might secure their cooperation. Kollek's ideas were well received by their primary target audience, international opinion and Diaspora Jewry. They did not, however, persuade many Arabs and had little effect on Israeli policy-making. Neither Labour- nor Likud-dominated governments in Israel embraced Kollek's plan; both were fearful that it might lead to a redivision of the city.[80] Even some of Kollek's closest colleagues in the municipality shared that view.[81] Over the years, Kollek became increasingly frustrated and disaffected with what he saw as neglect of Jerusalem by successive Israeli governments. 'We are not recognized by any government in the world as the capital of Israel,' he said, 'and only half by the Israeli Government.'[82]

The left-wing Mapam party, after many years of discussion, finally endorsed something like Kollek's plan at a party convention in 1980. But Mapam added several riders. Some, such as the call for extra-territorialization of the Temple Mount, went a little further than the general Israeli consensus; but others represented a retreat from the status quo towards a more assertive Israeli position – for example, the clause providing that 'one condition for the exercise of full educational autonomy in the municipality or in the Arab sub-municipalities is that the school children be educated in a spirit of loyalty to the State of Israel, good citizenship, mutual tolerance and a firmer fraternity of the two peoples'.[83] This might be read (and was probably intended) as a call for the imposition of the Israeli Arab school curriculum in east Jerusalem.

Neither these ideas nor Kollek's, nor the more radical suggestions of one of Kollek's deputy mayors, Meron Benvenisti, were translated into government policy. But in August 1977 Moshe Dayan, Foreign Minister in the recently installed government of Menahem Begin, flew an intriguing diplomatic kite. He recalled that when Ben Gurion had been Prime Minister he had been ready to sign a peace treaty that would have provided for continued partition of Jerusalem (he was referring to the negotiations of 1948–51 with King Abdullah in which he himself had participated). Dayan announced that even east Jerusalem was not excluded as a possible subject of bargaining.[84] Although the hint was given in public it was little noted at the time. But it was one of the signals that led to President Anwar Sadat's peace initiative a few weeks later.

The question of Jerusalem inevitably figured in the discussions during the Egyptian President's dramatic visit to the Israeli capital in November. The Israelis were disappointed by Sadat's references to Jerusalem in his speech to the Knesset. He insisted on Israeli withdrawal from all occupied territory 'including Arab Jerusalem', which, he said, 'must be a free city, open to all the faithful'.[85] In private talks with the Israelis, the Egyptians indicated slightly more flexibility. When the Israeli Foreign Minister suggested that it would be best to begin not with the question of sovereignty but with the status of the holy places, Butros Ghali, the Egyptian Minister of State for Foreign Affairs and later UN Secretary-General, said (according to Dayan's account) that 'we should look ahead and try to come up with a new concept as an alternative to sovereignty'.[86]

In the course of negotiations over the next ten months, the Israelis tried to draw the Egyptians out on the subject. During discussions at Leeds Castle in England in July 1978, Dayan 'confided' in the Egyptian Foreign Minister, Mohamed Ibrahim Kamel, that 'the Jerusalem issue presented no difficulty so long as everybody agreed that it contained Holy Places for all religions; that there was a need for free movement and access to the Holy Places; and that it should not be divided. A formula for Jerusalem satisfactory to all parties could be found.'[87] But while moving towards a settlement of other, bilateral issues, the two sides remained far apart on Jerusalem.

It proved to be one of the thorniest issues during the thirteen days of the conference at Camp David in September 1978. While Egypt agreed to sign a peace treaty in return for a staged Israeli withdrawal from Sinai, discussion of the Palestinian problem and of Jerusalem became bogged down. The Egyptians' basic negotiating document called for the restoration of east Jerusalem to 'Arab sovereignty and administration', though they were prepared to agree to a 'joint municipal council'.[88] Sadat insisted that a 'Muslim flag' must fly over the Dome of the Rock immediately – that is, in advance of any Palestinian autonomy agreement. American officials, who tried to avoid involvement in the Jerusalem question, debated half-amusedly the design of the proposed flag.[89] But Sadat's demand was rejected out of hand by Menahem Begin, who saw such a concession as the thin end of a wedge that would dilute Israeli sovereignty over the whole city. Disagreement over Jerusalem on the last day of the summit very nearly scuttled the entire agreement. A formula was finally conjured up by US Secretary of State, Cyrus Vance, and the Israeli Attorney-General (later Chief Justice of the Israeli Supreme Court), Aharon Barak. They proposed that the agreement, which contained no reference to Jerusalem, be accompanied by side-letters in which Presidents Carter and Sadat and Prime Minister Begin would each state his country's unchanged position on Jerusalem. Sadat wrote to Carter:

1 Arab Jerusalem is an integral part of the West Bank. Legal and historical Arab rights in the City must be respected and restored.
2 Arab Jerusalem should be under Arab sovereignty.
3 The Palestinian inhabitants of Arab Jerusalem are entitled to exercise their legitimate national rights, being part of the Palestinian people in the West Bank.
4 Relevant Security Council resolutions, particularly Resolutions 242 and 267, must be applied with regard to Jerusalem. All the measures taken by Israel to alter the status of the City are null and void and should be rescinded.
5 All peoples must have free access to the City and enjoy the free exercise of worship and the right to visit and transit to the holy places without distinction or discrimination.
6 The holy places of each faith may be placed under the administration and control of their representatives.
7 Essential functions in the City should be undivided and a joint municipal council composed of an equal number of Arab and Jewish members can supervise the carrying out of these functions. In this way, the City shall be undivided.

Begin's letter was shorter. It simply recalled the Knesset legislation of

28 June 1967 and reiterated that 'Jerusalem is one city, indivisible, the Capital of the State of Israel.'[90]

Dayan felt the dispatch of these letters, marking, in effect a postponement of the whole issue, was acceptable since 'the American and Egyptian letters were not of an operational character. They did not commit Israel to withdrawing from this territory. The practical question as to who would control Jerusalem would be discussed within the framework of the negotiations for a peace treaty with Jordan five years after the establishment of autonomy in the West Bank. Time would tell.'[91] The Egyptian Foreign Minister, Mohamed Ibrahim Kamel, who resigned in protest against the accords, saw the letters as 'a merry-go-round or a children's see-saw, where the wooden horses never catch up and the see-saw is never at rest!'[92] Events over the following few years suggested that both Dayan and Kamel were right.

7   Towards Palestinian Autonomy

Between 1979 and 1991 the Jerusalem question marked time. Egyptian-Israeli talks about Palestinian autonomy ground down and finally stopped altogether. The mainly right-wing Israeli governments of the period dug in their heels and refused to discuss the possibility of any change in Jerusalem's status. Meanwhile, they continued to 'create facts' on the ground by land confiscations, residential construction for Israelis, attempts to reinforce Jerusalem's status as Israel's capital and restriction of Arab development within the municipal boundary. Meanwhile, the PLO did not, in these years, lay great stress on Jerusalem as a priority for the Palestinian cause. The outbreak in December 1987 of the civil rebellion known as the *intifada* radicalized Palestinian opinion in the West Bank and Gaza, as well as in east Jerusalem, to which disturbances also spread. The following year King Hussein decided to cut off his remaining ties to the West Bank, thus accelerating the trend towards independent political action by the Palestinians. Jerusalem now moved to the forefront of their thinking and, at their insistence, the question of representation for Jerusalem Arabs figured in preparatory discussions for the Middle East peace conference that opened in Madrid in 1991. With the end of the Cold War, regional conflicts in several parts of the world died down. The PLO, weakened by the loss of support from the USSR and from Arab regimes, moderated its stance towards Israel and indicated willingness to abjure terrorism. Opinion evolved in Israel too, leading, after the election in 1992 of a left-wing government under Yitzhak Rabin, to direct, secret negotiations between Israel and the PLO. These culminated in an outline agreement in September 1993. But this still did not resolve the Jerusalem issue.

Diplomacy by declaratory gesture

Following the signature of the Israel–Egypt peace treaty in March 1979, the Israeli Prime Minister, Menahem Begin, hoped that the Jerusalem issue could simply be left on one side. In July, reporting to the Cabinet on talks with Sadat in Alexandria, he said that Jerusalem was not currently a matter for discussion with the Egyptians.[1] He was soon disabused of this notion. The Egyptian Vice-President, Hosni Mubarak, insisted publicly that Jerusalem was an integral part of the West Bank and must therefore be included in the arrangements for Palestinian autonomy.[2] But efforts by Egypt and the USA to move the issue forward met a brick wall in Israel. When the Egyptians floated 'ideas', such as that east Jerusalem should be the seat of the proposed Palestinian autonomous council, these were met, according to the Israeli government spokesman, Dan Pattir, with a 'flat rejection'.[3] By the spring of 1980 the topic had become a recurring bone of contention in Israeli-Egyptian negotiations.[4] Successive sessions broke down on the issue, with the Israelis repeatedly insisting that it should not even be discussed. 'It is not a matter to be negotiated in the autonomy talks ... We don't raise issues which should not be negotiated ... and, in all friendship, we don't touch on the issue of the capital of Egypt,' declared the head of the Israeli delegation at the talks, Shmuel Tamir.[5]

Begin's post-Camp David policy regarding east Jerusalem had a core of internal contradiction. On the one hand, he accepted the principle of autonomy for the West Bank Arabs, which, he said, should apply to the population rather than to any particular territory; but on the other, he argued that the Arabs of east Jerusalem must not be included in the autonomy arrangement lest that impair Israeli sovereignty over the city. This potentially left the east Jerusalem Arabs in limbo – neither Israeli Arabs, nor included in Palestinian autonomy, they would presumably remain Jordanian citizens, enemy aliens with only limited rights in Jerusalem.

The United States position on this issue had been clarified shortly after the Camp David agreements. In response to an inquiry from King Hussein, the State Department declared that the USA would 'support proposals that will permit Arab inhabitants of East Jerusalem who are not Israeli citizens to participate in the elections to constitute the Self-Governing Authority and in the work of the Self-Governing Authority itself'.[6] On this as on other issues, however, the USA failed to persuade its recalcitrant client.

Begin's inflexible approach was criticized by his Foreign Minister, Moshe Dayan, and his Defence Minister, Ezer Weizman. Dayan resigned as Foreign Minister in October 1979; in a newspaper interview a few months later he said that 'Israel could hardly tell 100,000 people [in east Jerusalem] that while they could vote for the Jerusalem municipality, not being Israeli they could not take part in the Knesset elections, and also not cast their ballots for the Amman assembly.'[7] Dayan remained ambiguous on the issue of inclusion of east Jerusalem Arabs in the Palestinian autonomy arrangements. Other Israelis were a little more adventurous. For example, the political scientist Amos Perlmutter, in an article in the *New York Times* in October 1980, advocated new thinking on the point.[8] The government, however, would not be moved.

The Iranian revolution of 1979 produced a new outpouring of Muslim passion and propaganda on Jerusalem. One of the first official foreign visitors to Tehran after the revolution was Yasir Arafat. He secured an undertaking that its leader, Ayatollah Khomeini, would summon an International Congress 'to examine ways to liberate the city of Jerusalem from Israeli occupation'.[9] In May a conference of Islamic Foreign Ministers, from which Egypt was barred, announced that Jerusalem was the capital of Palestine and declared the Muslim year 1400 (starting in the following November) a 'year of Palestine and al-Quds'.[10] A committee of the Islamic Conference was established, under the presidency of King Hassan II of Morocco, to 'set in motion a political and information programme'.[11] Its products included a lavish, colour-printed booklet containing many photographs of King Hassan. The campaign stretched to the ends of the Islamic world – including non-Arab Muslims in Indonesia, South Africa and the United States. Among the more far-fetched accusations hurled against Israel was a report in the Pakistani paper *Dawn* that 'a conspiracy is being hatched in Israel to move the old city of Jerusalem to a new site in the Mediterranean seashore north of Tel Aviv'. The plan was said to have been approved by the Israeli Cabinet and to have been costed at £33 million.[12] Such flights of fancy might be dismissed as the far edge of paranoia. But they demonstrated the resonance of the Jerusalem issue for Muslims.

The Israeli response to this diplomatic pressure and propagandist clamour was similar to that of David Ben Gurion three decades earlier – a declamatory act. In July 1980 the Knesset passed the Jerusalem Law, which stated that 'Jerusalem, complete and united, is the capital of Israel'. Its initiator, the ultra-nationalist Knesset member Geula Cohen, made it clear that her purpose was to foreclose any negotiations about Jerusalem by ring-fencing it with a basic (i.e. entrenched, quasi-constitutional) law. She taunted Begin with the speculation that his attachment to Jerusalem did not extend further east than the Western Wall.[13] The bill embarrassed both the government and the Labour opposition. The general mood in the Knesset was expressed by Moshe Dayan, who said that the bill was 'unnecessary' – before he proceeded to vote for it. Begin did not wish to allow himself to be outflanked on the Jerusalem issue by his extreme-right opponents. Most Likud members therefore voted in favour, albeit unenthusiastically. The Labour Alignment decided to support the bill, though a number of members, including Yitzhak Rabin and Abba Eban, were absent during the vote on the first reading. Only a scattering of left-wingers opposed it. The Knesset vote was sixty-two to twelve in favour.[14] When the bill was discussed in an Alignment faction meeting, Rabin got into a bitter wrangle with Shimon Peres over the tactics they should adopt.[15] In the Knesset Law Committee, however, the bill was amended to delete a reference to the city 'in its limits determined by the Six Day War'; instead it referred simply to 'Jerusalem, complete and united'.[16] It was noted that, in spite of the furore that it aroused, the bill, as finally approved, contained nothing that precluded Jerusalem serving also as a Palestinian capital.[17] In the final Knesset vote, the bill was passed by sixty-nine votes to fifteen. Most Labour members, including Peres, supported it, though Rabin and Eban again absented themselves.

Unlike earlier legislation concerning Jerusalem, the bill was widely criticized within Israel. Even before it was passed, the dean of Tel Aviv University Law School, Professor Yoram Dinstein, had caused something of a sensation by his public insistence that the Israeli annexation of east Jerusalem was not lawful.[18] Other Israeli legal experts suggested that the law 'did not change the city's legal status' and merely had a 'declarative effect', though exactly what this was remained obscure.[19] Political opposition tended to be founded on tactical rather than principled considerations. Only those regarded as beyond the fringe, such as the leftist former Knesset member Meir Pail, defied the consensus by suggesting a redivision of sovereignty in Jerusalem.[20] Mayor Kollek, while welcoming the amendments introduced at committee stage, expostulated that 'all in all Jerusalem will benefit nothing from the law'.[21] 'Whom did it help?' he asked. 'I see what confusion it has created even among our friends.'[22]

Within a few weeks he was proved right. The law was criticized by all the major powers. On 20 August the UN Security Council passed a resolution of censure on Israel by fourteen votes to zero (the USA abstaining). The New York Times called the law 'capital folly'.[23] All the remaining thirteen diplomatic missions in Jerusalem, including those of countries that had traditionally been most friendly to Israel, such as the Netherlands, Guatemala and the Dominican Republic, moved to Tel Aviv (those of Costa Rica, Honduras and El Salvador subsequently returned). Turkey closed its consulates-general on both sides of the city. The Israeli Foreign Ministry pronounced itself 'deeply hurt' by the decisions, which represented a serious setback for Israel's efforts to secure international legitimation of Jerusalem as its capital.[24]

The Jerusalem Law thus had a counter-productive effect. Likud Knesset members had sought to anticipate these diplomatic consequences of the Jerusalem Bill by introducing a bill to make it mandatory for foreign missions to be stationed in Jerusalem and to withdraw diplomatic immunity from envoys who failed to conform.[25] Whether they contemplated prosecuting and imprisoning diplomats who failed to comply with such further 'declaratory' legislation is not recorded. Wisely, more prudent counsels prevailed in this instance and a diplomatic showdown was averted by the abandonment of the proposal.

At the same time as the Jerusalem Bill was moving through the Knesset, Menahem Begin, anxious to demonstrate that he was second to none in his devotion to Israel's capital, let it be announced that his office would move to the eastern part of the city. The news evoked some domestic criticism. The chairman of the World Zionist Executive, Aryeh Dulzin, a moderate right-winger, called the move 'great folly'.[26] The former Director-General of the Foreign Ministry, Walter Eytan, argued that 'the proposed transfer suggests uncertainty, a hidden fear that we may yet lose East ("Arab") Jerusalem.'[27] Diplomatic reaction was sharp. The American ambassador, Samuel Lewis, warned Begin that he would be unable to call on him in east Jerusalem.[28] The British Foreign Secretary, Lord Carrington, appearing on Israeli television, said the move would be 'a great mistake', adding, 'I think it will make things very much more difficult for your friends and very much easier for your enemies.'[29] Begin hated that sort of tone in critics, particularly British ones, and responded in characteristic manner in a prepared statement:

> It is not his business to advise the Prime Minister of
> Israel where to site his office ... Jerusalem was a capital,
> a Jewish capital, long before London became the capital
> of the United Kingdom. When King David moved the

capital of his kingdom from Hebron, where he reigned
for seven years, to Jerusalem, where he reigned for thirty-
three years (Kings I, 2: xi), the civilized world had not yet
heard of the city of London.[30]

(This was an old Anglo-Zionist theme: in 1906, Chaim Weizmann,
during his first meeting with Balfour, had said, 'Suppose I give you
London instead of Paris, would you take it?' Balfour said, 'We have
London.' To which Weizmann responded, 'Mr Balfour, we had
Jerusalem when London was a swamp.'[31])

A building was prepared in east Jerusalem, refurbished by
plumbers, plasterers and carpenters, and desks and office equipment
were moved in.[32] But following admonitory messages from President
Carter and Secretary of State Muskie, backed up by advice from
American Jewish leaders, members of Begin's Cabinet suggested he
think again.[33] In the end, he backed down; the move did not take
place. The Supreme Court, which had originally been set to move
from cramped quarters on the Russian compound to Mount Scopus,
was instead given a palatial new home in west Jerusalem by the Rothschild family. Altogether, only four ministries and the national police
headquarters moved to east Jerusalem.

Passage of the Jerusalem Law and the threat to move the Prime
Minister's office had the further consequence that Egypt suspended
talks with Israel on Palestinian autonomy. Sadat was moved in part by
growing domestic disquiet and condemnation throughout the Arab
world. He sent Begin an eighteen-page letter urging that 'the historic
and legal rights of Arabs and Moslems in Jerusalem should be respected while keeping the utilities of the city unified and guaranteeing the freedom of movement and worship'. 'No issue,' he wrote,
'should be considered, or rendered, not negotiable.'[34] In a lengthy
reply on 4 August, Begin claimed to speak, on the subject of
Jerusalem, 'for ninety-five percent of the Israeli people'. He made it
clear that he would not give an inch of the city that was 're-united and

indivisible for all generations'.[35] Begin was not, in truth, greatly upset by the suspension of the talks: he had never been enthusiastic about Palestinian autonomy.

With Sadat's assassination on 6 October 1981, the most determined proponent of the idea of Israeli-Egyptian peacemaking was removed from the scene. His successor, Hosni Mubarak, did not repudiate Sadat's legacy but moved much more cautiously. His aim, eventually successful, was to end Egypt's diplomatic isolation in the Arab world. President Reagan's special Middle East envoy, Sol Linowitz, tried to breathe new life into the talks in early 1982 but without success. Reagan himself, in his 'peace initiative' of 1 September 1982, reaffirmed support for 'participation by the Palestinian inhabitants of East Jerusalem in the election of the West Bank-Gaza authority' – although he did not use these words in his televised speech but merely in a list of 'talking points sent to Begin and to Arab governments'.[36] The omission hardly bespoke resolve. But Israel's reaction was immediate and rendered in the barrack-room lawyer style of the Prime Minister: 'No mention is made in the Camp David agreement of such a voting right. The single meaning of such a vote is the repartition of Jerusalem ...'[37]

But by now all this was purely theoretical. Even the Arab world's attention was diverted from Jerusalem by the intensification of warfare to the north and the east. The Israeli invasion of Lebanon in June that year had destroyed any prospect of a further agreement between Egypt and Israel on the autonomy issue. And a communiqué from Iran in July proclaimed that its counter-attack on Iraq was the first stage in a campaign 'to liberate Jerusalem from Zionist domination'. For the remainder of the decade Palestinian autonomy, and with it the question of Jerusalem, remained stuck in a diplomatic logjam.

Meanwhile, Israel continued to 'create facts' by reinforcing the ring of new Jewish housing and connecting roads around Jerusalem, both within and beyond the municipal precincts. To the north-west large Jewish suburbs were built at Neve Yaakov and Pisgat Zeev. In the north-east new developments were planned at Psagot, near El-Bira, and Anatot. About seven miles east of the city, in 1975, a handful of young nationalists established an unofficial caravan site on a hillside overlooking the desert; over the next twenty years this grew into the town of Maaleh Adumim. South of Jerusalem large housing estates were built at Har Gilo and planning began for a large new housing development at Har Homa, near the Arab village of Sur Bahir. Declaratory diplomacy and legislation brought no respite in terrorist attacks in Jerusalem and other parts of Israel. In December 1983 a bomb attack on a Jerusalem bus killed five Jews and wounded forty-six. Other such incidents followed, outraging Israeli public opinion and enabling Begin to persuade the United States government that the PLO leadership were not *interlocuteurs valables*.

Jerusalem: an American problem?

Although the Israelis could generally count on strong support from the United States, they had always had more friends in Congress than in the State Department. Israel and its American supporters were irritated throughout these years by the dogged refusal of successive United States administrations to shift the American position and recognize Israeli sovereignty in Jerusalem. After the 1967 war, as Israel became heavily dependent on American arms and economic aid, great efforts were devoted to strengthening the Israeli lobby in Washington. By the 1970s AIPAC (America-Israel Public Affairs Committee) was regarded with awe as second only to the National Rifle Association in its capacity to wield political influence in both houses of Congress. Most of its work was devoted to hard-edged military and economic rather than diplomatic issues. Jerusalem, however, became an exception and from the 1970s a determined campaign was launched to change American foreign policy on Jerusalem by mobilization of political pressure in Congress. From here it was but a short step to the injection of the issue into American electoral politics.

Over the years a ritual dance around Jerusalem became almost *de rigueur* in American politics. Presidential candidates were obliged to declare a commitment to moving the embassy to Jerusalem; yet every president, once elected, decided not to do so. Even George McGovern, the Democratic candidate in 1972, widely regarded as unsympathetic to Israel, was obliged to take the pledge.[38] In 1976 Jimmy Carter had some misgivings about repeating the promise; he was persuaded against his better judgement to do so. After his election the US embassy stayed put. In the 1980 election campaign Carter, under pressure from his Democratic rival, Senator Edward Kennedy, was compelled to agree to the reinsertion of the pledge in the party platform.[39] His Republican opponent, Ronald Reagan, had fewer inhibitions. Questioned about Jerusalem, he said: 'An undivided city of Jerusalem means sovereignty for Israel over that city.' When challenged as to whether he would really move the embassy in the face of State Department advice to the contrary, the candidate added some disobliging comments about the State Department and its personnel.[40] But even before the election, Reagan's robust position crumpled. His foreign policy advisers warned him not to repeat the mistake of the short-lived Canadian Conservative Prime Minister Joe Clark, who had solemnly undertaken to move the Canadian embassy, only to change his mind three days after taking office in June 1979. The Republican platform accordingly watered down Reagan's forthright undertaking.[41] In the later stages of the campaign an apparently confused Reagan argued simultaneously for a Vatican-type arrangement and for Israeli sovereignty throughout the city.[42] Under the Reagan administration too, the embassy remained in Tel Aviv.

In June 1980 the House of Representatives had voted against any embassy move – the Israel lobby and strongly pro-Israel representatives, on tactical grounds, had opposed a move at that time.[43] But in early 1984 Senator Daniel Patrick Moynihan of New York and Representatives Tom Lantos and Benjamin A. Gilman introduced legislation in both houses of Congress requiring the removal of the embassy to

Jerusalem. The administration opposed the bills and Secretary of State Shultz said they raised 'very serious separation-of-powers questions'.[44] On this occasion, AIPAC backed the measure, which secured broad support in both parties.[45] Press opinion was mostly negative: half of the 'big 50' newspapers in the country commented on the issue and all but three opposed the move.[46] President Reagan, forgetful of his own earlier enthusiasm for the idea, scolded Congress for favouring it and threatened to veto any such bill.[47] A Jerusalem Embassy Act finally became law in 1995 but President Clinton repeatedly invoked a national security clause to prevent implementation of the embassy move.

The domestic debate in the United States seemed predicated on the assumption that American Jews cared deeply about the Jerusalem issue. It undoubtedly struck a chord for many, even if few bothered to inform themselves about the intricacies of the matter. Most took their lead from the Israeli government, though at times of stress some American Jewish leaders urged caution on Israel. While most Jews in North America and western Europe tended in general terms to support a unified Israeli Jerusalem, there was little evidence that the issue aroused the degree of passion that erupted from time to time in the Muslim world. A few Diaspora Jewish leaders expressed mildly heretical views: for example, the British Chief Rabbi, Immanuel Jakobovits, who supported Kollek's 'borough' plan and wrote that he 'could envisage Vatican-type enclaves' for non-Jews in the city.[48]

While argument about the location of the US embassy continued, a gradual change took place in the function of the US consulate-general in Jerusalem. Although it maintained offices in both east and west Jerusalem, the consulate's main emphasis was placed on the east. This remained an autocephalous consulate, responsible not to the US embassy in Tel Aviv, but directly to the State Department. In this it was not quite unique among US consulates anywhere in the world (since a similar arrangement existed in Hong Kong) but it was very unusual. By the 1980s the consulate's main function had become relations with the Palestinians in east Jerusalem and the West

Bank; eventually it developed, in all but name, into the US embassy to the Palestinians. Israeli governments, particularly right-wing ones, accordingly distanced themselves from it. When Molly Williamson took up her post as consul-general in 1990, the Foreign Ministry let it be known that it would not meet her – a strange reversal of roles from earlier days, when foreign diplomats would not meet the Foreign Minister in Jerusalem.

Palestinians and Jerusalem

Although the Palestine Liberation Organization held its founding conference in Jerusalem in 1964, the movement placed curiously little emphasis on the city in the early stages of its development – in this as in other ways mimicking the early Zionists. Perhaps for fear of upsetting Jordanian susceptibilities, Jerusalem was not even mentioned in the Palestinian National Charter – in neither its 1964 nor its 1968 version. It was similarly ignored in the ten-point political programme adopted at the twelfth session of the Palestinian National Council held in Cairo on 8 June 1974.[49]

Only in the mid-1970s did the PLO's attitude begin to change. In 1977 the Saudi Crown Prince (later King) Fahd visited Washington and laid a PLO memorandum before President Carter. This stated, among other things, that east Jerusalem, under Palestinian sovereignty, must be the capital of the future Palestinian state, with access to the holy places guaranteed to all.[50] The fact that it should have been a Saudi prince who thus released the Palestinians from thrall to the Hashemite obsession with Jerusalem was sadly indicative of the PLO's dependence on external patronage. The episode also illustrated the degree to which Jerusalem remained a symbolic prestige item and political shuttlecock in Arab and Muslim rivalries.

The Saudis, no doubt seeking to outbid their old rivals, the Hashemites, as protectors of the Islamic holy places, seem to have taken a special interest in Jerusalem at this time. King Khalid, in a major speech to pilgrims during the *hajj* in Mecca, called for the 're-gaining of the third holiest mosque [al-Aqsa] in Jerusalem and noble Jerusalem itself, and for cleansing them of all the impurities that have been attached to them'.[51] Shortly afterwards, it was reported that Saudi Arabia had offered $12 million for a new Palestinian university to be built on the Mount of Olives.[52] Israel betrayed some interest in encouraging Saudi pretensions, if only as a counterweight to Jordan. On 'Jerusalem Day' in 1979, for example, the World Zionist Organization distributed a memorandum by Walter Eytan that proposed offering sovereignty over the Muslim holy places to the King of Saudi Arabia 'in the same way as the Pope enjoys sovereignty over the Vatican City'.[53] The WZO was not a government body and Eytan was no longer a public servant; the Israeli government could therefore disclaim any responsibility for the idea. But it nevertheless served a useful function for Israeli diplomacy in fanning inter-Arab competition over Jerusalem.

Following Sadat's peace initiative in November 1977, Palestinian leaders began to think seriously about the future of the city and tried to define their political aims for it. In July 1978 Walid Khalidi, an exiled intellectual from an old Jerusalem family, published an article in the influential American journal *Foreign Affairs*. Setting out what he called a 'personal inventory' for a solution of the Palestine problem, he called for the creation of a Palestinian state that would include the West Bank, Gaza and east Jerusalem. He admitted that this was a reversion to the old concept of partition and that 'in some Palestinian and Arab quarters' it might be seen as treason. But he maintained that a new generation of Palestinian and Arab leaders now accepted the concept. East Jerusalem, which he called the 'navel' of the West Bank, was 'the natural capital of Arab Palestine'. There should be no rebuilding of the wall there. West Jerusalem should remain the capital of Israel. There should be freedom of movement and residence. The city should be administered by a joint inter-state municipal council. And there should be a 'grand inter-faith council' for the holy places.

Jews should have an 'irreversible right of access' to the Western Wall. And, while Khalidi rejected demilitarization of the Palestinian state as a whole, he urged that it would be 'supremely fitting' if Jerusalem (both east and west) were demilitarized.[54] Khalidi's proposals included several elements certain to be unacceptable to the Israelis: for example, the reference to freedom of residence would have opened the door to the return of Palestinian refugees. The article nevertheless represented a sign of new thinking among Palestinians and was widely discussed.

The following year the PLO produced for the first time a considered official statement of its position on Jerusalem. Entitled 'Status of Jerusalem', the document was presented to the UN Committee for the Exercise of the Inalienable Rights of the Palestinian People. After rehearsing the history of the city from a Palestinian nationalist angle of vision, it avoided any recommendation for the future of the city other than to suggest that a settlement would be possible 'only within the context of a global settlement of the Middle East question which must necessarily conform to the resolutions of the General Assembly concerning the rights of the Palestinian people'.[55]

From 1979 onwards evidence multiplied that the Arabs of east Jerusalem, far from succumbing at last to annexation by Israel, were, on the contrary, becoming more politically conscious, more insistent on preserving their identity and more ready to defy Israeli occupation. In July 1979 a Palestinian Social Congress in the city, financed by the Jordanian government, heard children in folk costumes sing nationalist songs such as 'We Will Redeem You in Blood and Fire'. The conference ended with a call for the establishment of an independent Palestinian state.[56] The following May, unrest in the West Bank spread to Jerusalem: clashes broke out between Arab youths; a Palestinian flag was raised in the old city; and east Jerusalem shopkeepers joined those of the West Bank in a commercial strike.[57] The former Jordanian governor of Jerusalem Anwar al-Khatib, at this time practising as an attorney in east Jerusalem, declared that thirteen years of Israeli rule had not unified the city.[58]

In November 1986 serious Arab-Jewish riots broke out in Jerusalem following the murder of a Jew, Eliahu Emadi, by four members of Fatah. Arab and Jewish youths stoned each other, Arab-owned cars and homes were torched. The funeral of Emadi turned into a riot. A few days later the funeral of the local Arab notable and former Jordanian minister Anwar Nusseibeh turned into a counter-demonstration by Palestinian nationalists. Only after a week did the troubles die down, to be succeeded by a sullen, menacing calm. Analysis of the motives of rioters and the objects of attack indicated that this was more than a straightforward ethnic contest between Arabs and Jews. The mass-circulation Hebrew paper *Yediot Aharonot* commented that the riots exposed three layers of conflict: between Arabs and Jews, between religious and secular Jews, and between rich and poor Jews – the last often running parallel with conflict between Ashkenazim and Sephardim.[59] It warned that the animosities among these groups were deep-seated and would not readily disappear. The Hobbesian prospect of a struggle of all against all was borne out by what followed.

In the course of the following year several manifestations of Palestinian assertiveness indicated the coming political eruption. In June 1987 Hanna Siniora, a Christian Arab, supporter of Fatah and editor of the newspaper *al-Fajr*, announced that he would run for office in the next municipal elections. 'I want to show that Jerusalem is inhabited by real people, not ghosts,' he said. *Al-Fajr* had been outspoken in its support for the PLO and for Palestinian self-determination since the early 1970s. But Siniora, as a Christian, might have had some difficulty in garnering electoral support even if an election boycott were not still in place. The mayor of Bethlehem, Elias Freij (also a Christian), declared the candidacy 'a brilliant idea', but it was criticized by the PLO and eventually withdrawn.[60] The episode was nevertheless a straw in the wind, one of many indicating a heightened readiness by Palestinians under occupation to take their destiny into their own hands.

Later that summer the Israeli government decided to end the right of the Jerusalem District Electric Company to supply Jewish districts in east Jerusalem. Behind this decision lay a legal and political saga of epic proportions. The company was Arab-owned and had come to be regarded by Palestinians as a national asset. Its origins lay in an Ottoman concession granted to a Greek citizen, Euripides Mavromatis, to supply electricity within a radius of twenty kilometres of the top of the rotunda of the Church of the Holy Sepulchre. Under the British mandate the concession became the subject of a tortuous legal case that dragged on for years and was the subject of endless appeals. The concession was nevertheless renewed by the British and Jordanians and the company remained the primary supplier of electricity to Jordanian Jerusalem. After June 1967 the question arose whether the company's concession would give it also the right to supply electricity to the new Jewish suburbs within its concessionary area. As the deputy mayor, Meron Benvenisti, described it, 'the notion that Jews should consume "Arab electricity" appeared fantastic'.[61] But fearing legal complications, the government decided to recognize the company's continuing rights under the concession.

The approaching end of the sixty-year period of the concession on 31 December 1987 gave the Israelis an opportunity to act. The Israel Electric Corporation, a monopolist power supplier within Israel proper, had been trying to take its little competitor over for years. It now got half its wish – that is, it was authorized to supply all Jewish areas of the city. The Arab company was limited to supplying Arab-inhabited areas of east Jerusalem. The government's order compelled the company to sack half its workforce. Paradoxically, however, the government's decision had the unintended effect of reinforcing the tendency towards Palestinian autonomy in a divided city since electricity supplies in Arab and Jewish areas of the city were now strictly divided along ethnic lines. The order to the company, under emergency defence regulations dating back to the mandatory period, to switch off supply to Jewish areas took effect on 8 December. One thousand police stood by as the neighbourhoods were linked to the Israeli company's national grid. The 'Arab electricity' was cut off and the partition of the city's power supply was complete.[62] If the Israeli authorities had but known it, they could hardly have chosen a more apposite symbol of the division of the city and of the imminent explosion.

Intifada and after

Conclusive proof that Israel's annexation of Jerusalem had failed came in the course of the *intifada*, the series of widespread civil disturbances that erupted in Gaza in December 1987. During the first few days of the troubles the government hoped to prevent the spread of violence to the capital. On 19 December, however, rioting broke out in Jerusalem. Shopkeepers observed a commercial strike. PLO pamphlets were widely distributed, Israeli and American flags burned, Palestinian flags raised and nationalist slogans daubed on walls. Burials of those killed by the Israeli security forces turned into demonstrations and then into pitched battles. In January Israeli police engaged in a running fight with Palestinians on the Haram al-Sharif after a 'victims' day' service in memory of protesters who had been killed. Soldiers entered al-Aqsa mosque, fired tear-gas canisters and clubbed Arab worshippers.[63]

The Israeli authorities, at first taken aback by the scale of the violence, seemed at a loss how to react. They oscillated between repressive measures and attempts to pacify the protesters. In Jerusalem they were at first hesitant about using the harsh tactics deployed in Gaza and the West Bank, both because of the presence of the international press and because they wished to differentiate between occupied territory on the one hand and the supposedly unified Israeli capital on the other. But they rapidly found that this distinction had no meaning. They were never able fully to resolve the ensuing dilemma: severe counter-measures would deepen the lines of separation running through the city; passivity would give *carte blanche* to the Palestinian nationalists to demonstrate the strength of their support in Israel's capital city.

Conversely, from the Palestinian point of view, the special status of east Jerusalem presented certain tactical advantages. Since it was part of Israel, its Palestinian residents were subject to fewer legal restrictions than those in the occupied territories. They could move about somewhat more freely and censorship was less tight. As a result, Jerusalem's role as political-cultural centre of Arab Palestine was further strengthened by the *intifada*.

On 13 January 1988 prominent Jerusalem Arab figures, including several regarded as moderates, were arrested. In a phrase that became notorious, the Defence Minister, Yitzhak Rabin, declared he would suppress the disturbances 'with force, power and blows'.[64] On 19 January a meeting of police and army officers and municipal officials made contingency arrangements for the invocation of emergency police powers in east Jerusalem for the first time since 1967. Three days later the powers were invoked when a curfew was declared for twenty-two hours in the neighbourhood of a-Tur on the Mount of Olives. The newspaper *al-Quds* was banned for forty-five days and Hanna Siniora was prosecuted for publishing an interview with Yasir Arafat in *al-Fajr*. But the rioting, stone-throwing, roadblocks, tyre-burning, commercial and school strikes, and open defiance of Israeli authority continued unabated.

As the disturbances went on and on, Israeli politicians gradually began to realize that they faced a deep-seated national revolt against Israeli occupation. Jerusalem, they grew to understand, could not be insulated from the *intifada* (literally 'shaking-off') as the uprising came to be called. Teddy Kollek, more realistic than most, acknowledged in early February 1988 that 'the situation in Jerusalem has changed in a fundamental way'.[65] The *intifada* marked the collapse of his two-decade-long effort to unify the city under Israeli rule, though he could not quite bring himself to accept this.

The division between Arab and Jewish areas of the city became an almost impassable psychological wall. A 'geography of fear' prevailed.[66] Already in the 1980s many Jews had stopped venturing into Arab areas. Now hardly any did so. Jewish taxi drivers refused to go there. Israeli private car owners heading for Jewish areas of east Jerusalem took long detours. The already small number of Arabs living in west Jerusalem was reduced to a handful; this applied even to Israeli Arabs (i.e. Palestinians who were Israeli citizens, generally of pre-1967 vintage), many of whom moved to Palestinian neighbourhoods such as Bet Hanina. Others left Jerusalem altogether.[67] Similarly Jews, other than ideologically motivated settlers, found it prudent to move out of Arab areas. Residential segregation, which had always been a characteristic of Jerusalem, thus became ever more strictly defined.

By the end of 1988 the Jerusalem police had made more than 2,000 arrests. Still the disturbances continued, sometimes taking new forms, petrol-bomb attacks and occasional knifings, as well as the ubiquitous stone-throwing. Although repression was generally less heavy-handed in Jerusalem than in the West Bank, Arab bitterness and alienation grew. In August 1990 the murder of two Jewish teenagers led to Jewish riots against Arabs. As communal relations became more poisoned in the autumn of 1990, with ever-increasing violence and counter-violence, the Israeli security forces placed roadblocks all around Jerusalem to prevent Palestinians from the West Bank entering the city. Thousands of border police also appeared at intersections along the now no longer so invisible boundary between Arab and Jewish sections of the 'unified' city.

The actions of some Israelis added to the atmosphere of tension and embitterment in the city. On 15 December 1987, in a demonstrative move, the right-wing politician Ariel Sharon moved into a refurbished apartment in the Muslim quarter. He was followed by several dozen *yeshiva* students. Similarly provocative moves were staged by religio-nationalist groups in other Arab districts of the city.

In a typical incident, in October 1991 a group of ultra-nationalist religious Jews, acting with the support of the Housing Ministry, headed by Sharon, installed themselves in a house in Silwan, an Arab village within the municipal boundary of Jerusalem. 'We have set a goal for ourselves of not leaving one neighborhood in East Jerusalem without Jews, not even one,' Sharon announced in May 1992. Teddy Kollek denounced Sharon's views and behaviour as 'a kind of messianism which has always been extremely harmful to us in history'. But the mayor's calls for reasonableness seemed out of tune with the times and politically he was by now a spent force.[68]

The hardening of sectoral boundaries in the city applied not only to Jews and Arabs but also to secular and ultra-orthodox Jews (*haredim*). The rapid growth in numbers of the orthodox Jewish population led, in the later years of Kollek's mayoralty, to fierce conflicts arising from the orthodox population's need for new areas of housing and consequent expansion into hitherto secular areas. A heightened militancy was discernible in orthodox demands that streets that had hitherto carried traffic on the Sabbath should now be closed on that day. Occasional violence, and even riots, erupted over other controversies such as the sale of non-kosher meat, 'immodest' advertisements on bus shelters and the opening of cafés on the Sabbath. Critics of the Israeli government noted that although orthodox Jewish rioters characteristically resorted to stone-throwing against Sabbath-breakers and police, they, unlike Palestinian rioters, were never fired upon by the security forces with live ammunition. The acrimony of relations between secular and religious Jews was greater in Jerusalem than in any other part of Israel and led to secular 'white flight' from Jerusalem to neighbouring areas outside the municipal boundary, such as the rapidly growing suburb of Mevasseret Zion to the west of the city.

In the winter of 1992–3 serious rioting by ultra-orthodox activists broke out. The issues once again seemed minor: objections to archaeologists digging in supposed ancient Jewish burial sites, demands for the closing of roads near orthodox areas on the Sabbath, and suchlike. But they were symbolic rallying cries for a submerged and poverty-stricken group in Israeli society that felt on the defensive against a wave of secularization. In these feelings (although not in the riots) the Ashkenazi *haredim* were joined by large numbers of Jews of north African (particularly Moroccan) origin, traditional rather than hyper-punctilious in their religious observance and, unlike the *haredim*, ultra-nationalist in their political outlook. The confluence of these two groups was to have a powerful effect on both municipal and national politics in Israel over the next few years.

On the diplomatic level the *intifada* produced an intensification of United States efforts to revive the stalled Palestinian autonomy talks. American policy now began a historic shift towards openness to dialogue with the Palestinian political leadership. In February 1988 the Secretary of State, George Shultz, on a visit to Israel, invited Arab representatives from east Jerusalem to meet him. As on his previous visit, in October 1987, they refused to do so. On this occasion Shultz, at the American Colony Hotel in Jerusalem, addressed a statement specifically 'to East Jerusalem'. Stressing that 'Palestinian participation [was] essential to success in the peace process', he declared that 'Palestinians must be active participants in negotiations to determine their future.' 'Legitimate Palestinian rights,' he said, 'can be achieved in a manner which protects Israeli security.'[69] The change in the United States position was clear: while not yet prepared to deal officially with the PLO, the Americans, evidently shocked by the scale and intensity of the rising, were ready to invite Palestinian representatives from within the occupied territories to speak for the Palestinian people.

A no less dramatic change in policy was announced by another interested party a few months later. On 31 July 1988, in a speech in Amman, King Hussein reversed his long-standing hostility to the PLO. He declared his acceptance of its aim to establish an independent state in the West Bank and Gaza. In consequence, the 'legal and administrative links between the two banks' of the Jordan would be dismantled. This cutting of the umbilical cord that bound many members of the Palestinian élite in the West Bank and east Jerusalem to Amman accelerated the political and psychological movement among the Palestinians towards autonomy. The speech did not, however, refer to Jerusalem. It therefore remained doubtful whether Hussein intended to disinterest himself altogether from the city that was so closely tied to his family's and his own history.[70]

But if Hussein wished to leave some ambiguity on this point, others had no such interest. In the Declaration of Independence issued from exile by the Palestine Liberation Organization on 15 November 1988 Jerusalem was at last mentioned – for the first time in a major PLO document: 'The Palestine National Council hereby declares, in the Name of God and on behalf of the Palestinian Arab people, the establishment of the State of Palestine in the land of Palestine with its capital at Jerusalem.'[71] The declaration was followed by a series of public statements issued by Yasir Arafat renouncing terrorism and accepting Israel's right 'to exist in peace and security'.[72] At first these were hesitant and mealy-mouthed. But eventually even many critics of the PLO had to admit that, if only for reasons of tactics, a change in rhetoric and perhaps more fundamentally in outlook had taken place. This turn by the PLO towards a new pro-American orientation was met half-way by the US administration. President Reagan announced that a 'dialogue' would now be initiated with the PLO.

In the early 1990s, the fall of the Soviet Union, the Gulf War and the continuing *intifada* radically changed the nature of the Jerusalem question. Although Israeli leaders of both major parties continued to declaim loudly their devotion to the maintenance of Israeli sovereignty over the united city, in fact they found themselves boxed in, constrained by the demographic realities, by the continuing social and institutional vitality of the east Jerusalem Arabs' collective identity, and by the rapidly shifting diplomatic context.

American efforts to revive Israeli-Arab negotiations on a new track moved into a high gear under US Secretary of State James Baker. The Jerusalem issue once again proved a stumbling block. Likud members of Israel's National Unity government refused to negotiate with any Palestinian delegation that included a Jerusalem Arab, considering that this would weaken Israel's claim to have unified Jerusalem definitively under Israeli sovereignty. For parallel reasons, Palestinian leaders in the West Bank, acting in concert with the PLO, insisted that a Jerusalem Arab must participate in any such talks. Labour members of the Israeli government were prepared to compromise on the issue, which helped bring about the breakup of the unity government in 1990 and the formation of a right-wing government headed by Yitzhak Shamir and dominated by the Likud. Baker nevertheless persisted with his efforts. In March 1991 he held a meeting, the first of its kind, with leading Palestinians, avowed supporters of the PLO from Jerusalem. In July that year, when he visited Jerusalem, he spent four hours at the American consulate in east Jerusalem with Arab leaders from the occupied territories, among them Faisal Husayni.

The son of Abd al-Qader Husayni, the Arab military commander who was killed in the battle for Jerusalem in 1948, Faisal was a distant kinsman of the mufti and derived some of his authority and popularity from his lineage. Riding the increasing militancy of the *intifada*, Husayni had emerged, since the death of Anwar Nusseibeh in 1986, as the leading political figure among the Palestinians of east Jerusalem. Unlike Nusseibeh, Husayni, a former Fatah activist, was an open supporter of the PLO. In 1987, together with Nusseibeh's son Sari, he held talks with a maverick Israeli Likud politician, Moshe Amirav. Shortly afterwards he was placed under administrative detention for nine months. Later he was arrested again. On his release he continued to foster contacts with Israeli politicians, including Yael Dayan, daughter of the general and herself a Labour member of the Knesset. He learned Hebrew sufficiently well to be interviewed on

Israeli television. Husayni's readiness for political links with Israelis, which resulted in a number of joint statements, demonstrations and public meetings, was a new phenomenon in Jerusalem and encouraged American hopes that he was a man with whom they and the Israelis could deal.

In return for an undertaking from Baker that a Palestinian from Jerusalem would be allowed to participate in the joint Palestinian-Jordanian delegation to the peace talks, the Palestinians agreed that the question of Jerusalem would not be raised in the initial stages of the negotiations. The Israeli Foreign Minister, David Levy, for his part indicated that the Israelis would be prepared to accept this semi-fictive arrangement. 'We will not inquire closely into the history of personalities nominated by King Hussein,' he said.[73] Later the Israelis drew back from this position. After much humming and hawing, a compromise was reached on a format for negotiations. The Palestinians would have their own delegation composed of leaders from the West Bank and Gaza. This would nominally form part of a joint Jordanian-Palestinian delegation. It would not represent the Palestine Liberation Organization. And it would not include Jerusalemites. But it would be aided by a committee of 'advisers' approved by the PLO which would include Faisal Husayni.

The peace conference opened in Madrid in October 1991. Jerusalem was not on the agenda. The opening session of the conference was not promising: all the Middle Eastern participants made speeches indicating total immobility. A framework had, however, been created that would facilitate diplomatic movement when the time was ripe. The election of Yitzhak Rabin as Israeli Prime Minister in June 1992, at the head of a Labour-dominated coalition, brought a radical change in Israel's posture. In April 1993 the Foreign Minister, Shimon Peres, indicated a shift in the Israeli position on the ground rules for the peace talks: Faisal Husayni would now be accepted as head of a Palestinian delegation. The offer of formal contact was a significant departure from the Israeli insistence, at the time of the opening of the Madrid conference, that no east Jerusalemites should participate in the Palestinian delegation. At the same time as making the announcement, Peres declared that there was no change in the substance of Israeli policy on Jerusalem – 'that Jerusalem will remain united as the capital of Israel under Israeli sovereignty'. Notably absent from this formulation was any commitment to specific boundaries for Israeli Jerusalem.[74] A Likud member of the Knesset, Eliahu Ben-Elissar objected, 'We started here this day, negotiating on Jerusalem.'[75]

Shortly afterwards, the Israelis made another gesture towards accommodation when they permitted the return of eleven Palestinian deportees, among them Rawhi al-Khatib, the former mayor of Jordanian Jerusalem, by this time in his eighties. He was given a hero's welcome on his return to the city he had last seen in 1968. More surprisingly, the Israelis also offered to allow the return of the former Greek Catholic bishop of Jerusalem, Hilarion Capucci, who had been arrested in 1974 on charges of arms smuggling and expelled in 1977. Capucci, who had become something of a Palestinian hero, rejected the offer, claiming that it had been 'tied to me not saying anything regarding the Palestinian cause or giving my opinion when I return'. He would not go back, he said, until Jerusalem was liberated and the capital of the state of Palestine.[76]

Meanwhile, secret talks between Israelis and Palestinian representatives had begun in Oslo under Norwegian auspices. This so-called 'back channel' had more success than the parallel public negotiations. It eventually resulted in the Palestinian-Israeli 'Declaration of Principles', signed on the White House lawn on 13 September 1993 (later, because of its origins, this came to be known as the 'Oslo Agreement'). The document said little about Jerusalem. The 'Palestinian Interim Self-Government Authority' that was to be created under the agreement would have no jurisdiction over east Jerusalem. Nevertheless, the Israelis made an important concession in agreeing that Palestinians resident there could vote in the elections that were to be held for a Palestinian Council, though the question whether Jerusalemites might stand as candidates in such elections remained open. The agreement postponed the fate of Jerusalem. Like other intractable issues such as the Arab refugee problem and Jewish settlements in occupied territories, it was to be dealt with in so-called 'final status negotiations', which were to begin 'as soon as possible but not later than the beginning of the third year of the interim period'. An optimistic Yasir Arafat said that the agreement was 'merely the first step' towards 'the total withdrawal from our land, our holy sites and our holy Jerusalem'.[77] But an Israeli spokesman insisted, 'Jerusalem is not part of the deal and there has been no weakening on that.'[78]

In spite of the improved diplomatic atmosphere, the *intifada* spluttered on. At the municipal level, the atmosphere of inter-communal relations of Jews and Arabs deteriorated after the defeat of Teddy Kollek in the mayoral election of November 1993. Although he cut a considerable international figure and was popular among secular and even some religious Jews in Jerusalem, Kollek's age (he was eighty-two) counted against him. So did the growing electoral weight of orthodox Jews in the city, most of whom voted for his opponent. Kollek had hoped that in the new atmosphere engendered by the Oslo Agreement he might at last persuade large numbers of Arabs to vote for him in the municipal election. In the event, only 8,000 participated in the election. This was double the number who had done so in the previous election and most supported Kollek, but not nearly enough to save him. The Likud candidate, Ehud Olmert, secured 60 per cent of the vote against Kollek's 34 per cent. The victory was explained in part by differential turnout: voting among the ultra-orthodox was estimated to have been as high as 90 per cent, whereas barely a third of secular voters had gone to the polls. Many of Kollek's former supporters, it appeared, had abstained, feeling that his long reign had reached its natural term but unable to bring themselves to vote for his opponent.

Kollek's twenty-eight-year mayoralty, the longest in the history of the city, thus ended sadly. For all Kollek's palpable decency, realism and imagination, and in spite of the personal popularity and international acclaim that he enjoyed during much of his term of office, his administration of the city must be judged a failure by the central criterion that he set himself at the moment of victory in June 1967: unification. At the end of his term Jerusalem was more, not less, divided than it had been in those heady days just after the Six Day War. Whatever the shortcomings and blind spots of his policy, Kollek could not be accused of failing to work single-mindedly and energetically to hold the divided city together. If he could not achieve this, it was doubtful anybody could.

8   Christian Jerusalem in Eclipse

Viewed in historical perspective, perhaps the most significant change in Jerusalem over the past century has been the decline in numbers and influence of Christianity in the city. At the end of the Ottoman period Christians outnumbered Muslims in Jerusalem. In 1946 there were still almost as many Christian as Muslim residents (see Table 1, page 46). But with the end of rule by a Christian power in 1948, the city's Christian population fell precipitously both in absolute numbers and relative to Muslims and Jews. From 31,400 in 1946, their numbers fell to 14,100 in 1995 (of these only 10,800 were reckoned to be Palestinians; the remainder were expatriates[1]). Proportionately the drop was even more precipitate: from 19 per cent in 1946 to only 2 per cent by 1995.

At the same time significant internal shifts took place in the balance of population among the Christian sects. By the 1990s, for the first time in the modern period, the Greek Orthodox were in danger of being overtaken by the Latins as the largest Christian community in the city.[2] Towards the end of the decade each was estimated to have about 4,000 adherents in the city. The other major Orthodox community, the Armenians, also declined. From a peak of between 5,000 and 7,000 in 1945, their numbers dwindled to an estimated 1,500 by 1990.[3] A small but steady trickle of emigration to the United States, to the Soviet Union and, after 1991, to the newly independent Armenian republic further reduced the Armenian population to barely 1,000. Most still lived in the Armenian quarter of the old city, although even here Armenians were in danger of becoming a minority by the 1990s.

'My fear,' said the Archbishop of Canterbury, Dr George Carey, on a visit in 1992, 'is that Jerusalem, Bethlehem – once centres of a strong Christian presence – might become a kind of Walt Disney Christian theme park.'[4] His words seemed dangerously close to prophecy. By 1996 all but five of the shops selling religious ornaments in the Christian quarter were rented out to Muslims.[5] The decline was particularly felt in Bethlehem, where it was said that, owing to emigration, there were more Bethlehemites in Santiago in Chile than in Bethlehem itself. By the end of the millennium, for the first time in history, Muslims outnumbered Christians in the birthplace of Jesus.

Demographic decline reflected a collapse of power. France's role as protector of Latin Christendom had been rudely crushed by the British, Russia's as patron of Orthodoxy reduced to a thin simulacrum by the revolution. As a result, the Christian triumphalism of the period after the First World War gave way by mid-century to a realistic recognition on the part of the Churches that the best that Christians could hope for in Jerusalem was shared crumbs at the table – hence the retreat by the Vatican and the Protestant Churches into pleas for internationalization. By the end of the century, the Christian position had deteriorated further. Christian institutions and 'Christian powers', as such, were now little more than bit players in the struggle for Jerusalem. Muslims and Jews, overwhelmingly dominant demographically, would determine the destiny of the city. The most the Churches could hope for was to maintain control over their institutions and holy places in Jerusalem while their numbers dwindled, in the case of some of the smaller eastern Churches to the brink of oblivion.

Christians under Jewish rule

Christian Jerusalem under Israeli rule after 1967 exhibited contradictory and even paradoxical aspects. On the one hand, many Christians, a well-educated, westernized and politically sophisticated élite among the Palestinians, naturally gravitated towards nationalism and furnished some of the Palestinian movement's most articulate and effective leaders and advocates. On the other, as a decreasing minority among Muslims, they felt a certain unease that set them apart from the mass of the population.

Israel began its new relationship with the Christians of Jerusalem with some built-in advantages. Many elements in the Christian communities had little reason to recall Jordanian rule with affection. The various restrictive laws and regulations had made life difficult for Christian institutions in east Jerusalem between 1949 and 1967. Israeli propaganda over the next few years dwelt on the release of east Jerusalem Christians from these constraints.[6] The very fact that the city was unified eased problems for communities that had hitherto been divided from their co-religionists in west Jerusalem and in Israel in general. In several respects Christian institutions found Israeli bureaucracy less irksome than Jordanian.

For all these reasons, Christians were generally unwilling, at the start of Israeli rule, to participate in anti-Israeli activity. In July and August 1967 Christian leaders succumbed to Israeli pressure, in the form of an order from the District Commissioner for Jerusalem, and refused to sign public protests against Israeli rule.[7] By December the official in charge of Jerusalem affairs in the Israeli Foreign Ministry could note with satisfaction that the heads of the Churches were 'privately thankful that things have changed since the unification of the city in which freedom of religion and religious education are now secured'.[8] At the end of the year the heads of all the Churches in east Jerusalem were invited to the Israeli President's annual reception for heads of Christian communities in Israel. The Greek and Armenian Patriarchs both accepted; the Latin did not, though he held friendly conversations with Israeli officials.

In Bethlehem, which had been allocated to the greater Jerusalem *corpus separatum* by the UN in 1947, there were calls from Christian (and some Muslim) notables in July 1967 for the town to be incorporated into an expanded Jerusalem municipality – and therefore into Israel. After the petition became public, however, it was explained that the main object of the Bethlehemites was not annexation by Israel but rather 'their wish not to be separated from Jerusalem with which the life of Bethlehem was bound up'.[9] The Israelis rejected the idea of incorporating Bethlehem in Jerusalem, given the large accretion of Arab population (including a growing Muslim element) that this would have brought to Israel's capital, though in later years Shimon Peres tried half-heartedly to revive the idea.[10]

As in the period between 1949 and 1967, Israel initially developed happier relations with the Greek Patriarchate than with the Latin, reflecting the former's conflict with its Arab laity and the latter's greater Arabization. Initial Greek complaints about Israeli policy subsided as it emerged that the new rulers had no intention of interfering with the status quo at the holy places.[11] In November 1967, after a meeting with Prime Minister Eshkol, Patriarch Benediktos submitted a long memorandum recapitulating the history of the Greeks' rights at the holy places and affirming that Israel's 'absolute respect and protection to the Holy Shrines' and 'eager disposition to enlarge the rights and privileges of the Religious Communities, such as the Diplomatic Immunity, the use of foreign currency for dealings abroad etc' brought 'great honour to the State of Israel'.[12] The Hellenic Brotherhood were restored to their position of dominance in the Church and the limited moves towards Arabization undertaken in the Jordanian period were reversed.[13] When a new Patriarch had to be elected in 1980, an Arabic-speaking Greek was elected, Israel and Jordan cooperating happily in the arrangements. Once again demands for representation by the Arab laity were swept aside.[14]

The Israelis made a particular effort to cultivate the Armenian Patriarchate. In the early 1980s, however, they, like the Jordanians in their day, became damagingly entangled in the complex internal politics of the Armenian community.[15] A bitter dispute between the Armenian Patriarch, Yeghishe Derderian, and the Archbishop of Jerusalem, Shahe Ajamian, rent the Armenian community. Ajamian, who was regarded as particularly close to the Israelis, was deposed by the Patriarch. His successor, an Australian citizen, was threatened with deportation by the Israelis. In 1985 Ajamian's house was set on fire and one of his supporters stabbed.[16] On the other hand, growing prosperity and large donations from the Armenian Diaspora facilitated renovation of the historic buildings of the quarter. In 1990 the election as Patriarch of Torkom Manookian, who had spent many years in the United States, brought an American style of modernization to the Patriarchate. Israel valued good relations with the Armenians, both as a non-Arab Christian element in the old city and on account of their connections with the Armenian homeland. But they lost their way in the labyrinth of Armenian politics and found it hard to capitalize on the investment they made in cultivating Armenian friendship.

Israel encountered even greater difficulties in its relations with the Roman Catholic Church and those other Churches (such as the Greek Catholics) that recognized the authority of the Pope. The Israeli Foreign Ministry had at first hoped that the Vatican was moving towards the idea that only the holy places and not the city as a whole should be internationalized.[17] This hope was initially dashed. A note circulated by the Vatican observer at the United Nations on 24 June 1967 explained, 'The Holy See remains ... convinced that the only solution which offers a sufficient guarantee for the protection of Jerusalem and of its holy places is to place that city and its vicinity under an international regime.' An Israeli representative had visited Rome a little earlier to try to persuade the Vatican of the merits of the Israeli scheme for 'functional internationalization' of the holy places only, but the Vatican note made it clear that this was not acceptable: 'In Jerusalem the holy places are so numerous throughout the city that it is not possible to separate the two questions, namely that of Jerusalem and that of the holy places.'[18]

The Vatican did, however, offer various hints suggesting that it would be satisfied with internationalization of a much more limited area than that envisaged by the *corpus separatum* of 1948. On 16 June Pope Paul VI told a meeting of Cardinals that Jerusalem must have 'its own internationally guaranteed constitution'.[19] Subsequent quasi-official announcements by the Vatican conformed to this more restricted line on internationalization.[20] In a private conversation with a British diplomat the Deputy Secretary of State, Monsignor Casaroli, explained that:

> they realized that there was no likelihood of the Israelis relinquishing control, at least of the New City. For the Old City, present Vatican thinking was that in the long term something more would be necessary than a simple Israel guarantee of free access to the holy places. The Old City should be treated as a whole and given some form of international regime. The Vatican had an open mind as to the form of any such regime but they did not place much confidence in the United Nations after its recent show of impotence.

The diplomat gathered that the Vatican was thinking instead of working out an arrangement directly with Israel, Jordan and 'representatives of the various religious bodies interested in the City.'[21]

In July 1967 a special delegate, Monsignor Angelo Felici, an Under-Secretary of State, was sent by the Vatican to hold discussions with the Israelis and with the eastern Church leaders in Jerusalem on the subject of the holy places and Jerusalem in general. The Israelis discussed with him their ideas for the transfer of the Christian holy places to a committee comprised of representatives of the various Christian communities. From these talks and other contacts with the Vatican, the Israelis learned of a significant evolution in the Vatican's position. It no longer insisted on complete internationalization of Jerusalem or even of part of it, but would be satisfied with an international statute that would guarantee the Christian holy places and also the rights of the Christian communities in the city. Significantly, Pope Paul VI, in his consistorial allocution on 22 December 1967, spoke about the holy places and about religious and civil rights but did not call for internationalization of the city.[22]

Felici tried but failed to secure the support of the Armenian and Greek Patriarchs. The Armenian Patriarch, Yeghishe Derderian, took care to report his discussion with Felici to the Israelis.[23] The Greek Patriarch Benediktos took exception to Felici's mission and addressed a strongly worded message to the Israeli Prime Minister, Levi Eshkol, insisting that 'the Pope and the Vatican have no competence to discuss questions of the holy places'.[24] Benediktos told an Israeli official that if the Vatican concluded an agreement with Israel on the subject, then he, as owner of two-thirds of the holy places, would oppose it. He added that he was opposed to internationalization, whether of the city or of the holy places alone.[25] The two Patriarchs, concerned at the apparent danger that the Vatican might conclude a separate agreement directly with the Israelis, persuaded the Anglican Archbishop to go to London with a message to the Archbishop of Canterbury, pleading for his support and complaining that Felici had come to Jerusalem 'to take and not to give.'[26] The Secretary-General of the World Council of Churches also expressed disquiet over Felici's mission and declared that his body (comprising most Protestant Churches) could 'not silently tolerate any deal with Rome that subordinates [the] position [of] ancient churches'.[27]

Israel came to no such arrangement with the Vatican or any of the other Churches. Instead it clung, like its predecessors, to the sacred principle of the status quo, both at the holy places and more generally in its relations with Christian institutions in Jerusalem.

The trend towards Arabization of the Churches, with the significant exception of the Greek Orthodox, accelerated under Israeli rule. In 1976 the first Arab Anglican bishop, Faiq Haddad, was consecrated and in December 1987 Michel Sabbah became the first Arab (also the first non-Italian) Latin Patriarch of Jerusalem. In the long term Arabization had political consequences that were unwelcome to Israel. The *intifada* was marked by a pronounced surge of Islamic fervour that tended to alarm Christian Arabs, who generally held aloof from the violence. Nevertheless, Christian Arabs, both lay and clerical, were prominent as spokespersons of the Palestinian cause – most notably Hanan Ashrawi of Bir Zeit University near Ramallah. Sabbah, born in Nazareth, had succeeded the Italian Giacomo Giuseppe Beltritti. He openly supported the rebellion, declaring at Easter 1988, 'It is normal for the people to rebel and say "enough" after twenty years of occupation.'[28] The Israelis sought to censor Sabbah's sermons and entered vigorous complaints with the Vatican about his endorsement of the *intifada*. According to the Israeli Ministry of Religious Affairs, he was reprimanded by the Vatican. He nevertheless remained outspoken in his public utterances and Israeli-Vatican relations were adversely affected. Even the Armenian Patriarch, Derderian, signed a collective statement of protest with the heads of other Churches in Jerusalem at Easter 1989.[29]

In April 1990 Israeli relations with the Christian communities in east Jerusalem took a further turn for the worse when armed right-wing Israeli diehards, protected by 150 policemen, occupied the Hospice of St John, a seventy-two-room building near the Church of the Holy Sepulchre. The new residents hung a star of David over the cross in the door-frame. In response to indignant Christian protests, they claimed to have permission from the Armenian leaseholder of the building. Later the Israeli government admitted that it had provided $1.8 million to a 'Panamanian' company that had sub-let the building.[30] The Prime Minister, Yitzhak Shamir, backed the occupation publicly and his spokesman described the government's contribution as 'an ordinary real-estate transaction'.[31] Although the hospice was not on the official list of holy places, Christian opinion was outraged. The Greek Orthodox Patriarch, Diodoros I, who claimed ownership of the site, hung out black flags on his headquarters and other Church heads signed a joint statement of solidarity.[32]

The prelate was overcome by tear-gas fumes when he joined a demonstration against the occupation of the hospice. Teddy Kollek, left-wing Israelis and Palestinian Muslims joined the protests. The affair took on an international character as the Pope, the US State Department, the *New York Times*, American Jewish organizations, President Saddam Hussein of Iraq, the Greek Orthodox Archdiocese of North and South America and the European Parliament all joined the chorus of criticism of the Israeli government on the issue. Although most of the militants were evicted in early May, after a Supreme Court order, twelve were still living there in February 1991. Meanwhile similar occupations and counter-protests continued over the next few years in other Arab areas of the city.

Israel's relations with the Vatican nevertheless took a dramatic turn for the better in the early 1990s. The main reason was the opening of the Madrid peace conference and the Vatican desire not to be left without a say in any settlement of the question of Jerusalem and the holy places. Another reason, perhaps the most historically significant, was the evolution of Catholic theological attitudes towards the Jews since the Second Vatican Council.[33] A third was the desire of the aged and ailing Pope John Paul II to go on a pilgrimage to the Holy Land before his death. (Pope Paul VI had visited the Holy Land in 1964 but, since most of the holy places were then in Jordanian hands, he had spent barely twenty-four hours in Israel, hardly acknowledged his Israeli hosts and did not utter the word 'Israel'. The Israelis would not countenance a second such snub.) A fourth reason was pressure from Italian politicians, driven by public sympathy for Israel's endurance and forbearance in the face of Iraqi missile attacks during the Gulf War in early 1991. And a fifth was the formalization of the Vatican's withdrawal from sponsorship of internationalization of Jerusalem. When Cardinal O'Connor of New York visited Israel in January 1992 he confirmed that the Vatican 'ha[d] no particular interest in who controls Jerusalem' but simply sought free access to the holy places and 'equal rights for everyone'.[34]

Secret Israeli-Vatican talks began in 1991. In July 1992 the two states announced the formation of a joint commission. After lengthy but cordial negotiations, an accord was reached on 30 December 1993 that provided for the first time for the establishment of diplomatic relations between Israel and the Holy See. As if to show balance, the Vatican announced that it was also opening talks with a view to establishing diplomatic relations with Jordan. Jerusalem was not mentioned in the text of the treaty. But it was understood that the Vatican was now seeking no more than what Monsignor Claudio Celli, the Vatican representative at the signing ceremony, called 'an international warranty in order to protect, to save, to recognize the particularity of the city for the three monotheistic religions'.[35] The agreement stirred some concern among Latin Christians in Jerusalem. The Patriarch stressed that the Vatican had not recognized Israeli sovereignty over the city.[36] The Vatican envoy to be sent to Israel would reside in Jaffa rather than Jerusalem. In October 1994 the Vatican announced that it had reached agreement on the establishment of formal relations with the PLO.[37] These took even longer to conclude but in February 2000 the Vatican and the Palestinian Authority signed a treaty to 'normalize relations'. With the establishment of diplomatic relations with both Israel and the Palestinians, and against the background of the end of the *intifada* and Israeli-Palestinian diplomatic détente, the way was now open for the Pope to visit the Holy Land.

John Paul II's pilgrimage to Jerusalem the following month was the climax of millennial-year celebrations by the Latins in Palestine and by Catholics worldwide. It reinforced the centrality of Jerusalem in the spiritual life of Christians throughout the world. It demonstrated to all that the era of Christian triumphalism was long past. And it sealed the difficult reconciliation between the Church and Judaism. The Pope took care to show sensitivity to the concerns of Jews as well as Muslims. On a visit to Yad Vashem, the memorial to the victims of Nazi genocide, he acknowledged the historic failings of the Christian

Church in its conduct towards Jews. By prior arrangement, he was not accompanied by an Israeli government official when he visited holy places in the old city, including the Muslim shrines on the Temple Mount (though several hundred mainly religious Jews demonstrated against him). A few discordant notes were struck at an inter-faith meeting with leaders of all three faiths: the Ashkenazi Chief Rabbi of Israel, Yisrael Meir Lau, thanked the Pope for his 'recognition of Jerusalem as Israel's united, eternal capital'. The Vatican had issued no such recognition. The mufti of Jerusalem, Sheikh Akram Sabri, on the other hand, boycotted the ceremony on the ground that it involved recognition of Israeli sovereignty over Jerusalem. His stand-in, Sheikh Tatzir Tamimi, head of the Palestinian Authority's Muslim religious courts, used the occasion to denounce Israel for committing 'genocide' as well as 'strangling Jerusalem and oppressing its residents'.[38]

The new relationship between Israel and the Vatican fuelled concern among Orthodox Christians that their interests might be ignored. The Greek Orthodox Patriarch, Diodoros I, pointed out in 1994, 'The Vatican does not represent us.'[39] Another historic fault-line emerged in a statement from the senior Greek Orthodox bishop in Jerusalem, Metropolitan Timotheos. Evidently worried by the new tone of relations between Israel and Russia, he declared, 'Only the Greek Orthodox Church is the local church and self-administering, with no other authority outside of Jerusalem.'[40] But from the Russian ambassador to Israel, Alexander Bovin, came echoes of the past: 'In this question, the Russian church has got to be involved,' he said in a newspaper interview.[41] The old protectorate of the Orthodox, it appeared, was not yet quite dead.

Reds and whites

Although cut off from their homeland by the Great War, the revolution and then the civil war, the Russian institutions in Palestine somehow survived intact and with their intense, inward-looking religiosity unimpaired. The last patroness of the Imperial Orthodox Palestine Society, the Grand Duchess Elizabeth Feodorovna, suffered a terrible fate. Two days after the murder of the Tsar, she, together with members of her family, was thrown down a mine shaft in Siberia, shot and wounded, then left to die. Their remains were found by advancing forces of the counter-revolutionary Admiral Kolchak, who sent them to China. In 1920–21 they were brought to Jerusalem in a British navy vessel and buried near the Russian Church of Gethsemane. The solemn occasion was symbolic of the travails of Russian imperialism in Palestine, but also of its enduring spiritual essence. About the same time the Palestine government agreed to allow several hundred Russian women refugees to settle in convents in Palestine. The Russian priests, monks and nuns, stranded in Jerusalem, came to regard themselves as guardians of a sacred cause. Like many other exiles from the French revolution onwards, their *ancien regime* style of life and way of thought congealed for the next three-quarters of a century.

By 1927 the Russian Orthodox Church had split into several jurisdictions: a communist-controlled 'red' Church ruled from Moscow and three separate 'white' Orthodox groups supported by Russian exiles hostile to the revolution. One of the 'white' groups, the Synod of the Russian Church in Exile, based initially at Sremski-Karlovci (Karlovtzy) in Yugoslavia, attracted the support of the Russian ecclesiastical mission in Palestine.

Following British recognition of the Soviet government in 1924, the mandatory administration in Palestine was presented with an immediate demand by the Soviets for recognition of their rights of ownership over all Russian Church and government property in Palestine. These included important buildings in the old city of Jerusalem, the onion-domed Church of St Mary Magdalene near the Garden of Gethsemane, and the beautiful white-and-green Orthodox cathedral and large surrounding compound in the heart of west Jerusalem –

not to mention extensive real estate elsewhere in Palestine. The government resisted the demand, taking cover behind article 13 of the mandate, which, as a later Foreign Office memorandum put it, 'laid upon His Majesty's Government a clear duty to protect these ecclesiastical properties against a Government which had no claim to be regarded as a protector of Christian interests'.[42] For fear that the Russians might have recourse to law to regain their property, an ordinance was passed removing from the jurisdiction of the courts any matter involving holy places. The effect of this was to leave the properties in the hands of the 'whites'.

There the matter remained for two decades. It was reopened in 1943. By then the British government found itself the ally of a Soviet Russia in which the Orthodox Church was mobilized by Stalin on behalf of the patriotic war effort. The British now reconsidered their view. Churchill decided that, 'in the light of our present relations with the Soviet Government and of the changed status of the Orthodox Church', renewed Russian claims 'would be difficult to resist'.[43] Rather than handing over the property, however, British officials resorted to the time-honoured Whitehall tactic of sending the thing for further study. Investigations were protracted and in due course wartime alliance gave way to Cold War and the thought of transferring holy places to a godless regime again appeared out of the question. When the Russians presented their demands anew in March 1945, the Foreign Office, after further study lasting thirteen months, rejected the claim.[44]

Meanwhile, however, in May 1944 the Soviets had achieved a partial victory by winning the allegiance of some of the surviving Russian clergy in Jerusalem. A year later, after the end of the war in Europe, Patriarch Alexii of Moscow visited Jerusalem, where he met Russian and Greek clergy, although he was reported to have been 'not too successful' with the latter.[45] In early 1948, with the end of the mandate in sight, the Palestine government decided to promulgate a law vesting control of the Russian properties in Palestine in British-appointed trustees. The *Vaadat Ha-matzav* (situation committee) of the Jewish Agency discovered this; shortly afterwards the Haganah blew up the government printing press. The law was thus never gazetted.[46] It seems never to have taken effect. In May 1948, just before the end of the mandate, the Soviet government applied unsuccessfully to the British government for the handing over to their diplomatic mission in Egypt of all Russian property in Palestine.[47] In the chaos that ensued the Soviets tried to get the Czechoslovak, Yugoslav and Polish consuls-general to secure 'temporary custodianship of moveable property, real estate, archives and documents belong to the Russian Orthodox Society' – but to no avail.[48]

The result, after the dust cleared, was a divided Russian Church in a divided city. Following the Israel–Jordan armistice agreement of April 1949, the Russian properties in Jerusalem were separated by barbed wire and minefields. Those in the old city and the Gethsemane Church on the Mount of Olives were held by Jordan, which had no diplomatic relations with the Soviet Union. With the approval of the British, Jordan decided to maintain the status quo and recognized the rights of the 'whites'. The Russian compound and cathedral in west Jerusalem found themselves in the centre of what became Israel's capital. Archimandrite Antonii, head of the Russian Ecclesiastical Mission, was placed under house arrest by the Israelis. After pressure from the International Red Cross, he was released and left for east Jerusalem.[49] Other Russian priests and monks abandoned the buildings in west Jerusalem and fled to east Jerusalem. The Israelis took over the empty structures for use by government offices and the Supreme Court. As early as August 1949, diplomatic rumours were circulating that the reason for Russian opposition to internationalization of Jerusalem was that 'they would much sooner deal directly with the Israelis over Russian property in Jerusalem than with an international body'.[50] In fact, the Israelis had promised informally, even before the establishment of the state, that they would recognize Soviet rights to the Russian properties in Palestine. Shabtai Rosenne, who later became legal adviser to the Israeli Foreign Ministry, had held a meeting on the subject with a Soviet representative in London in December 1947 at which such an assurance was given. Negotiations on the details, however, dragged on for many years.

In early 1950 the Israelis, seeking to maintain the favour of the Soviet Union, formally recognized the representatives of the Soviet-controlled Moscow Patriarchate as having administrative authority over the Russian ecclesiastical mission in Jerusalem. Thenceforth the Israeli government paid rent to the Soviets for Russian-owned buildings that it occupied.

The Israelis offered to buy most of the properties and the Soviets agreed in principle. But a number of complications prevented speedy agreement. Some of the properties were registered in the name of the Tsarist government, of which the USSR claimed to be the legal successor; others in the name of the Romanov family or the Grand Duke Sergei as representative of the Imperial Orthodox Palestine Society; and the remainder in the name of the Russian Orthodox Church. Eventually, in October 1964 agreement was reached on the sale to Israel of the greater part of the Russian compound, with the exception of the cathedral in its centre and one other building. Other Russian properties were also sold at about the same time. Part of the price was a shipload of oranges.[51] The rest of the payment was in dollars, but the Soviets asked for a guarantee against devaluation. Israel then asked in reciprocity for a guarantee against third-party claims. A ceremony took place at the Israeli Foreign Ministry at which the Soviet ambassador and the Foreign Minister, Golda Meir, signed the treaty. A little later the telephone rang in the office of the ministry's legal adviser. A lady who claimed to be the daughter of Anastasia, the Romanov princess who had allegedly survived the murder of the royal family in 1918, was on the line demanding her property back. She was told to submit her application in triplicate, but was never heard from again, although reports appeared in 1966 that persons purporting to be heirs of the Grand Duke Sergei were planning to lodge claims.[52]

The question of properties was only part of a larger complex of issues connected with the Orthodox Church that exercised the Israelis between 1949 and 1967. They followed with fascination the relationship between the Soviets and the Greek Orthodox hierarchy in Jerusalem. In a 'top secret' memorandum in September 1949, the Israeli diplomat Jacob Herzog wrote to Reuven Shiloah, head of the Israeli intelligence service, noting a remarkable historic rapprochement: the Greek Orthodox Patriarchate in the old city was drawing close to the representatives of the (pro-Soviet) Russian Orthodox Church in west Jerusalem, headed since the previous November by the Archimandrite Leonid. Friendly visits had been exchanged and a joint service had even been celebrated in west Jerusalem in the presence of Soviet and Greek consuls. In spite of the long hostility between the Patriarchate and the Russian communists, the two sides were reportedly being drawn together by their common opposition to the internationalization of Jerusalem.[53]

But a British consular report a few months later suggested that the Patriarchate was playing something of a double game: 'There has been considerable intrigue over this matter within the Greek Patriarchate here. The Patriarch himself, who is very anti-Russian, is perfectly content that the Holy Places should remain under King Abdullah's protection, and is against internationalisation on the ground that this will inevitably lead to Russian dominance in the Orthodox Church here.'[54]

In January 1952 it was reported that the Soviets had re-established the Russian Palestine Society (the word 'imperial' had apparently been dropped from the title). A little later the Archimandrite Ignatius Polykarp, accompanied by five assistants, arrived to head the Russian ecclesiastical mission in Jerusalem. He was said to be 'one of the most brilliant products of the Soviet-controlled theological academies', and more subtle than his predecessor in Jerusalem, who had tried, without success, to bribe the Greek Orthodox Patriarch Timotheos with a large sum in gold. In the febrile atmosphere of the Cold War, the inevitable consequence was an effort in New York to raise funds for the impoverished Patriarchate from impeccably anti-communist sources.[55] In spite of this competitive bidding war, however, neither reds nor whites seem to have been able to solve the patriarchate's perennial financial problems.

Suddenly, in June 1952, the British consulate-general reported the appearance of potential salvation from a new quarter:

> The opportunity offered to the Russians by the extreme poverty of the Orthodox Patriarchate will soon disappear if certain current negotiations between the Patriarchate and the Israelis succeed. The Israelis are at present, incredible as it may seem, offering the Patriarchate something like £300,000 in *sterling cash down* for a 99-year lease of certain lands in Israeli-held Jerusalem. Other lands may come under the same treatment, and the Patriarchate is already benefiting very substantially, or will very soon do so from yet another lease signed earlier: they are due to get from this about £50,000 *sterling* a year for two years, and £17,000 *sterling* a year for 13 years thereafter. The expenditure which they have to meet amounts to about £50,000.[56]

Thereafter the Greek Patriarchate in Jerusalem recognized only the 'red' Church and had no dealings with its competitors, based in New York.[57]

As a result of the 1967 war Israel faced new complications regarding the Russian properties in east Jerusalem. Within a few days of the end of the war the 'white' Orthodox Church, based in New York, sent two clergymen to Jerusalem to establish contact with the Israelis and try to ensure that the properties they controlled in east Jerusalem would not be turned over to Soviet control.

Logical consistency, one might have thought, would dictate that the

Israelis apply the same rule to east as to west Jerusalem and hand over the Russian properties there to the Soviets – particularly since the Israeli government incorporated east Jerusalem within Israel and insisted that it was not occupied territory and that the normal rules concerning maintenance of the status quo under military occupation should not apply there.

But in the meantime a revolution had occurred in Israeli-Soviet relations. The USSR had broken off relations with Israel, leaving behind as the only Soviet representatives there a small group of nuns, three priests, an administrative secretary and a driver. All were kept under close scrutiny by the Israeli security service, which suspected that some at least were intelligence agents. The USSR was conducting a propaganda war against Israel and encouraging its allies to do the same. Moscow was also rearming Israel's sworn enemies. The Israeli government had no reason to reward the Soviets by handing over any property in east Jerusalem. It therefore decided to maintain the status quo on the express condition that the 'whites' undertook not to contest the agreement that Israel had signed with the Soviets recognizing 'red' ownership of the properties in west Jerusalem and elsewhere in Israel.[58]

The visiting 'white' emissaries were accordingly given a warm welcome by the Israeli authorities and the Minister of Religious Affairs personally took them in his car to their shrines on the Mount of Olives. Shortly afterwards Metropolitan Philaret, the head of the 'white' Church, put in a formal request, in its capacity as successor to the Russian Palestine Society, for confirmation of 'white' ownership of the holy places that his Church had hitherto controlled under Jordanian rule.[59] In his reply, the Israeli ambassador in Washington, Abraham Harman, assured the Metropolitan 'that the Holy Places of your Church are safe'.[60] This was, of course, cunningly worded: on the one hand, it half suggested recognition of the whites' claims. And indeed the Israelis did not interfere with the status quo at the white-controlled shrines in east Jerusalem. At the same time they gave no explicit confirmation of ownership to the whites, thus keeping a card up their sleeves for possible dealing with the reds – who, after all, potentially had much more to offer the Israelis.

The Soviet Union, however, found itself awkwardly situated in pressing the red claim. In the first place, it did not recognize the Israeli annexation of east Jerusalem. Moreover, since the Soviets had withdrawn their diplomatic representatives from Israel they could not present any claim directly. After a year or so of wrestling with this quandary, they therefore took the only course open to them and did so indirectly. In 1968 the head of the 'red' ecclesiastical mission in Jerusalem submitted a claim to the Israeli Ministry of Religious Affairs, demanding that the 'white'-controlled properties in east Jerusalem be handed over to his mission. The Israelis, who had rushed with such alacrity to satisfy the Soviets in 1950, now adopted a standoffish approach. The head of the Christian Communities Department in the Ministry of Religious Affairs, Dr Saul Colbi, declared publicly, 'To adjudge claims and counter-claims between the two rival churches at this stage is not our business.'[61] Following this rebuff, TASS issued a statement denying that any such demand had even been presented. All the Archimandrite had done, it was explained, 'was to inform the Israeli authorities that the "émigré group" [i.e. the 'whites'] had no right to sell land or buildings or negotiate for new building'.[62]

The Israelis would not budge and the strange consequence was Israeli maintenance of the status quo in favour of the 'whites' in east Jerusalem and of the 'reds' in the west of a city which Israel insisted was united, with no legal difference between its parts. The Russian ecclesiastical mission remained one of the few official links between Israel and the USSR and it was rumoured that the cathedral in Jerusalem had been turned into a KGB intelligence station. From time to time in the 1970s and 1980s the Soviets utilized this tenuous connection and sent Church emissaries to Israel – the only official Soviet representatives to visit the country.

Meanwhile, the Russians continued to use the Jerusalem issue in other ways as a kind of bait to tempt the Israelis. As in the past, they appeared to indicate a less rigid position on Jerusalem than the western powers. For example, at a very low point in Israeli fortunes, in December 1973, when the Soviet Foreign Minister, Andrei Gromyko, met his Israeli counterpart at the United Nations, he took the opportunity to mention that Jerusalem was low down on the list of Soviet concerns, implying a readiness to accept the de facto position of Israeli rule over the whole city.[63] In September 1980 an international Islamic conference, convened in Tashkent by the Grand Mufti of Central Asia, Ziayutdin Babakhanov, was abruptly closed when Arab delegates proposed resolutions on Jerusalem regarded as too extreme by their Soviet hosts.[64]

In the late 1980s came another turn of the wheel. Following the accession to power of Mikhail Gorbachev, the USSR cautiously moved towards a renewal of relations with Israel. In 1987 the USSR sent a consular delegation to Israel, the first of its kind for twenty years, supposedly to survey Russian properties and renew the passports of Soviet citizens. The visit eventually resulted in a resumption of diplomatic relations, which was announced on 18 October 1991 – two months before the collapse of the Soviet Union. In the short time that was left to it, the USSR did not press any claim for Russian properties in east Jerusalem, Hebron or Jericho; it did not, in any case, wish to appear to give recognition to the Israeli occupation of Jerusalem and the West Bank. After the fall of the Soviet Union turmoil ensued in the 'white' Russian Church as a result of attempts to reunite it with the Moscow Patriarchate. The Israeli government now began to hint that it might resolve the issue by recognizing the rights of the Moscow Patriarchate to all Russian Church property in Israel and the occupied territories. Israel, however, took no action against the 'whites' in Jerusalem and the occupied territories.

Matters came to a head again as a result of the 1993 Israel-Palestinian agreement and the subsequent withdrawal of Israeli forces from parts of the West Bank. Some of the 'white' Russian property, though not yet any in east Jerusalem, now found itself under Palestinian authority. In June 1997 the Russian Orthodox Patriarch Alexii II visited Yasir Arafat and secured from him a commitment to support the Moscow Patriarchate in its claims to property in Palestinian-held areas. Arafat owed a great deal to the Soviet Union and after 1991 maintained good relations with Russia. He therefore complied with the request. As an earnest of his intentions, he ordered a police assault on the 'white' Russian-held Abraham's Oak Monastery in Hebron, in which several monks and nuns were beaten about and evicted. In January 2000 there was a similar incident at a monastery near Jericho: two 'white' nuns based at the Mary Magdalene Convent in Jerusalem resisted attempts by Palestinian police to remove them. 'I rushed to the Jericho monastery. I saw the head of the ['red'] Russian patriarchate there with a whole load of Palestinian soldiers. I saw two monks taken away. They tried to take me but I fought back and eventually the police let me go,' said Sister Maria Stephanopoulos (a sister of George Stephanopoulos, a former senior assistant to President Clinton). The nuns started a hunger strike in protest. Eventually, after the intervention of the US consul-general, a compromise was reached whereby they were permitted to stay in an empty hut near the monastery 'until the issue is resolved'.[65]

The fate of the Russian holy places in Jerusalem remained open. Their future would depend on whether the Russian Orthodox Church would reunite and whether sovereignty in Jerusalem would redivide. Like everything else in the city, the crux of the matter was the feasibility of an agreement about Jerusalem between Israel and the Palestinians.

9   Creeping Partition

The Oslo Agreement left the Jerusalem question open for discussion. This, in itself, represented a dramatic change. Ever since 1967 the position of all Israeli governments, at least as presented to the Israeli population, had been that the Jerusalem question was closed: Jerusalem had been 'unified', was the 'eternal capital' of Israel and could not be a subject for negotiation. Now, suddenly, Jerusalem was back on the table. While the determination of its future was nominally postponed for two years, pending the start of 'final status' negotiations for a comprehensive Israeli-Palestinian settlement, the reality was that both sides immediately began jostling for position.

The Beilin-Abu Mazen agreement

The euphoria that surrounded the handshake between Rabin and Arafat on the White House lawn in September 1993 soon dissipated. The nationalist right in Israel launched a bitter campaign against Rabin, accusing him of betraying the national interest and vowing to resist territorial withdrawal. Some hot spirits called for violent action; other even more extreme elements began planning to carry it out. On 25 February 1994 an Israeli fanatic, Baruch Goldstein, carrying an M-16 rifle, entered a mosque at the Cave of the Patriarchs in Hebron, a holy place shared by Muslims and Jews, and shot dead twenty-nine people while they were at prayer. Over 100 more were injured before he was overpowered and killed. His supporters among the Jewish settler community in Hebron turned his grave into a shrine, visited by hundreds of admirers, and published a memorial book celebrating his deed. The massacre led to protest demonstrations and a riot on the

Haram al-Sharif, which was cleared and closed for a time by the Israeli police.

Palestinian anguish over this incident was fanned by the policies of the municipality in Jerusalem, now headed by the right-wing Ehud Olmert, and also by some actions of the Rabin government. In its policies on residential construction in and around Jerusalem, the Labour-dominated government did not seem very different from its right-wing predecessor: it continued to expropriate land and to lay plans for large-scale Jewish housing developments in the 'Greater Jerusalem' area beyond the municipal limits. Olmert's decision in 1994 to close down the municipality's Arab Affairs office, which had been set up by Kollek in 1967 in an effort to maintain some links with east Jerusalem Arab leaders, had little practical effect, but it was seen as symbolic of the difference in outlook of the two mayors. Another was Olmert's encouragement of Jewish settlement in mainly Arab areas of east Jerusalem, including the Muslim quarter of the old city, Silwan, Ras al-Amud and Wadi Joz.

In 1995–6 the Israeli position in Jerusalem suffered a setback. In an effort to increase tourism and strengthen Israel's international position in Jerusalem, plans had been initiated some years earlier by then-mayor Kollek for an elaborate programme of celebration of the supposed three-thousandth anniversary of the foundation of the city by King David. The scheme was taken up with enthusiasm by his successor and its emphasis was turned in a political direction. The jollifications attracted some ridicule and opposition. It was pointed out that the dating seemed more politically opportunistic than historically accurate. Old-timers recalled that the city had, in fact, already marked its three-thousandth birthday forty years earlier. Arab Jerusalemites refused to have anything to do with what they saw as a Zionist propaganda scheme. And ultra-orthodox Jews also opposed the project. They took exception to a proposed show about King David, written by Tim Rice (librettist of *Jesus Christ Superstar*), that was to be staged in connection with the festivities. A city councillor for the ultra-orthodox Yahadut Ha-Torah party expressed fear lest David's relationship with Jonathan be portrayed 'in distorted ways'. And the deputy mayor, Haim Miller, a member of the same party, complained that Jerusalem was being 'transformed into a jungle' and demanded that the show be dropped from the programme.[1] The year-long event dwindled into an embarrassment and ended as a flop.

Nor were Israelis reassured by renewed terrorist attacks, wild anti-Israeli propaganda by the Muslim Hamas movement and provocative anti-Israeli demonstrations in Gaza and the West Bank. In May 1994 the atmosphere was further soured after Yasir Arafat, in a speech at a mosque in South Africa, called for a *jihad* to liberate east Jerusalem. Arafat's remarks were recorded and broadcast on Israel radio, leading to predictably outraged Israeli responses. Against this background, the prospects for further progress towards a comprehensive settlement seemed bleak.

The designation of Jerusalem as a 'final status' issue did not, however, prevent informal discussions among Israeli and Palestinian intellectuals and politicians to try to lay the groundwork for such an agreement. These disclosed some surprising areas of common ground. Talks of this kind predated the Oslo Agreement and began in a similar 'back-channel', informal manner. One set of informal discussions took place in London in the summer of 1992. The Israeli participants included Moshe Amirav, a maverick member of the Jerusalem municipality who had crossed over from the Likud to the left-wing Meretz party. The Palestinians included Hanna Siniora, the journalist who had briefly considered running for the municipality in 1987.

Shortly after the signature of the Oslo Agreement, an intriguing kite was flown in public by the Israeli Deputy Foreign Minister, Yossi Beilin. A confidant of the Foreign Minister, Shimon Peres, who was his chief political patron, Beilin had on previous occasions been ready to test public opinion by stretching the bounds of the sayable beyond the usual constraints of government policy and conventional wisdom.

On this occasion he mused about the possibility of Israel's agreeing to Palestinian administrative control of parts of east Jerusalem. Although this did not sound very different from the long-dormant 'borough' proposal, Beilin was immediately reprimanded by its originator, Teddy Kollek, who wrote to him, 'Your [ideas] are totally incomprehensible. We saw in the reunification of the city in 1967 the practical realization of the Zionist movement's goals. Will we now, with such ease, give up on a united Jerusalem?'[2]

Later it emerged that Beilin's remarks were no mere academic speculations. They reflected secret talks that he had begun with a Palestinian leader, Mahmoud Abbas (better known by his *nom de guerre* Abu Mazen), a close adviser to Arafat who, like Beilin, had played a major role in the discussions leading to the Oslo Agreement. Beilin and Abu Mazen held about twenty meetings between the autumn of 1993 and the spring of 1995 in Jerusalem, Cyprus and various places in Europe. The discussions focused on all aspects of a possible 'final status' agreement, but it was the conclusions that were reached regarding Jerusalem that came to excite the greatest interest – and criticism. On 31 October 1995 the two men agreed in Tel Aviv on the text of a 'framework for the conclusion of a final status agreement between Israel and the Palestine Liberation Organization'.

This remarkable document boldly attempted to resolve all outstanding issues between Israel and the Palestinians. It called for the creation of a Palestinian state within agreed borders. Israeli forces would withdraw from 94 per cent of the West Bank, including the Jordan valley and the whole of the Gaza Strip. A land bridge would be created between Gaza and the West Bank. The Palestinian state would be demilitarized and Israel would maintain three early warning stations and agreed levels of forces on its territory pending peace treaties with neighbouring Arab states. Israeli settlements in the area of the Palestinian state would be dismantled ('There will be no exclusive civilian residential areas for Israelis in the state of Palestine'). Israel acknowledged 'the moral and material suffering caused to the

Palestinian people as a result of the war of 1947–9' and further acknowledged 'the Palestinian refugees' right of return to the Palestinian state and their right to compensation and rehabilitation for moral and material loss'. No such agreed statement between responsible Israeli and Palestinian leaders had ever been achieved before during the previous century of conflict.

The Beilin-Abu Mazen draft also came close to providing a blueprint for a solution of the Jerusalem problem. The two men agreed that Jerusalem should 'remain an open and undivided city with free and unimpeded access for people of all faiths and nationalities'. The borders of the city would be expanded to include Abu Dis (some 10 per cent of which was already within the city), al-Azariya, a-Ram, a-Zaim, Maaleh Adumim, Givat Zeev, Givon and some adjacent areas. Within this expanded area, neighbourhoods inhabited by Israelis would become 'Israeli boroughs' and neighbourhoods inhabited by Palestinians would be 'Palestinian boroughs'. The number of Israeli boroughs and of Palestinian boroughs would reflect the Jewish-Arab demographic balance of 2:1. A unified umbrella municipality would be formed for the whole city to be known as the Joint Higher Municipal Council and to consist of representatives of the boroughs. Those representatives would elect the mayor of the city. Given the larger number of Israeli boroughs (reflecting the demographic balance), this would presumably have guaranteed the Jews the mayoralty for the foreseeable future.

The document went on to specify that

> in all matters related to the areas of the 'City of
> Jerusalem' under Palestinian sovereignty, the Joint Higher
> Municipal Council shall seek the consent of the
> Government of Palestine. In all matters related to the
> areas of the 'City of Jerusalem' under Israeli sovereignty,
> the Joint Higher Municipal Council shall seek the consent
> of the Government of Israel.

The effect of this would be to ensure that the built-in Israeli majority on the council could not legislate for the Arab areas of the city. A further safeguard in the same direction was provided by the creation of two sub-municipalities, one Israeli, the other Palestinian. To these would be delegated strong local powers, including local taxation, local services, 'an independent education system', 'separate religious authorities' and 'housing planning and zoning'.

The western (Israeli) part of the city was to be known by its Hebrew name Yerushalayim, and the 'Arab Eastern part of the city, under Palestinian sovereignty' would be called by its Arabic name, al-Quds. Israel would recognize al-Quds as the capital of Palestine. Palestine would recognize Yerushalayim as the capital of Israel.

Now came a crucial clause that indicated continuing lack of agreement on a critical point:

> The ultimate sovereignty of the area outside Yerushalayim
> and al-Quds, but inside the present municipal boundaries
> of Jerusalem, shall be determined by the parties as soon
> as possible. Each party maintains its position regarding
> the sovereign status of this area.

This clause referred to the new Arab city outside the walls but within the municipal area as it had been expanded by Israel since 1967. Beilin felt that, given the Israeli government's commitment to maintain the 'unity' of the city under Israeli sovereignty, he could not agree to its becoming part of the Palestinian state. Abu Mazen felt that, given its centrality to Arab Jerusalem, he could not agree that it should remain permanently part of Israel. The issue of the ultimate sovereignty of this area was therefore postponed for further discussion without prejudice to the rest of the agreement.

Of course, no agreement on Jerusalem could be complete without reference to the Holy Places:

> The Parties acknowledge Jerusalem's unique spiritual and religious role for all three great monotheistic religions. Wishing to promote interfaith relations and harmony among the three great religions, the Parties accordingly agree to guarantee freedom of worship and access to all Holy Sites for members of all faiths and religions without impediment or restriction.

That much was a standard formula to which all could give assent. More difficult to resolve were the details, particularly concerning the old city:

> In recognition of the special status and significance of the Old City area ... for members of the Christian, Jewish and Muslim faiths, the Parties agree to grant this area a special status.

What was this 'special status' to be? This, alas, was not defined in the agreement: nor was the issue of sovereignty in the old city settled. That too would form a subject for ongoing discussions. Some guiding principles for those talks were, however, agreed: the Palestinian sub-municipality was to be responsible for the municipal concerns of the Palestinian citizens residing in the old city area and their local property; the Israeli sub-municipality was to be responsible for the municipal concerns of the Israeli citizens residing in the old city area and their local property. A 'Joint Parity Committee' was to be appointed 'to manage all matters related to the preservation of the unique character of the Old City Area' and to resolve disputes. And for the holy places lying at the heart of Jerusalem and the Jerusalem problem:

> The State of Palestine shall be granted extra-territorial sovereignty over the Haram ash-Sharif under the administration of the al-Quds Awqaf. The present status quo regarding the right of access and prayer for all will be secured.

> The Church of the Holy Sepulchre shall be managed by
> the Palestinian sub-Municipality. The Joint Parity
> Committee shall examine the possibility of assigning extra-
> territorial status to the Church of the Holy Sepulchre.

A little strangely, no mention was made of the Western Wall. Presumably it was taken for granted that this would continue to be administered as sovereign territory by Israel.

A final clause of the Jerusalem section of the agreement concerned
security: 'Supervision of persons and goods transported through the
"City of Jerusalem" shall take place at the exit points.'[3] Again this was
unclear. Would Jerusalem be an open city or a closed one with barriers around it? Would the Israelis still have the right to 'close' the city
to Palestinians wishing to enter it to pray or work, as had frequently
happened since the start of the *intifada*?

In spite of the questions that it raised and the lacunae in certain
central clauses, the agreement represented a surprising achievement.
Even on those points where full agreement had not been achieved
(principally the issue of sovereignty in Arab areas of east Jerusalem
and in the old city), it set out a framework for potential resolution.
Probably no more clearly articulated settlement of the Jerusalem
problem was attainable at that time by leaders wishing to maintain the
support of the broad constituencies that would be necessary to turn
such a deal from a draft into a treaty that could be signed by Yasir
Arafat for the PLO and Yitzhak Rabin for the Israeli government. We
cannot now know whether this agreement could have been turned
into a final peace treaty. Yet the experience of its negotiators in relation to the Oslo Agreement, which had also started out as a similar
'back-channel' document, gave them some ground for optimism.

On 4 November 1995, just four days after the Beilin-Abu Mazen
agreement was finalized, Yitzhak Rabin was shot dead in Tel Aviv. His
successor, Shimon Peres, was no less determined to reach a final
settlement of the Israeli-Palestinian conflict. He had been Beilin's

political patron and the draft agreement undoubtedly reflected his basic approach to the issues involved. But Peres had been demonized by the right as an appeaser of the Arabs. As an unelected Prime Minister, he did not dare proceed immediately to sign such an agreement. Better, he thought, to wait and secure a mandate on his own account from Israeli voters. In the aftermath of the assassination, there had been a huge revulsion from the shrill political rhetoric of the right. No comparable event had ever taken place in Israel and its effect on the entire population was profound. Opinion polls at the time suggested that if Peres called an election immediately he would have been elected at the head of a commanding parliamentary majority. But he felt it dangerous to appear to be exploiting the assassination or riding on the coat-tails of his former Labour Party rival and, more recently, uneasy partner in government. It would be more decent, he thought, and also in the long run more effective, to wait a while and be able later to claim convincingly that he had won the election in his own right. It was one of the most disastrous political calculations in Israel's history.

As rumours about the Beilin-Abu Mazen agreement (at first thought to refer only to Jerusalem) began to circulate, the right seized on the alleged 'threat to Jerusalem' as a stick with which to beat Beilin, his patron Peres and the Labour Party in general. Without releasing the text of the agreement, Beilin defended its compatibility with standing government policy:

> Israel would retain sovereignty over united Jerusalem in
> its current boundaries and can add Maaleh Adumim,
> Givon, and Givat Zeev to the city. Yet the Palestinians
> would be able to take over villages outside Jerusalem such
> as Abu Dis, al-Azariya, or even Ramallah and call it al-
> Quds. Palestinians might retain their right to discuss
> other parts of Jerusalem, but they know this could take a
> generation.[4]

This, however, rather than reassuring critics, inflamed the opposition. Peres felt obliged to distance himself from Beilin. Nevertheless, the Likud announced that their slogan in the forthcoming election would be 'Peres will divide Jerusalem.'[5] An election was finally called for 29 May 1996. But confidence in Peres's leadership was already ebbing.

On 25 February 1996 twenty-five people were killed and fifty injured when a device attached to an Arab suicide-bomber exploded on the number 18 bus in Jerusalem. On 3 March another suicide bomb on the same bus route killed eighteen more people. Further bombings, carried out by Palestinian Muslim fanatics in Jerusalem and elsewhere in Israel, caused additional bloodshed and deeply affected the political psychology of an Israeli population already profoundly shaken by the Rabin assassination. The right capitalized on the bomb attacks, claiming that their tough line and resistance to further territorial concessions would be more effective in preventing further terrorism.

The election resulted in a victory for the Likud candidate for Prime Minister, Binyamin Netanyahu, who proceeded to form a government of right-wing and religious parties. Although the Netanyahu government, under considerable American pressure, agreed to a withdrawal of Israeli troops from most of Hebron, the peace process foundered thereafter. For the next three years diplomatic progress on the Jerusalem issue was suspended. Meanwhile, another set of elections had introduced a new political dynamic into the region.

Palestinian elections

The elections for the Palestinian Authority, the first approach to a nationwide poll in Palestinian history, aroused considerable enthusiasm and pride among the participants and much interest in the rest of the world. The question of participation by Jerusalem Arabs had greatly exercised the Israelis and the Rabin government withdrew only gradually and reluctantly from the exposed positions that had been adopted by Begin and Shamir on this issue. At one point in the first phase of autonomy talks with the Begin government the Americans had suggested that non-Israeli Arabs in Jerusalem be granted an 'absentee ballot' in such elections, with the provisos that the Palestinian body would have no authority over Jerusalem and that the question of the city's future would be left open.[6] Relics of this concept were retained in the agreement that was finally reached in September 1995 on arrangements for the elections which were to be held in January 1996.[7] Palestinians in Jerusalem would have the right to vote and be represented on the council. Jerusalem residents would not be permitted to stand for election unless they could also demonstrate residence outside the city. The Palestinians decided to accept that since, as Faisal Husayni pointed out, most Palestinians in the city could list an address of a family member elsewhere.[8] Neither the council nor the Palestinian Authority was to have administrative power in Jerusalem. Nevertheless, the participation of Jerusalem Arabs in the elections (in spite of several Israeli expedients designed to prevent such participation) reinforced the Authority's legitimacy among the Arab population of the city. Jerusalem was allocated four (later increased to six, later still to seven) seats on the council, of which two were reserved for Christians.

Although the Rabin government had given way to the American view on the issue of Jerusalem Arabs' voting rights, they were by no means clear in their own minds where this would lead – or happy about the potential ammunition that the concession would give to their opponents, particularly the Likud mayor of the city. They therefore decided to try to limit both the turnout and the visibility of Jerusalemites' participation in the election by reducing the number of polling stations to a minimum. It was spread about that Jerusalemites who registered to vote might in consequence be deprived of their Israeli identity cards (which carried with them valued social benefits and other rights). Partly for this reason, only about half of those Arabs in Jerusalem eligible to vote registered to do so. At first, the Israelis argued that all the polling stations should be outside the city limits, so as not to appear to place Israeli sovereignty in question. In the end, five polling stations were set up at post offices within the city boundary. But when Hanan Ashrawi, a candidate for one of the Christian seats, tried to enter Jerusalem in a car covered with campaign posters, she was stopped by Israeli police and prevented from proceeding. The confrontation was shown on television around the world and turned effectively to advantage by Ashrawi.[9]

Mayor Olmert and some other Israelis argued that the elections demonstrated the low level of support for Arafat among Jerusalem Arabs.[10] This interpretation was doubtful. Of the members elected from Jerusalem, three were reckoned to be Arafat supporters: Ahmad Hasim al-Zghayar and Emile Jarjou were Fatah members; Ahmad al-Batsh was elected as an independent but was a member of Fatah. Two others were counted as 'critical supporters': Hatim Abd al-Qadar, a Fatah member who acted as spokesman in Jerusalem, and Ahmad Khuri (Abu Ala), one of the most prominent Palestinian leaders, also a Fatah member, who had acted as chief negotiator at Oslo. The last two belonged to the opposition to Arafat: Hanan Ashrawi and Ziyad Abu Zayad, who, like Ashrawi, was elected as an independent.[11]

The relative success of the Palestinians in incorporating Jerusalem into the election process for the Palestinian Council heightened concern on the Israeli right lest the eastern sector of the city be lost to Israel by default. The development of Palestinian autonomy in east Jerusalem had been noticed – and denounced – by the Israeli right even before the Oslo Agreement. In April 1993, for example, Ariel Sharon condemned 'a Palestinian state operating in East Jerusalem'.[12] Although denied by the Rabin and Peres governments, the accusation had a large basis in fact.

By 1995 the PLO and the as yet unelected Palestinian Authority had already acquired effective control over large areas of day-to-day life in the Arab-inhabited areas of Jerusalem. Gradually this was extended to cover almost every aspect of daily life, including the Muslim religious establishment, private schools (serving 40 per cent of Palestinian pupils in the city), the Arabic press and even (under a secret agreement with Israel concluded on 21 June 1995 between Israeli Brigadier-General David Shahaf and the Palestinian Authority's Finance Minister, Atef Alawneh) tax collection. Al-Quds University, headed by the Oxford-educated scholar-politician Sari Nusseibeh, was certified by the Palestinian Ministry of Higher Education and conducted its activities openly in Abu Dis and Bet Hanina (outside the municipal boundaries), as well as in buildings in central Jerusalem. The Israeli civil administration in the occupied territories had tried unsuccessfully to bar West Bank students from attending. The university enjoyed influential support, however, both internationally and from some Israeli academics, and the government chose not to court further criticism by closing it down. It was left to an Israeli 'security source' to issue a plaintive comment that 'the university does not have the requisite certification from the Israeli Council on Higher Education to operate and grant degrees, as required by law'.[13] In addition to all this, east Jerusalem was still receiving 'Arab electricity' from the Jerusalem District Electric Company.

Most importantly, the Palestinian Authority controlled the streets through large numbers of ubiquitous plain-clothes security personnel. The Israeli Police Minister, questioned in a Knesset committee in January 1995, denied that Palestinian police were serving in Jerusalem, but at the same time he admitted that what he called 'shock squads' were 'sporadically operating against pimps, prostitutes and drug rings'.[14] In fact, the Israelis faced a dilemma in suppressing such activity, since they relied on covert policing by Palestinian security organs for help in the suppression of terrorist groups in Jerusalem as in the West Bank. In July 1995 the Israelis arrested alleged Palestinian Authority policemen operating in Jerusalem, but the PA's security branch remained active in the city, albeit more discreetly. In addition to all this, several official and quasi-official Palestinian institutions had their headquarters in Jerusalem, among them the

Ministry of Religious Affairs, the Palestinian Broadcasting Corporation and, most importantly, Orient House.

The siege of Orient House

A former hotel in the Sheikh Jarrah district, Orient House had first opened as an office for the 'advisory' committee to the Palestinian delegation to the Madrid Peace Conference in 1991. It soon developed into the political bureau of Faisal Husayni and became a kind of town hall of Arab east Jerusalem. Following the Oslo Agreement, the Palestinian Authority's Ministry of Jerusalem Affairs, headed by Husayni, set up its headquarters there.

The appearance of this Palestinian office in the heart of the Israeli capital aroused uproar on the Israeli right. In a series of public statements Mayor Olmert denounced its presence as a provocation and a violation of Israeli law and he demanded that it be closed down. When Rabin mooted the idea that Yasir Arafat might visit Jerusalem to pray at al-Aqsa, Olmert threatened to mobilize a million Jews from around the world to stop the visit. In August 1994 employees of Orient House were interrogated by Israeli police and a number of administrative obstacles were placed in the way of the functioning of Palestinian institutions there.[15]

The issue came to a head when several official visitors to Israel made a point of calling at Orient House. At first the Israelis lodged no objection and even facilitated such visits, but they backtracked when these assumed a political dimension that seemed to indicate recognition of a PLO presence in Jerusalem. In November 1994 the Turkish Prime Minister, Tansu Çiller, who was paying an official visit to Israel, called on Husayni in his office without previously coordinating the meeting with the Israeli authorities. Rabin called the encounter a 'trick' and commented, 'Private visits, yes. But here they tried to turn [Orient House] into an independent Palestinian representation for meetings with international figures.'[16] Hardly had he said this than the visiting French Minister for Social Affairs, Simone Weil (a Jewish survivor of Auschwitz), called at the building on what was explicitly termed an 'official visit'.[17]

Right-wing politicians capitalized on these episodes and called for Orient House to be closed. The Likud politician Yehoshua Matza complained that it had become the Palestinians' Foreign Ministry, but Husayni denied this and claimed, rather bizarrely, that no Palestinian Authority business was discussed at Orient House.[18] A group of right-wing Knesset members demonstrated outside the building and one of them, Rafael Eitan, a former Israeli army chief of staff, told reporters, 'This is sad. Here we see the Palestinian state in the middle of Jerusalem.'[19] Some right-wing extremists (including an Israeli army officer, Oren Edri, and Ben David, formerly Ja'abari, a convert from Islam to Judaism) even contemplated physical assault on Orient House.[20] On the other hand, left-wing Knesset members, with whom Husayni maintained cordial relations, visited the building to urge that it remain open.

Embarrassed by these events, the Rabin government reacted with administrative and legislative actions. Roadblocks were set up outside the building, checking the identities of persons who wished to enter. The Minister of Police, Moshe Shahal, announced that official visits that had not been prearranged with the Israelis would be stopped.[21] In December 1994 the Knesset passed an Orient House Law that supposedly barred PLO political activity in Israel. But the law, once passed, was hardly invoked; although Israeli police investigated 'illegal activity' in the building, it was not closed down. The opposition, which had manoeuvred the government into proposing the law, taunted it with failing to use it. When a visiting group of European Union ministers called at the building in February 1995, Israeli right-wingers asked for a Supreme Court injunction to forbid the visit, but without success. Between May 1994 and August 1995, representatives of twenty-nine countries held fifty diplomatic meetings at Orient House. The Palestinian success in cocking a snook at the

Israelis on this issue divided the Israeli government, leading to a row in the Cabinet between Peres and Shahal in August 1995.

The man at the centre of the controversy, Faisal Husayni, suggested that the issue was simple: 'We can go two ways: the way of Orient House or the way of Hamas.'[22] Over the next few months, discussion of the issue revolved round such esoteric points as whether the building housed PLO or Palestinian Authority institutions (the distinction was almost invisible, but the Israeli government hoped somehow to shelter behind it). The question was also raised whether Husayni was or was not a minister in the Authority. On this there was a certain ambiguity. He was not a member of the first PA Cabinet, formed in May 1994; in the second, formed in May 1996, he appeared as 'minister without portfolio'; in the third, formed in August 1998, he was listed as minister for Jerusalem; he was included in the official list of ministers in August 2000, but whereas all other names were designated as 'minister' with their portfolios, Husayni's appeared only with the words 'Jerusalem file'.[23] The reality was that throughout this period Husayni was widely regarded as the leading Palestinian political figure in the city.

His rise to this status and success in the struggle over Orient House occasioned some friction with Arafat, who was said to be jealous that many high-level visitors were calling on Husayni at Orient House without, in every case, also visiting Arafat in his office in Gaza.[24] Rumours that Husayni was seeking direct funding from Arab states, independently of the Palestinian Authority, further troubled the relationship.[25] Disagreement between the two men came to a head in June 1995, when the Palestinian Authority Cabinet was reported to have decided to form a municipal council for east Jerusalem.[26] The Israeli police considered invoking the military order that had been issued on 29 June 1967, dismissing the council of Jordanian Jerusalem.[27] It subsequently turned out that the proposal had been a bright idea of Arafat's which Faisal Husayni, considering it an affront to his own authority in Jerusalem, promptly squashed.[28]

Why did neither the Likud mayor, Ehud Olmert, nor the Netanyahu government, in office from 1996 to 1999, close the building
– particularly since they had promised, when in opposition, to shut
these offices down? The reason lay in an adjunct to the 1993 Oslo
Agreement: an at first secret side-letter sent by Foreign Minister Peres
to the Norwegian Foreign Minister, Johan Jurgen Holst, and dated 11
October 1993 – that is, a month after the signature of the Israeli-
Palestinian Declaration of Principles in Washington. In this document, which came to be of critical importance in the post-Oslo
jostling for position in Jerusalem, Peres wrote:

> I wish to confirm that the Palestinian institutions of East
> Jerusalem and the interests and well-being of the
> Palestinians of East Jerusalem are of great importance
> and will be preserved. Therefore, all the Palestinian
> institutions of East Jerusalem, including the economic,
> social, educational, and cultural, and the holy Christian
> and Muslim places are performing an essential task for
> the Palestinian population. Needless to say, we will not
> hamper their activity; on the contrary, the fulfillment of
> this important mission is to be encouraged.[29]

In the light of this document, the insistence of an Israeli spokesman
that 'Jerusalem is not part of the deal and there has been no weakening on that' rang false – as was subsequently noted by some Israeli
commentators.[30] Given the right-wing attacks on Peres over the
Jerusalem issue, it is hardly surprising that he kept the letter secret
for as long as possible.

The origins of the document and its subsequent history, as recounted by a Jerusalem research organization, the Palestinian Academic Society for the Study of International Affairs (itself one of the
institutions covered by the letter), shed much light on the peace
process and on the Israeli government's secret readiness, as far back

as 1993, to compromise over Jerusalem. According to this account, the letter was one of three side-documents, to be exchanged between the two sides, that were made a condition by the PLO for signature of the agreement in Washington in September 1993. One was a letter from Arafat to Rabin undertaking to secure a revision or cancellation of certain articles in the Palestine Covenant that were abhorrent to Israel. Upon Arafat's signature of this on 9 September, Rabin signed a letter to Arafat recognizing the PLO as the representative of the Palestinian people. The Peres letter, unlike the other two, was supposed to remain secret, although, like the other two, it formed part of the package deal. Although it bore the date 11 October, it was apparently delivered to Holst, and by him to the Palestinians, only in mid-October.

The letter became public in May 1994 as a result of a statement by Arafat in South Africa. At first, Rabin and Peres seemed to deny its existence. Whereupon Faruq Qaddumi, head of the Political Department of the PLO (who had been far from enthusiastic about the Oslo Agreement), wrote to US Secretary of State Warren Christopher quoting the whole text of the letter and claiming, 'This letter is an integral part of the commitments by the government of Israel. Israel has failed to comply with this commitment which is most important and sensitive.' Publication of the letter produced an uproar in Israel. Likud leaders denounced it fiercely. Ariel Sharon said it was 'madness' and Benny Begin (son of Menahem and a respected Likud parliamentarian) said that it 'severely impairs Israel's sovereignty over its capital'. Peres defended himself lamely, explaining that 'a letter is not a document' and that he regretted it had become public.[31] Nevertheless, secret or public, integral or separate, the letter represented a formal commitment by Israel to a friendly government (Norway) and even the right-wing Netanyahu government, elected in 1996, did not feel able to repudiate it.

Apart from this international obligation, there may have been a no less significant political reason for the failure of successive governments to close Orient House and the other Palestinian offices in Jerusalem. As Faisal Husayni had pointed out, that would have left the field open for the growth in influence of radical Muslim groups such as Hamas – a development that Israelis, whether of right or left, certainly did not desire.

Orient House was more than vivid political theatre; it was a major political and public-relations victory for the Palestinians. Their triumph lay not only in the fact that the building remained open even under the Netanyahu and Olmert administrations that had undertaken to close it down; Faisal Husayni's real success was achieved elsewhere – in the arena of Israeli public opinion. The very fact that what was in effect a Palestinian organ of government could function in Jerusalem without Israel's existence thereby appearing to be in any way endangered presented the whole issue of a Palestinian state and the Palestinian presence in Jerusalem in a new light to many Israelis. Husayni appeared as a human face of Palestinian nationalism, far removed from the Israeli image of Arafat as a *kefiyah*-wearing terrorist. By 1997 it was clear that the siege of Orient House was over. With its lifting, the still half-conscious basis had been laid in the minds of many Israelis for recognition of a Palestinian political dimension in east Jerusalem.

By then the Palestinian Authority had taken over effective control of many of the levers of government in east Jerusalem. This was illustrated in an Israeli security service report leaked in February 1997. The report painted a striking picture of the near-total collapse of Israeli authority in the Arab-inhabited areas of the city. More than twenty institutions were said to be operating under the aegis of the Palestinian Authority in east Jerusalem. The Palestinian Ministry of Religious Affairs, headed by Dr Hassan Tahboub, which supervised all 180 mosques in and around Jerusalem, had its offices on the Haram al-Sharif. The al-Mokassad and Augusta Victoria hospitals, which served an exclusively Arab clientele, were funded by the Palestinian Ministry of Health and their personnel were said to obey 'presidential decrees' promulgated by Arafat. Most private Arab schools in east Jerusalem were functioning under the control of the Palestinian Ministry of Education: Palestinian Authority inspectors regularly visited them and pupils received diplomas stamped by the ministry. Most tellingly, the report indicated that 'plainclothesmen belonging to the Palestinian General Security Service, to [Colonel] Jibril Rajoub's Preventive Security Service, and the Force 17 Presidential Guard conduct patrols, intelligence-gathering and enforcement activities, and operate on the major thoroughfares of eastern Jerusalem'. Examples of Palestinian police activities included threats to thwart real-estate deals between Jews and Arabs, measures to enforce strikes in businesses and schools, intimidation against Arab journalists who criticized Arafat or the Palestinian Authority, 'arrests' and abductions of suspect persons from Jerusalem and their detention and interrogation in territory directly controlled by the Palestinian Authority.[32]

In case any further evidence of the enforcement powers of the Authority were required, it was furnished in May 1997: an Arab land dealer in Jerusalem who was accused of 'intimate dealings with the Israel Lands Administration' was found dead from a blow on the back of the head a week after Arafat had ordered his security forces to stop land sales to Jews and three days after the Palestinian Justice Minister had said publicly that the death penalty should be enforced against such dealers.[33] Shortly afterwards two more bodies of land dealers were discovered, another man was reported to be 'missing' and yet another was released after Israeli police intercepted a convoy of Palestinian police cars escorting him for interrogation to Ramallah.[34]

That such a collapse of Israeli authority in east Jerusalem should take place under a government wedded to maintaining Israeli sovereignty was particularly galling to the Israeli right. In order to try to reassure supporters that policy on Jerusalem was unchanged, the Netanyahu government heightened its rhetoric on the issue and took some new steps. In February 1997 it decided to proceed with the long-planned Har Homa housing development south of Jerusalem.

This called for the construction of 6,500 apartments for Israelis on an area of 460 acres, about a third of it expropriated from Arabs. Palestinians demonstrated against the project, which was widely condemned outside Israel – only the United States' veto saved Israel from renewed condemnation by the UN Security Council. President Clinton nevertheless criticized the development.

The government also pursued a policy of revoking the residency status of Palestinian Arabs formerly living in the city who had not returned there for a certain period. In 1996, according to Interior Ministry data, the residency status of 689 Palestinians was revoked; in 1997 that of 606 was revoked; and in 1998 of 788. These figures compared with a total of 327 for the period 1987 to 1995.[35] This policy, combined with the continued withholding of building permits to Palestinians and other such administrative procedures, was plainly designed to limit the growth of Palestinian Arab population within the city. It did not, however, prevent a continued increase in the Palestinian proportion of the city's population.

In April 1999 the Israeli Cabinet finally decided to close down Orient House. The decision was a palpable manoeuvre to win popularity on the nationalist right (an election had been called for 17 May). The Cabinet authorized the Police Minister, Avigdor Kahalani, to act. A closure order was issued and a Palestinian lawyer immediately lodged a petition to the High Court seeking a revocation of the order. Whereupon, greatly to Netanyahu's annoyance, the minister, who was ploughing his own political furrow, announced that he would delay implementing the order pending a court decision. Palestinians gathered in front of the building in demonstrations of support. On 11 May an order for a temporary stay was issued. The matter was to be postponed until after the elections. But with the ousting of the Netanyahu government in those elections and the installation of a new coalition government headed by the Labour leader Ehud Barak, the closure order was soon forgotten as the lumbering caravan of the peace process once again resumed forward motion.

Camp David and beyond

In spite of the policies of the Netanyahu government and the apparent impasse regarding the final status of Jerusalem, the Israeli establishment's ideas on the subject continued to evolve between 1996 and 1999. An important sign of such new thinking was a memorandum submitted to the Cabinet in 1998 by the Jerusalem Institute for Israel Studies, a think-tank that had devoted careful study to the Jerusalem issue. The report analysed a number of possible solutions to the question and outlined several alternatives:

> The first alternative, known as 'functional sovereignty', would divide metropolitan Jerusalem between Israel and the Palestinian Authority. Under this plan, Israel would have sovereignty over Jewish localities in the metropolitan area, including Maaleh Adumim, Har Adar, Efrat, Betar Illit and the Etzion Bloc settlements. Two 'umbrella municipalities', one Israeli and one Palestinian, would be set up under this scenario ... The Israeli government and the Palestinian Authority would set up a supreme body to coordinate and supervise metropolitan affairs. This body would exercise authority on sensitive issues, such as 'demographic balance' and residential construction ... Israeli sovereignty would be maintained within the city of Jerusalem. The Palestinian capital would be located outside of Jerusalem's present municipal boundaries.

A second alternative involved a kind of shared sovereignty with what was termed 'sliding sovereignty in the seam areas between Israel and the Palestinian Authority'. And a third alternative, described as 'qualified symmetry', would establish Palestinian sovereignty over most of the eastern part of metropolitan Jerusalem, except for Jewish localities, which would become sovereign Israeli enclaves. Meanwhile, the Palestinian community in Jerusalem (presumably this referred to the Muslim and Christian quarters of the old city and areas outside the walls such as Sheikh Jarrah and Wadi Joz) would constitute an enclave possessing limited sovereignty inside Israel.

> An umbrella municipality would be established in the eastern metropolitan area in which the Palestinian and Jewish localities would be represented. The Palestinian Authority would be given qualified sovereignty in the area of the Temple Mount, including responsibility for maintaining order and security. The Christian holy places would be granted extraterritorial status under the authority of the churches.[36]

The Netanyahu government was not prepared to consider such ideas, which bore the clear imprint of the Beilin-Abu Mazen draft agreement of 1995. But the voicing of proposals like these, almost unthinkable to Israelis a few years earlier, suggested an increased flexibility in Israeli opinion.

As Prime Minister, Ehud Barak displayed similar qualities to those that he had demonstrated earlier in his career as an army officer: boldness, ability to see through to the heart of a problem and readiness to take calculated risks. But he also exhibited lamentable political maladroitness. He presided over a rambunctious coalition that stretched from the leftist Meretz party to the National Religious Party. Labour, although the leading element, counted for less than half of the government's support base in the Knesset.

The new government tried to demonstrate its concern for Jerusalem by appointing, for the first time, a minister with special responsibility for the city. In this capacity Haim Ramon did not wholly reverse the policies of the previous government. The Har Homa development continued, although another controversial project at Ras al-Amud in east Jerusalem was halted. The Barak government, like its predecessors, made growling noises about Orient House and

Palestinian Authority activities in Jerusalem without doing much to counter them: 'We'll act as a sovereign state against anyone who violates the law, so these violations will not occur. Faisal Husayni heard about this policy from the Public Security Minister, Shlomo Ben-Ami, and he'll also hear about it from me,' said Ramon in July 1999.[37]

Under some pressure from the press and international opinion, the government took measures designed to ease the bureaucratic lot of Palestinians in east Jerusalem. The Interior Minister, Natan Sharansky, partially reversed the policy of seeking to deprive Arabs of residency rights. He also announced that more resources would be allocated to the ministry's east Jerusalem office, where shocking scenes of overcrowding and endless queueing had been recorded. 'As someone who believes that Jerusalem must remain under Israeli sovereignty, we must look after the human rights of all citizens, including those who live in east Jerusalem,' he said.[38]

The commendable sentiment failed, however, to address the central issue: the fact that the persons involved were not 'citizens' but subjects who had no say in their destiny and little even in some aspects of their daily lives. The problem was not merely one of civil rights; nor was it only political in a narrow sense; it was also one of identity. 'The lack of reference for Palestinian residents of Jerusalem is one of the most difficult aspects of our lives,' said Dr Zakaria al-Quq, co-director of the Israel/Palestine Centre for Research and Information, a Jerusalem think-tank. 'We are neither fully Israeli, nor are we allowed to be fully Palestinian, and so we live in a sort of no man's land. It is intolerable.'[39]

More important than such administrative measures were the government's new political initiatives. Barak reopened 'back-channel' discussions with Palestinian leaders, including Faisal Husayni, in an effort to resolve the 'final status' issues, including Jerusalem. The Beilin-Abu Mazen proposals surfaced again as the starting point for discussions. Tentative agreement was reached on some issues: for example, the location of the Palestinian parliament in Abu Dis, which

would be included in the expanded Jerusalem as part of the Palestinian 'al-Quds'. The proposal attracted some public support in Israel:
for example, from the Likud Knesset member Michael Eitan, who
had held discussions with Yossi Beilin as far back as 1997 in an effort
to establish a left-right consensus on Jerusalem. Mayor Olmert at first
opposed the idea:

> We cannot allow the PA full control over Abu Dis,
> because that would put it just one mile from the heart of
> the main Jewish part of Jerusalem, the Temple Mount
> [sic]. PA control over Abu Dis would also mean the
> creation of a stepping-stone, a corridor through which
> the Palestinians would seek to overturn Israeli sovereignty
> in the city.[40]

Most of the sticking points that had eluded agreement between
Beilin and Abu Mazen remained unresolved. Official negotiations on
a permanent settlement began in November 1999, but these too
failed to make much progress on the Jerusalem question. A variety of
inventive solutions were considered by the negotiators – only to rub
up again and again against the hard rock of sovereignty. A 'Ramadan
goodwill gesture' by the Israelis in December 1999 of releasing Palestinian prisoners from east Jerusalem improved the atmosphere, but
the negotiations still limped along inconclusively.

As the negotiations proceeded, noises off from the Israeli right
grew in volume. But the decision by some Likud leaders to identify
themselves with more extreme elements, such as those seeking Jewish
prayer rights on the Temple Mount, tended to alienate centrist Israeli
opinion. The bizarre antics of the nationalist far right tended to
isolate it rather than attract support – at least so long as Palestinian
terrorist attacks did not resume. A case in point was the discovery, in
April 2000, of a new Jewish holy place: the supposed tomb of
the thirteenth-century rabbinical scholar Nahmanides, conveniently

situated in a cave in the Arab district of Sheikh Jarrah in east Jerusalem. Led by Knesset member Benny Elon, a group of fanatics tried to enter the site and engaged in scuffles with Arab residents and Palestinian leaders, led by Faisal Husayni, who rushed to the scene.[41] Pursuing the by now familiar Janus-headed strategy of physical force and legalistic manoeuvres, the group secured a ruling in the following month from the District Court that the cave was a holy place and that Jews must be permitted to enter it for prayer.[42] Palestinians announced an appeal to the High Court.

The Israelis devoted much thought to subtle distinctions between different types of sovereignty and administrative control – partly with a view to disabling critics from the right, partly perhaps to convince themselves that they were not yielding on fundamentals. This pattern followed that of the earlier post-Oslo negotiations, in which territories surrendered by Israel were divided into different categories, A (full Palestinian control) and B (Israeli security control, Palestinian civilian control). But as a writer in *Ha-aretz* pointed out in January 2000, these distinctions made less sense in real life than on paper:

> The only trouble is that in Abu Dis, where the
> Palestinians have been granted only 'civil' powers, all the
> PA's security mechanisms are already operating, and there
> is nothing that really differentiates it from Area A (full
> Palestinian control). From Abu Dis, the Palestinian
> security units [already] extend their arms into Jerusalem,
> long before anyone has permitted them to operate in the
> city.[43]

In the spring of 2000 Barak tried to secure Cabinet agreement to an early handover to full Palestinian control of the greater part of Abu Dis, as well as the villages of al-Azariya and Suwarha. But he encountered opposition in his increasingly rickety coalition and was compelled to abandon the idea. A short time later the local planning commission, dominated by right-wing and religious party members, voted by seven to one to build 200 new Jewish apartments in the 10 per cent of Abu Dis that lay within the Jerusalem municipal boundary.[44]

In July 2000 Barak, Arafat and Clinton held a summit meeting at Camp David that, it was hoped, would replicate the success of the meeting hosted by President Carter that had led to the Israeli-Egyptian agreement of 1978. As on that occasion the Americans decreed casual dress and seclusion from the rest of the world in the hope of creating a dynamic for agreement. Although the preparatory Israeli-Palestinian talks had failed to resolve several central issues, the Americans hoped that by involving the President and setting an implicit deadline (given the impending elections and end of his period of office), an agreement might be secured. Both Barak and Arafat were conscious of the danger that further partial agreements might invite violent intervention from extremists determined to ambush and destroy the peace process; they therefore shared a determination to try and reach a conclusive settlement of all outstanding issues. But both faced internal difficulties. Arafat was under pressure not to give way on the Palestinian demand for an Israeli withdrawal from the whole of Arab east Jerusalem. Barak's coalition was crumbling and he arrived at the conference at the head of a government that seemed on the verge of collapse. Only the opportune summer recess of the Knesset gave him a breathing space until the end of October, when parliament was expected to resume.

Jerusalem was the core issue that was discussed at Camp David and Jerusalem was what ultimately prevented an agreement. On the seventh day of the talks, after the Israelis and Palestinians had failed to agree among themselves, the Americans proposed ideas of their own. These were broadly along the lines of the Beilin-Abu Mazen compromise, with some modifications and additions. Israel would withdraw from 91 per cent of the West Bank; the remaining 9 per cent would be annexed to Israel. Jerusalem's boundaries would be expanded to include the post-1967 Jewish settlements of Givat Zeev and Maaleh Adumim. Some Palestinian-inhabited areas – Shuafat, Bet Hanina and the Qalandiya refugee camp – would become part of the Palestinian state. The Palestinian capital would be established at Abu Dis. The old city would be under Israeli sovereignty: the Jewish and Armenian quarters would be directly ruled by Israel; the Palestinians would administer the Muslim and Christian quarters. The Haram al-Sharif would remain under Israeli sovereignty but Muslim (Palestinian) control and a Palestinian flag would fly there. Jews, however, would for the first time be permitted to pray there, possibly in a designated section.[45]

The proposal represented an advance towards specificity in that it spelled out ideas for the old city, left open for future discussion by Beilin and Abu Mazen. The Palestinians, in essence, were prepared to concede the Jewish quarter. The Armenians were reported to be unhappy about being transferred to the Jewish state, though their anxiety may have been tactical rather than sincere. Certainly the Republic of Armenia, given its ancient and continuing animosity to surrounding Muslim states, had little reason to seek to place the Armenian quarter under the rule of a predominantly Muslim Palestinian state.

Questions remained about the nature of administrative control that would be allowed to the Arab 'boroughs' under this scheme. In Israeli-Palestinian talks in Stockholm in May 1997, when a similar plan had been broached by the Israelis, they had sought to retain control over planning and housing in the Arab boroughs – or so the Palestinians understood it. These too had formed part of the local powers envisaged in the Beilin-Abu Mazen document. Now it seemed that the matter was not so clear cut.

As the talks moved close to breakdown, increasingly odd ideas were produced to try to resolve the differences: it was suggested that the Palestinians should hold 'vertical sovereignty' over the Temple Mount – apparently meaning over everything above ground level –

while the Israelis would retain sovereignty on the ground and everything below it. Perhaps appropriately this concept was discussed in a
side-meeting in New York, home of the legal concept of 'air rights' in
property.

Barak indicated broad readiness to accept the American proposals
for Jerusalem. He was also ready to withdraw from 91 per cent of the
West Bank, to accept the creation of a Palestinian state and to go
some way towards meeting Palestinian demands on the refugee issue.
These were far-reaching concessions, particularly on Jerusalem. They
surprised and disconcerted many Israelis, including members of his
own party, such as Shimon Peres. The key to Barak's change of position was undoubtedly the Beilin-Abu Mazen draft and the various
plans that had been drawn up over the years by think-tanks such as
the Jerusalem Institute for Israel Studies and the Jaffee Centre for
Strategic Studies – whose director, Joseph Alpher, was present at
Camp David. Alpher had long advocated an arrangement whereby
Israel would withdraw from most of the West Bank but annex post-
1967 areas of Israeli development, near Jerusalem and within the
West Bank, such as Maaleh Adumim and Givat Zeev. The concessions
in east Jerusalem were to be offered as a kind of recompense for these
areas. Some Palestinian spokesmen over the previous few years had
given indications of openness to this way of thinking and their response had been noted by the Israelis.[46]

Arafat's reply to these proposals was negative. Towards midnight
on the last evening of the talks, Clinton put forward final proposals on Jerusalem. According to a later account by one of Arafat's
aides, Akram Hanieh, corroborated by other sources, these were as
follows:

- A committee that included the Security Council and Morocco
  would grant Palestine 'sovereign custody' of the Haram, while
  Israel would retain 'residual sovereignty.'
- The Muslim and Christian quarters of the Old City would come

under Palestinian sovereignty. The Jewish and Armenian quarters would come under Israeli sovereignty.
- The Palestinians would have functional jurisdiction in what was called the internal neighborhoods, including Musrara and Wadi Joz.
- Palestinian sovereignty would extend to the external neighborhoods of Jerusalem, or Palestinian sovereignty would cover the internal neighborhoods of Jerusalem and a special regime would be adopted in the Old City, the details of which would have to be agreed.[47]

Arafat, however, was adamant that this was unacceptable. Among other things he insisted that the Armenian quarter must fall under Palestinian sovereignty. More broadly, he said he could not take on himself the responsibility of a decision of this magnitude on Jerusalem with its Muslim holy places. He would have to consult 'with the Sunnis and the Shiites and all Arab countries'.

Towards the end, when a frustrated Clinton accused Arafat of being unyielding, Arafat's reply echoed that of Saladin to Richard the Lionheart's demand for the surrender of Jerusalem in 1191. According to Hanieh, Arafat said, 'Do you want to attend my funeral? I will not relinquish Jerusalem and the holy places.'[48] He also rejected three alternative suggestions by President Clinton, that an agreement be signed that would postpone the entire issue of Jerusalem for determination later, that just the question of the old city be postponed or that the deferment relate just to the problem of the Temple Mount.

After fifteen days the conference ended in failure. Arafat returned to a hero's welcome in Ramallah. A depressed Barak blamed Arafat for the collapse of the talks and said all offers that had been made were now off the table. A frustrated Clinton said it had been 'like going to the dentist without having your gums deadened'.[49]

10 Trouble on the Temple Mount

Although it was not the only issue that prevented agreement at Camp David, the Temple Mount was the straw that broke the camel's back. On 28 September 2000, a month after the failure of the summit, the Israeli opposition leader, Ariel Sharon, walked into the area, surrounded by a phalanx of Israeli policemen, to deliver what he called 'a message of peace'. His visit sparked off riots on the Haram al-Sharif that spread to Arab areas of east Jerusalem, the West Bank, Gaza and, for the first time, to Nazareth, Haifa, Jaffa and other Arab-inhabited areas of Israel. Within ten days the death toll in what Palestinians called the 'al-Aqsa *intifada*' approached 100. Prospects for a permanent peace settlement suddenly looked worse than at any point since 1993.

Why has the Temple Mount assumed this critical role in the struggle between Jews and Arabs for the Holy Land? What are the special religious associations of this area with Islam and Judaism? How has its status changed over the past century? Why is it that two secular nationalist political movements have repeatedly come to blows over a religious site? Is this holy of holies destined to prevent any resolution of the Jerusalem question as a whole – and perhaps of the larger Israeli-Arab conflict?

Palimpsest

The Temple Mount is a kind of religious palimpsest. It has been the home successively of pagan, Jewish, Roman, Muslim, Christian and again Muslim shrines. Except during the Byzantine period, when it was left as waste land, it has always, since ancient times, held a

317

religious shrine of high importance. For twelve of the past thirteen centuries (apart, that is, from the Crusader period) it has been a Muslim holy place. Until 1967 that status was not challenged by religious claims from any other quarter.

In its plural religious origins, it was not unique. As we have seen, holy places in Palestine, as elsewhere, have often had a competitive character. The construction of a shrine on the ruins of that of another faith was a frequent phenomenon. The Church of the Holy Sepulchre, for example, was built on the site of Hadrian's temples of Venus and Jupiter, the Church of the Nativity in a grove that had been consecrated to Adonis.[1]

In Muslim tradition, the Haram was not only the destination of the Prophet's miraculous 'night journey' from Mecca.[2] It was regarded (adopting a Jewish and Christian view that derived from Greek thought) as the *omphalos* or navel of the earth. Tradition further relates that all the prophets of God up to Muhammad came to pray at the Rock, which is daily surrounded by a bodyguard of 70,000 angels.

One aspect of the matter that is often misunderstood by non-Muslims is the nature of the Haram in Muslim tradition. The Aqsa mosque and the nearby Dome of the Rock are often thought of as sacred Muslim shrines that are on the Temple Mount. Since the latter includes a large amount of open paved space it is sometimes assumed that it is unreasonable for Muslims to claim exclusive rights there. But in fact the whole of the Temple Mount is a mosque. *Masjid* in Arabic means 'a place of prostration (in prayer)'. It refers to the entire Haram area. This was well understood by western specialists by the end of the late nineteenth century. Guy Le Strange pointed it out in 1890, long before the matter was one of controversy between Jews and Muslims.[3] It was also appreciated by Israeli orientalists when Israel captured east Jerusalem in 1967. To this day, Muslims participating in Friday morning prayers on the Temple Mount often spread out beyond al-Aqsa in a vast throng in the open air.

There are many attested cases of non-Muslims, both Christians and Jews, ascending to the Haram in the pre-modern period. By the early nineteenth century, however, Muslims had become suspicious of the purpose of such visits and they were forbidden. From the time of the Crimean War, under pressure from the powers, the ban was relaxed. The first infidel permitted to ascend in modern times was the Duke of Brabant, later King of the Belgians, who visited Jerusalem in 1855, armed with a *firman* from the Sultan granting him permission to enter the Haram. It is an indication of the alarm his visit occasioned that the local pasha deemed it advisable, just before the duke set foot on the Mount, to employ a ruse whereby the entire guard of the Haram area, Africans of ferocious repute, were locked up in the pasha's house until the eminent visitor had gone.

Various other distinguished tourists followed, among them the leading English Jew of the day, Sir Moses Montefiore. His visit to the Mount evoked a vigorous protest from orthodox Jews in Jerusalem, who denounced him for treading on sacred soil and took the extreme step of pronouncing a *herem* (excommunication) against him. Another incident, in the early years of the twentieth century, illustrates Muslim and Jewish attitudes concerning the Temple Mount:

> The story is current in Jerusalem that only a year or two ago some Moslem children, playing in the Temple courts, fell into one of the immense reservoirs which underlie a large portion of the Haram area, the storage of millions of gallons of water. The last time one of these storehouses for the water supply had been cleaned out, human remains had been discovered, and this recent event had made the Moslems sensitive on the score of pollution. A Jew in the neighbourhood volunteered to search for the bodies on condition that he was carried to and from the cistern on another man's back so as not to set foot on the sacred soil.[4]

Here we have, then, two occasions when Jews were permitted to enter the Haram.

Christians were allowed in the late Ottoman period to gather to pray on the Mount and Consul Finn noted that 'they were able to do so undisturbed by any uncourteous act or gesture on the part of the Moslem guardians or frequenters of the Sanctuary'.[5] In fact, once the precedent had been established of non-Muslim entry to the area, the Ottoman authorities appear to have been remarkably complaisant, and, as the consul reported, entry became 'principally a matter of paying a pound for each person' – a large sum in those days.[6]

Of course, at that time there was no suspicion of non-Muslim designs on the Temple Mount. The subject came up, however, in a discussion in May 1896 between Theodor Herzl and Sultan Abdul Hamid II. The Ottoman emperor said 'that he would never give up Jerusalem. The Mosque of Omar must remain forever in the hands of Islam.' Herzl responded: 'We can get around that difficulty. We shall extraterritorialize Jerusalem, so that it will belong to nobody and yet everybody; and with it the Holy Places which will become the joint possession of all Believers – a great condominium of culture and morality.'[7] This part of Herzl's dream remained unfulfilled. In the twentieth century the Haram, like other holy places in Palestine but more so, became a lightning conductor for religious antagonisms. As a result, the question of access to it was transformed into a political issue of major importance – in the struggle for control of Jerusalem, in the Arab-Israel conflict and in relations between the Muslim and Jewish worlds.

Riots at the Wailing Wall

Judaism, historically speaking, does not encourage cults of holy places. If anything, it has something of a horror of such practices as akin to anthropomorphism. Whereas the two younger monotheistic faiths sanctified particular spots in and around Jerusalem and elsewhere, the Jewish attitude was different. As Shemaryahu Talmon of

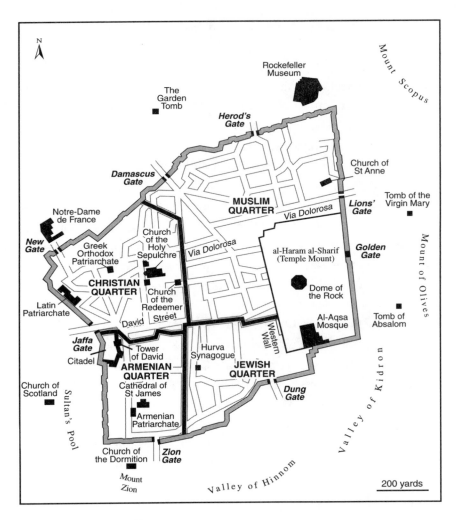

Map 12: Jerusalem: the old city

the Hebrew University wrote in 1974, 'In Jewish tradition ... it is the whole circumference of the city which is held and will be held, holy. In distinction from other religions, that have pinned their pious reverence for Jerusalem on select localities in her, on particular *topoi* which are connected with specific events in their *Heilsgeschichte*, Judaism has sanctified the city as such.'[8] One conspicuous exception to this doctrine nevertheless held special significance: the Western Wall.

Lying immediately next to the Temple Mount, though at a lower level, the Western (or 'Wailing') Wall is generally held to be a last vestige of the outer wall of Herod's temple. Because of this association, Jewish pilgrims to Jerusalem formed a profound attachment to it and the rabbis of old held that the *shekhinah* (the spirit or presence of God among men) had never deserted it. Until 1967 the wall was accessible only by a narrow passageway through a Muslim-inhabited area of the old city. The wall was not, however, a holy place in quite the sense that this phrase conveys in Christianity and Islam. It did not have theophanic connections as did those Christian holy places connected with the life of Jesus Christ. Nor was pilgrimage to it an indispensable religious duty – as in the case of the *hajj* to Mecca. On the other hand, its singular character, the fact that, leaving aside some tombs of famous rabbis in eastern Europe and North Africa, it was the *only* place of pilgrimage and veneration known to Judaism (unless one counts the three lesser 'holy cities', Hebron, Safed and Tiberias) gave it a unique standing in the hearts of Jews.

Although holy to the Jews, it did not belong to them. The owners, both of the wall and of the passage and houses in front of it, was the Abu Midyan Muslim trust (*waqf*). *Awqaf* can be 'public' (administered by the state) or 'private' – or some combination of the two. They can be founded for a religious or a secular purpose. The fact that the wall belonged to such a trust, established under Muslim law, did not render it a Muslim holy place. The *waqf* had been founded in 1320 to help North African Muslim pilgrims to Jerusalem. The wall area was only one of its several property holdings in Jerusalem.[9] Descendants of the original beneficiaries still lived in the slum-like houses in front of the wall – sometimes known as the Maghrebi quarter. Because the founder of the trust had been an Algerian, the French government took upon itself the protection of the trust's rights, an interest that continued until the 1960s.

Before the First World War unsuccessful attempts had been made by the Baron Edmond de Rothschild to buy the wall from its owners (a Muslim trust is theoretically inalienable but modern Muslim law has developed means of preventing such properties being entirely *extra commercium*, for example by the device of 'exchange' [*istibdal*]). In 1918 the Zionist leader, Chaim Weizmann, tried to arrange Jewish purchase of the wall through the good offices of the British Military Governor of Jerusalem, Ronald Storrs. But strong Muslim opposition prevented the sale going through, even though a purchase price of £100,000 (equivalent to around £5 million in modern terms) was spoken of. In 1926 another abortive effort was made, this time to buy up property adjacent to the wall in order to make a new entrance to it. The chairman of the Palestine Zionist Executive, Colonel F. H. Kisch, wrote privately that his 'further plans, which cannot, of course, be realized immediately' aimed at 'securing the whole of the shaded area facing the Wall so that it may be possible to make an open space of it with seats for aged worshippers to sit on'.[10]

Although rebuffed in their efforts to secure ownership of the wall, the Jews nevertheless tried to extend their rights there, after the time-honoured fashion of such matters in Jerusalem – by the piece-meal establishment of a new status quo. They brought along benches, religious appurtenances and a screen to separate men from women, as in a synagogue. In April 1922 the mufti complained that Jews were bringing benches to the wall. Two months later Storrs ordered such benches removed. In January 1923 the mufti complained again and a ritual was established whereby the benches appeared, the Muslims complained, the benches were removed, a little time elapsed and they appeared again. In September 1925, on the Day of Atonement, the holiest day of the Jewish year, they were removed yet again after a complaint by the mufti. As the cycle continued, Muslim suspicion of Jewish intentions grew. *Al-Sabah*, a Jerusalem Arabic newspaper sub-sidized by the Husaynis, wrote that the Jews would not be satisfied until al-Aqsa and the 'Holy Rock' were 'in their custody'.[11]

On 24 September 1928, the Jewish Day of Atonement, another serious incident disrupted prayers at the wall. The previous day Muslims had complained to the Deputy District Commissioner, Edward Keith-Roach, that a screen had been erected illegally at the wall to separate men and women at prayer. Keith-Roach, an official with an inflated sense of his own self-importance, proceeded to the wall and ordered the screen to be removed. The Jewish *shammes* (beadle) at the wall, one William Ewart Gladstone Noah, promised this would be done by the following morning. When it emerged the next day that the promise had not been kept, the screen was removed by the police amid some scuffles. Keith-Roach told the Acting High Commissioner that 'nothing more would be heard of' the matter.[12] No forecast could have been less accurate. A storm of outrage was let loose. Colonel Kisch complained that the authorities 'had treated the religious furniture of the Western Wall as if it were a kiosk in a municipal garden'.[13] Strenuous Jewish protests were heard from as far away as the United States.

The Jewish innovations aroused Muslim anger and were exploited in a demagogic manner by Hajj Amin al-Husayni. The mufti successfully bound together the forces of Muslim traditionalism and of political anti-Zionism. The glue that he used was the accumulating Muslim anxiety about the wall. Round about this time the claim began to be heard loudly that the wall was not only a Jewish holy place but a Muslim one as well. It was identified as the spot where the Prophet Muhammad had tethered his miraculous winged steed, Buraq, before climbing the adjacent hill and ascending to the Seventh Heaven. Hence the wall was known eponymously among Muslims as al-Buraq. Some scholars suggest that this alleged tradition was a relatively recent discovery. Rashid Khalidi has disputed this, tracing the tradition back to the fourteenth century.[14] This, of course, is fairly late in Islamic history. In any case, no less important than dating is location. A careful study by Amikam Elad suggests that 'towards the end of the seventeenth century the place where al-Buraq was fastened was still identified as that on the outside south-west corner of the wall of the *Haram*, just as it was described by Ibn al-Faqih and Ibn Abd Rabbihi in the tenth century'.[15] This location is *not* identical with the Western Wall.

The mufti's campaign in defence of al-Buraq was closely connected with his efforts on behalf of the adjacent Haram al-Sharif. International Muslim interest in the alleged threat to the Haram dated back to the early days of the British occupation. Fears were then expressed that the Jews were planning to take over the whole area and rebuild the Temple. These were far-fetched, although in 1914 in his first conversation with Chaim Weizmann Herbert Samuel had spoken of rebuilding the Temple – 'of course, in a modernized form'.[16] But he soon thought better of this. As early as January 1919 the All-India Muslim League had sent a telegram of protest to the British government on the issue. Always concerned about Muslim sensitivities in India, the Foreign Office found this cable 'very important'.[17] Muslim concern did not abate and in 1922 Samuel, now High Commissioner, felt obliged to issue an official announcement denying the rumour that the Haram was to be turned over to the Jews.[18]

In the winter of 1928–9 the mufti launched an ambitious campaign focusing on the wall. Under his aegis an Association for the Protection of al-Aksa Mosque and the Islamic Holy Places in Jerusalem was formed and issued a series of fiery propaganda statements.[19] In October 1928 the organ of the Supreme Moslem Council, *al-Jamia al-Arabiyya*, called on 'all our Moslem brethren' to rally to the defence of al-Buraq.[20] The following February it declared that the Muslims would 'not hesitate even for a moment to restore their holy places by force, as they are ordered to do by the Muslim religion'.[21] Efforts to internationalize the issue intensified: in May 1929 the Intelligence Bureau of the Home Department in India intercepted a letter from the mufti to Shawkat Ali of the Central Khalifat Committee in Bombay, seeking support for defence of al-Buraq.[22]

The Zionist Organization's mostly secular leadership cared little one way or another about the wall. If anything, they tended to see it as a symbol of all that was retrograde in the 'old *yishuv*'. But they were outflanked by more militant Jewish elements who, like the mufti, were spoiling for a fight and who played into the mufti's hands. The nationalist newspaper *Doar Hayom* denounced the 'robbery of the Holy Places', urged the destruction of a new mosque next to the wall and suggested the rebuilding of the Temple.[23] The nationalist Jewish youth movement Betar, which was *not* religious in orientation, organized provocative demonstrations to assert Jewish rights at the wall. Its leaders were quite open about their wish to change the status quo there. This was not, after all, a concept that had ever been endorsed by the Jews. When first enunciated, in the nineteenth century, it had applied exclusively to Christian holy places. Muslims might appeal to the traditional Islamic legal objection to new developments of churches and synagogues in Muslim states. But Palestine was no longer under Muslim rule and in any case Jews could not feel bound by Muslim law. The mainstream Zionist leadership tried, but failed, to restrain the aggressive behaviour of the young nationalists.

Counter-demonstrations by Muslims followed the Jewish ones, and an escalating series of scuffles and disturbances culminated in an explosion of communal violence. Some time in the week starting 18 August 1929 the Association for the Protection of al-Aksa Mosque and the Islamic Holy Places in Jerusalem issued a notice in Arabic complaining bitterly of Jewish demonstrations and attacks which revealed 'hidden hatred' of Muslims. 'Muslim brethren in all lands of the earth' were summoned 'to stand as an impregnable barrier against the frightful ambitions of the Jews with regard to the Muslim holy places'.[24]

On 23 August, after Friday prayers in al-Aqsa, thousands of Muslims poured down from the Haram and attacked the Jewish quarter. The carnage extended beyond the walls. Among the targets were the homes in the Talpiot district of the Hebrew writers S. Y. Agnon and Joseph Klausner, whose libraries were destroyed. The conflagration spread throughout Palestine: 133 Jews and 116 Arabs were killed and hundreds wounded. The atmosphere in the city remained inflammable for weeks and half the Jewish population of the old city fled their homes. The riots marked a decisive turning point in the history of Palestine: the end of any realistic hope of Arab-Jewish peace under the British mandate.

In December 1930 an international commission, appointed by the British government, issued an adjudication on the Wailing Wall controversy. With a view to ensuring impartiality, the three men appointed by the British government to assess the merits of the Muslim-Jewish dispute were all Christians: a former Swedish foreign minister, a Swiss jurist and a Dutch former governor of East Sumatra. The findings were a disappointment to the Jews. The commission concluded that the wall and the pavement in front of it were Muslim property and that the wall was sacred to Muslims as well as Jews. The commission affirmed a Jewish right of access but strictly limited the prayer appurtenances that might be brought to the wall by Jews.[25]

The wall affair has been called the 'crowning achievement' of the mufti's campaign to enhance the status of the Haram al-Sharif.[26] The mufti succeeded in further exploiting his position and in advancing his claim to be a defender of Muslim rights in Jerusalem by turning the Haram into a kind of international Islamic Pantheon. King Hussein, leader of the Hashemite Arab revolt in the First World War, was buried there, as were other Muslim leaders from as far afield as India.[27]

Under British rule, the government took great care not to appear in any way to infringe the sanctity of the Haram. That was why there was no attempt to arrest the mufti when he took refuge there in 1937. After the mufti's flight the following year, a police post was established there for the first time.[28] But until the end of the mandate the government respected Muslim sensibilities and permitted the Supreme Moslem Council to administer it without any obtrusive interference.

The Temple Mount under Israeli rule

When the Israeli army captured the Temple Mount on 7 June 1967, an Israeli flag was hoisted on the Dome of the Rock. The Israeli Defence Minister, Moshe Dayan, immediately ordered it removed. The same day the Chief Rabbi of the Israeli Army, Shlomo Goren, went up to the Temple Mount, where he exchanged the following thoughts with General Uzi Narkiss, the OC Central Command in the Israeli army:

> GOREN: Uzi, this is the time to put a hundred kilograms of explosives in the Mosque of Omar – and that's it, we'll get rid of it once and for all.
> NARKISS: Rabbi, stop it!
> GOREN: You'll enter the history books by virtue of this deed.
> NARKISS: I have already recorded my name in the pages of the history of Jerusalem.

As Narkiss recounted it years later, Goren then walked off without a word.[29] Shortly afterwards Dayan ordered Israeli paratroops to be withdrawn from the Haram; the area was sealed off and its internal security restored to Muslim guards. The keys to eight of the nine gates to the compound (the exception was the Maghrebi Gate, near the Western Wall) were returned to the Muslim authorities and the Israeli presence was reduced to a small police post, generally manned by former members of the Jordanian police force. Outside the Maghrebi Gate a notice was posted in Hebrew, English and French:

Notice and Warning
Entrance to the area of the Temple Mount is forbidden to everyone by Jewish law owing to the sacredness of the place.
The Chief Rabbinate of Israel

Over the next few weeks the Israeli military authorities engaged in a tussle with sections of the Jewish religious establishment who were anxious to affirm Jewish rights on the Mount. On 15 August, in the Hebrew calendar the fast of the ninth of Av, commemorating the destruction of the Temple, Chief Rabbi Goren again ascended the Mount, this time with a scroll of the Law, an ark and a pulpit, in order to conduct prayers. The army tried but failed to stop him.[30] The next day the Israeli Minister of Religious Affairs, Dr Zerah Warhaftig, a member of the National Religious Party, stated that the Temple Mount was Jewish property: he pointed out that King David had bought it for fifty shekels from Araunah king of the Jebusites.[31] Goren wrote a bitter letter to the ministerial committee on the protection of holy places, complaining that, of all places in the world, the Temple Mount was the only one in which there was an explicit ban on Jewish prayer.[32] He and his allies tried to secure Jewish rights to hold prayer meetings on the Mount but eventually they were forced to yield to a government ruling which maintained that the status quo barred Jewish prayer there.

In the initial phase of Israeli rule, officials hoped to vest control of the Haram in a committee of Israeli Muslim leaders that would include Muslims from east Jerusalem.[33] But the initiative was seized by the east Jerusalem Muslim establishment and the Israelis were compelled to come to terms with it. The entire administration of the Haram therefore remained firmly in the hands of the Muslim Council. Public order in the area was assigned to guards employed by the council and the small unit of Israeli police.

One of the first acts undertaken by the Israeli authorities after the Six Day War in June 1967 was the razing of 135 houses in the Maghrebi area immediately in front of the Western Wall. The clearance began on the evening of Saturday 10 June and was completed within two days. The action was justified as necessary in order to accommodate the hundreds of thousands of Jews who thronged to the wall from June 1967 onwards, after nineteen years during which they had been deprived of access by the Jordanian government. The 650 inhabitants in the demolished houses, all Muslims, were summarily evicted. Clearance of the area fulfilled an ambition that had been voiced by Zionist leaders as far back as 1926.[34] The demolitions transformed the area in front of the wall from a narrow passageway to a great, open plaza. This was given over to the control of the Ministry of Religious Affairs, which administered it as a Jewish shrine and synagogue. Services were held there round the clock. Men and women were segregated. Increasingly, symbolic state events of national significance were staged at the plaza, for example, swearing-in ceremonies by military and scout units – this in spite of some resistance from ultra-orthodox elements, who disapproved of such gatherings.

Muslims were outraged by the summary confiscation of a *waqf* property and some feared that this might be merely the start of Jewish encroachment on the Haram itself. In November 1967 the following statement was issued (whether from Jerusalem or from outside Israeli-occupied territories remains unclear):

> *Statement Signed, 'A Call from Near Al-Aqsa Mosque', on the*
> *Pollution of the Holy Places*
>
> The Zionist authorities, including the Minister of
> Religious Affairs, have announced that the site of the *Aqsa*
> mosque is their property.
>
> The Zionists have also announced that they intend to
> rebuild the Temple on the ruins of the Dome of the
> Rock.
>
> They have appropriated by force one of the gates of the
> *Haram al-Sharif*, the gate adjacent to the Wall of the *Buraq*.
>
> Moslems all over the world: Jerusalem cries out to you,
> the *Aqsa* mosque needs your aid ... Who will respond?
> We have pledged ourselves to resistance, we have vowed
> that we shall never submit ... We cry out as the Moslem
> woman cried out to the Caliph al-Mu`tasim, and we say
> as she said, 'Help, O Mu`tasim! Help, O Mu`tasim!',

and al-Mu`tasim answered her call and saved her from her enemies.

Will the Kings, Presidents, peoples and organizations of the Moslems likewise answer, and exert all their strength to save Jerusalem, the *Aqsa* mosque, and all the Holy Places?[35]

In the early years of Israeli rule, government policy was very clear that the Temple Mount in its entirety was to be regarded as a Muslim holy place, that no Jewish claims on it would be entertained and that, as with the Christian holy places, it should remain under Muslim control. In September 1969 the Foreign Minister, Abba Eban, told the UN General Assembly that, pending an agreed status negotiated 'in such a manner as to promote Middle East peace and ecumenical harmony', Israel's policy was 'that the Moslem and Christian Holy Places should always be under the responsibility of those who hold them sacred'.[36] Israel emphasized its commitment to freedom of access to the holy places and, under the 'open bridges' policy instituted by Moshe Dayan, hundreds of thousands of Muslims, many citizens of countries at war with Israel, visited the Haram.

But starting in 1969, a long series of violent episodes set a question mark over Israel's ability to function effectively as custodian of the Muslim holy places in Jerusalem. On 21 August 1969 al-Aqsa mosque was set on fire by a deranged Australian Christian. The arson attack caused extensive damage and destroyed a precious work of Muslim art – the pulpit in which Saladin was said to have stood after the recapture of the city from the Crusaders in 1187. The fire evoked an outpouring of anguish among the Muslims of Jerusalem. The Jerusalem Muslim Council complained that 'Israel was invading Sanctuaries and desecrating sacred beliefs'.[37] A foreign observer recorded:

I arrived on the spot immediately after [the fire] is said to

have started. It was like a scene from Dante's *Inferno*. As I
entered the Haram young Arab men rushed at me
shouting, grabbing my arm, weeping, 'The Jews have
done it!', they yelled and sobbed, their faces contorted.
'They want to kill us all! Even to destroy our holy
places.'[38]

Expressions of wrath were heard throughout the Muslim world. An
Islamic summit was called. There were riots in Kashmir, calls in
Malaysia for a holy war. The leading Pakistani newspaper *Dawn* complained, 'While Jerusalem is burning, the Muslims are fiddling.'[39] An
Egyptian paper explained that the 'arson was made possible only after
occupation authorities had allowed semi-nude girls, hippies, and all
types of social rejects to turn the Mosque's courts into a meeting
place and *al Aqsa* into a tourist attraction'.[40] Even the Soviet news
agency TASS, not normally conspicuous in its concern for Muslim
religious feelings, declared that Israel could 'not escape responsibility
for this act of aggression'.[41] The UN Security Council passed a resolution condemning Israel (the vote was eleven to zero with four
abstentions, among these the USA; the UK voted in favour). The Israeli representative at the UN explicitly denied to the Security Council on 12 September 1969 that his country had 'any plans for the
rebuilding of the Temple'.

While that statement certainly reflected government policy, small
groups of Jewish religio-nationalist enthusiasts sought to change the
status quo, and in particular to establish Jewish rights to pray on the
Temple Mount. The efforts were led by Rabbi Goren, who was ele-
vated to the Ashkenazi Chief Rabbinate of Israel in 1972. In that
capacity, he engaged in a fierce vendetta against his Sephardi counterpart, the Rishon Le-Zion, Rabbi Ovadia Yosef. Unlike Goren, Yosef
belonged to the rabbinical camp that opposed Jewish entry to the
Mount. In later years Yosef became the charismatic leader of the tra-
ditionalist religious Shas party, supported in particular by Jews of Mo-

roccan origin. His pronouncements were regarded by his followers as dogma and his stance on this issue therefore had great influence in preventing a stampede by religious Jews towards the Goren view.

Advocates of Jewish prayer rights on the Mount resorted to three forms of action: incursions into the Haram al-Sharif, applications to the courts, and plans for armed attacks on the Muslim shrines.

An early example of the first was described by one of the participants, Rabbi Louis Rabinowitz, a former Chief Rabbi of South Africa, who had moved to Jerusalem. In 1973, on the Fast of the Tenth of Tevet, Rabinowitz went up to the Mount and, as he later narrated, 'led a *minyan* [Jewish prayer quorum of ten adult men] in prayer on a spot of the Mount which I was convinced after an exhaustive examination of the *halakhic* aspect, was beyond the area of prohibition'.[42] Shortly afterwards Rabinowitz ran for election as mayor of Jerusalem on the nationalist Herut party ticket, losing to Teddy Kollek.

The Israeli courts generally upheld the right of the government, on security grounds, to prevent or restrict Jewish prayer in the area. In a judgement in 1970, the High Court rejected an application for an order *nisi* against the Minister of Police to show cause why he should not protect Jewish worshippers on the Temple Mount.[43] But on 28 January 1976 an Israeli magistrate, Ruth Or, presiding over the trial of a group of Betar youths, acquitted them and declared, 'If I hadn't heard this with my own ears, I wouldn't have believed it – that the ban on Jews praying on the Temple Mount has existed only since the Israeli Government took control of it!'[44] This was initially taken to mean that Jews did after all have the right to pray in the area. Demonstrations and riots followed throughout the West Bank for the next three months. The magistrate's decision was eventually overruled by the District Court and the Supreme Court subsequently reaffirmed that the police were entitled to prevent Jews praying on the Mount.

In the face of these legal decisions, the battle gradually moved to the extra-legal arena. Groups of nationalist youth, often, as in the prelude to the 1929 riots, members of the Betar movement or its affiliates, repeatedly sought to enter the compound and on each occasion were ejected by Israeli police, amid much shouting and kicking. Sometimes Jews would go in with prayer books, sit down and claim that they were merely reading. On one occasion, two men ran in at the end of the Day of Atonement and blew a shofar (ram's horn).

In the course of the 1970s a number of radical groups were formed with the specific object of advancing Jewish claims on the Temple Mount. The best known, with a fluctuating estimated membership of around 1,500, was the Temple Mount Faithful, led by Gershon Salomon. His followers provoked repeated affrays in which Jews attempted to enter the area to pray and were prevented from doing so by the Israeli police.

One of the founders of the Temple Mount Faithful, Stanley Goldfoot, later split away to form his own group. A former South African, who had been a member of Lehi (the Stern Gang) in 1948, Goldfoot set up the Jerusalem Temple Foundation with financial support from fundamentalist Christians in the United States. He was reported to have made plans to hover in a helicopter at dawn above the Temple Mount 'to X-ray and probe the innards of the mount with ... [an] induced polarization set, Cesium Beam magnetometer, downhill Borescope television and high-power Dipole-Dipole Restitivity Set'. A mixture of fantast and fanatic, Goldfoot was also reported to have channelled funds to Jewish terrorists bent on blowing up the Muslim holy places on the Temple Mount.[45]

Another fringe group, known as the Ateret Kohanim (literally 'crown of priests'), initiated preparations for the restoration of the Temple, including the weaving of ceremonial vestments. They claimed to trace their origins to the ideas of the Chief Rabbi of Palestine in the mandatory period, Avraham Kook, although it is doubtful whether that saintly, semi-mystical but moderate-spirited leader would have endorsed their notions. His son Rabbi Zvi Yehuda Kook, however, gave the group legitimacy on the nationalist-religious right. The younger Kook was a founder of the Gush Emunim ('Bloc of the

Faithful') movement that spearheaded Jewish settlement in the West Bank in this period. The Ateret Kohanim yeshiva was established in the Muslim quarter of the old city in 1978. It promoted the study of all aspects of Jewish law concerning the Temple. The head of the yeshiva, Rabbi Shlomo Aviner, publicly eschewed violent methods, but some of his students had fewer scruples. They were arrested for arson, attacks on Arabs and an attempt to burrow under the Temple Mount in order to discover supposed hidden treasure from the First Temple.

Ateret Kohanim enjoyed support from a number of right-wing Israeli politicians, including Binyamin Netanyahu, Benny Begin and Ehud Olmert, as well as from militantly nationalist rabbis such as Nachum L. Rabinovich and the Ashkenazi Chief Rabbi of Israel, Avraham Shapira.[46] Another supporter was Ariel Sharon. When he spoke at a dinner in support of the group in New York in 1993, he was hailed in a full-page advertisement in the *New York Times* as 'a resident of the Old City Western Wall quarter' – a reflection of the group's desire to blot out even the name of the Muslim quarter.[47] Ateret Kohanim received financial support from wealthy American, Canadian and British Jews, including Cyril Stein, a London bookmaker, Marc Belzberg, a Canadian investment banker, and Irving Moskowitz, a Miami-based real-estate developer.[48] The group also resorted to a tried and tested device of right-wing American Zionists and included in their publicity, without authorization, the names of well-known bigwigs, among them Senator Joseph Lieberman of Connecticut and the Nobel laureate Elie Wiesel. In 1988 they received a secret 5.6 million shekel (at the time $2.3 million) loan from the Israeli government to finance mortgages that would facilitate the purchase of properties in Arab areas of east Jerusalem.

Out of the activity of such groups, a fringe element emerged that was ready to resort to extreme measures. On 11 April 1982 an American-born Israeli soldier, Alan Harry Goodman, burst into the Dome of the Rock, firing an M-16 rifle. Two Arabs were killed and thirty wounded. Goodman then mounted the rock in the centre of the shrine and fired four shots into the dome above. A search of Goodman's apartment revealed propaganda leaflets of the extreme-nationalist Kach movement led by Rabbi Meir Kahane. Goodman later explained that he had felt he 'had to do this' because of Palestinian terror attacks on Israelis.[49] Once again, fierce protests erupted throughout the Muslim world and riots broke out in the West Bank and Gaza. Troops were called out to quell rioters on the Temple Mount. David Shipler of the *New York Times* reported:

> Eventually the troops withdrew but returned when a small police contingent was stoned. They shot into the air and used tear gas, driving the demonstrators towards Al-Aqsa Mosque. Most of them left the mount and the soldiers were ordered to withdraw.
>
> Just before going, one of them, with a laugh, threw a tear gas grenade near the mosque, upwind from the main door. Smoke from the perfectly placed canister blew into the mosque, and worshipers came out coughing and wiping their eyes. One elderly man was carried to an ambulance. A few of the troops walked away laughing.[50]

As in the case of the 1969 arson, Israeli spokesmen sought to explain the event as an isolated attack by a madman. But tension remained high: two people were killed, at least 184 injured and 200 arrested in a week of violence in Jerusalem after the shooting.

Further incidents between 1982 and 1984 could not be brushed aside as the work of mentally ill individuals. In October 1982 Yoel Lerner, an activist in Kahane's Kach movement, was convicted of planning to blow up the Dome of the Rock. In 1983 thirty-eight Jewish zealots, led by Rabbi Yisrael Ariel, another follower of Kahane, were arrested and charged with planning to storm and occupy the Temple Mount. In January 1984, in what was clearly an attack by an organized group, two men climbed the eastern wall of the Haram carrying twenty-two pounds of explosives and eighteen hand grenades. They fled when the alarm was raised. Nor were these the only instances of plots to destroy the Muslim shrines.[51]

While these terrorist groups were an unrepresentative extremist fringe, a much larger body of opinion within the legitimate political spectrum supported the assertion of Jewish prayer rights on the Temple Mount. In January 1986 the Knesset Interior Committee, headed by Dov Shilansky, a Likud member, visited the mount 'to investigate charges that illegal construction ha[d] taken place'. Accompanying the committee were right-wing Knesset members and other nationalist figures, including Gershon Salomon of the Temple Mount Faithful. They got into a brawl with *waqf* guards and workmen. Shilansky complained, 'It was like a pogrom. They could have finished us off in a flash.'[52]

What happened on 8 October 1990, at the height of the Palestinian *intifada*, was even more serious. Behind this episode lay a tangle of provocation and hatred. One element was the announcement, a fortnight earlier, by the Temple Mount Faithful that they intended to lay a symbolic cornerstone for the Third Temple. Muslims called for counter-demonstrations and resistance. The police initially told the Jewish group that they would be permitted to enter the Mount in pairs with a police escort, though that permission was later rescinded. Violence ensued when Arabs began throwing stones and bottles at the police, some of which landed on Jews praying at the Western Wall. Nobody was seriously hurt but police and soldiers responded with disproportionate force. Twenty-one Arabs were killed, several shot in the back, and more than 100 wounded during clashes on the Haram with Israeli security forces. It was the largest death toll on a single day in the course of the *intifada* and its location was a huge symbolic provocation to all Muslims.

On 13 October the UN Security Council voted unanimously to condemn 'especially the acts of violence committed by the Israeli security forces resulting in injuries and loss of life'. The resolution ordered Israel to comply with the Fourth Geneva Convention, which, it said, was 'applicable to all the territories occupied by Israel since 1967'. The Security Council also voted to send a UN mission to the Middle East to report on the situation.[53] The Israeli government's response to the announcement of the UN mission was unrepentant. The Cabinet Secretary, Yossi Ahimeir, announced, 'We will not cooperate with them.'[54] The decision was endorsed by the Cabinet two days later, in spite of a letter from US Secretary of State James Baker warning that by non-cooperation Israel would risk comparison with 'Saddam Hussein and his rejection of Security Council decisions'.

In the wake of the massacre, the atmosphere of seething inter-communal hatred in Jerusalem reached a peak. In the Baqa district of west Jerusalem a Jewish woman, a gardener and a policeman were stabbed to death by a Palestinian shouting 'God is Great.' At the funeral of one of the victims the Israeli Police Minister, Roni Milo, said, 'He who comes to kill you, rise up and kill him first.'[55] An Israeli judicial commission, appointed to investigate the causes and handling of the riots, concluded nine months later that the police had initially provoked the violence and that some of the shooting deaths were clearly unjustified.[56] No charges were preferred against any of the police officers involved. Shortly after the appearance of the commission's initial findings, the police commander on the scene at the time of the episode, whose handling of the affair had been the object of severe rebuke by the commission, was promoted by the National Police Commander – whose own conduct had also been criticized.[57]

The battle of the muftis

Controversy over the Temple Mount moved to the diplomatic realm in 1994 as a result of the signature of a peace treaty between Israel and Jordan. The agreement was sponsored by the United States and preceded by a joint declaration in Washington. The Israelis infuriated the Palestinian Authority by inserting a clause declaring, 'Israel respects the present special role of the Hashemite Kingdom of Jordan in Muslim Holy shrines in Jerusalem. When negotiations on the permanent status will take place, Israel will give high priority to the Jordanian historic role in these shrines.'[58] The clause was said to have been championed by Prime Minister Rabin and opposed by Foreign Minister Peres, who regarded it as an unnecessary 'poke in the eye' for the Palestinians.[59] Yasir Arafat described the clause as 'a scandalous infringement' of the Israel–PLO agreement.[60] But the Israeli Housing Minister, Benjamin Ben Eliezer, a close associate of Prime Minister Rabin, asserted that, unlike King Hussein, Arafat had 'no rights over the holy sites of Jerusalem, which have always been under the sole responsibility of the Jordanians'.[61] Peres denied that the clause was an attempt by the Israelis to stir up renewed hostility between Jordan and the PLO or to undercut the Palestinian position in Jerusalem, but it was difficult to interpret it in any other way. If so, it backfired badly.

The PLO lodged two formal letters at the UN objecting to the clause.[62] The Palestinians also sent a delegation, headed by Faisal Husayni, to Amman to contest the Jordanian claim that they were merely representing the 'higher Islamic interest' in the city – a function the Palestinians felt they could quite as easily perform themselves. Meanwhile, they took immediate steps to assert their control at the local level. The PLO's Minister for Information and Culture, Yasser Abed Rabbo, was dispatched to Jerusalem to instruct the officials of the *waqf* to cease accepting salaries from Jordan. King Hussein's response was, on the face of things, unapologetic: 'The issue of Islamic Wakf is too important and dangerous to be abused and played with … Jordan will continue to perform its role until it is fully assured that all rights are preserved.'[63] But the statement, like many of the king's Delphic utterances, could be read more ambivalently: while suitably assertive of Jordanian prerogatives, it might be seen as hinting at the possibility of a Jordanian withdrawal, provided it could be achieved without loss of face.

The Palestinians, however, were in no mood to provide Jordan with an elegant route of retreat. Instead, the Palestinian Authority issued a declaration on 17 September 1994 that all the Islamic shrines, as well as mosques and schools in east Jerusalem, the West Bank and Gaza, were under its authority. It set a date of 1 October for the transfer from Jordanian to Palestinian control and appointed the veteran *waqf* official Dr Hassan Tahboub as Minister of Islamic Affairs, responsible for all the Muslim institutions, including the Haram al-Sharif.[64] The Palestinians' reaction hardened the Jordanian position and provoked a fiery response from Hussein. In an obvious allusion to the assassination by a Palestinian of his grandfather King Abdullah on the Haram in 1951, an event that he himself had witnessed, Hussein told the Jordanian parliament:

> Jordanians have never bowed at the gates of Jerusalem
> and its holy al-Aqsa mosque except to kneel before God,
> or to die as martyrs for the sake of its glory. Jerusalem
> remains a trust with the Hashemites, who are resolute on
> its patronage and reconstruction and on the supervision
> of its holy sites. We will never relinquish our religious
> responsibilities toward the holy sites under all
> circumstances.[65]

At the height of this controversy the mufti of Jerusalem, Suleiman Jaabari, died. As in the case of the appointment of Hajj Amin al-Husayni as mufti in 1920, the appointment of a successor became the focus for a contest that revealed a new power balance in Arab Jerusalem. The comparison with 1920 is instructive in another way too. In 1920 the British mandatory authorities had been punctilious in preserving the outward form of election according to the law inherited from the Ottoman period – while privately taking measures to ensure that the result met British political needs.[66] In 1994 no elective tincture was given to the proceedings. Both Jordan and the

Palestinians proceeded to direct appointment of a new mufti. The Jordanians appointed Sheikh Abd al-Qadder Abdeen; the Palestinians Sheikh Ikrima Sabri, a former *waqf* official.

A fierce competition for precedence ensued between the rival muftis. Sabri, who had previously served as a preacher in al-Aqsa, succeeded in gaining access to the mufti's official suite of offices. Abdin, by contrast, was confined to a small room next door to al-Aqsa mosque, where, it was reported, 'no one visits him'.[67] Mass demonstrations took place throughout the West Bank, with Fatah supporters chanting slogans such as 'Jerusalem is ours' and 'Hussein, you coward, you agent of the Americans'.[68] After several months of acrimonious exchanges, an agreement was patched up: Jordan would retain a role, mainly in paying the salaries of Jerusalem *waqf* officials, but the Palestinian Authority would take over once there was a permanent settlement with Israel.[69]

Yet hardly was the ink on the agreement dry than controversy erupted anew. The start of Ramadan on the Haram was observed on the date approved by Sabri, the Palestinian-appointed mufti; he followed the reported sighting of the new moon by Saudi Arabian experts rather than observations of the Jordanian meteorological office. Lest there be any doubt about the broader significance of these findings, he announced, 'The Palestinians control *al-Aqsa* and no longer take orders from the Jordanians.'[70] The 'Jordanian' mufti was ignored and humiliated – and soon faded away altogether. Sabri's authority quickly expanded. His fiery sermons drew him wide support; he took to calling himself 'mufti of Palestine' rather than merely of Jerusalem – a position unknown in history but one that struck a chord with Palestinian Islamists and nationalists alike. Against this background of Palestinian nationalist self-assertiveness in relation to the Haram and the Muslim institutions in Jerusalem, the Israelis took another incautious step.

On 25 September 1996 Israel opened a 400-foot archaeological tunnel underneath the western edge of the Temple Mount. The opening of the tunnel had been approved by Prime Minister Netanyahu and by Mayor Olmert, who called it 'a great present for humanity'. Palestinians, and much of the rest of the world, saw it rather as a provocation. Violent demonstrations broke out again in Jerusalem and throughout the West Bank and the Gaza Strip. Seventy-five Palestinians were killed by Israeli troops; fifteen Israeli soldiers were also killed. The Palestinian Authority called for mourning for the 'martyrs of al-Aqsa'. A few weeks later, in a retaliatory burst of excavatory activity, the Palestinian Authority announced its intention of opening a new prayer hall under al-Aqsa mosque.

By 1997 the struggle over the Temple Mount had even reached the level of virtual reality, as rival Palestinian and Israeli internet websites issued competing versions of the controversy. Jewish groups continued to target the Temple Mount both for peaceful protest, especially attempted prayer meetings, and for terror attacks. In February 1999 Israeli police reported that they had foiled five attacks on the Temple Mount in the previous two months.[71] In April that year the Temple Mount Faithful carried out a 'Paschal sacrifice' of a young goat on a hilltop overlooking the Temple Mount. The repeated outbreaks of communal violence at the Temple Mount and the Western Wall indicated the profound symbolic attachments to these spots of both Islam and Judaism. Clearly any permanent resolution of the Jerusalem question would have to address not only the old issue of the Christian holy places but also this newer and even more burning problem of Muslim and Jewish ones.

The logic of haggle

Hence the importance attached at the Camp David conference to its resolution. The really revolutionary proposal introduced there was the Israeli-American one for allowing Jews to pray on the Mount and the possible designation of a special section for that purpose. This marked a dramatic break with the status quo and a radical departure from both Muslim and Jewish tradition – as well as from the policy of every Israeli government since 1967. Prime Minister Barak's motives in advocating it are not known. It must be surmised that he saw this demand, if attained, as an achievement that might help damp down nationalist opposition to his concessions on other more substantial points, such as territorial withdrawal on the West Bank, the refugee issue and Jerusalem. Muslims immediately saw the demand for Jewish prayer rights as a foot in the door for ultimate attempts by Jews to secure control of the whole Temple Mount. It was also noted that the proposal for a designated Jewish prayer section was based on a misunderstanding of the nature of the sanctity of the area in the eyes of Muslims: it was not this or that building on the Haram but the whole of the enclosed platform that was a mosque and an Islamic holy place.[72]

In the aftermath of the failure of the Camp David conference, Barak tried to court favour among his political opponents by insisting that he would never surrender 'our holy assets' to the Palestinians (it was later noted that he had *not* said that he would never surrender them to some other body – such as the UN Security Council. On a whirlwind tour of friendly states, Arafat was gently pushed by Russia towards compromise. But any hope he might have had of obtaining cover from Arab states for concessions was dashed. The Egyptian President, Hosni Mubarak, warned 'Any compromise over Jerusalem will cause the region to explode in a way that cannot be put under control and terrorism will rise again ... No single person in the Arab or Islamic world can squander east Jerusalem or *al-Aqsa* Mosque.'[73] Saudi Arabia was reported to be opposed to any concessions on Jerusalem. In Iran the Foreign Minister, Kamal Karrazi, told Arafat, 'No Muslim can allow holy Jerusalem to remain under occupation, and the Organization of the Islamic Conference will never let any deal be made over Jerusalem.'[74] And the Syrian newspaper *al-Thawra* argued that 'the dangerous thing ... is to make the occupied al-Quds subjecting to the logic of haggle'.[75]

Among the concepts floated in the wake of the summit was the suggestion by the Latin Patriarch of Jerusalem, Michel Sabbah, that sovereignty in the Temple Mount should be vested in God. Both Mayor Olmert and President Mubarak of Egypt expressed interest and the idea aroused wide international discussion – until legal experts pointed out certain technical difficulties. Another proposal, advanced by the Americans, called for the Mount to be divided into four sections, each under the control of a different 'mix' of authorities. The four areas were 1. the Dome of the Rock and al-Aqsa mosque; 2. the plaza of the Haram al-Sharif; 3. the external wall; and 4. the 'subterranean spaces'.[76] Yet another idea, apparently from the Israelis, was for a tunnel to be built between the Haram and Arab areas of eastern Jerusalem in order to facilitate access for Muslims without passing through Israeli security control. 'Are we mice, that we must crawl through underground passageways to get to our holy sites?' asked a Palestinian spokesman.[77]

The more such far-fetched proposals were offered, the more distant seemed any prospect of a resolution of this great symbolic dispute at the very heart of divided Jerusalem. Then came 28 September 2000 and the start of the 'al-Aqsa *intifada*'.

Epilogue   The Earthly City

Can the Jerusalem question be resolved? Or is the struggle for Jerusalem doomed to pitch its inhabitants, and their champions elsewhere, against one another in an unending war, rendered ever more bitter by the apparent impossibility of total victory for either side? Is there still, in spite of the volcanic outpouring of collective hatred since September 2000, some path towards a peaceful settlement?

Jigsaw-puzzle solutions

Can law and political science help? Discussion of the position of Jerusalem in international law has generally taken the form of partisan special pleading. Literature of this kind, setting out both Israeli and Arab 'cases', is extensive but depressingly blinkered and unrealistic.[1] It has had little influence on the main political actors engaged in the Jerusalem problem — save where, for political reasons, they have sometimes chosen to fall back on legalistic arguments. As the international lawyer Rodman Bundy has suggested, 'while each side should be doing its legal "homework" to justify its claims ... the matter is more likely to require a creative diplomatic solution freed from the strict constraints of law.'[2]

What of such creative solutions? Political scientists and others have offered an almost dizzying number and variety in recent years. One study in 1995 amassed sixty-three such proposals.[3] Among those that have not already been discussed in this book were:

- Jerusalem to serve as capital of an Arab-Israeli confederation (Professor Joëlle Le Morzellec, 1979).

- Three-way division: west Jerusalem to Israel; east Jerusalem to be capital of Palestine; old city to be placed under international control (Professor Gerald Draper, 1981).
- Jerusalem to remain unified capital of Israel but to become the seat of common institutions of an Israel-Jordan-Palestinian confederation (Israeli Ambassador Gideon Rafael, 1983).
- Jerusalem to be condominium of Israel and Palestine as well as joint and undivided capital of both states (John V. Whitbeck, international lawyer, 1989).
- Jerusalem to remain under Israeli sovereignty but with 'city-county arrangements', 'federated municipalities' and/or 'neighborhood district programs' or other means of meeting needs of 'different ethnic, religious, and/or ideological groups' (Professor Daniel Elazar, 1991).
- City to be capital of Israel and of Palestine, divided by 'imaginary, sovereign lines' with two separate municipal councils plus a roof municipality (Sari Nusseibeh and Mark Heller, respectively Palestinian and Israeli intellectuals, 1991).
- Area of city to be quadrupled by adding land from both Israel and West Bank; twenty municipalities to be established; source of authority to be a 'Charter of Jerusalem'; Israeli, Palestinian and/or Jerusalem flags to be flown (Cecilia Albin, doctoral student, Moshe Amirav, Shinui party Jerusalem councillor, and Hanna Siniora, Palestinian Christian, editor of *al-Fajr* newspaper, 1992).

Nor does this list exhaust the human ingenuity and creative imagination that have been applied to the Jerusalem question. Professor Saul Cohen of Queen's College, New York suggested a 'five-tier Jerusalem' in which the city's various ethnic groups would enjoy autonomy under Israeli sovereignty. King Hussein of Jordan called for Jerusalem to be 'an open city of peace.' Professor Walid Khalidi continued to press his scheme for an undivided city that would be capital of both Israelis and Palestinians. The prominent Israeli Arab, Ahmad

Table 3 **Population of old city of Jerusalem (1914–99)**

Year	Population
1914	35,000
1922	22,247
1931	25,183
1967	27,675
1999	32,488

Sources: for 1914, Yehoshua Ben-Arieh, *Jerusalem in the 19th Century: Emergence of the New City* (Jerusalem, 1986), p. 448; for 1922 and 1931, Government of Palestine census; for 1967, Gideon Weigert, *Israel's Presence in East Jerusalem* (Jerusalem, 1973), p. 18; for 1999, *Ha-aretz*, 27 September 2000.

Tibi, who served for a time as an adviser to Yasir Arafat, suggested in 1991 postponing the issue of sovereignty, 'but establishing a separate Palestinian municipal government in East Jerusalem as a first step.'[4] Chaia Beckerman of the Truman Institute for Peace at the Hebrew University suggested the model of the city of Chandigarh in India, which serves as the capital of two Indian states, Haryana and Punjab because Lahore, the original capital of Punjab, became part of Pakistan in 1947.[5] Others have proposed making Jerusalem a capital district, like Washington DC or Canberra.

Many of these ideas have merit. But in the last resort, they all look like flimsy jigsaw-style solutions applied to a profound problem of human relations. None has been embraced even by one party to the conflict, let alone both.

The Clinton legacy

In a meeting at the White House with Israeli and Palestinian representatives on 23 December 2000 President Clinton presented his own ideas for bridging the gaps between the two sides. The basis of his proposals was an understanding that a Palestinian State would be created in the West Bank and Gaza and that Israelis would withdraw altogether from Gaza. Israel would withdraw from 94 to 96 per cent of the West Bank. She would annex the remainder of the West Bank, containing some 80 per cent of Israeli settlers. The Palestinian State would be 'compensated by a land swap of 1 to 3 per cent in addition to territorial arrangements such as a permanent safe passage' between the West Bank and Gaza. The new state would be subject to limitations on armaments and three Israeli warning stations would be maintained in the West Bank. Israel would 'acknowledge the moral and material suffering caused to the Palestinian people as a result of the 1948 war' and the Palestinian refugee problem would be solved on the basis of 'the guiding principle that the Palestinian state should be the focal point for the Palestinians who choose to return to the area.' Both sides would accept that 'the agreement clearly marks the end of the conflict and its implementation puts an end to all claims.'

On Jerusalem, the President proposed:

> The general principle is that Arab areas are Palestinian and Jewish ones are Israeli. This would apply to the Old City as well. I urge the two sides to work on maps to create maximum contiguity for both sides.
>
> Regarding the Haram/Temple Mount, I believe that the gaps are not related to practical administration but to symbolic issues of sovereignty and to finding a way to accord respect to the religious beliefs of both sides.
>
> I know you have been discussing a number of formulations ... I add to these two additional formulations guaranteeing Palestinian effective control over the Haram while respecting the conviction of the Jewish People. Regarding either one of those two formulations will be international monitoring to provide mutual confidence:
>
> 1. Palestinian sovereignty over the Haram and Israeli sovereignty over (a) the Western Wall and the space

sacred to Judaism of which it is a part or (b) the Western Wall and the Holy of Holies of which it is a part.

There will be a firm commitment by both not to excavate beneath the Haram or behind the Wall.

2. Palestinian sovereignty over the Haram and Israeli sovereignty over the Western Wall and shared functional sovereignty over the issue of excavation under the Haram and behind the Wall such that mutual consent would be requested before any excavation can take place.[6]

The President's suggestions were not set out in a formal document but were delivered orally and 'not written down' (though, in fact, verbatim minutes were kept). The intention was to indicate that the proposals represented a framework for further detailed discussion rather than a cut-and-dried treaty. Many subsidiary problems were left open for further negotiation: on Jerusalem, for example, the President did not broach such vexed issues as the location of the municipal boundary or the form of municipal government.

The Israeli response was broadly positive – though Barak stated publicly that he would not transfer sovereignty over the Temple Mount to the Palestinians. The Palestinians accepted the plan with more substantial reservations. The immediate reaction to the Clinton proposals of both Israeli and (even more) Palestinian public opinions was negative – raising the question whether mutual hostility was now so deeply rooted as to preclude any early possibility of a diplomatic settlement.

Israeli and Palestinian public opinions

Both Israel and Palestine are seriously flawed democracies. Nevertheless, in both public opinion counts for a great deal. Notwithstanding the interests of outsiders, including the great powers, the United

Nations, the Vatican, the Orthodox and Protestant churches, the Arab and Muslim countries, world Jewry, and many more, the destiny of Jerusalem is today essentially in the hands of the Israeli and Palestinian peoples – or rather, in the case of the latter, primarily of that section of the Palestinian people living in Jerusalem, the West Bank and Gaza. What can be said of these two public opinions?

First, they are both highly volatile. The experience of the past two decades in particular suggests that they are both prone to wild, collective emotional swings – particularly in response to violence. The huge shift in Israeli public opinion between November 1995 (the assassination of Rabin) and May 1996 (the election of Binyamin Netanyahu), clearly caused mainly by the terrorist bomb attacks in the interim, is one illustration of this. Another is the tremendous effect on Palestinian feeling of such events as the Temple Mount massacre of 8 October 1990 and the al-Aqsa *intifada*.

Secondly, both public opinions are divided into distinct sectors that react differentially to external stimuli. In the case of Israel one must distinguish, in particular, between secular and religious opinion – or perhaps, more specifically, among secular, traditional, and ultra-orthodox. Among Palestinians, the old divide between Muslims and Christians hardly counts any more: Christians form barely 2 per cent of the Arab population of Jerusalem and the West Bank. The barriers between Israeli Arabs and other Palestinians remain important – although the al-Aqsa *intifada* helped propel them closer. More significant are the deep social and cultural rifts between inhabitants of the refugee camps and other Palestinians, the psychological schism between the Palestinians of the diaspora and those still resident in the land, the geographical divide between Gaza and the West Bank, and the socioeconomic gap between townspeople and *fellahin* (peasants). The Arab population of Jerusalem and its neighbouring towns of Ramallah and Bethlehem represents something of an élite: by and large they are the best educated, most westernized, most economically advanced and politically sophisticated segment of the Palestinian popu-

Table 4	Population of old city of Jerusalem by quarter (1997)			
Quarter	Jews	Muslims	Christians	Total
Christian	140	892	3,830	4,862
Armenian	653	351	1,195	2,199
Jewish	2,112	292	0	2,404
Muslim	168	20,653	1,265	22,086
Total	3,073	22,188	6,290	31,551

Source: Israel Central Bureau of Statistics.

lation. But they alone cannot decide the Jerusalem issue.

As the Jerusalem question has moved to the forefront of the Is-raeli-Palestinian negotiations, several currents in Palestinian opinion have become discernible:

First, and perhaps most potent, is Islam – not that perversion of Islam by an extremist minority that seeks sainthood in suicide bomb-ing, but the solemn simplicity of faith of the adherents of a great world religion. Jerusalem represents for Muslim Palestinians of what-ever background a central religious reference point.

Secondly, Jerusalem, for Palestinian Arabs, is essentially the old city and the Haram al-Sharif. The reasons are partly historical and partly demographic. Muslims are today an overwhelming majority of the population of the old city (see table above). An *al-Quds* that did not include the Haram and at least those quarters of the old city in which Arabs form a majority (i.e. the Muslim and Christian quarters) would be, in Palestinian eyes, a stunted travesty.

Thirdly, the special characteristics of the Arab population of Jerusalem, to some extent reflected in political leaders such as Faisal Husayni, as well as in the fact that they, more than any other part of the Palestinian people, including even most Israeli Arabs, live cheek by jowl with the Israeli cultural and political élite, offer them the opportunity to play a unique role. But that can be realized only if they do not remain politically neutered as they were from 1967 until the early 1990s.

Public opinion polls among Palestinians have shown sharp variations and gyrations in attitudes towards the peace process. This
volatility has reflected, particularly, collective reactions to violence.
The most reliable polls conducted in the West Bank and Gaza are
generally held to be those of the Jerusalem Media and Communication Center. One conducted in June 2000 provided data that gave
some inkling of the general mood at that time among Palestinians.
Respondents were drawn from the West Bank, Gaza and Jerusalem.
Among the main findings were:

- Low confidence in the Palestinian leadership: while Arafat remained the most popular leader, only 32 per cent of those questioned said they placed trust in him.
- Ninety per cent believed there was corruption within the Palestinian Authority.
- One third of those questioned believed that the Palestinian leadership 'should resort to means other than peace negotiations such as
  confrontations and resistance, if the Palestinian and Israeli sides
  can't reach a final agreement by September 2000'.[7]

The poll also asked the following question on Jerusalem:

> During the current final status negotiations on Jerusalem
> there are suggestions of compromised [sic] solutions
> including: the Palestinian Authority will have total
> responsibility over religious sites, the Aqsa and Holy
> Sepulchre, as well as administrative responsibilities over
> East Jerusalem. The capital of Palestine will become parts
> of Jerusalem neighbourhoods such as Abu Dis while
> postponing final resolution of the political future of East
> Jerusalem to the future. What is your opinion of this
> suggested solution?

Only six per cent of those questioned were prepared to endorse this approach. A further 26 per cent agreed it 'should be studied and deeply thought of before making a viewpoint on it.' But the overwhelming majority, 62 per cent, responded that the proposal was 'unacceptable.'

A further poll, carried out in the West Bank and Gaza Strip by the Development Studies Program of Bir Zeit University in November 2000, provided evidence of the radicalization and polarization of Palestinian opinion after the outbreak of the al-Aqsa *intifada*. Three quarters of those questioned supported the continuation of the *intifada* – though some said it should be waged by 'peaceful means'. Sixty per cent thought there was no 'chance for peaceful coexistence between Palestinians and Israelis', while only 33 per cent still believed there was such a chance. Ninety-two per cent said that peace was impossible without east Jerusalem as capital of a Palestinian state. Even more strikingly, 74 per cent said that even if East Jerusalem came under Palestinian sovereignty, they would not accept Israeli sovereignty over west Jerusalem; only 21 per cent pronounced in favour of such a partition of sovereignty over the city. Yet even now there were some limited grounds for optimism among peacemakers: 58 per cent said that they supported the continuation of the peace process on the basis of UN resolutions.

These results show the constraints within which the Palestinian leadership operate and also something of the frustration that sustained the renewed Palestinian rebellion. Nevertheless, it should be stressed that such polls provide no more than a snapshot of a moving train. Since 1993, a majority of Palestinians have shown a general readiness to go along with agreements when these are presented effectively by the leadership of the Palestinian Authority – and when emotions have not been roused by acts of violence.

Israeli opinion is divided into five camps: secular-left, nationalist-right, national-religious, ultra-orthodox, and Israeli Arab. Nevertheless, there is a minimal position regarding Jerusalem that, broadly speaking, unites most members of the first two of these, representing the most powerful political forces in Israel, as well as some of the others. That consensual basis was defined in January 1997 by a bipartisan committee of Labour and Likud members of the Knesset, headed by Yossi Beilin of the Labour Party and Michael Eitan, a leading Likud Knesset member. The agreed document, which covered the broad range of peacemaking issues, dealt with Jerusalem as follows:

> 1. Jerusalem, the capital of Israel, with its existing municipal borders, will be a single unified city within sovereign Israel.
> 2. The Palestinians will recognize Jerusalem as the capital of Israel and Israel will recognize the governing center of the Palestinian entity which will be within the borders of the entity and outside the existing municipal borders of Jerusalem.
> 3. Muslim and Christian holy places in Jerusalem will be granted special status.
> 4. Within the framework of the municipal government, the Palestinian residents of Arab neighborhoods in Jerusalem will receive a status that will allow them to share in the responsibility of the administration of their lives in the city.[8]

This formulation might be argued to be compatible with the Beilin-Abu Mazen agreement, albeit in a limited and reserved sense. Although it did not receive the formal endorsement of either the Likud or the Labour Party, it was generally accepted as representing a basis of understanding for a potential national unity government.

In spite of all that was said at the time of the Camp David conference about the bravery of Ehud Barak in moving ahead of public opinion regarding Jerusalem, evidence had been building for several years of growing flexibility on the subject in Israel. A survey conducted between September 1995 and January 1996 by Professor Elihu Katz of the Hebrew University and Shlomit Levy of the respected, non-political Guttman Centre of Applied Social Research produced some striking figures in this direction. The survey revealed that while 80 per cent of Israelis were not willing to contemplate negotiation with the Palestinians on the future of Jerusalem, their attachment to the city was more abstract than specific. When invited to identify those areas that were 'important to you as part of Jerusalem', the Western Wall scored over 90 per cent, old-established Jewish areas of the city more than 80 per cent, and newer Jewish neighbourhoods more than 70 per cent. But the non-Jewish quarters of the old city scored only 40 per cent, downtown Arab east Jerusalem around 30 per cent, and outlying Arab areas even less.[9] Several subsequent polls suggested that a sizable body of Israeli Jewish opinion, varying between 45 and 54 per cent, was prepared to contemplate a Palestinian capital with a parliament at Abu Dis and Palestinian control over the Islamic holy places on the Temple Mount.

The shift in feeling becomes clear if one looks back over a longer period. In December 1973, a public opinion poll showed 99 per cent of Israeli Jews opposing a return of east Jerusalem to Jordan.[10] In a poll in January 1997, 45 per cent declared themselves ready to consider Palestinian sovereignty over the 'periphery' of Jerusalem. According to the same poll, no fewer than 59 per cent approved revision of the borders of the city such that Arab villages currently within the municipal boundary were excluded – if that were required to maintain a Jewish majority.[11] Even in December 2000, Israeli public opinion polls, while hostile to the Clinton plan as a whole, showed a majority ready to agree to Arab rule over Arab-inhabited areas of east Jerusalem.

Demographic Diktat?

When Israel took over east Jerusalem in 1967 the population of the city was 267,800, within which the balance was 74 per cent Jewish and 26 per cent non-Jewish. After 1967 the Israelis set about expanding the Jewish population of the city by building new suburbs in incorporated areas around its fringes. By 1996 the Jewish population of east Jerusalem, at about 160,000, had begun to overtake that of Arabs. This policy thus succeeded in one of its central aims, shifting the centre of gravity of the Jewish population eastwards.

But in spite of that geographical success, the Israeli policy failed to alter the relative balance of the city's population in favour of the Jews or even (a declared governmental policy aim) to hold the Jewish/Arab proportions stable. By December 1999 Jerusalem had a population of 646,000 (68 per cent Jews, 32 per cent others).[12] Thus, after three decades of Israeli rule, the population of the city had more than doubled but the Jewish proportion of the total had shrunk.

The main reason for this is that the Arab rate of natural increase has generally been much higher than the Jewish one. Although the fertility rate of Muslim women in east Jerusalem has decreased significantly over the past thirty years, it remains significantly higher than that for Jews in the city – this in spite of the large ultra-orthodox Jewish population. In 1998 the number of live births per thousand of population for Jews in Jerusalem was 25.2; for Arabs it was 34.7. The Arab rate has been significantly higher than the Jewish in each of the past twenty years.

What renders these figures even more striking is the failure of large-scale Jewish immigration, promoted by government policy, including the construction, at great political cost, of huge housing estates, to compensate for the gap between Arab and Jewish rates of natural increase. In recent years there has been significant Jewish emigration from Jerusalem to extra-municipal suburbs or to other parts of Israel, leading, in some years, to a net outflow of Jews from the city.

The migration can be explained in part as 'white flight' of secular Jews from what they perceive as ultra-orthodox domination. A survey in 1998 found that only 40 per cent of Jerusalem's secular Jewish population planned to stay in the city no matter what happened; by contrast, some 80 per cent of the ultra-orthodox said they would stay. Most of the secular respondents who said they intended to leave cited relations with the ultra-orthodox as the main reason. The composition of the Jewish population was estimated at that time as about 29 per cent secular, 25 per cent 'traditional', 20 per cent orthodox, and 26 per cent ultra-orthodox. But the much higher fertility of ultra-orthodox women led some experts to predict that within a generation the ultra-orthodox might gain an overall majority among Jews in the city.

One recent projection for population growth in Jerusalem in 2020 suggests a total of 947,000 of whom 589,000 would be living in Jewish areas and 358,000 in Arab ones. That would give a population balance of 62:38.[13] This is based on assumptions of declining fertility and continuing internal and international migration. On other assumptions the balance of population would range between 65:35 and 57:43.[14] On almost any reasonable assumptions, therefore, the Jewish proportion of the population is heading steadily downwards.

These projections are restricted to the municipal area of the city. Beyond the boundary is a further burgeoning population, Arab as well as Jewish, that forms part of Jerusalem in many social and economic senses. A realistic view must consider the balance of population in the whole Jerusalem region, considered as a geographical unit rather than a political one. The city in this sense stretches from Ramallah in the north to Bethlehem in the south; and from Maaleh Adumim in the east to Mevasseret Zion in the west. Estimates of the population of the metropolitan area suggest that in 1967 47 per cent of the total of 427,000 were Arab.[15] Another estimate in 1990 indicated a proportion of 58 per cent Jewish to 42 per cent Arab.[16] But this probably overstated the Jewish majority. By 2000 the two populations were roughly equal – with Arabs overtaking Jews to become a majority in the metropolitan area. The gap was set to grow in the Arabs' favour as a result of differential rates of natural increase.

We therefore have four central demographic trends: 1. Large-scale absolute growth in population; 2. Faster population growth among Arabs than among Jews in spite of heavy Jewish immigration and in spite of the large proportion of ultra-orthodox Jews with a high rate of natural increase; 3. A shift in the geographical distribution of Jews and Arabs, with large numbers of Jews now living in east Jerusalem and with Arabs increasingly concentrated on the northern and southern fringes of the metropolitan area, outside the municipal boundaries; 4. A growing Arab majority in the Jerusalem region considered as a whole.

One clear conclusion emerges from these statistics: the dream of many Israelis, after 1967, of Jerusalem as a predominantly Jewish city has been shattered by demographic reality.

Must heaven wait?

The late Israeli diplomat Gideon Rafael liked to tell the story of a visit he made in the late 1950s to the then Belgian Congo. One day, he stopped in a remote village and went into the post office to mail some postcards. The clerk accepted them with a friendly smile, but when he examined their destination his face froze. 'Monsieur, you mean to send these cards to Jerusalem?' he asked. 'What's wrong with that?' said Rafael. 'But mon cher Monsieur, Jerusalem is in heaven.'

Even Jerusalem cannot yet be moved that far. But there is now a general consensus that Jerusalem's municipal boundaries do not reflect social, economic or demographic reality. Several of the plans for the future of Jerusalem in recent years have included proposals for expansion of the city's boundaries. In the case of the Beilin-Abu Mazen draft, which clearly influenced the Clinton proposals of December 2000, such expansion was offered as a possible path towards a political solution. Essentially, the inclusion in Israeli Jerusalem of the new Jewish suburbs in the east was proposed in return for Palestinian acquisition of the Arab-inhabited areas of east Jerusalem and its environs. Some Palestinians see this as the burglar offering to return half the loot in exchange for permission to keep the other half. Some Jews see it as a betrayal of the promise of an eternally unified city under Israeli sovereignty. To the Palestinians the answer can be given that the areas of greater Jerusalem that will become part of Israel are not now (and in large measure have never been) inhabited by significant numbers of Arabs. To the Israelis one can say that the promise that they were given in 1967 has *already* been betrayed by forces that experience has shown are beyond Israeli control: Jerusalem today is not unified and Israel does not and cannot in the long term exercise effective sovereignty in its Arab parts.

The Beilin-Abu Mazen formula is the only one that has ever been agreed between senior accredited political leaders of the Israelis and the Palestinians. The tragedy of the Rabin assassination prevented its implementation in 1995. Yet while it was never endorsed by the Israeli government and the Palestinian Authority, its creators did not repudiate it. Their proposal, in the updated form of the Clinton 'legacy', is the only one that addresses current social, ideological, and demographic realities in Jerusalem – and that, at the same time, bears some colour of political viability. It is the only one that offers any realistic hope of an end to the long torment of the holy city.

The outbreak of the al-Aqsa *intifada* and the harsh Israeli response abruptly halted the peace process in its tracks. By January 2001 more than 350 people, most of them Palestinians, had been killed and thousands injured. Prospects for a settlement, whether of the Jerusalem question or of the larger conflict of which it is the heart, suddenly looked more bleak than for years. But violence cannot deliver a long-term solution; it cannot prevent it; it can only delay it. Sooner or later divided Jerusalem must somehow learn to live with herself. Italy and the Vatican had to wait two generations before they could bring themselves to sign the Lateran Treaty that finally settled the Roman question. Jerusalem has already waited that long for diplomacy to catch up with reality. How much longer must she wait?

Notes

Abbreviations

AMAEN	Archives du Ministère des Affaires Etrangères, Nantes
AMAEP	Archives du Ministère des Affaires Etrangères, Paris
BN	Bibliothèque Nationale, Paris
CZA	Central Zionist Archives, Jerusalem
FRUS	*Foreign Relations of the United States*
IHT	*International Herald Tribune*
ISA	Israel State Archives, Jerusalem (FM = Foreign Ministry papers; RAM = Religious Affairs Ministry papers)
JP	*Jerusalem Post*
NYT	*New York Times*
PRO	Public Record Office, Kew
UNGA	*United Nations General Assembly Official Records*
UNSC	*United Nations Security Council Official Records*
UNTC	*United Nations Trusteeship Council Official Records*
UNTSO	United Nations Truce Supervision Organization
USNA	United States National Archives

Preface

1   Arthur Koestler, *Promise and Fulfilment: Palestine 1917–1949* (London, 1949), p. 243.
2   Ronald Storrs, *Orientations* ('Definitive edition', London, 1943), p. 304.
3   Quoted in George Macaulay Trevelyan, *Garibaldi's Defence of the Roman Republic* (London, 1907), p. 112.
4   Memorandum by A. E. Saunders (Foreign Office), 24 October 1967, PRO FCO 17/251.

Prologue

1   Abraham Wasserstein, ed., *Flavius Josephus: Selections from His Works* (New York, 1974), p. 235.
2   Quoted in Jonathan Frankel, *Prophecy and Politics: Socialism, Nationalism, and the Russian Jews, 1862–1917* (Cambridge, 1981), p. 85.
3   Text of speech,1 December 1948, Barnett Litvinoff, ed.,*The Letters and Papers of Chaim Weizmann*, series B, vol. 2 (New Brunswick, NJ, 1984), pp. 700–702.
4   Moshe Gil, *A History of Palestine, 634–1099* (Cambridge, 1992), pp. 68–9.
5   Moshe Gil, 'Dhimmi Donations and Foundations for Jerusalem (638–1099)', *Journal of the Economic and Social History of the Orient*, 27: 2 (1984), pp. 156–74.
6   Joshua Prawer, *The History of the Jews in the Latin Kingdom of Jerusalem* (Oxford, 1988), p. 46 ff.

7   Jacob Barnai, *The Jews in Palestine in the Eighteenth Century* (Tuscaloosa, Alabama, 1992), p. 47.
8   Ibid., p. 5.
9   Theodor Herzl, *Tagebücher* (3 vols., Leipzig, 1925), vol. II, p. 212.
10 See Ron Aaronsohn, 'Yerushalayim Be-'Einei Anshei Ha-`Aliyah Ha-Rishonah', in Hagit
    Lavsky, ed., *Yerushalayim Ba-Toda`ah U-Va-`Asiyah Ha-Tsiyonit* (Jerusalem, 1989), pp. 47–65;
    and Margalit Shilo, 'Mi-Yafo Lirushalayim: Yahasah shel Ha-Histadrut Ha-Tsiyonit
    Lirushalayim Bi-Tkufat Ha-`Aliyah Ha-Shniyah', ibid., pp. 91–106.
11 See Dan Miron, 'Depictions in Modern Hebrew Literature', in Nitza Rosovsky, ed., *City of the
    Great King: Jerusalem from David to the Present* (Cambridge, Mass., 1996), pp. 241–87.
12 Quoted in Walter Zander, *Israel and the Holy Places of Christendom* (London, 1971), p. 7.
13 Quoted ibid., p. 6.
14 P. W. L. Walker, *Holy City, Holy Places? Christian Attitudes to Jerusalem and the Holy Land in the
    Fourth Century* (Oxford, 1980), p. xii.
15 Ze'ev Rubin, 'The Church of the Holy Sepulchre and the Conflict between the Sees of
    Caesarea and Jerusalem', in Lee I. Levine, ed., *The Jerusalem Cathedra*, vol. 2 (Jerusalem,
    1982), pp. 79–105.
16 Walker, *Holy City*, p. 351.
17 Ibid., p. 314.
18 Amnon Linder, 'Jerusalem as a Focus of Confrontation between Judaism and Christianity', in
    Richard I. Cohen, ed., *Vision and Conflict in the Holy Land* (Jerusalem, 1985), p. 19.
19 See Prawer, *History of the Jews*, Chapters 1 and 2.
20 For both traditions and the background, see M. J. Kister, ' "You Shall Set Out Only for Three
    Mosques": A Study of an Early Tradition', in M. J. Kister, *Studies in Jahiliyya and Early Islam*
    (London, 1980), pp. 173–96.
21 Ibid.
22 Richard Ettinghausen in Joseph Schacht and C. E. Bosworth, eds., *The Legacy of Islam* (2nd
    edn., Oxford, 1974), p. 279.
23 I. Goldziher, *Muslim Studies,* vol. 2 (London, 1971), pp. 44–6. See also M. Gaudefroy-
    Demombynes, *Mahomet* (Paris, 1969), p. 93.
24 S. D. Goitein, 'Jerusalem in the Arab Period (638–1099)', in Levine, ed., *The Jerusalem
    Cathedra*, vol. 2, pp. 168–96. For a third view see entry on 'al-Kuds' in *Encyclopaedia of Islam*
    (2nd edn., vol. V, Leiden, 1980), pp. 322 ff. See also Amikam Elad, *Medieval Jerusalem and
    Islamic Worship: Holy Places, Ceremonies, Pilgrimage* (Leiden, 1995), pp. 158–61.
25 See Goitein, 'Jerusalem', p. 187.
26 E. Sivan, 'Le caractère sacré de Jérusalem dans l'Islam aux XIIe–XIIIe siècles', *Studia
    Islamica*, 27 (1967), pp. 149–82.
27 Ibid., p. 161.
28 Isaac Hasson, 'Muslim Literature in Praise of Jerusalem: *Fada'il Bayt al-Maqdis*', in Lee I.
    Levine, ed., *The Jerusalem Cathedra*, vol. 1 (Jerusalem, 1981), pp. 168–84.
29 Quoted ibid., p. 171.
30 See M. H. Burgoyne and D. S. Richards, *Mamluk Jerusalem: An Architectural Study* (London,
    1987).

Chapter 1   **The Wars of the Consuls**

1   Dror Ze'evi, *An Ottoman Century: The District of Jerusalem in the 1600s* (Albany, NY, 1996), p. 20.

2 Amy Singer, *Palestinian Peasants and Ottoman Officials: Rural Administration Around Sixteenth-century Jerusalem* (Cambridge, 1994), pp. 30–31.

3 Ze'evi, *Ottoman Century*, p. 23.

4 Benjamin Braude, 'Foundation Myths of the Millet System', in Benjamin Braude and Bernard Lewis, eds., *Christians and Jews in the Ottoman Empire: The Functioning of a Plural Society* (2 vols., New York, 1982), vol. 1, pp. 69–88; Amnon Cohen, ed., *A World Within: Jewish Life as Reflected in Muslim Court Documents from the Sijill of Jerusalem (XVIth Century)* (2 vols., Philadelphia, 1994), vol. 1, pp. 18–19.

5 *Firmans Ottomans émanés pour les Lieux-Saints de la Palestine* (3 vols., Jerusalem, 1934), vol. 1, pp. 1–2.

6 Ibid., pp. 3–11.

7 Quoted in Zander, *Israel and the Holy Places*, p. 24.

8 Louis XIII to ambassador in Constantinople, 14 July 1621, in P. A. Arce OFM, ed., *Documentos y Textos para la Historia de Tierra Santa y sus Santuarios 1600–1700*, vol. 1 (Jerusalem, 1970), p. 327.

9 Jean Lempereur to C. Balthazar, 20 September 1620, ibid., pp. 327–9.

10 Ibid.

11 Quoted in Father La Bretesche to Balthazar, 21 September 1621, ibid., pp. 329–31.

12 'Noticias del "voyage de Levant" del embajador Louis des Hayes, 1621, en Jerusalem del 1 al 22 de octubre', ibid., pp. 340–46.

13 Louis des Hayes to General of Jesuit Order, n.d. [1621/2], ibid., pp. 351–3.

14 English translation of *firman*, dated 17 May 1622, ibid., pp. 362–3.

15 See René Neuville, 'Heurs et Malheurs des Consuls de France à Jérusalem aux XVIIe, XVIIIe et XIXe Siècles', *Journal of the Middle East Society*, I: 2 (1947), pp. 3–34. See also Ze'evi, *Ottoman Century*, pp. 21–2.

16 H. C. Luke, *Prophets, Priests and Patriarchs: Sketches of the Sects of Palestine and Syria* (London, 1927), p. 46.

17 See Ze'evi, *Ottoman Century*, pp. 166–7.

18 François Charles-Roux, *Les Echelles de Syrie et de Palestine au XVIIIe Siècle* (Paris, 1928), pp. 10–11.

19 Ibid.; see also Neuville, 'Heurs et Malheurs', pp. 20–24.

20 Mordechai Abir, 'Local Leadership and Early Reforms in Palestine, 1800–1834', in Moshe Ma`oz, ed., *Studies on Palestine during the Ottoman Period* (Jerusalem, 1975), p. 293.

21 Zander, *Holy Places*, pp. 46–7.

22 Paschal Baldi, *The Question of the Holy Places* (Rome, 1919), pp. 62–3.

23 Ibid., pp. 64–5.

24 Quoted in Zander, *Holy Places*, p. 47.

25 Quoted in H. W. V. Temperley, *England and the Near East*, vol. 1: *The Crimea* (London, 1936), p. 284.

26 Abir, 'Local Leadership', in Ma`oz, ed., *Studies*, pp. 297–310.

27 See Baruch Kimmerling and Joel S. Migdal, *Palestinians: The Making of a People* (Cambridge, Mass., 1993), pp. 3–35.

28 See A. J. Rustum, *The Royal Archives of Egypt and the Disturbances in Palestine, 1834* (Beirut, 1938).

29 Rachel Simon, 'The Struggle over the Christian Holy Places during the Ottoman Period', in Richard I. Cohen, ed., *Vision and Conflict*, p. 33.

30   Moshe Ma`oz, 'Changes in the Position of the Jewish Communities of Palestine and Syria in Mid-Nineteenth Century', in Ma`oz, ed., *Studies*, pp. 146–7.

31   Mayir Vereté, 'Why was a British Consulate Established in Jerusalem?', *English Historical Review*, 85 (1970), pp. 316–45.

32   James Finn, *Stirring Times or Records from Jerusalem Consular Chronicles of 1853 to 1856* (London, 1878), vol. I, p. 98.

33   Mayir Vereté, 'A Plan for the Internationalization of Jerusalem, 1840–41', in *From Palmerston to Balfour: Collected Essays of Mayir Vereté* (London, 1992), pp. 143–4.

34   Quoted ibid., p. 145.

35   Ibid.

36   William H. Hechler, *The Jerusalem Bishopric: Documents* (London, 1883), p. 27.

37   Quoted in R. W. Greaves, 'The Jerusalem Bishopric', *English Historical Review*, 64 (1949), pp. 328–52.

38   Quoted ibid.

39   Quoted in Barnai, *Jews in Palestine*, p. 14.

40   Quoted in *The Jerusalem Bishopric and Its Connection with the London Society for Promoting Christianity amongst the Jews* (London, 1887), pp. 7–9.

41   Entry in Lord Shaftesbury's diary, quoted in G. E. A. Best, *Shaftesbury* (London, 1975), pp. 29–30.

42   John Henry Newman, *Apologia Pro Vita Sua*, first pub. 1864 (London, 1949), p. 143.

43   Geoffrey Faber, *Oxford Apostles: A Character Study of the Oxford Movement* (Harmondsworth, 1954), p. 292.

44   A. H. Grant, 'Michael Solomon Alexander', in *Dictionary of National Biography* (London, 1885), vol. I, p. 274.

45   W. T. Young (Jerusalem) to Earl of Aberdeen, 22 May 1843, PRO FO 618/2.

46   Quoted in A. L. Tibawi, *British Interests in Palestine 1800–1901: A Study of Religious and Educational Enterprise* (Oxford, 1961), p. 60.

47   Young (Jerusalem) to Aberdeen, 13 [January ?] 1843, PRO FO 618/2.

48   Quoted in Greaves, 'Jerusalem Bishopric', p. 351.

49   Young (Jerusalem) to Sir Stratford Canning (Constantinople), 8 January 1844 (copy), PRO FO 617/1.

50   Theofanis George Stavrou, *Russian Interests in Palestine 1882–1914: A Study of Religious and Educational Enterprise* (Thessaloniki, 1963), pp. 29–30.

51   Memoranda by Young, 19 and 20 July 1844, PRO 617/1.

52   Foreign Secretary to James Finn, 8 June 1852, PRO FO 78/913.

53   Karl Marx, 'Declaration of War – On the History of the Eastern Question' (28 March 1854), in Karl Marx and Frederick Engels, *Collected Works*, vol. XIII (London, 1980), p. 105.

54   Quoted in Norman Rich, *Why the Crimean War? A Cautionary Tale* (Hanover, NH, 1985), p. 214.

55   Quoted ibid., pp. 20–21.

56   See Earl Cowley (Paris) to Earl Malmesbury, 8 March 1852, in *Correspondence Respecting the Rights and Privileges of the Latin and Greek Churches in Turkey*, vol. 1 (London, 1854), p. 35.

57   Text in Bernardin Colin, ed., *Recueil de Documents concernant Jérusalem et les Lieux Saints* (Jerusalem, 1982), pp. 91–3.

58   Canning to Earl Granville, 18 February 1852, *Correspondence*, vol. 1, p. 33.

59   Sir G. H. Seymour to Lord John Russell, 11 January 1853, *Correspondence*, vol. 1, pp. 875–8.

60 Seymour to Russell, 13 January 1853, *Correspondence*, vol. 1, p. 61.
61 Memorandum by M. E. Pisani, 25 March 1853, *Correspondence*, vol. 1, p. 119; 'Project of Secret Treaty proposed to the Porte by Prince Menschikoff', enclosed with Lord Stratford de Redcliffe to Earl of Clarendon, 11 April 1853, ibid., pp. 146–9.
62 Russell to Cowley, 28 January 1853, *Correspondence*, vol. 1, pp. 69–70.
63 De Redcliffe to Clarendon, 22 April 1853, and Cowley to Clarendon, 8 May 1853, *Correspondence*, vol. 1, pp.171–2 and 175–6.
64 Texts of *firmans* enclosed with de Redcliffe to Clarendon, 25 May 1853, *Correspondence*, vol. 1, pp. 267–70.
65 Memorandum, Direction Politique, Paris, 1 March 1856, AMAEN, Consulat Jérusalem, série B, carton 37.
66 See David Kushner, 'Intercommunal Strife in Palestine during the Late Ottoman Period', *Asian and African Studies*, 18 (1984), pp. 187–204.

Chapter 2 Old City, New City

1 Yehoshua Ben-Arieh, *Jerusalem in the 19th Century: Emergence of the New City* (Jerusalem, 1986), p. 448.
2 Earlier dates are sometimes given but these are generally based on impressionistic evidence such as consular reports. A painstaking analysis by Adar Arnon, 'The Quarters of Jerusalem in the Ottoman Period', *Middle Eastern Studies*, 28: 1 (January 1992), pp. 1–65, based on Ottoman census materials and adjusted for non-Ottoman citizens (not counted in the censuses), reaches this conclusion.
3 Barnai, *Jews in Palestine*, p. 21.
4 See above p. 3.
5 See U. O. Schmelz, 'Some Demographic Peculiarities of the Jews of Jerusalem in the Nineteenth Century', in Ma`oz ed., *Studies*, pp. 119–41.
6 Yehoshua Ben-Arieh, *Jerusalem in the 19th Century: The Old City* (Jerusalem, 1984), pp. 131, 194 and 279, and *New City*, p. 466.
7 Arnon, 'Quarters of Jerusalem', p. 48.
8 For a comprehensive survey of the growth of the new city, see Ben-Arieh, *New City*.
9 Ben-Arieh, *Old City*, pp. 378 ff.
10 Herzl, *Tagebücher*, vol. II, p. 215.
11 Ben-Arieh, *New City*, p. 241.
12 Ibid., pp. 354–5.
13 See Robert Blake, *Disraeli's Grand Tour: Benjamin Disraeli and the Holy Land 1830–1831* (London, 1982).
14 Mordechai Eliav, 'German Interests and the Jewish Community in Nineteenth-century Palestine', in Ma`oz, ed., *Studies*, p. 438.
15 Clarendon to de Redcliffe, 24 June 1853, *Correspondence*, vol. 1, pp. 316–18.
16 Text in George Young, *Corps de Droit Ottoman*, vol. 2 (Oxford, 1905), pp. 3–9.
17 Ibid., pp. 11–12.
18 Hechler, *Jerusalem Bishopric*, pp. 43 ff.
19 Baldi, *Holy Places*, p. 73.
20 French ambassador (Constantinople) to consul (Jerusalem) 20 June 1862, AMAEN, Consulat Jérusalem, série B, carton 32, dossier 1862.

21 Dispatch dated 30 January 1872, AMAEN, Consulat Jérusalem, série B, carton 32, dossier 1872.

22 Text in Michael Hurst, ed., *Key Treaties for the Great Powers 1814–1914* (Newton Abbot, 1972), vol. 2, pp. 551–77.

23 Dispatch dated 9 September 1891, AMAEN, Consulat Jérusalem, série B, carton 32, dossier 1891.

24 *Les Pyramides*, 4 November 1902.

25 Consul Wiet to Father Giannini, 13 January 1902, AMAEN, Consulat Jérusalem, série B, carton 33, dossier 1902.

26 *Il Giornale d'Italia*, 21 October 1902.

27 See *L'Orient*, 8 November 1902, *Débats*, 15 November 1902.

28 *Les Pyramides*, 4 November 1902.

29 Memorandum by Jules Cambon, 28 June 1909, AMAEN, Consulat Jérusalem, série B, carton 27, dossier 1906–7, 1909–10.

30 Mordechai Eliav, *Die Juden Palästinas in der Deutschen Politik: Dokumente aus dem Archiv des deutschen Konsulats in Jerusalem 1842–1914* (Tel Aviv, 1973), pp. xiv and xvi–xviii.

31 French consul (Jerusalem) to ambassador (Constantinople), 24 June 1874, AMAEN, Consulat Jérusalem, série B, carton 27, dossier 1874.

32 *Norddeutsche Zeitung*, 18 August 1887.

33 French ambassador (Constantinople) to consul (Jerusalem), 23 October 1898, AMAEN Consulat Jérusalem, série B, carton 27, dossier 'Voyage de l'Empereur de l'Allemagne 1898'.

34 Quoted in Derek Hopwood, *The Russian Presence in Syria and Palestine 1843–1914: Church and Politics in the Near East* (Oxford, 1969), pp. 50–51.

35 Baudin (St Petersburg) to Count Walewski, 3 December 1857, AMAEN, Consulat Jérusalem, série B, carton 44, dossier jaune.

36 Memorandum entitled 'La Société Impériale Orthodoxe de Palestine', enclosed with dispatch from French Foreign Ministry to Consul Ledouly in Jerusalem, 30 January 1894, AMAEN, Consulat Jérusalem, série B, carton 44, dossier jaune.

37 Quoted in Hopwood, *Russian Presence*, p. 63.

38 Jacob C. Hurewitz, 'Britain and Ottoman Palestine: An Impressionistic Retrospect', in Ma`oz, ed., *Studies*, p. 410.

39 Foreign Minister to Ledouly, 30 January 1894, AMAEN Consulat Jérusalem, série B, carton 44, dossier jaune.

40 *Les Pyramides*, 4 November 1902.

41 Etienne Flandin to Aristide Briand, 18 April 1916, AMAEP Guerre 1914–18, Turquie 17/44.

42 Quoted in John James Moscrop, *Measuring Jerusalem: The Palestine Exploration Fund and British Interests in the Holy Land* (London, 2000), p. 70.

43 Foreign Office to Palestine Exploration Fund, PEF archive, PEF/JER/WAR/17, 26 August 1869.

44 Moscrop, *Measuring Jerusalem*, pp. 110–11.

45 Claude Conder (Constantinople) to Walter Besant (PEF), 10 February 1882, PEF Archive, PEF/ES/CON/42.

46 Consul Langlais to Ministry of Foreign Affairs (Paris) 26 January 1883, AMAEN, Consulat Jérusalem, série B, carton 28.

47 Consul in Jerusalem to French ambassador (Constantinople), 4 May 1884, AMAEN, Consulat Jérusalem, série B, carton 7.

48   `Aref al-`Aref, 'The Closing Phase of Ottoman Rule in Jerusalem', in Ma`oz, ed., *Studies*, p. 337.

49   Daniel Rubinstein, 'The Jerusalem Municipality under the Ottomans, British, and Jordanians' in Joel L. Kraemer, ed., *Jerusalem: Problems and Prospects* (New York, 1980), pp. 72–99; see also Haim Gerber, *Ottoman Rule in Jerusalem 1890–1914* (Berlin, 1985), pp. 114 ff.

50   Quoted in Ruth Kark, 'The Jerusalem Municipality at the End of Ottoman Rule', *Asian and African Studies*, 14: 2 (July 1980), p. 140.

51   For the background, see Albert Hourani, 'Ottoman Reform and the Politics of Notables', in W. R. Polk and R. L. Chambers, eds., *The Beginnings of Modernization in the Middle East: The Nineteenth Century* (Chicago, 1968), pp. 41–68.

52   Quoted in Neville J. Mandel, *The Arabs and Zionism before World War I* (Berkeley, 1976), pp. 47–8.

53   David Kushner, ed., *Moshel Hayiti Birushalayim: Ha-`Ir Ve-Ha-Mahoz be-`Einav shel `Ali Ekrem Bey 1906–1908* (Jerusalem, 1995).

54   See Eliezer Tauber, *The Emergence of the Arab Movements* (London, 1993), pp. 61, 62, 102, 125 and 290–92.

55   Ibid., p. 280.

56   Text of Decision of Ottoman Council of Ministers, 20 June 1909, in David Farhi, 'Documents on the Attitude of the Ottoman Government Towards the Jewish Settlement in Palestine after the Revolution of the Young Turks', in Ma`oz, ed., *Studies*, pp. 190–210.

57   Rashid Khalidi, *Palestinian Identity: The Construction of Modern National Consciousness* (New York, 1997), p. 31.

58   Quoted in Mandel, *Arabs and Zionism*, p. 185.

59   See N. T. Moore (Jerusalem) to Sir A. White (Constantinople), 1 March 1890, in Albert M. Hyamson, ed., *The British Consulate in Jerusalem in Relation to the Jews of Palestine 1838–1914*, vol. 2 (London, 1941), pp. 451 ff.

60   W. Hough, 'History of the British Consulate in Jerusalem', *Journal of the Middle East Society* [Jerusalem], 1 (1946), p. 11.

61   P. J. C. McGregor (Jerusalem) to Sir Gerard Lowther (Constantinople), 23 November 1912 and Home Office to Foreign Office, 19 May 1913, in Hyamson, ed., *British Consulate*, pp. 579–80 and 582.

62   McGregor to Lowther, 29 January 1913, in Hyamson, ed., *British Consulate*, pp. 580–81.

63   George Antonius, *The Arab Awakening* (New York, 1965), pp. 147–8.

64   Hough, 'British Consulate'.

65   See Mordechai Eliav, 'Po`olam shel Netsigei Germanyah Ve-Austriyah Lema`an Ha-Yishuv Ha-Yehudi Be-Eretz Yisrael', in Mordechai Eliav, ed., *Be-Matzor U-Ve-Matzok: Eretz-Yisrael Be-Milhemet Ha-`Olam Ha-Rishonah* (Jerusalem, 1991), pp.157–167; and Nathan Efrati, *Mi-Mashber Le-Tiqvah: Ha-Yishuv Ha-Yehudi Be-Eretz Yisrael Be-Milhemet Ha-`Olam Ha-Rishonah* (Jerusalem, 1991).

66   Michael Brown, *The Israeli-American Connection: Its Roots in the Yishuv 1914–1945* (Detroit, 1996), pp. 27–8.

67   Text in J. C. Hurewitz, ed., *Diplomacy in the Near and Middle East: A Documentary Record* (Princeton, NJ, 1956), vol. 2, pp. 2–3.

68   Briand to François Georges-Picot, 2 November 1915, AMAEP Guerre 1914–18, vol. 871, ff. 32–6.

69   Briand to Paul Cambon (London), 5 January 1916, AMAEP Guerre 1914–18, vol. 871.

70   Text in J. A. S. Grenville, *The Major International Treaties 1914–1973* (London, 1974), pp. 30–32.

71   Sir George Macdonogh to Sir Arthur Nicolson, 6 January 1916, PRO FO 371/2767.

72   Paul Cambon to Paris, 9 December 1916, AMAEP Guerre 1914–1918, Turquie vol. 20 (Syrie et Palestine IX), no. 22.

73   P. de Margerie to Président du Conseil, 14 December 1916, AMAEP Guerre 1914–18, Turquie vol. 20 (Syrie et Palestine IX), no. 42.

74   Stéphan Pichon to French ambassador (London), 21 November 1917, AMAEP Guerre 1914–18, Turquie vol. 25, no. 15.

75   Sergio Minerbi, *The Vatican and Zionism: Conflict in the Holy Land 1895–1925* (New York, 1990), p. 22.

76   Ibid., pp. 23 and 187–8.

77   Quoted in C. Ernest Dawn, *From Ottomanism to Arabism: Essays on the Origins of Arab Nationalism* (Urbana, 1973), p. 30.

78   Djemal Pasha, *Memoirs of a Turkish Statesman 1913–1919* (London) [1922]), pp. 165 and 201.

79   Leonard Stein, *The Balfour Declaration* (London, 1961), pp. 538–9.

80   See Isaiah Friedman, *German, Turkey and Zionism 1897–1918* (Oxford, 1977).

81   Quoted in Stein, *Balfour Declaration*, p. 628.

82   Kress von Kressenstein to Yilderim headquarters, 29 September 1917, text in W. T. Massey, *How Jerusalem Was Won: Being the Record of Allenby's Campaign in Palestine* (London, 1919), appendix IV, pp. 273–4.

83   Quoted in Friedman, *German, Turkey, and Zionism*, p. 352.

84   Ibid., p. 377.

85   See Bernard Wasserstein, *The British in Palestine: The Mandatory Government and the Arab–Jewish Conflict 1917–1929* (2nd edn, Oxford, 1991), p. 1.

86   Douglas Duff, *Palestine Picture* (London, 1936), p. 56.

87   Massey, *How Jerusalem Was Won*, p. 33.

88   Text ibid., p. 286.

89   Sir Mark Sykes to Brigadier G. F. Clayton, 16 January 1918, PRO FO 371/3383/13.

90   Minute by Sykes, 16 January 1918, PRO FO 371/3383/18.

91   Massey, *How Jerusalem Was Won*, pp. 195–6.

92   Ibid., p. 254.

93   David Lloyd George, *War Memoirs* (London [1936]), vol. 2, p. 1092.

94   Attrib. (courtesy of Sir Martin Gilbert).

Chapter 3   Jerusalem under the Mandate

1   'Note pour le Ministre' by P. de Margerie, 14 December 1917 and accompanying note by Pichon, 15 December 1917, AMAEP Guerre 1914–18, Turquie vol. 25, nos. 223–4.

2   Paul Cambon to Foreign Ministry, Paris, 21 December 1917, AMAEP Guerre 1914–18, Turquie vol. 26, no. 99.

3   Lord Bertie of Thame to Pichon, 21 December 1917, AMAEP Guerre 1914–18, Turquie vol. 26, no. 103.

4   Gilbert Clayton to Sykes, 26 January 1918, PRO FO 371/3398/605.

5   Translated from French. Picot to French Foreign Ministry, 26 January 1918, PRO FO 371/3383/336.
6   Teleprinter exchanges, 26 January 1918 and later, AMAEP, Guerre 1914–18, Turquie, vol. 27, nos. 229–33.
7   'Projet de Sir Mark Sykes', 31 January 1918, AMAEP Guerre 1914–18, Turquie vol. 27, nos. 295–6.
8   P. de Margerie to Picot, 4 February 1918, AMAEP Guerre 1914–18, Turquie vol. 28, nos. 33–4; Picot to French Foreign Ministry, [?] February 1918, AMAEP Guerre 1914–18, Turquie vol. 28, nos. 113–14.
9   Sykes to Clayton [3 March?] 1918, PRO 800/221/106–112.
10   Foreign Office to Clayton, 6 April 1918, PRO FO 371/3383/373.
11   See Jean-Dominique Montoisy, Le Vatican et le Problème des Lieux Saints (Jerusalem, 1984), p. 46.
12   See Sergio Minerbi, L'Italie et la Palestine 1914–1920 (Paris, 1970), pp. 141 ff.
13   Tuozzi to Carlo Sforza (Under-Secretary at Italian Foreign Ministry), 19 December 1919, quoted ibid., p. 149.
14   'Extract from memorandum enclosed with Foreign Office letter to Colonial Office of 31 May 1944', PRO CO 733/461/14.
15   Norman and Helen Bentwich, Mandate Memories 1914–1948 (London, 1965), p. 37.
16   Chaim Weizmann to Vera Weizmann, 18 April 1918, quoted in David Vital, Zionism: The Crucial Phase (Oxford, 1987), p. 321.
17   Clayton to Foreign Office, 7 May 1918, PRO FO 371/3391/351.
18   Clayton to Foreign Office, enclosing report by William Ormsby-Gore, 19 April 1918, PRO FO 371/3395/2 ff.
19   Clayton to Foreign Office, 22 July 1918, PRO FO 371/3391/418.
20   A. Albina to Sykes [June 1918], 'Secret Report no. 15', PRO FO 800/221/62 ff.
21   J. N. Camp to Chief Administrator, 12 August 1918, PRO FO 371/4182/352.
22   Protest letter dated 20 August 1918, PRO FO 371/4183/302.
23   A. J. P. Taylor, ed., Lloyd George: A Diary by Frances Stevenson (New York, 1971), p. 202.
24   Text of dispatch, 11 December 1917, in Massey, How Jerusalem Was Won, p. 209.
25   Quoted in Vital, Zionism: The Crucial Phase, p. 299.
26   Quoted in H. Eugene Bovis, The Jerusalem Question 1917–1948 (Stanford, 1971), pp. 6–7.
27   Text of Latin memorandum, dated Christmas 1918, in Colin, ed., Recueil, pp. 52–61; text of Greek Orthodox memorandum, 29 June 1919, ibid., pp. 217–25.
28   Text ibid., p. 18.
29   L. G. A. Cust, The Status Quo in the Holy Places (Jerusalem, 1929).
30   See Finn, Stirring Times, vol. I, p. 29; and Storrs, Orientations , p. 402.
31   H. C. Luke, Cities and Men (3 vols., London, 1953–6), vol. 2, p. 208.
32   Minerbi, Vatican and Zionism, p.142.
33   Minute by Sykes, 1 September 1918, PRO FO 371/3393.
34   See documents relating to relations between government and Patriarchate in ISA 2/215.
35   Southard (Jerusalem) to State Department, Washington, 6 September 1921, USNA State Department records, microcopy 353, roll 79, frame 109.
36   Minerbi, Vatican and Zionism, p. 35.
37   Bulletin de Renseignements, no. 23, French consulate-general, Jerusalem, 4 January 1923, AMAEN, Consulat Jérusalem, série B, carton 101, dossier 1923. See also note of French

consulate-general, Jerusalem, 29 January 1922, AMAEN, Consulat Jérusalem, série B, carton 20.

38   Ronald Storrs to consul-general, 15 April 1925, AMAEN, Consulat Jérusalem, série B, carton 153, dossier 1925.

39   Sir Anton Bertram and Harry Charles Luke, *Report of the Commission Appointed by the Government of Palestine to Inquire into the Affairs of the Orthodox Patriarchate of Jerusalem* (London, 1921), p. 38.

40   Ibid., p. 20.

41   Sir R. Wingate to A. J. Balfour, 13 February 1918, PRO FO 371/3400; see also Captain A. Abramson to GHQ, Intelligence, 1 February 1918, ibid.

42   Bertram and Luke, *Report*, pp. 219–20.

43   Storrs, *Orientations*, p. 405.

44   Stavrou, *Russian Interests*, pp. 210–11.

45   J. H. H. Pollock (Colonial Office) to J. G. T. Sheringham (Foreign Office), 23 February 1950, PRO FO 371/82233.

46   Storrs to Occupied Enemy Territory Administration headquarters, 24 November 1918, PRO FO 371/3386/267.

47   Uri Kupferschmidt, *The Supreme Muslim Council: Islam under the British Mandate for Palestine* (Leiden, 1987), p. 231.

48   See L. A. Meyer, 'Two Inscriptions of Baybars', *Quarterly of the Department of Antiquities of Palestine*, 2 (1932); Yosef Sadan, 'Ha-Maqam Nabi Musa bein Yeriho le-vein Damesek: Le-Toldoteha shel Taharut Bein Shnei Atarei Kodesh', *Ha-Mizrah He-Hadash*, 28: 1–2 (1979), pp. 22–38, and 'Ha-Mahloket Be-Sugiyat Maqam Nabi Musa Be-Einei Ha-Mekorot Ha-Muslemiyin', *Ha-Mizrah He-Hadash*, 28: 3–4 (1979), pp. 220–38; G. E. von Grünebaum, *Muhammadan Festivals* (London, 1976), pp. 81–3.

49   *Palestine Weekly*, 25 June 1920.

50   See David Wasserstein, *The Rise and Fall of the Party Kings* (Princeton, 1985), pp. 243–4; also Spyros Vryonis, *The Decline of Medieval Hellenism in Asia Minor and the Process of Islamisation from the Eleventh through the Fifteenth Century* (Berkeley, 1971); and F. W. Hasluck *Christianity and Islam under the Sultans* (Oxford, 1929).

51   Storrs, *Orientations*, p. 329.

52   Interim report of Commission of Inquiry under Major-General P. C. Palin, 7 May 1920, PRO FO 371/5119/181 ff.

53   See Bernard Wasserstein, *British in Palestine*, pp. 64–5.

54   Bentwich, *Mandate Memories*, p. 195.

55   See Kupferschmidt, *Supreme Muslim Council*, p. 22.

56   See Zvi Elpeleg, *The Grand Mufti: Haj Amin al-Hussaini, Founder of the Palestinian National Movement* (London, 1993), p. 2; and *infra* p. 165.

57   Norman Bentwich, *My Seventy-seven Years* (London, 1962), p. 74.

58   See Kupferschmidt, *Supreme Muslim Council*, pp. 159–67.

59   See list ibid., pp. 69–70.

60   Ibid., pp. 193–5.

61   Ibid., p. 202.

62   Ibid., pp. 207–8.

63   Ibid., p. 209.

64   Rubinstein, 'Jerusalem Municipality', p. 79; see also Neil Caplan, *Futile Diplomacy*, vol. 1

(London, 1983), pp. 74–6.

65   Yehoshua Porath, *The Palestinian Arab National Movement: From Riots to Rebellion 1929–1939* (London, 1977), pp. 63–4.

66   Quoted in Moshe Hirsch, Deborah Housen-Couriel and Ruth Lapidoth, *Whither Jerusalem? Proposals and Positions Concerning the Future of Jerusalem* (The Hague, 1995), p. 27; see also Chaim Arlosoroff, *Yoman Yerushalayim* (Tel Aviv [1949]), pp. 170–71 (Arlosoroff diary entries for 6 and 7 January 1932).

67   Porath, *Palestinian Arab National Movement*, p. 188.

68   Record of discussion on 17 February 1934 in Litvinoff, ed., *Letters and Papers of Chaim Weizmann*, series B, vol. 2, pp. 38–40.

69   See Michael Romann, 'Maavaro shel Ha-Mercaz Ha-Demografi Ve-Ha-Kalkali Miyrushalayim Le-Tel-Aviv Bi-Tkufat Ha-Mandat', in Lavsky, ed., *Yerushalayim*, pp. 217–34.

70   These figures refer to 1939: D. Gurevich et al., *Statistical Handbook of Jewish Palestine 1947* (Jerusalem, 1947), p. 48.

71   Quoted in Yossi Katz, 'The Political Status of Jerusalem in Historical Context: Zionist Plans for the Partition of Jerusalem in the Years 1937–1938', *Shofar*, 11: 3 (Spring 1993), p. 45.

72   Porath, *Palestinian Arab National Movement 1929–1939*, p. 219.

73   Katz, 'Political Status', pp. 46–50. See also Motti Golani, 'Jerusalem's Hope Lies Only in Partition: Israeli Policy on the Jerusalem Question, 1948–67', *International Journal of Middle East Studies*, 31: 4 (November 1999), pp. 577–604.

74   *Palestine Partition Commission Report* (Cmd 5854, London, 1938), p. 75.

75   See Bernard Wasserstein, *Secret War in Shanghai* (London, 1998), p. 7.

76   *Palestine Partition Commission Report*, pp. 76–9.

77   Report published on 29 July 1937, quoted in Yehuda Taggar, *The Mufti of Jerusalem and Palestine Arab Politics, 1930–1937* (New York, 1986), p. 446.

78   Ibid., p. 451.

79   Porath, *Palestinian Arab National Movement 1929–1939*, p. 240.

80   W. Battershill, Officer Administering the Government of Palestine, Jerusalem, to Colonial Secretary, 2 November 1937, PRO CO 733/337/17.

81   See minute by Ormsby-Gore, 22 November 1937, ibid.

82   Memorandum by Middle East Department of Colonial Office on 'The Mayoralty of Jerusalem', 31 August 1944, PRO CO 733/458/4.

83   See Gavriel Cohen, 'Harold MacMichael and Palestine's Future', *Zionism*, 3 (April 1981), pp. 133–55.

84   *Olympian Odes*, VI: 3–4.

85   Memorandum by High Commissioner on 'The Nature and Constitution of the Succession States', February 1944, PRO CO 733/461/13.

86   Minute by E. B. Boyd, 8 March 1944, PRO CO 733/461/13.

87   'Extract from Report of Cairo Conference held on 6th–7th April, 1944, enclosed with Resident Minister's letter to Secretary of State of 9th May 1944', PRO CO 733/461/14.

88   Minute by Boyd, 28 June 1944, PRO CO 733/461/14.

89   Memorandum by A. Eden, 15 September 1944, PRO CAB 95/14.

90   Extract from Foreign Office memorandum, 6 October 1944, PRO CO 733/461/14.

91   Minutes of meetings and maps of proposals in PRO CAB 121/51.

92   Quoted in Yossi Katz, 'The Marginal Role of Jerusalem in Zionist Settlement Activity Prior to the Founding of the State of Israel', *Middle Eastern Studies*, 34: 3 (July 1998), pp. 121–45.

93   Rubinstein, 'Jerusalem Municipality', p. 86.

94   *Jewish Chronicle*, 8 September 1944; see also R. M. Graves, *Experiment in Anarchy* (London, 1949), p. 12.

95   George Kirk, *The Middle East in the War* [Royal Institute of International Affairs, *Survey of International Affairs 1939–1946*] (London, 1952), pp. 319–20.

96   Lord Gort to Colonial Secretary, 20 April 1945, PRO CO 733/458/4.

97   *The Times*, 13 July 1945.

98   *Palestine Royal Commission Report* (Cmd 5479, London, 1937), p. 368.

99   Yossi Feintuch, *US Policy on Jerusalem* (Westport, Conn., 1987), p. 6.

100 Motti Golani, 'Zionism without Zion: The Jerusalem Question, 1947–1949', *Journal of Israeli History*, 16: 1 (Spring 1995), pp. 39–52.

101 Quoted in Michael Brecher, *Decisions in Israel's Foreign Policy* (London, 1974), p. 14.

102 See comparative tables of official figures in *Supplementary Memorandum by the Government of Palestine, including Notes on Evidence given to the UN Special Committee on Palestine up to 12 July 1947* (Jerusalem, 1947), p. 56.

103 Haim Levenberg, *Military Preparations of the Arab Community in Palestine 1945–1948* (London, 1993), p. 80.

104 Silvio Ferrari, 'The Holy See and the Postwar Palestine Issue: The Internationalization of Jerusalem and the Protection of the Holy Places', *International Affairs*, 60: 2 (Spring 1984), p. 264.

105 Golani, 'Zionism without Zion', p. 41.

106 *Report to the General Assembly by the United Nations Special Committee on Palestine* (London, 1947).

107 Loy Henderson to John H. Hillering (telegram), 10 November 1947, USNA, RG 59, Palestine Reference Files of Dean Rusk and Robert McClintock 1947–1949, Dean Rusk Reference 'Book', 1 October 1947–15 February 1948.

108 Warren Austin (New York) to Secretary of State (telegram), 11 November 1947, ibid.

109 UN General Assembly resolution 181/II, 29 November 1947.

Chapter 4   **Division**

1   Graves, *Experiment*, pp. 104–5.

2   Ibid., p. 106.

3   Ibid., p. 116.

4   Ibid., p. 122.

5   Levenberg, *Military Preparations*, p. 187.

6   See Benny Morris, *Righteous Victims: A History of the Zionist-Arab Conflict, 1881–1999* (New York, 1999), p. 201; and Elpeleg, *Grand Mufti*, p. 87.

7   *UNSC, Third Session* (New York, 1948), 253rd meeting, 24 February 1948, pp. 255–73.

8   Pablo de Azcárate, *Mission in Palestine 1948–1952* (Washington, 1966), p. 6.

9   *UNTC, Second Session* (New York, 1947–8), Second Part, 19th meeting, 18 February 1948, pp. 1–5.

10   *UNTC, Second Session* (New York, 1947–8), Second Part, 29th meeting, 4 March 1948, pp. 122–30.

11   Trafford Smith (New York) to W. A. C. Mathieson (Colonial Office), 23 January 1948, PRO CO 537/3892A.

12   'Statute for Jerusalem: Report on the Second Part of the Second Session of the Trusteeship Council' [March 1948], PRO CO 537/3892B.

13 G. B. Shannon (Commonwealth Relations Office) to Mathieson (Colonial Office), 17 January 1948, PRO CO 537/3892A.

14 Unidentified British diplomat to A. N. Galsworthy (Colonial Office), 30 January 1948, PRO CO 537/3892B.

15 Minute by J. M. Martin, 16 February 1948, PRO CO 537/3892A.

16 British Delegation at UN to Foreign Office, 18 February 1948, PRO CO 537/3892A.

17 Memorandum of telephone conversation between Robert McClintock and Benjamin Gerig, 11 December 1947, USNA, RG 59, Palestine Reference Files of Dean Rusk and Robert McClintock 1947–1949, Dean Rusk Reference 'Book', 1 October 1947–15 February 1948.

18 Azcárate, *Mission in Palestine*, p. 22.

19 *UNSC, Third Year, Special Supplement No. 2,* Document A/AC.21/7 (United Nations Palestine Commission: first monthly progress report to the Security Council, 29 January 1948), p. 6.

20 Sir Alan Cunningham to Sir Thomas Lloyd, 15 January 1948, PRO CO 537/3892A.

21 Menahem Kaufman, *America's Jerusalem Policy: 1947–1948* (Jerusalem, 1982), pp. 12–13.

22 *UNSC, Third Session* (New York, 1948), 271st meeting, 19 March 1948, pp. 154–72.

23 *UNSC, Third Session* (New York, 1948), 275th meeting, 30 March 1948, pp. 245–54.

24 See Michael Brecher, 'Jerusalem: Israel's Political Decisions, 1947–1977', *Middle East Journal*, 32: 1 (Winter 1978), pp. 13–34.

25 Partial text of statement in Meron Medzini, ed., *Israel's Foreign Relations: Selected Documents 1947–1974* (Jerusalem, 1976), pp. 217–19.

26 Diary entry dated 28 September 1947, in Graves, *Experiment*, p. 88.

27 *UNTC, Second Session* (New York, 1947–8), Second Part, 32nd meeting, 8 March 1948, p. 156.

28 Feintuch, *US Policy*, pp. 23–5.

29 *Manchester Guardian*, 6 March 1948.

30 Memorandum by J. H. H. Pollock, 20 March 1948, PRO CO 537/3893.

31 For a discussion of the circumstances of his death, see Danny Rubinstein, 'Unsolved Mystery: The Death of Abd al-Kader al-Husseini', *Ha-aretz*, 6 November 1998.

32 Graves, *Experiment*, p. 185.

33 Israel Foreign Ministry memorandum, 13 October 1948, ISA FM 1814/1 I.

34 Meron Benvenisti, *Jerusalem: The Torn City* (Minneapolis, 1976), pp. 41–2.

35 Graves, *Experiment*, p. 191.

36 See Leo Kohn (Jewish Agency) to Lt.-Gen. G. H. A. MacMillan (GOC British Troops in Palestine), 16 April 1948, PRO CO 733/484/4; Cunningham to Colonial Office, 21 April 1948, ibid.; and correspondence between J. L. Magnes and MacMillan, April 1948, ibid.

37 Minute by Mathieson, 28 July 1948, PRO CO 733/484/4.

38 Cunningham (Jerusalem) to British Delegation at UN, 25 April 1948, PRO CO 537/3893.

39 *UNSC, Third Session*, 283rd meeting, 16 April 1948.

40 Cunningham (Jerusalem) to Colonial Office, 16 April 1948, PRO CO 537/3893.

41 Ibid.

42 Cunningham (Jerusalem) to British Delegation at UN, 25 April 1948, PRO CO 537/3893.

43 See Kaufman, *America's Jerusalem Policy*, pp. 139–41.

44 *UNTC, Second Session* (New York, 1947–8), Third part, 38th meeting, 27 April 1948, pp. 117–30, 39th meeting, 28 April 1948, pp. 30–42, 40th meeting, 29 April 1948, pp. 43–52.

45 *UNTC, Second Session* (New York, 1947–8), Third Part, 37th meeting, 27 April 1948, pp. 10–17. British Delegation at UN to Foreign Office, 29 April 1948, PRO CO 537/3893.

46 *UNTC, Second Session* (New York, 1947–8), Third Part, 41st meeting, 30 April 1948, pp. 52–63.
47 *UNTC, Second Session* (New York, 1947–8), Third Part, 42nd meeting, 30 April 1948, pp. 63–75.
48 See Cunningham to Colonial Office, 11 May 1948, PRO CO 537/3893.
49 Cunningham (aboard HMS *Euryalus*) to Colonial Office, 16 May 1948, PRO CO 537/3893.
50 Foreign Office to British Delegation to UN (New York), 17 May 1948, PRO CO 537/3893; Mathieson to D. Balfour, 19 May 1948, PRO CO 537/3893.
51 Quoted in Amitzur Ilan, *Bernadotte in Palestine, 1948, A Study in Contemporary Humanitarian Knight-Errantry* (London, 1989), p. 77; *The Times*, 22 June 1948.
52 Truce Commission to President, Security Council, 10 May 1948 (read out by President in *UNSC*, 291st meeting, 12 May 1948).
53 *UNSC*, 291st meeting, 12 May 1948.
54 Foreign Office minute quoted in Ilan, *Bernadotte in Palestine*, p. 267.
55 Minute on 'The Status of Jerusalem' by Foreign Office Research Dept, Middle East Section, 18 December 1962, PRO FO 371/164323.
56 Nigel Clive quoted in A. J. Sherman, *Mandate Days: British Lives in Palestine 1918–1948* (London, 1997), p. 243.
57 Golani, 'Zionism without Zion', pp. 45–6.
58 Memorandum by Vivian (later Chaim) Herzog, 21 May 1948, ISA FM 2451/4.
59 See Avi Shlaim, *Collusion across the Jordan: King Abdullah, the Zionist Movement, and the Partition of Palestine* (New York, 1988), pp. 134–8; but cf. Levenberg, *Military Preparations*, pp. 225–7.
60 William Roger Louis, *The British Empire in the Middle East 1945–51* (Oxford, 1984), pp. 366–72.
61 *UNSC, Third Session*, 283rd meeting, 16 April 1948.
62 *UNSC, Third Session*, 287th meeting, 23 April 1948.
63 Shlaim, *Collusion*, pp. 177–8.
64 Moshe Shertok (Jerusalem) to President, UN Security Council, 13 May (read out in Council by President, 15 May) *UNSC*, 292nd meeting, 15 May 1948.
65 Ibid.
66 George Kirk, *The Middle East 1945–1950* (London, 1954), p. 273.
67 Abdullah to Trygve Lie, 16 May 1948, UN Security Council document S/748.
68 Ahmad Hilmi to Government of Transjordan, [c. 16] May 1948, quoted in Shlaim, *Collusion*, p. 241.
69 Quoted ibid.
70 Feintuch, *US Policy*, p. 38.
71 Kirk, *Middle East 1945–1950*, pp. 273–4.
72 See Shlaim, *Collusion*, p. 248.
73 Feintuch, *US Policy*, pp. 37–8.
74 Azcárate, *Mission in Palestine*, p. 58.
75 Memorandum by Herzog, 21 May 1948, ISA FM 2451/4.
76 *UNSC*, 295th meeting, 18 May 1948.
77 This and much of the following paragraphs are based on *Progress Report of the United Nations Mediator on Palestine, Rhodes, 16th September 1948* (Cmd 7530, London, 1948).
78 Text of agreement in Rosalyn Higgins, *United Nations Peacekeeping 1946–1967: Documents and Commentary 1. The Middle East* (London, 1969), p. 76.

79   Kaufman, *America's Jerusalem Policy*, pp. 56–7.
80   Joseph Heller, 'Bernadotte's Mission to Palestine (1948)', *Middle Eastern Studies*, 20: 4 (October 1984), p. 226; Cary David Stanger, 'A Haunting Legacy: The Assassination of Count Bernadotte', *Middle East Journal*, 42: 2 (Spring 1988), p. 261; Ilan, *Bernadotte in Palestine*, pp. 132–8.
81   Text of letter in Folke Bernadotte, *To Jerusalem* (London, 1951), pp. 149–52.
82   *Progress Report*, pp. 51–2.
83   Kaufman, *America's Jerusalem Policy*, pp. 83–4; Ilan, *Bernadotte in Palestine*, pp. 183–91; Feintuch, *US Policy*, pp. 51–4.
84   George C. Marshall to US embassy, London, 12 August 1948, quoted in Shlomo Slonim, 'The United States and the Status of Jerusalem, 1947–1984', *Israel Law Review*, 19: 2 (Spring 1984), pp. 186–7. See also Shlomo Slonim, *Jerusalem in America's Foreign Policy, 1947–1949* (The Hague, 1998), p. 115.
85   Marshall to James G. McDonald, 1 September 1948, quoted in Ferrari, 'Holy See', p. 275.
86   Quoted in Slonim, *Jerusalem*, p. 117.
87   Ibid.
88   Text in Medzini, ed., *Documents*, pp. 219–20.
89   Quoted in Golani, 'Zionism without Zion, pp. 49–50.
90   Gabriel Sheffer, *Moshe Sharett: Biography of a Political Moderate* (Oxford, 1996), p. 389; see also Heller, 'Bernadotte's Mission', p. 230.
91   Shlaim, *Collusion*, pp. 357–8.
92   Quoted in Mary C. Wilson, *King Abdullah, Britain and the Making of Jordan* (Cambridge, 1988), p. 180.
93   Joseph Nevo, *King Abdullah and Palestine: A Territorial Ambition* (London, 1996), p. 166.
94   Haggai Eshed, *Reuven Shiloah: The Man behind the Mossad* (London, 1997), p. 143.
95   Ibid., p. 144; and Shlaim, *Collusion*, pp. 375–7.
96   Text of proclamation, 4 February 1949, in Medzini, ed., *Documents*, p. 222.
97   Feintuch, *US Policy*, pp. 61–2.
98   Text of agreement in John Norton Moore, ed., *The Arab–Israeli Conflict*, vol. 3 (Princeton, 1974), pp. 397–406.
99   UN General Assembly resolution 194, 11 December 1948.
100 Azcárate, *Mission in Palestine*, p. 141.
101 Quoted in James G. McDonald, *My Mission in Israel 1948–1951* (London, 1951), pp. 184–5.
102 Quoted in Feintuch, *US Policy*, p. 74.
103 Quoted in Kirk, *Middle East*, p. 305.
104 Ferrari, 'Holy See', p. 266.
105 *Acta Apostolicae sedis*, 16: 5 (25 April 1949), pp. 161–4.
106 Ferrari, 'Holy See', p. 269.
107 Text of speech, 12 September 1949, in Litvinoff, ed., *Letters and Papers of Chaim Weizmann*, series B, vol. 2, pp. 715–17.
108 Ferrari, 'Holy See', p. 281.
109 See Kaufman, *America's Jerusalem Policy*, p. 52.
110 Memorandum by Avraham Biran, October 1948, ISA FM 1814/1 II.
111 Memorandum by Herzog, 7 September 1949, ISA FM 2451/4.
112 Memorandum, n.d., October 1949, left by Mordechai Eliash with Archbishop of Canterbury, ISA 100/27.

113 Memorandum, 31 October 1949, printed in *UNGA Fifth Session,* Supplement No. 18 (A/1367/Rev. 1), *General Progress Report and Supplementary Report of the United Nations Conciliation Commission for Palestine* (New York, 1951), pp. 9–11.

114 Draft by Shabtai Rosenne, 29 September 1949, ISA FM 1885/4.

115 Memorandum by Rosenne, 30 September 1949, ISA FM 1885/4.

116 Walter Eytan to Israeli Ambassador (Brussels), 14 November 1949, quoted in Uri Bialer, 'The Road to the Capital – The Establishment of Jerusalem as the Official Seat of the Israeli Government in 1949', *Studies in Zionism*, 5: 2 (Autumn 1984), p. 278.

117 Quoted in Zander, *Israel and the Holy Places*, p. 80.

118 Sir H. Dow (Tel Aviv) to Foreign Office, 7 October 1949, PRO FO 371/75352.

119 Cabinet minutes, 5 December 1949, ISA.

120 Text of statement to Knesset, 5 December 1949, in Medzini, ed., *Documents*, pp. 223–4.

121 UN General Assembly resolution 303 (IV), 9 December 1949.

122 Brecher, *Decisions*, pp. 28–32.

123 See Golani, 'Zionism without Zion', pp. 51–2; Bialer, 'Road to the Capital', pp. 294–6; Sheffer, *Sharett*, pp. 507–8.

124 Quoted in Tom Segev, *1949: The New Israelis* (New York, 1986), pp. 41–2.

125 Text of statement in Medzini, ed., *Documents*, p. 226.

126 Secretary of State to embassy in Israel, 4 January 1950, *FRUS 1950,* vol. V (Washington, 1978), pp. 667–8.

127 Quoted in Shlaim, *Collusion*, p. 537.

128 Sheffer, *Sharett*, p. 510.

129 Shlaim, *Collusion*, pp. 527–8.

Chapter 5 **Two Jerusalems**

1 Population breakdown in ISA FM 4032/17.

2 *NYT*, 30 May 1950.

3 *Le Monde*, 31 May 1950; *The Times*, 1 June 1950.

4 British Delegation to UN to Foreign Office, 19 January 1950, PRO FO 371/82183.

5 Foreign Office to British delegation (Geneva), 9 February 1950, ibid.

6 US Chargé in Amman to Secretary of State (Washington), 25 January 1950, *FRUS 1950*, vol. V (Washington, 1978), pp. 703–4.

7 US Chargé in Amman to Secretary of State (Washington), 13 February 1950, ibid., pp. 741–2.

8 Report in Jerusalem Arabic newspaper, *Filastin*, 21 April 1950, quoted in US Consul General in Jerusalem to State Department, 24 April 1950, ibid., p. 872.

9 Copy in ISA FM 1814/4.

10 Avi Plascov, *The Palestinian Refugees in Jordan 1948–1967* (London, 1981), p. 177; Wilson, *King Abdullah*, p. 209.

11 Shlaim, *Collusion*, pp. 395–6.

12 Ibid., pp. 607–8; and Naim Sofer, 'The Political Status of Jerusalem in the Hashemite Kingdom of Jordan 1948–1967', in E. Kedourie and S. G. Haim, eds., *Palestine and Israel in the 19th and 20th Centuries* (London, 1982), pp. 255–76.

13 See Michael Comay (Tel Aviv) to Aubrey (Abba) Eban (Washington), 12 November 1951, ISA FM 2451/5.

14   British Legation (Tel Aviv) to Foreign Office, 5 August 1952, PRO FO 371/98488.
15   Memorandum by Stuart W. Rockwell of meeting with Eban and Eliahu Elath, 19 April 1950, *FRUS 1950*, vol. V (Washington, 1978), pp. 861–4.
16   Dean Acheson to US embassy (London), 22 August 1950, ibid., p. 977.
17   Memorandum, 29 July 1952, text in Caplan, *Futile Diplomacy*, vol. 4 (London, 1997), pp. 291–2.
18   Quoted ibid., p. 64.
19   Memorandum by Evelyn Shuckburgh, 15 December 1954, text ibid., pp. 294–5.
20   Memorandum, 10 March 1955, text ibid., pp. 296–303.
21   UNRWA table of 'Monthly Distribution Return of Refugee Population, Jordan District, June 1953' in Stewart Perowne, *The One Remains: A Report from Jerusalem* (London, 1954), Appendix 1.
22   Roderick Parkes (Amman) to R. S. Crawford (Foreign Office), 7 December 1962, PRO FO 371/164323.
23   Minute by P. H. Lawrence (Levant Dept, Foreign Office), 15 March 1956, PRO FO 371/121851.
24   Thomas Wikeley (Jerusalem) to E. M. Rose (Foreign Office), 5 June 1956, PRO FO 371/121851.
25   Perowne, *The One Remains*, p. 61.
26   Wikeley (Jerusalem) to Rose (Foreign Office), 7 April 1955, PRO FO 371/115663.
27   Quoted in Avi Plascov, 'The Palestinians of Jordan's Border', in Roger Owen, ed., *Studies in the Economic and Social History of Palestine in the Nineteenth and Twentieth Centuries* (London, 1982), p. 233.
28   Moshe Ma`oz, *Palestinian Leadership on the West Bank: The Changing Role of the Arab Mayors under Jordan and Israel* (London, 1984), pp. 54–5.
29   Plascov, 'Palestinians of Jordan's Border', p. 237.
30   C. B. Duke (Amman) to Rose (Levant Dept, Foreign Office), 24 September 1956, PRO FO 371/121850.
31   Wikeley (Jerusalem) to Foreign Office, 29 September 1956, no. 352, PRO FO 371/121850.
32   British consulate-general, Jerusalem (East) to Foreign Office, 19 January 1967, PRO FCO 17/563.
33   Wikeley (Jerusalem) to Foreign Office, 29 September 1956, no. 353, ibid.
34   Wikeley (Jerusalem) to Foreign Office, 1 October 1956, PRO FO 371/121850.
35   Sir G. Jebb (Paris) to Foreign Office, 9 October 1956, PRO FO 371/121850.
36   Wikeley (Jerusalem) to Foreign Office, 8 October 1956, PRO FO 371/121850; Foreign Office aide-mémoire (apparently prepared for submission to Jordanian government), 11 October 1956, ibid; Wikeley (Jerusalem) to Foreign Office, 23 October 1956, ibid; and minute on 'the status of Jerusalem' by Foreign Office Research Dept, Middle East Section, 18 December 1962, PRO FO 371/164323.
37   Minute by R. M. Hadow, 5 November 1956, PRO FO 371/121767; see also minute by P. H. Lawrence, 3 November 1956, ibid.
38   Barry Rubin, *Revolution Until Victory: The Politics and History of the PLO* (Cambridge, Mass., 1994), p. 2; Uriel Dann, *King Hussein and the Challenge of Arab Radicalism: Jordan 1955–1967* (New York, 1989), p. 196.
39   Israel Kimhi and Benjamin Hyman, 'Demographic and Economic Developments in Jerusalem since 1967', in Kraemer, ed., *Jerusalem*, p. 137. The reference area used for these figures is the post-1967 Israeli municipal borders.

40   Daphne Tsimhoni, *Christian Communities in Jerusalem and the West Bank since 1948: An Historical, Social, and Political Study* (Westport, Conn., 1993), pp. 1–9.

41   Wikeley (Jerusalem) to Rose (Foreign Office), 30 November 1955, PRO FO 371/115663.

42   Rose (Jerusalem) to Sir Charles Peake (British Ambassador, Athens), 5 December 1955, PRO FO 371/115614.

43   John Nicholls (Tel Aviv) to Rose (Levant Dept, Foreign Office), 6 February 1956, PRO FO 371/121442.

44   Minute by B. Miller, 31 October 1955, PRO FO 371/115617.

45   Tsimhoni, *Christian Communities*, pp. 36–43.

46   Eytan and Herzog (Tel Aviv) to Sharett (New York), 10 November 1950, ISA FM 1814/5; and Herzog to Sharett, 29 November 1950, ibid.

47   Tsimhoni, *Christian Communities*, pp. 68–9; see also Victor Azarya, *The Armenian Quarter of Jerusalem: Urban Life Behind Monastery Walls* (Berkeley, 1984), pp. 114–15.

48   Ibid., p. 116.

49   See Bovis, *Jerusalem Question*, pp. 97–8.

50   A. R. Walmsley (Jerusalem) to G. H. Baker (Levant Dept, Foreign Office), 11 January 1954, PRO FO 371/110853.

51   Memorandum by J. F. Brewis, 18 March 1954, PRO FO 371/110583.

52   Secretary of State (Washington) to US Embassy in Israel, 4 January 1950, *FRUS 1950*, vol. V (Washington, 1978), pp. 667–8.

53   See editorial note in *FRUS 1961–1963*, vol. XVII (Washington, 1994), p. 738.

54   Walmsley (Jerusalem) to Eastern Department, Foreign Office, 31 August 1953, enclosing report on 'heads of career consular posts in Jerusalem, August 1953', PRO FO 371/104484.

55   Israeli Foreign Ministry note, n.d. [December 1950], ISA FM 1814/5.

56   Minutes of extraordinary meeting of consular corps, Jerusalem, 13 January 1951, ISA FM 1814/5; A. Biran to Director-General, Israel Foreign Ministry, 17 January 1951, ibid.; Foreign Ministry Research Department to Foreign Minister, 29 January 1951, ibid.

57   Ibid.

58   Text of note from Soviet representative at UN, Y. A. Malik, to UN Secretary-General Trygve Lie, 17 April 1950, in PRO FO 371/82186.

59   Knox Helm (Tel Aviv) to Foreign Office, 25 April 1950, PRO FO 371/82186.

60   See memorandum by Y. Ilsar, n.d. [January 1966], ISA FM 4032/17.

61   See Sharett to John Foster Dulles, 27 July 1953, ISA FM 1817/3.

62   Extract from UK record of Anglo-American conversations held in State Department, 14 July 1953, PRO FO 371/104738; see also Department of State press release, 28 July 1953, *FRUS 1953*, vol. IX (Washington, 1986), pp. 1263–4.

63   M. T. Walker (Amman) to Foreign Office, 30 July 1953, PRO FO 371/104739.

64   A. R. Moore (Tel Aviv) to P. S. Falla (Levant Dept, Foreign Office), 22 December 1953, PRO FO 371/104842.

65   US ambassador (London), to Eden (conveying message from Dulles), 9 October 1954, PRO FO 371/111132.

66   Nicholls (Tel Aviv) to Rose (Levant Dept, Foreign Office), 1 and 8 August 1955, PRO FO 371/115938.

67   See State Department to President's Special Assistant for National Security Affairs, 31 May 1962, *FRUS 1961–3*, vol. XVII (Washington, 1994), pp. 688–91.

68   Memorandum of conversation at State Department with Faiz al-Khouri, 28 August 1950,

FRUS 1950, vol. V (Washington, 1978), p. 981.

69 Caplan, *Futile Diplomacy*, vol. 4, p. 185.

70 British consulate-general (Jerusalem), to Levant Dept, Foreign Office, 27 January 1955, PRO FO 371/115615.

71 J. G. S. Beith (Foreign Office) to P. F. Hancock (Tel Aviv), 12 February 1960, PRO FO 371/164322.

72 Memorandum on 'France and the problem of Jerusalem' by West European Dept of Israel Foreign Ministry, 16 April 1966, ISA FM 4032/17.

73 Text of agreement in Moore, *Arab-Israeli Conflict*, vol. 3, pp. 397–406.

74 'Top secret' report by Baruch Neumark, 8 October 1948, ISA FM 2451/4.

75 Shlaim, *Collusion*, p. 460.

76 Report by UNTSO Chief of Staff quoted in Higgins, *United Nations Peacekeeping*, p. 164.

77 Text of statement by General Vagn Bennike, UNTSO Chief of Staff to UN Security Council, ibid., pp. 120–21.

78 See Baruch Gil`ad, ed., *Te'udot Li-Mediniut Ha-Hutz shel Medinat Yisrael*, vol. 14 *1960* (Jerusalem, 1997), p. 11.

Chapter 6 **Annexation**

1 Text of statement in Medzini, ed., *Documents*, p. 343.

2 See e.g. Israel Ministry of Foreign Affairs, *Jerusalem: Issues and Perspectives* (Jerusalem, 1972).

3 Quoted in Dann, *King Hussein*, p. 200.

4 Quoted in Brecher, 'Jerusalem', p. 23.

5 Based on extract from verbatim minutes in Brecher, 'Jerusalem', pp. 23–4.

6 Quoted in Morris, *Righteous Victims*, p. 324.

7 Abraham Rabinovich interview with Motta Gur, *JP*, 21 July 1995.

8 Golani, 'Jerusalem's Hope', pp. 594–6.

9 Quoted in Randolph S. and Winston S. Churchill, *The Six Day War* (London, 1967), p. 141.

10 Martin Van Creveld, *The Sword and the Olive: A Critical History of the Israeli Defense Force* (New York, 1998), pp. 188–91.

11 Benvenisti, *Jerusalem*, p. 86.

12 Richard H. Pfaff, *Jerusalem: Keystone of an Arab-Israeli Settlement* (Washington, 1969), p. 35.

13 Memorandum by Comay, 9 June 1967, ISA FM 4089/15.

14 Memorandum on Jerusalem by A. Levontin, 10 June 1967, ISA FM 4089/15.

15 Michael Hadow (Tel Aviv) to Foreign Office, 14 June 1967, PRO FCO 17/251.

16 *IHT*, 23 June 1967.

17 Feintuch, *US Policy*, pp. 125–7.

18 R. Ze'evi to Y. S. Shapiro, Minister of Justice, 22 June 1967, ISA FM 4089/14. Population data from Maya Choshen and Naama Shahar, *Statistical Yearbook of Jerusalem 1997* (Jerusalem, 1998), pp. 25–9.

19 Record of decisions of meeting on 23 June 1967, ISA RAM 6306/1115, file 1.

20 Texts of decisions ibid.

21 Text of law in Medzini, ed., *Documents*, p. 245.

22 Text ibid, pp. 245–6.

23 Text ibid., p. 247.

24 See Benvenisti, *Jerusalem*, pp. 95–104.

25 Memorandum by I. C. Alexander (British Consulate-General, Jerusalem), 29 June 1967.

26 Translated copy of order, PRO FCO 17/253.

27 *NYT*, 30 June 1967.

28 Eban, letter to editor, *Daily Telegraph*, 8 September 1980.

29 Benvenisti, *Jerusalem,* p. viii.

30 John Lewen (Jerusalem) to Foreign Office, 26 January 1968, PRO FCO 17/640.

31 See report on this case in *Israel Law Review*, 5: 1 (January 1970), pp. 120 ff.

32 Ruth Lapidoth, 'Jerusalem and the Peace Process', *Israel Law Review*, 28: 2/3 (Spring/Summer 1994), p. 416.

33 Zerah Warhaftig to Levi Eshkol, 1 October 1967, ISA RAM 6304/1067.

34 Arthur Kutcher, *The New Jerusalem: Planning and Politics* (London, 1973), p. 54.

35 *NYT*, 12 January 1968.

36 *NYT*, 3 July 1968.

37 David Ben Gurion's conversation with Eric Rouleau of *Le Monde* quoted in Pfaff, *Jerusalem*, p. 41.

38 *Ha-aretz*, 9 and 29 August 1968.

39 Quoted in B'Tselem (Israel Information Center for Human Rights in the Occupied Territories), *A Policy of Discrimination: Land Expropriation, Planning and Building in East Jerusalem* (Jerusalem, 1995), p. 36.

40 Ibid., p. 19.

41 Ibid., p. 49.

42 Meron Benvenisti, *City of Stone: The Hidden History of Jerusalem* (Berkeley, 1996); and Amir S. Cheshin, Bill Hutman and Avi Melamed, *Separate and Unequal: The Inside Story of Israeli Rule in East Jerusalem* (Cambridge, Mass., 1999); also *JP*, 11 July 1995 and *Ha-aretz*, 25 March 1999.

43 Lewen (Jerusalem) to W. Morris (Foreign Office), 6 July 1967, PRO FCO 17/253.

44 Rawhi al-Khatib et al. to R. Levy, Assistant Administrative Officer for Jerusalem, 23 July 1967, copy in PRO FCO 17/251.

45 Lewen (Jerusalem) to Morris (Foreign Office), 12 July 1967, PRO FCO 17/251.

46 On Aref's mandatory career see Bernard Wasserstein, *British in Palestine*, pp. 179–82.

47 *JP*, 25 and 26 July 1967; *NYT*, 26 July 1967.

48 UN Security Council document S/8109 and General Assembly document A/6782, 3 August 1967; cf. the version of the statement reproduced as item C of annexe 1 of UN Security Council document S/8146 (Report of Secretary-General dated 12 September 1967), pp. 266–8.

49 Hadow (Tel Aviv) to Foreign Office, 1 August 1967, PRO FCO 17/253.

50 Hebrew translation in ISA FM 4089/13.

51 *NYT*, 26 July 1967.

52 The following is based in large measure on David Farhi, 'Ha-Moatza Ha-Muslemit Be-Mizrah Yerushalayim U-Vihuda Ve-Shomron Meaz Milhemet Sheshet Ha-Yamim' ('The Muslim Council in East Jerusalem and in Judea and Samaria since the Six-Day War'), *Hamizrah Hehadash,* 28 (1979), pp. 3–21. Also Aharon Layish, 'The Status of the Shari`a in a Non-Muslim State: The Case of Israel', *Asian and African Studies*, 27: 1/2 (March/July 1993), pp. 171–88.

53 Ibid.

54 Meron Benvenisti, 'Status and Law', *JP*, 22 February 1980; see also Lapidoth, 'Jerusalem and the Peace Process', p. 408.

55 *JP*, 12 March 1980.

56 Romann and Weingrod, *Living Together Separately*, p. 66.

57   Director, West European Dept, Israel Foreign Ministry, to chargé (Paris), 6 August 1967, ISA FM 4089/12.
58   Elpeleg, *Grand Mufti*, p. 154.
59   *NYT*, 9 March 1968.
60   *NYT*, 8 March 1968.
61   UN General Assembly resolution 2253, 4 July 1967.
62   Text in Medzini, ed., *Documents*, p. 248.
63   UN Security Council document S/8146 and General Assembly document A/6793 (Report of Secretary-General dated 12 September 1967).
64   UN General Assembly resolution 252, 21 May 1968.
65   E.g. UN Security Council resolutions 267, 3 July 1969 and 298, 29 September 1971.
66   H. N. Pullar (Jerusalem) to Foreign Office, 13 June 1967, PRO FCO 17/213.
67   United States Information Service paper, 29 June 1967.
68   UN Security Council resolution 267, 3 July 1969.
69   See statement by Yost in Security Council, 1 July 1969, text in Moore ed., *Arab-Israeli Conflict*, vol. 3, pp. 992–5.
70   Quoted in Slonim, 'United States and the Status of Jerusalem', p. 218.
71   Quoted ibid., p. 216.
72   Interview of author with Lord Caradon, New York, 6 April 1970; *The Times*, 14 June 1974; *NYT*, 24 November 1974; *Guardian*, 27 August 1979.
73   *The Times*, 13 September 1974.
74   Quoted in Edward R. F. Sheehan, *The Arabs, Israelis, and Kissinger: A Secret History of American Diplomacy in the Middle East* (New York, 1976), pp. 74–5.
75   *NYT*, 15 March 1974; *Le Figaro*, 20 February 1975; *Egyptian Gazette*, 22 February 1977.
76   *NYT*, 3 April 1975.
77   Brookings Institution, *Towards Peace in the Middle East* (Washington, 1975); see also William Quandt, *Decade of Decisions: American Policy Toward the Arab-Israeli Conflict 1967–1976* (Berkeley, 1977), p. 291.
78   *IHT*, 31 December 1973.
79   *The Times*, 12 February 1974, *Guardian*, 14 February 1974.
80   Interview with Teddy Kollek, Israel radio, 17 May 1980.
81   *JP*, 9 and 14 May 1980.
82   *The Times*, 27 April 1977.
83   Ya'akov Hazan, 'Peace and the Future of Jerusalem', *Progressive Israel*, 6: 8 (June 1980).
84   *NYT*, 12 August 1977.
85   *The Times*, 21 November 1977.
86   Moshe Dayan, *Breakthrough: A Personal Account of the Egypt-Israel Peace Negotiations* (London, 1981), p. 85.
87   Mohamed Ibrahim Kamel, *The Camp David Accords: A Testimony* (London, 1986), p. 218.
88   Ibid., p. 297.
89   Interview with Harold Saunders, Washington, 14 June 1982. See also Kamel, *Camp David Accords*, p. 346.
90   Texts in J. A. S. Grenville and Bernard Wasserstein eds., *The Major International Treaties since 1945* (London, 1987), p. 379.
91   Dayan, *Breakthrough*, p. 179.
92   Kamel, *Camp David Accords*, p. 374.

Chapter 7   **Towards Palestinian Autonomy**

1   Israel Radio news broadcast, 17 July 1979.
2   Israel Radio news broadcast, 22 July 1979; see also *JP*, 22 December 1979.
3   Israel Radio news broadcast, 19 January 1980.
4   *JP*, 11, 23 and 25 April 1980; *The Times*, 3 April 1980.
5   *JP*, 16 July 1980.
6   Quoted in Slonim, 'United States and the Status of Jerusalem', p. 236.
7   *JP*, 18 January 1980.
8   *NYT*, 24 October 1980.
9   *Dawn*, 26 February 1979.
10   *Dawn*, 13 May 1979; *IHT*, 14 May 1979; *Observer* Foreign News Service report, 29 June
     1979.
11   See *Comité al Qods sous la présidence de Sa Majesté le Roi Hassan II: Réalisations et Perspectives*
     (Rabat, 1984).
12   *Dawn*, 28 March 1979.
13   *JP*, 1 August 1980.
14   *JP*, 24, 25 and 27 July 1980.
15   *JP*, 29 July 1980.
16   Text of 'Basic Law: Jerusalem the Capital of Israel', issued by Embassy of Israel, London,
     30 July 1980.
17   *JP*, 1 August 1980.
18   *Ma'ariv*, 15 June 1979.
19   See Hirsch, Housen-Couriel and Lapidoth, *Whither Jerusalem?*, passim.
20   *JP*, 15 September 1980.
21   Israel Army Radio, 29 July 1980.
22   *JP*, 1 August 1980.
23   *NYT*, 3 August 1980.
24   *JP*, 17 August 1980.
25   *Daily Telegraph*, 6 February 1979.
26   *JP*, 12 August 1980.
27   *JP*, 29 July 1980.
28   *JP*, 21 July 1980; see also *JP*, 25 July 1980.
29   *JP*, 13 July 1980.
30   *JP*, 14 July 1980.
31   Speech by Weizmann to Central Asian Society, London, 12 November 1929, in Litvinoff,
     ed., *The Letters and Papers of Chaim Weizmann*, Series B, vol. 1, pp. 570–81.
32   *JP*, 24 July 1980.
33   *JP*, 29, 30 and 31 July, 1 September 1980.
34   *JP*, 13 August 1980.
35   *JP*, 12 August 1980.
36   Texts of speech and 'talking points' in Moore, ed., *Arab-Israeli Conflict*, vol. 4, part 2
     (Princeton, 1991), pp. 1,131–41.
37   Ibid., pp. 1,142–5.
38   *The Times*, 5 January 1973.
39   *JP*, 4 July 1980.
40   *JP*, 25 March 1980.

41 *JP*, 11, 13 and 21 July, 8 August 1980.

42 *JP*, 16 September 1980.

43 *JP*, 22 June 1980.

44 *NYT*, 11 March 1984.

45 *NYT*, 27 March 1984.

46 'Big 50 Survey', unpublished memorandum by Anti-Defamation League of B'nai B'rith, 15 May 1984.

47 *NYT*, 29 March 1984.

48 *JP*, 9 October 1980.

49 Texts from Office of Permanent Observer Mission of Palestine to the United Nations.

50 *Guardian*, 2 August 1977.

51 Colin Legum, ed., *Middle East Contemporary Survey*, vol. 1 (1976–7) (New York, 1978), p. 581.

52 *Christian Science Monitor*, 25 July 1977.

53 'Reflections on the Political Future of Jerusalem' by Walter Eytan, 5 June 1979.

54 Walid Khalidi, 'Thinking the Unthinkable: A Sovereign Palestinian State', *Foreign Affairs*, 56: 4 (July 1978), pp. 695–713.

55 Text in Colin, ed., *Recueil*, pp. 273–301.

56 Report by Ian Black, *New Statesman*, 27 July 1979.

57 *JP*, 9 May 1980.

58 *Al-Fajr*, 18 May 1980.

59 *Yedi`ot Aharonot*, 28 November 1986.

60 *NYT*, 18 June 1987.

61 Benvenisti, *Jerusalem*, p. 192.

62 *Guardian*, 10 August 1987; *JP*, 8 and 11 December 1987.

63 *NYT*, 16 January 1988; *Guardian Weekly*, 24 January 1988 (reprinting *Washington Post* report).

64 *NYT*, 20 January 1988.

65 *NYT*, 12 February 1988.

66 Romann and Weingrod, *Living Together Separately*, p. 240.

67 See Ahmad Tibi, 'The Other Side of Jerusalem', *Jerusalem Report*, 4 July 1991; also Alex Weingrod and `Adel Manna, 'Living along the Seam: Israeli Palestinians in Jerusalem', *International Journal of Middle East Studies*, 30 (1998), pp. 369–86.

68 *NYT*, 1 June 1992.

69 Text of Shultz statement, 26 February 1988, in Moore, ed., *Arab-Israeli Conflict*, vol. 4, part 2, pp. 1,883–5.

70 Text of speech ibid., pp. 1,889–94.

71 Text from Office of Permanent Observer Mission of Palestine to the United Nations.

72 Text of Yasir Arafat speech to UN General Assembly, 14 December 1988, in Moore, ed., *Arab-Israeli Conflict*, vol. 4, part 2, pp. 1,913–16; statement by Arafat, 14 December 1988, ibid., pp. 1,917–18.

73 *Le Monde*, 4–5 July 1991.

74 *NYT*, 11 April 1993.

75 Ibid.

76 *NYT*, 10 April 1994.

77 *NYT*, 20 September 1993.

78 *NYT*, 7 October 1993.

Chapter 8   **Christian Jerusalem in Eclipse**

1   *JP*, 17 September 1997.
2   See Table 2.5 in Tsimhoni, *Christian Communities*, p. 26.
3   Ibid., p. 65.
4   *NYT*, 12 February 1992.
5   Report by Patrick Cockburn in *Independent on Sunday*, 14 May 1995.
6   See, e.g., *Jerusalem: Issues and Perspectives*.
7   See R. Levy (Ministry of Interior) to Director-General, Foreign Ministry, 23 July 1967, ISA FM 4089/14; and Levy to Director-General of Interior Ministry, 6 August 1967, ISA FM 4089/12.
8   Memorandum by Y. Ilsar, 8 December 1967, ISA FM 4089/13.
9   Hadow (Tel Aviv) to Foreign Office, 5 July 1967, PRO FCO 17/253; and Hadow to Foreign Office, 2 August 1967, PRO FCO 17/255.
10 See *The Times*, 23 October 1974.
11 See E. Ben-Horin (Foreign Ministry representative in West Bank) to Director-General, Israel Foreign Ministry, 19 June 1967, ISA FM 4089/15.
12 Patriarch Benediktos to Eshkol, 7/20 November 1967, ISA FM 4089/13.
13 Tsimhoni, *Christian Communities*, p. 44.
14 Ibid., pp. 44–5.
15 Ibid., pp. 70–71; Azarya, *Armenian Quarter*, p. 218.
16 See Naomi Shepherd, *Teddy Kollek, Mayor of Jerusalem* (New York, 1988), pp. 76–7.
17 Ilsar to Director-General of Foreign Ministry, 15 June 1967, ISA FM 4089/15.
18 *NYT*, 24 June 1967.
19 M. S. Williams (British Minister to Holy See) to Foreign Office, 27 June 1967, PRO FCO 17/252.
20 See *Osservatore Romano*, 22–3 March 1971, 30 June–1 July 1980; *The Times*, 11 April 1974; *IHT*, 8 March 1976 (but see also *IHT*, 10 March 1976); *NYT*, 13 January 1978; *Le Monde*, 8 February 1978; *JP*, 22 June, 1 July 1980.
21 Williams to Foreign Office, 6 July 1967, PRO FCO 17/252.
22 Joëlle Le Morzellec, *La Question de Jérusalem devant l'Organisation des Nations Unies* (Bruxelles, 1979), pp. 400–401.
23 Ben-Horin to Foreign Minister, 9 July 1967, ISA FM 4089/12.
24 Benediktos to Eshkol, 12 July 1967, ISA FM 4089/12.
25 Ilsar to Deputy Director-General, Israel Foreign Ministry, 14 July 1967, ISA FM 4089/12.
26 Foreign Office note, 13 July 1967, PRO FCO 17/252.
27 Quoted in Israel Foreign Ministry to Rome embassy, 16 July 1967, ISA FM 4089/12.
28 *NYT*, 4 April 1988.
29 Tsimhoni, *Christian Communities*, pp. 168–9.
30 *NYT*, 13, 16 ,19, 23 and 24 April 1990. See also Robert I. Friedman, 'Making Way for the Messiah', *New York Review of Books*, 11 October 1990.
31 *Time*, 7 May 1990.
32 Tsimhoni, *Christian Communities*, p. 177.
33 See Bernard Wasserstein, *Vanishing Diaspora* (London, 1996), ch. 6.
34 *NYT*, 7 and 8 January 1992.
35 *NYT*, 31 December 1993.
36 *NYT*, 1 January 1994.

37 *Ha-aretz,* 26 October 1994.
38 *JP*, 25 March 2000.
39 *JP*, 20 July 1994.
40 Ibid.
41 *JP*, 11 November 1994.
42 C. W. Baxter (Foreign Office) to Under-Secretary of State, Colonial Office, 3 November 1943, PRO CO 733/444/30.
43 Ibid.
44 See *Documents on Israeli-Soviet Relations 1941–1953: Part I: 1941–May 1949* (London, 2000), pp. 112–7.
45 Harry J. Psomiades, 'Soviet Russia and the Orthodox Church in the Middle East', *Middle East Journal*, 11: 4 (Autumn 1957), pp. 371–81.
46 Interview with Shabtai Rosenne, Jerusalem, 27 May 2000.
47 Soviet embassy, London, to Foreign Office, 4 May 1948, PRO FO 1040/3.
48 See *Documents on Israeli–Soviet Relations* I, p. 282, n. 2.
49 V. A. Zorin (Soviet Deputy Foreign Minister) to G. G. Karpov (Tel Aviv), 10 September 1948, ibid., pp. 337–8.
50 British Minister, Tel Aviv, to Foreign Office, 4 August 1949, PRO FO 371/75343.
51 *Le Monde*, 15 July 1987.
52 Interview with Shabtai Rosenne, Jerusalem, 27 May 2000; Yaakov Doron to Eliezer Doron, 13 January 1966, ISA FM 4049/14.
53 Herzog to Reuven Shiloah, 28 September 1949, ISA FM 2451/4.
54 Consulate-General, Jerusalem, to Foreign Office, 8 February 1950, PRO FO 371/82183.
55 Psomiades, 'Soviet Russia', p. 379.
56 British Consulate-General, Jerusalem to Eastern Dept., Foreign Office, 23 June 1952, PRO FO 371/98503.
57 See report by Dr S. P. Colbi, head of Department of Christian Affairs, Israel Ministry of Religious Affairs, ISA Gimel 5805/3.
58 Ilsar to A. Eshel, 11 July 1967, ISA FM 4089/12.
59 Metropolitan Philaret, President of Synod of Bishops of the Russian Orthodox Church Outside of Russia, to Abraham Harman (Israeli ambassador, Washington), 24 June 1967, ISA FM 4089/13.
60 Harman to Philaret, 28 June 1967, ISA FM 4089/13.
61 *Christian Science Monitor*, 18 October 1968.
62 TASS report, 29 October 1968.
63 Interview with Gideon Rafael, Jerusalem, 19 July 1982.
64 *JP*, 14 September 1980.
65 *The Times*, 21 January 2000. See also Bernard Wasserstein, 'Red Alert for White Nuns', *JP*, 31 January 2000.

Chapter 9 **Creeping Partition**

1 *Ha-aretz*, 11 December 1994.
2 Quoted in Edward Norden, 'Jerusalem: What Next?', *Commentary*, 97: 1 (January 1994), pp. 44–9; see also *NYT*, 14 February 1991.
3 The full text of the Beilin-Abu Mazen agreement has never appeared in print. Summaries

and edited versions began to leak out in 1996 (see e.g. *Ha-aretz*, 22 February 1996, *JP*, 23 February 1996 and *Ha'aretz*, 5 August 1996). This summary and the quotations are based on the text of the main part of the agreement that appeared (without the accompanying annexes or map) on the internet site of *Newsweek* magazine on 18 September 2000. The somewhat similar proposals advanced by this author in a lecture in London in June 1995 (published in October 1995 as Institute of Jewish Affairs Report no. 3, *Jerusalem: Past, Present, and Future* – later also in Norwegian in Helge Aarflot, ed., *Fred for Jerusalem: Historisk, religiøs og politisk bakgrunn* [Oslo, 1996], pp. 251–70) were formulated without knowledge of the contemporaneous Beilin-Abu Mazen negotiations.

4   *JP*, 23 February 1996.
5   Ibid.
6   Interview with Harold Saunders, Washington, 14 June 1982.
7   Israeli-Palestinian Interim Agreement on the West Bank and the Gaza Strip, 28 September 1995: Annex II: Protocol Concerning Elections, text from Israel Foreign Ministry.
8   *JP*, 18 July 1995.
9   *NYT*, 19 January 1996.
10 Ehud Olmert in an exchange with the author at Königswinter, January 1997.
11 Based on the careful analysis by Barry Rubin in his *The Transformation of Palestinian Politics: From Revolution to State-Building* (Cambridge, Mass., 1999), pp. 206–12.
12 Quoted in full-page advertisement for American Friends of *Ateret Cohanim* in *NYT*, 6 June 1993.
13 See *Ha-aretz*, 12 July 1995.
14 *JP*, 17 January 1995.
15 *Le Monde*, 21–22 August 1994.
16 *JP*, 8 November 1994.
17 *Le Monde*, 9 November 1994.
18 *JP*, 10 and 11 November 1994.
19 *JP*, 15 November 1994.
20 *JP*, 30 September 1994.
21 *Le Monde*, 8 November 1994.
22 *JP*, 8 November 1994.
23 See lists of Palestinian Cabinets, 1994–9, in Rubin, *Transformation*, pp. 203–5; list for 2000 from office of Palestinian observer at United Nations.
24 *Ha-aretz*, 16 November 1994.
25 *Ha-aretz*, 3 February 1995; *JP*, 3 February 1995; Rubin, *Transformation*, p. 224.
26 Rubin, *Transformation*, p. 224.
27 *JP*, 7 July 1995.
28 *JP*, 21 July 1995.
29 Text from Israel Foreign Ministry.
30 *NYT*, 7 October 1993.
31 'The Jerusalem Letter', memorandum produced by Palestinian Academic Society for the Study of International Affairs. See also Marshall J. Breger, 'The New Battle for Jerusalem', *Middle East Quarterly*, 1: 4 (December 1994), p. 30.
32 *Ha-aretz*, 12 February 1997; see also *Ha-aretz*, 1 February 1998.
33 *JP*, 11 May 1997.
34 *Jerusalem Report*, 26 June 1997.

35   Figures supplied by B'Tselem; see also *Ha-aretz*, 8 and 16 April 1999 and *JP*, 23 April 1999.

36   *Ha-aretz*, 5 April 1998.

37   *Ha-aretz*, 1 August 1999.

38   *IHT*, 19 October 1999.

39   *JP* (international edn.), 26 November 1999.

40   *Jewish Chronicle*, 10 March 2000.

41   *JP*, 28 April 2000.

42   *Ha-aretz*, 23 May 2000.

43   *Ha-aretz*, 2 January 2000.

44   *Ha-aretz*, 23 May 2000.

45   *Guardian*, 22 August 2000; and other press reports in *Ha-aretz*, *JP*, *NYT*, *IHT*, *The Times*.

46   See e.g. Menahem Klein, *Yerushalayim Be-Masa U-Matan Le-Shalom: `Amadot `Araviyot* (Jerusalem, 1995).

47   *NYT*, 17 September 2000.

48   *NYT*, 17 September 2000.

49   *The Times*, 26 July 2000.

Chapter 10   **Trouble on the Temple Mount**

1   See Linder, 'Jerusalem as a Focus of Confrontation', p. 2.

2   See p. 10.

3   See Guy Le Strange, *Palestine under the Muslims* (Beirut, 1965 reprint), p. 96.

4   A. Goodrich Freer, *Inner Jerusalem* (London, 1904), p. 364.

5   Finn, *Stirring Times*, vol. 2, p. 423.

6   Finn (Jerusalem) to Clarendon, 1 January 1857, in Hyamson, ed., *British Consulate*, vol. I, p. 245.

7   Herzl diary entry, 7 May 1896, as translated by Marvin Lowenthal, *The Diaries of Theodor Herzl* (New York, 1956), p. 127.

8   Shemaryahu Talmon, 'The Biblical Concept of Jerusalem', in John M. Oesterreicher and Anne Sinai, eds., *Jerusalem* (New York, 1974), p. 202.

9   See Yitzhak Reiter, *Islamic Institutions in Jerusalem: Palestinian Muslim Organization under Jordanian and Israeli Rule* (The Hague, 1997), p. 41.

10   F. H. Kisch to Nathan Strauss, 4 November 1926, CZA S25/748.

11   *Al-Sabah*, 12 July 1922.

12   See Wasserstein, *British in Palestine*, p. 222.

13   Meeting of Jewish delegation with government officials, Jerusalem, 25 September 1928, CZA S25/2939.

14   Khalidi, *Palestinian Identity*, p. 216.

15   Amikam Elad, *Medieval Jerusalem and Islamic Worship: Holy Places, Ceremonies, Pilgrimage* (Leiden, 1995), p. 102.

16   See Bernard Wasserstein, *Herbert Samuel: A Political Life* (Oxford, 1992), p. 199.

17   See PRO FO 371/4164/124–6.

18   *The Times*, 24 July 1922.

19   See e.g. ISA 2/01182.

20   *Al-Jami`a al-`Arabiyya*, 1 October 1928.

21   *Al-Jami`a al-`Arabiyya*, 11 February 1929.

22 Copy of letter forwarded by Sir John Chancellor to Sir John Shuckburgh, Colonial Office, 15 May 1929, PRO CO 733/173 (67314/26).
23 *Doar Hayom*, 23 and 30 July, 1 August 1929.
24 Copy of statement in CZA S25/2948.
25 *Report of the Wailing Wall Commission* (London, 1931).
26 Yehoshua Porath, *The Emergence of the Palestinian-Arab National Movement 1918–1929* (London, 1974), p. 272.
27 Kupferschmidt, *Supreme Muslim Council*, p. 133.
28 Ibid., p. 55.
29 Avi Shlaim, *The Iron Wall: Israel and the Arab World* (New York, 2000), p. 245 (drawing on recollections by Narkiss published in *Ha-aretz*, 31 December 1997).
30 Moshe Dayan, *Story of My Life* (London, 1976), p. 314.
31 Bovis, *Jerusalem Question*, p. 108.
32 Shlomo Goren to Ministerial Committee for Protection of Holy Places, 31 August 1967, ISA FM 4089/13.
33 See S. Bar-Hayyim, Director of Middle East Dept, Israel Foreign Ministry, to Director-General of Ministry, 14 July 1967, ISA FM 4089/12.
34 See also memorandum by M. Eliash, 28 October 1929, CZA S25/3077.
35 Full (English) text of document in Institute for Palestine Studies, *The Resistance of the Western Bank of Jordan to Israeli Occupation 1967* (Beirut, 1967).
36 Quoted in Yehuda Zvi Blum, *The Juridical Status of Jerusalem* (Jerusalem Papers on Peace Problems, 2, Leonard Davis Institute for International Relations, Hebrew University of Jerusalem, 1974).
37 Zander, *Israel and the Holy Places*, pp. 2–3.
38 *Observer* Foreign News Service report by Gavin Young, Jerusalem, 21 August 1969.
39 *Daily Telegraph*, 23 August 1969, *Straits Times* (Malaysian edn.), 28 August 1969, *Dawn*, 21 August 1970.
40 *Egyptian Gazette*, 1 January 1970.
41 *Soviet News*, 2 September 1969.
42 *JP* (international edn.), 6 April 1973.
43 See Esther Cohen, *Human Rights in the Israeli-Occupied Territories 1967–1982* (Manchester, 1982), pp. 213–14.
44 *JP* (international edn.), 3 February 1976.
45 *JP* (international edn.), 17 June 1984.
46 Article by Robert I. Friedman in *Guardian Weekly*, 24 January 1988; see also *JP*, 21 October 1994.
47 *NYT*, 6 June 1993.
48 Article by Robert I. Friedman in *New York Review of Books*, 11 October 1990.
49 *NYT*, 13 April 1982.
50 *NYT*, 12 April 1982.
51 See Ehud Sprinzak, *Brother against Brother: Violence and Extremism in Israeli Politics from Altalena to the Rabin Assassination* (New York, 1999), pp. 146, 156–61 and 164–5.
52 *JP* (international edn.), 18 January 1986.
53 Text of resolution in *NYT*, 14 October 1990.
54 *NYT*, 14 October 1990.
55 *NYT*, 25 October 1990.

56 *NYT*, 19 July 1991.
57 Ibid.
58 Text of agreement, dated 26 October 1994, from Israel Ministry of Foreign Affairs.
59 *Ha-aretz*, 5 August 1996.
60 *JP*, 19 October 1994.
61 *IHT*, 26 July 1994.
62 Dr Nasser al-Kidwa, Permanent Observer of Palestine to the UN, to Secretary-General and President of Security Council, 29 July and 19 October 1994 (texts from Office of Palestinian Observer at UN).
63 *JP*, 18 September 1994.
64 *JP*, 30 September 1994.
65 *JP*, 23 October 1994.
66 See Wasserstein, *British in Palestine*, pp. 98–100.
67 *JP*, 28 October 1994.
68 *JP*, 30 October 1994.
69 *Ha-aretz*, 16 and 25 January 1995.
70 *JP*, 1 and 3 February 1995.
71 *JP*, 17 February 1999.
72 See p. 318.
73 *JP*, 13 August 2000.
74 *NYT*, 12 August 2000.
75 English translation as issued on the *al-Thawra* website, 18 August 2000.
76 *Ha-aretz*, 30 August 2000.
77 *Ha-aretz*, 1 September 2000.

Epilogue   The Earthly City

1 Examples include Henry Cattan, *Palestine and international law: the legal aspects of the Arab-Israeli conflict* (Harlow, 1973); Y. Z. Blum, *The Juridical Status of Jerusalem* (Jerusalem, 1974).
2 Rodman Bundy, 'Legal Approaches to the Question of Jerusalem' in Ghada Karmi, ed., *Jerusalem Today: What future for the peace process?* (Reading, 1996), pp. 45–50.
3 Moshe Hirsch, Deborah Housen-Couriel and Ruth Lapidoth, *Whither Jerusalem? Proposals and Positions Concerning the Future of Jerusalem* (The Hague, 1995), pp. 25–136.
4 Ahmad Tibi, 'The Other Side of Jerusalem', *Jerusalem Report*, 4 July 1991.
5 *JP*, 30 October 1994.
6 Based on 'minutes' of the meeting published in the English edition of *Ha'aretz*, 31 December 2000. These minutes may not record the precise words used in English by President Clinton.
7 JMCC Public Opinion Poll No. 37, June 2000: results from JMCC.
8 Text as issued by Knesset.
9 *Ha-aretz*, 6 January 1997; *IHT*, 8 Jan. 1997; *JP*, 10 January 1997.
10 *IHT*, 31 December 1973.
11 *Ha-aretz*, 6 January 1997; *IHT*, 8 January 1997; *JP*, 10 January 1997.
12 Most of the figures in this section are taken from Israeli census data and/or successive editions of the *Jerusalem Statistical Year Book* published annually since 1984 by the Jerusalem Institute for Israel Studies.

13 *Jerusalem Statistical Year Book 1999*, p. 53.

14 See Sergio DellaPergola, 'Jerusalem's Population, 1995–2020: Demography, Multiculturalism and Urban Policies', to appear in *European Journal of Population*, 2000. [I am grateful to Professor DellaPergola for making an advance copy of this paper available to me.]

15 Saul B. Cohen, *Jerusalem: Bridging the Four Walls: A Geopolitical Perspective* (New York, 1977), pp. 78–9.

16 See Ira Sharkansky, *Governing Jerusalem: Again on the World's Agenda* (Detroit, 1996), pp. 122–3.

Sources

Archives

Archives Nationales, Paris
Central Zionist Archives, Jerusalem
French Foreign Ministry Archives, Paris and Nantes
Israel State Archives, Jerusalem
Municipal Archives, Jerusalem
Ottoman Foreign Ministry Archives, Istanbul
Palestine Exploration Fund Archives, London
Public Record Office, London
United States National Archives, College Park, Maryland

Interviews

Aref al-Aref (Ramallah, 27 January 1971), David Ben Gurion (Sdeh Boqer, 16 January 1970), Professor Norman Bentwich (London, 20 November 1969), Dr Avraham Biran (Jerusalem, 9 January 1970), Dr Khalil Budeiri (Jerusalem, 1 April 1974), Dr Musa Budeiri (Jerusalem, 29 May 2000), Lord Caradon (New York, 6 April 1970), Sir William Fitzgerald (London, 1970), Mr and Mrs Henry Kendall (Weybridge, 6 September 1970), Anwar Nusseibeh (Jerusalem, 9 September 1969), J. H. H. Pollock (Bath, 2 March 1970), Gideon Rafael (Jerusalem, 19 July 1982), Shabtai Rosenne (Jerusalem, 27 May 2000), Harold Saunders (Washington, 14 June 1982), Dr Hassan Tahboub (Jerusalem, 5 December 1970)

Official and semi-official publications

A Brief Record of the Advance of the Egyptian Expeditionary Force under the Command of General Sir Edmund Allenby GCB, GCMG, July 1917 to October 1918 (London, 1919)
Comité Al Qods sous la présidence de Sa Majesté le Roi Hassan II: Réalisations et Perspectives ([Rabat, 1983])
Correspondence Respecting the Rights and Privileges of the Latin and Greek Churches in Turkey Presented to Both Houses of Parliament by Command of Her Majesty (4 vols., London, 1854–6)
Documents on the Foreign Policy of Israel
Documents on Israeli-Soviet Relations 1941–1953: Part I: 1941–May 1949 (London, 2000)
Firmans Ottomans émanés pour les Lieux-Saints de la Palestine (3 vols., Jerusalem, 1934)
Foreign Relations of the United States
Israel's Foreign Relations: Selected Documents 1947–1974, Meron Medzini, ed., (Jerusalem, 1976)

Palestine: Commission on the Disturbances of August 1929: Minutes of Evidence (Colonial No. 48, 3 vols., London, 1930)

Palestine Partition Commission Report (Cmd 5854, London, 1938)

Palestine Royal Commission Report (Cmd 5479, London, 1937)

Progress Report of the United Nations Mediator on Palestine, Rhodes, 16th September 1948 (Cmd 7530, London, 1948)

Report by Sir William Fitzgerald on the Local Administration of Jerusalem (Jerusalem, 1945)

Report of the Commission Appointed by His Majesty's Government in the United Kingdom ... to determine the Rights and Claims of Moslems and Jews in Connection with the Western or Wailing Wall at Jerusalem (London, 1931)

Report of the Commission Appointed by the Government of Palestine to Inquire into the Affairs of the Orthodox Patriarchate of Jerusalem (London, 1921)

Report of the Commission on the Palestine Disturbances of August 1929 (Cmd 3530, London, 1930)

Report to the General Assembly by the United Nations Special Committee on Palestine (London, 1947)

Statistical Yearbook of Jerusalem 1982– (Jerusalem, 1984–)

United Nations Official Records
> General Assembly
> Security Council
> Trusteeship Council

The Western or Wailing Wall in Jerusalem (Cmd 3229, London, 1928)

Books and articles

Anderson, M. S., *The Eastern Question 1774–1923* (London, 1966)

Anon., *Refutation of the Allegations Put Forward by Sir Anton Bertram Against the Patriarchate of Jerusalem* (Jerusalem, n.d. [c. 1925])

Arce, P. A., ed., *Documentos y Textos para la Historia de Tierra Santa y sus Santuarios 1600–1700* (vol. 1, Jerusalem, 1970)

Armstrong, Karen, *A History of Jerusalem: One City, Three Faiths* (London, 1996)

Arnon, Adar, 'The Quarters of Jerusalem in the Ottoman Period', *Middle Eastern Studies*, 28: 1 (January 1992), pp. 1–65

Azarya, Victor, *The Armenian Quarter of Jerusalem: Urban Life Behind Monastery Walls* (Berkeley, 1984)

Azcárate, Pablo de, *Mission in Palestine 1948–1952* (Washington, 1966)

Baldi, Paschal, *The Question of the Holy Places* (Rome, 1919)

Barkan, R., 'Pax Hierosolymitana', *International Problems*, 20: 2–4 (40) (Summer 1981), pp. 139–46

Barnai, Jacob, *The Jews in Palestine in the Eighteenth Century* (Tuscaloosa, Alabama, 1992)

Ben-Arieh, Yehoshua, 'Patterns of Christian Activity and Dispersion in Nineteenth-Century Jerusalem', *Journal of Historical Geography*, 2:1 (1976), pp. 49–69

– *Jerusalem in the 19th Century: The Old City* (Jerusalem, 1984)

– *Jerusalem in the 19th Century: Emergence of the New City* (Jerusalem, 1986)

Ben-Meir, Alon, 'Jerusalem's Final Status Must Reflect its Uniqueness', *Middle East Policy*, 3:3 (1994), pp. 93–109

Bentwich, Norman and Helen, *Mandate Memories 1918–1948* (London, 1965)

Benvenisti, Meron, *Jerusalem: The Torn City* (Minneapolis, 1976)

—— *City of Stone: The Hidden History of Jerusalem* (Berkeley, 1996)

Bercovits, Shmuel, *Milhamot Ha-Mekomot Ha-Kedoshim: Ha-Ma`avak `al Yerushalayim Ve-Ha-Mekomot Ha-Kedoshim Be-Yisrael, Yehuda, Shomron, Ve-Hevel `Aza* (Jerusalem, 2000)

Bernadotte, Folke, *To Jerusalem* (London, 1951)

Bialer, Uri, 'The Road to the Capital – the Establishment of Jerusalem as the Official Seat of the Israeli Government in 1949', *Studies in Zionism*, 5:2 (Autumn 1984), pp. 273–96

Biger, G., 'Trumat Ha-Shilton Ha-Briti Le-Hitpathutah shel Yerushalayim Be-Reshit Shiltono Ba-Aretz (1918–1925)', *Mehkarim Be-Geografiah shel Eretz-Yisrael*, 9 (1976), pp. 174–200

Blake, Robert, *Disraeli's Grand Tour: Benjamin Disraeli and the Holy Land 1830–1831* (London, 1982)

Blum, Yehuda Zvi, *The Juridical Status of Jerusalem* (Jerusalem Papers on Peace Problems, 2, Leonard Davis Institute for International Relations, Hebrew University of Jerusalem, 1974)

Blyth, Estelle, *When We Lived in Jerusalem* (London, 1927)

Bovis, H. Eugene, *The Jerusalem Question 1917–1948* (Stanford, 1971)

Braude, Benjamin, 'Foundation Myths of the Millet System', in Benjamin Braude and Bernard Lewis eds., *Christians and Jews in the Ottoman Empire: The Functioning of a Plural Society* (2 vols., New York, 1982), vol. 1, pp. 69–88

—— 'Councils and Community: Minorities and the *Majlis* in *Tanzimat* Jerusalem', in C. E. Bosworth, Charles Issawi, Roger Savory and A. L. Udovitch eds., *Essays in Honor of Bernard Lewis: The Islamic World from Classical to Modern Times* (Princeton, N J, 1989), pp. 651–60

Brecher, Michael, *Decisions in Israel's Foreign Policy* (London, 1974)

—— 'Jerusalem: Israel's Political Decisions, 1947–1977', *Middle East Journal*, 32: 1 (Winter 1978), pp. 13–34

Breger, Marshall J., 'The New Battle for Jerusalem', *Middle East Quarterly*, I: 4 (December 1994), pp. 23–34

Brookings Institution, *Towards Peace in the Middle East* (Washington, 1975)

Brown, Michael, *The Israeli-American Connection: Its Roots in the Yishuv 1914–1945* (Detroit, 1996)

B'tselem (Israel Information Center for Human Rights in the Occupied Territories), *A Policy of Discrimination: Land Expropriation, Planning and Building in East Jerusalem* (Jerusalem, 1995)

Burns, Lieutenant- General E. L. M., *Between Arab and Israeli* (London, 1962)

Caplan, Neil, *Futile Diplomacy* (4 vols., London, 1983–97)

Charles-Roux, François, *Les Echelles de Syrie et de Palestine au XVIIIe Siècle* (Paris, 1928)

Cheshin, Amir S., Hutman, Bill, and Melamed, Avi, *Separate and Unequal: The Inside Story of Israeli Rule in East Jerusalem* (Cambridge, Mass., 1999)

Cohen, Amnon, *Palestine in the 18th Century: Patterns of Government and Administration* (Jerusalem, 1973)

—— *Jewish Life under Islam: Jerusalem in the Sixteenth Century* (Cambridge, Mass., 1984)

—— ed., *A World Within: Jewish Life as Reflected in Muslim Court Documents from the Sijill of Jerusalem (XVIth Century)* (2 vols., Philadelphia, 1994)

Cohen, Esther R., *Human Rights in the Israeli-Occupied Territories 1967–1982* (Manchester, 1985)

Cohen, Gavriel, 'Harold MacMichael and Palestine's Future', *Zionism*, 3 (April 1981), pp. 133–55

Cohen, Richard I., ed., *Vision and Conflict in the Holy Land* (Jerusalem, 1985)

Cohen, Saul B., *Jerusalem: Bridging the Four Walls – A Geopolitical Perspective* (New York, 1977)

Colin, Bernardin, ed., *Recueil de Documents concernant Jérusalem et les Lieux Saints* (Jerusalem, 1982)

Connell, John, *The House by Herod's Gate* (London, 1946)

Cremonesi, Lorenzo, 'The Vatican and Israel: Theological Contempt to Political Confrontation', in

W. Frankel ed., *Survey of Jewish Affairs 1985* (Cranbury, NJ, 1985)

Cust, L. G. A., *The Status Quo in the Holy Places* (Jerusalem, 1929)

Dayan, Moshe, *Story of My Life* (London, 1976)

—— *Breakthrough: A Personal Account of the Egypt-Israel Peace Negotiations* (London, 1981)

Drory, Joseph, 'Jerusalem during the Mamluk Period', in Lee I. Levine, ed., *The Jerusalem Cathedra*, vol. 1 (Jerusalem, 1981), pp. 190–213

Efrati, Nathan, *Mi-Mashber le-Tiqvah: Ha-Yishuv Ha-Yehudi Be-Eretz Yisrael Be-Milhemet Ha-`Olam Ha-Rishonah* (Jerusalem, 1991)

Elad, Amikam, *Medieval Jerusalem and Islamic Worship: Holy Places, Ceremonies, Pilgrimage* (Leiden, 1995)

Eliav, Mordechai, *Die Juden Palästinas in der Deutschen Politik: Dokumente aus dem Archiv des deutschen Konsulats in Jerusalem 1842–1914* (Tel Aviv, 1973)

—— ed., *Be-Matzor U-Ve-Matzok: Eretz-Yisrael Be-Milhemet Ha-`Olam Ha-Rishonah* (Jerusalem, 1991)

Elon, Amos, *Jerusalem: City of Mirrors* (London, 1990)

Elpeleg, Zvi, *The Grand Mufti: Haj Amin al-Hussaini, Founder of the Palestinian National Movement* (London, 1993)

Falaize, Robert, *Le Statut de Jérusalem* (Paris, 1959)

Farhi, David, 'Ha-Mo`atza Ha-Muslemit Be-Mizrah Yerushalayim U-Vihuda Ve-Shomron Meaz Milhemet Sheshet Ha-Yamim', *Hamizrah Hehadash*, 28 (1979), pp. 3–21

Feintuch, Yossi, *US Policy on Jerusalem* (Westport, Conn., 1987)

Ferrari, Silvio, 'The Holy See and the Postwar Palestine Issue: The Internationalization of Jerusalem and the Protection of the Holy Places', *International Affairs*, 60: 2 (Spring 1984), pp. 261-83

Finn, E. A., *Reminiscences of Mrs Finn* (London, 1929)

Finn, James, *Stirring Times or Records from Jerusalem Consular Chronicles of 1853 to 1856* (2 vols., London, 1878)

Finnie, David H., *Pioneers East: The Early American Experience in the Middle East* (Cambridge, Mass., 1967)

Frankel, Jonathan, *The Damascus Affair: 'Ritual Murder', Politics, and the Jews in 1840* (Cambridge, 1997)

Freer, A. Goodrich, *Inner Jerusalem* (London, 1904)

Friedland, Roger, and Hecht, Richard, *To Rule Jerusalem* (Cambridge, 1996)

Friedman, Isaiah, *Germany, Turkey, and Zionism 1897–1918* (Oxford, 1977)

Frumkin, Gad, *Derekh Shofet Biyrushalayim* (Tel Aviv, 1954)

Garcia-Granados, Jorge, *The Birth of Israel: The Drama As I Saw It* (New York, 1949)

Gerber, Haim, *Ottoman Rule in Jerusalem 1890–1914* (Berlin, 1985)

Gil, Moshe, 'Dhimmi Donations and Foundations for Jerusalem (638–1099)', *Journal of the Economic and Social History of the Orient*, 27: 2 (1984), pp. 156-174

—— *A History of Palestine 634–1099* (Cambridge, 1992)

Gilbert, Martin, *Jerusalem in the Twentieth Century* (London, 1996)

Glaubach-Gal, Eliezer, *Yerushalayim: Hesder Ha-Keva` – Kol Ha-Hatsa`ot, Kol Ha-Mahshavot, Kol Ha-Pitronot* (Tel Aviv, 1996)

Goitein, S. D., 'Jerusalem in the Arab Period (638–1099)', in Lee I. Levine, ed., *The Jerusalem Cathedra*, vol. 2 (Jerusalem, 1982), pp. 168–96

Golani, Motti, *Tsiyon Be-Tsiyonut: Ha-Medinah Ha-Tsiyonit U-She'elat Yerushalayim 1937–1949* (Tel Aviv, 1992)

——— 'Zionism without Zion: The Jerusalem Question 1947–1949', *Journal of Israeli History*, 16: 1 (Spring 1995), pp. 39–52

——— 'Jerusalem's Hope Lies Only in Partition: Israeli Policy on the Jerusalem Question, 1948–67', *International Journal of Middle East Studies*, 31 (1999), pp. 577–604

Goldfrank, David M., *The Origins of the Crimean War* (London, 1994)

Graves, R. M., *Experiment in Anarchy* (London, 1949)

Gray, John, *A History of Jerusalem* (London, 1969)

Greaves, R. W., 'The Jerusalem Bishopric', *English Historical Review*, 64 (1949), pp. 328–52

Grindea, Myron, ed., *Jerusalem: The Holy City in Literature* (London, 1968)

Grünebaum, G. E. von, *Muhammadan Festivals* (London, 1976)

Halper, Jeff, *Between Redemption and Revival: The Jewish Yishuv of Jerusalem in the Nineteenth Century* (Boulder, Col., 1991)

Hassan Bin Talal, Crown Prince of Jordan, *A Study on Jerusalem* (London, 1979)

——— *Palestinian Self-Determination: A Study of the West Bank and Gaza Strip* (London, 1981)

Hasson, Isaac, 'Muslim Literature in Praise of Jerusalem: *Fadail Bayt Al-Maqdis*', in Lee I. Levine, ed., *The Jerusalem Cathedra*, vol. 1 (Jerusalem, 1981), pp. 168–84

Hechler, William H., *The Jerusalem Bishopric: Documents* (London, 1883)

Herling, David, 'The Court, the Ministry and the Law: *Awad* and the Withdrawal of East Jerusalem Residence Rights', *Israel Law Review*, 33: 1 (Winter 1999), pp. 67–105

Herzl, Theodor, *Tagebücher* (3 vols., Leipzig, 1925)

Heyberger, Bernard, *Les Chrétiens du Proche-Orient au temps de la réforme Catholique* (Rome, 1994)

Higgins, Rosalyn, *United Nations Peacekeeping 1946–1967: Documents and Commentary I. The Middle East* (London, 1969)

Hirsch, Moshe, Housen-Couriel, Deborah, and Lapidoth, Ruth, *Whither Jerusalem? Proposals and Positions Concerning the Future of Jerusalem* (The Hague, 1995)

Hopkins, I. W. J., *Jerusalem: A Study in Urban Geography* (Grand Rapids, Michigan, 1970)

——— 'The Four Quarters of Jerusalem', *Palestine Exploration Quarterly* (July–December 1971), pp. 68–84

Hopwood, Derek, *The Russian Presence in Syria and Palestine 1843–1914: Church and Politics in the Near East* (Oxford, 1969)

Hough, W., 'History of the British Consulate in Jerusalem', *Journal of the Middle East Society*, 1 (1946), pp. 3–14

Hurewitz, Jacob C., *The Struggle for Palestine* (New York, 1976)

Hyamson, Albert M., ed., *The British Consulate in Jerusalem in Relation to the Jews of Palestine 1838–1914* (2 vols., London 1939, 1941)

Ilan, Amitzur, *Bernadotte in Palestine, 1948: A Study in Contemporary Humanitarian Knight-Errantry* (London, 1989)

Islamic Council of Europe, *Jerusalem: The Key to World Peace* (London, 1980)

Jones, Martin, *Failure in Palestine: British and United States Policy after the Second World War* (London, 1986)

Jones, S. Shepard, 'The Status of Jerusalem: Some National and International Aspects', *Law and Contemporary Problems*, 33: 1 (1968), pp. 169–82

Joseph, Bernard, *The Faithful City: The Siege of Jerusalem, 1948* (New York, 1960)

Kamel, Mohamed Ibrahim, *The Camp David Accords: A Testimony* (London, 1986)

Kark, Ruth, 'The Jerusalem Municipality at the End of Ottoman Rule', *Asian and African Studies*, 14: 2 (July 1980), pp. 117–141

——— *American Consuls in the Holy Land, 1832–1914* (Jerusalem, 1994)

Karmi, Ghada, ed., *Jerusalem Today: What Future for the Peace Process?* (Reading, 1996)

Katz, David S., 'English Charity and Jewish Qualms: The Rescue of the Ashkenazi Community of Seventeenth-Century Jerusalem', in Ada Rapoport-Albert and Steven J. Zipperstein, eds., *Jewish History: Essays in Honour of Chimen Abramsky* (London, 1988), pp. 245–67

Katz, Yossi, 'The Political Status of Jerusalem in Historical Context: Zionist Plans for the Partition of Jerusalem in the Years 1937–1938', *Shofar*, 11: 3 (1993), pp. 41–53

—— 'Mekomah Shel Ha-`Ir Yerushalayim Be-Masekhet Pe`ulotav Shel Ha-Mimsad Ha-Tsiyoni Be-Shilhei Tequfat Ha-Mandat', *Zion*, 61: 1 (1996), pp. 676–90

—— 'The Marginal Role of Jerusalem in Zionist Settlement Activity Prior to the Founding of the State of Israel', *Middle Eastern Studies*, 34: 3 (July 1998), pp. 121–45

Kaufman, Menahem, *America's Jerusalem Policy: 1947–1948* (Jerusalem, 1982)

Keith-Roach, Edward, *Pasha of Jerusalem: Memoirs of a District Commissioner under the British Mandate* (London, 1994)

Kendall, Henry, *Jerusalem: The City Plan – Preservation and Development during the British Mandate, 1918–1948* (London, 1948)

Khalidi, Rashid, *British Policy Towards Syria and Palestine 1906–1914* (London, 1980)

—— *Palestinian Identity: The Construction of a Modern National Consciousness* (New York, 1997)

Khalidi, Walid, 'Thinking the Unthinkable: A Sovereign Palestinian State', *Foreign Affairs*, 56: 4 (July 1978), pp. 695–713

Kimmerling, Baruch, and Migdal, Joel S., *Palestinians: The Making of a People* (Cambridge, Mass., 1993)

Kinglake, A. W., *Eothen* (London, 1844)

Kirk, George, *The Middle East 1945–1950* (London, 1954)

Kister, M. J. ' "You Shall Set Out Only for Three Mosques": A Study of an Early Tradition', in M. J. Kister, *Studies in Jahiliyya and Early Islam* (London, 1980), pp. 173–96

Klein, Menahem, *Yerushalayim Be-Masa U-Matan Le-Shalom: `Amadot `Araviyot* (Jerusalem, 1995)

Kodaman, Bayram, *Les Ambassades de Moustapha Réchid Pacha à Paris* (Ankara, 1991)

Koestler, Arthur, *Promise and Fulfilment: Palestine 1917–1949* (London, 1949)

Kollek, Teddy, *For Jerusalem* (New York, 1978)

Kraemer, Joel L., ed., *Jerusalem: Problems and Prospects* (New York, 1980)

Kupferschmidt, Uri, *The Supreme Muslim Council: Islam under the British Mandate for Palestine* (Leiden, 1987)

Kushner, David, 'Intercommunal Strife in Palestine during the Late Ottoman Period', *Asian and African Studies*, 18 (1984), pp. 187–204

—— *Moshel Hayiti Biyrushalayim: Ha-`Ir Ve-Ha-Mahoz be-`Einav shel `Ali Ekrem Bey 1906–1908* (Jerusalem, 1995)

Kutcher, Arthur, *The New Jerusalem: Planning and Politics* (London, 1973)

Lapidoth, Ruth, 'The Camp David Agreements: Some Legal Aspects', *Jerusalem Quarterly*, 10 (Winter 1979)

—— 'Jerusalem and the Peace Process', *Israel Law Review*, 28: 2/3 (Spring/Summer 1994), pp. 402–34

Lavsky, Hagit, ed., *Yerushalayim Ba-Toda`ah U-Va-`Asiyah Ha-Tsiyonit* (Jerusalem, 1989)

Layish, Aharon, 'The Status of the Shari`a in a Non-Muslim State: The Case of Israel', *Asian and African Studies*, 27: 1/2 (March/July 1993), pp. 171–88

Le Morzellec, Joëlle, *La Question de Jérusalem devant l'Organisation des Nations Unies* (Bruxelles, 1979)

Le Strange, Guy, *Palestine under the Muslims* (first pub. 1890, reprinted Beirut, 1965)

Levallois, Agnès, and Pommier, Sophie, *Jérusalem: de la division au partage?* (Paris, 1995)

Levenberg, Haim, *Military Preparations of the Arab Community in Palestine 1945–1948* (London, 1993)

Levine, Lee I., ed., *Jerusalem: Its Sanctity and Centrality to Judaism, Christianity, and Islam* (New York, 1999)

Lewis, Bernard, *The Jews of Islam* (Princeton, 1984)

Lichfield, Nathaniel, 'Planning and Development of Jerusalem', *Encyclopaedia Judaica Year Book 1974* (Jerusalem, 1974)

Lippell, Israel, 'Jerusalem – City of Religions: The Universality of Jerusalem', *Christian-Jewish Relations*, 21: 2 (1988), pp. 6–16

Little, Donald P., and Turgay, A. Üner, 'Documents from the Ottoman Period in the Khalidi Library in Jerusalem', *Die Welt des Islams*, NS 20: 1–2 (1980), pp. 44–72

Louis, William Roger, *The British Empire in the Middle East 1945–1951* (Oxford, 1984)

Luke, H. C., *Prophets, Priests and Patriarchs: Sketches of the Sects of Palestine and Syria* (London, 1927)

Luke, H. C., and Keith-Roach, E., *The Handbook of Palestine and Transjordan*, 2nd edn (London, 1930)

—— *Cities and Men* (3 vols., London, 1953–6)

McCarthy, Justin, *The Population of Palestine: Population History and Statistics of the Late Ottoman Period and the Mandate* (New York, 1990)

McDonald, James G., *My Mission in Israel 1948–1951* (London, 1951)

Mandel, Neville J., *The Arabs and Zionism before World War I* (Berkeley, 1976)

Ma`oz, Moshe, ed., *Studies on Palestine during the Ottoman Period* (Jerusalem, 1975)

—— *Palestinian Leadership on the West Bank: The Changing Role of the Arab Mayors under Jordan and Israel* (London, 1984)

Massey, W. T., *How Jerusalem Was Won: Being a Record of Allenby's Campaign in Palestine* (London, 1919)

Mattar, Philip, *The Mufti of Jerusalem: Al-Hajj Amin al-Husayni and the Palestinian National Movement* (New York, 1988)

—— 'The Mufti of Jerusalem and the Politics of Palestine', *Middle East Journal*, 42: 2 (Spring 1988), pp. 227–40

Minerbi, Sergio, *L'Italie et la Palestine 1914–1920* (Paris, 1970)

—— *The Vatican and Zionism: Conflict in the Holy Land 1895–1925* (New York, 1990)

Molinaro, Enrico, 'The Holy Places of Jerusalem in International Law', *Civil Society* (January 1999), pp. 12–17

Montoisy, Jean-Dominique, *Le Vatican et le problème des Lieux Saints* (Jerusalem, 1984)

Moore, John Norton, ed., *The Arab-Israeli Conflict* (4 vols., Princeton, 1974–91)

Morris, Benny, *The Birth of the Palestinian Refugee Problem 1947–1949* (Cambridge, 1987)

—— *Righteous Victims: A History of the Zionist-Arab Conflict 1881–1999* (New York, 1999)

Moscrop, John James, *Measuring Jerusalem: The Palestine Exploration Fund and British Interests in the Holy Land* (London, 2000)

Nashashibi, Nasser Eddin, *Jerusalem's Other Voice: Ragheb Nashashibi and Moderation in Palestinian Politics, 1920–1948* (Exeter, 1990)

Neff, Donald, 'Jerusalem in U.S. Policy', *Journal of Palestine Studies*, 23: 1 (Autumn 1993), pp. 20–45

Neuville, René, 'Heurs et Malheurs des Consuls de France à Jérusalem aux XVIIe, XVIIIe et XIXe Siècles', *Journal of the Middle East Society*, 1: 2 (1947), pp. 3–34

Nevo, Joseph, *King Abdullah and Palestine: A Territorial Ambition* (London, 1996)

Norden, Edward, 'Jerusalem: What Next?', *Commentary*, 97: 1 (January 1994), pp. 44–9

Oesterreicher, John M., *Jerusalem the Free* (London, 1973)

Oesterreicher, John M., and Sinai, Anne, eds., *Jerusalem* (New York, 1974)

Pappé, Ilan, *The Making of the Arab-Israeli Conflict 1947–1951* (London, 1994)

Perowne, Stewart, *The One Remains: A Report from Jerusalem* (London, 1954)

Pfaff, Richard H., *Jerusalem: Keystone of an Arab-Israeli Settlement* (Washington, 1969)

Pierotti, Ermete, *Customs and Traditions of Palestine* (Cambridge, 1864)

Plascov, Avi, *The Palestinian Refugees in Jordan 1948–1967* (London, 1981)

Popoff, Alexandre, *La Question des Lieux Saints de Jérusalem dans la correspondance diplomatique Russe du XIXme siècle*, 1re partie (1800–1850) (St Pétersbourg, 1910)

Porath, Yehoshua, *The Emergence of the Palestinian-Arab National Movement 1918–1929* (London, 1974)

———— *The Palestine Arab National Movement: From Riots to Rebellion 1929–1939* (London, 1977)

Prawer, Joshua, *The History of the Jews in the Latin Kingdom of Jerusalem* (Oxford, 1988)

Psomiades, Harry J., 'Soviet Russia and the Orthodox Church in the Middle East', *Middle East Journal*, 11: 4 (Autumn 1957), pp. 371–81

Quandt, William B., *Decade of Decisions: American Policy Toward the Arab-Israeli Conflict 1967–1976* (Berkeley, 1977)

Rabinovich, A., *Jerusalem on Earth: People, Passions and Politics in the Holy City* (New York, 1988)

Rackauskas, Constantine, 'The Jerusalem Problem: A Note on Legality', *Thought: Fordham University Quarterly*, 25: 96 (March 1950), pp. 100–114

Rafael, Gideon, *Destination Peace: Three Decades of Israeli Foreign Policy: A Personal Memoir* (London, 1981)

Reiter, Yitzhak, *Ha-Waqf Biyrushalayim 1948–1990* (Jerusalem, 1991)

———— *Islamic Endowments in Jerusalem Under British Mandate* (London, 1996)

———— *Islamic Institutions in Jerusalem: Palestinian Muslim Organization under Jordanian and Israeli Rule* (The Hague, 1997)

Reynier, Jacques de, *A Jérusalem un Drapeau flottait sur la ligne de feu* (Neuchâtel, 1950)

Rich, Norman, *Why the Crimean War? A Cautionary Tale* (Hanover, N H, 1985)

Robinson, Edward, *Biblical Researches in Palestine and the Adjacent Regions: A Journal of Travels in the Years 1838 and 1856* (London, 1856)

Romann, Michael, and Weingrod, Alex, *Living Together Separately: Arabs and Jews in Contemporary Jerusalem* (Princeton, 1991)

Rosenne, Shabtai, 'Revisiting Some Legal Aspects of the Transition from Mandate to Independence, December 1947–15 May 1948', in Alfred E. Kellerman, Kurt Siehr and Talia Einhorn, eds., *Israel Among the Nations* (The Hague, 1998)

Rosovsky, Nitza, ed., *City of the Great King: Jerusalem from David to the Present* (Cambridge, Mass., 1996)

Rubin, Barry, *The Transformation of Palestinian Politics: From Revolution to State-Building* (Cambridge, Mass., 1999)

Rustum, A. J., *The Royal Archives of Egypt and the Disturbances in Palestine, 1834* (Beirut, 1938)

Sadan, Yosef, 'Ha-Maqam Nabi Musa Bein Yeriho le-vein Damesek: Le-Toldoteha shel Taharut Bein Shnei `Atarei Kodesh', *Hamizrah Hehadash* 28: 1–2 (1979), pp. 22–38

———— 'Ha-Mahloket Be-Sugiyat Maqam Nabi Musa Be-`Einei Ha-Mekorot Ha-Muslemiyim', *Hamizrah Hehadash* 28: 3–4 (1979), pp. 220–38

Safdie, Moshe, *Jerusalem: The Future of the Past* (Boston, 1989)

Saint-Chariton, Foulque de, 'L'Etoile de la grotte de la nativité à Bethléem', *Journal of the Middle East Society*, 1: 3–4 (Autumn 1947), pp. 13–22

Samuel, Edwin, *A Lifetime in Jerusalem* (London, 1970)

Schmelz, U. O., 'The Development of the Jewish Population of Jerusalem during the Last Hundred Years', *Jewish Journal of Sociology,* 2: 1 (1960), pp. 56–73

—— 'The Jewish Population of Jerusalem', *Jewish Journal of Sociology,* 6: 2 (1964), pp. 243–63

—— *Modern Jerusalem's Demographic Evolution* (Jerusalem, 1987)

Segev, Tom, *1949: The New Israelis* (New York, 1986)

Shaltiel, E., ed., *Prakim Be-Toldot Yerushalayim Ba-Zman He-Hadash* (Jerusalem, 1981)

Shapira, Yitzhak, *Yerushalayim Mihutz La-Homah* (Jerusalem, 1947)

Sharef, Zeev, *Three Days* (London, 1962)

Sharkansky, Ira, 'Governing a City that Some Would Like to Internationalize: The Case of Jerusalem', *Jerusalem Journal of International Relations,* 14: 1 (March 1992), pp. 16–32

—— *Governing Jerusalem: Again on the World's Agenda* (Detroit, 1996)

Sheehan, Edward R. F., *The Arabs, Israelis, and Kissinger: A Secret History of American Diplomacy in the Middle East* (New York, 1976)

Sheffer, G., *Moshe Sharett: Biography of a Political Moderate* (Oxford, 1996)

Shepherd, Naomi, *Teddy Kollek: Mayor of Jerusalem* (New York, 1988)

Sherman, A. J., *Mandate Days: British Lives in Palestine, 1918–1948* (London, 1997)

Shim`oni, Ya`akov, `Arviei Eretz-Yisrael* (Tel Aviv, 1947)

Shlaim, Avi, *Collusion across the Jordan: King Abdullah, the Zionist Movement, and the Partition of Palestine* (New York, 1988)

—— *The Iron Wall: Israel and the Arab World* (New York, 2000)

Shragai, Nadav, *Har Hameriva: Ha-Ma`avak `al Har Ha-Bayit* (Jerusalem, 1995)

Silberman, Neil Asher, *Digging for God and Country: Exploration, Archaeology, and the Secret Struggle for the Holy Land, 1799–1917* (New York, 1982)

Singer, Amy, *Palestinian Peasants and Ottoman Officials: Rural Administration Around Sixteenth-Century Jerusalem* (Cambridge, 1994)

Sivan, E., 'Le caractère sacré de Jérusalem dans l'Islam aux XIIe–XIIIe siècles', *Studia Islamica,* 27 (1967), pp. 149–82

Slonim, Shlomo, 'The United States and the Status of Jerusalem, 1947–1984', *Israel Law Review,* 19: 2 (Spring 1984), pp. 179–252

—— *Jerusalem in America's Foreign Policy, 1947–1949* (The Hague, 1998)

Sofer, Naim, 'The Political Status of Jerusalem in the Hashemite Kingdom of Jordan 1948–1967', in E. Kedourie and S. Haim, eds., *Palestine and Israel in the 19th and 20th Centuries* (London, 1982), pp. 255–76

Spolsky, Bernard, and Cooper, Robert L., *The Languages of Jerusalem* (Oxford, 1991)

Sprinzak, Ehud, *Brother against Brother: Violence and Extremism in Israeli Politics from Altalena to the Rabin Assassination* (New York, 1999)

Stavrou, Theofanis George, *Russian Interests in Palestine 1882–1914: A Study of Religious and Educational Enterprise* (Thessaloniki, 1963)

Stein, Kenneth W., *Heroic Diplomacy: Sadat, Kissinger, Carter, Begin, and the Quest for Arab-Israeli Peace* (New York, 1999)

Storrs, Ronald, *Orientations* (London, 1943)

Taggar, Yehuda, *The Mufti of Jerusalem and Palestine Arab Politics, 1930–1937* (New York, 1986)

Tauber, Eliezer, *The Emergence of the Arab Movements* (London, 1993)

Tessler, Mark, *A History of the Israeli-Palestinian Conflict* (Bloomington, 1994)

Tibawi, A. L., *British Interests in Palestine 1800–1901: A Study of Religious and Educational Enterprise*

(Oxford, 1961)

Tsimhoni, Daphne, *Christian Communities in Jerusalem and the West Bank since 1948: An Historical, Social, and Political Study* (Westport, Conn., 1993)

Vatikiotis, P. J., 'The Greek Patriarchate of Jerusalem between Hellenism and Arabism', *Middle Eastern Studies*, 30: 4 (October 1994), pp. 916–929

Vereté, Mayir, 'Why was a British Consulate Established in Jerusalem?', *English Historical Review*, 85 (1970), pp. 316–45

—— *From Palmerston to Balfour: Collected Essays of Mayir Vereté* (London, 1992)

Vester, Bertha Spafford, *Our Jerusalem: An American Family in the Holy City 1881–1949* (Beirut, 1954)

Vilnay, Zev, *Yerushalayim Birat Yisrael* (4 vols., Jerusalem, 1970–76)

Walker, P. W. L., *Holy City, Holy Places? Christian Attitudes to Jerusalem and the Holy Land in the Fourth Century* (Oxford, 1980)

Wardi, Chaim, 'The Latin Patriarchate of Jerusalem', *Journal of the Middle East Society*, 1: 3–4 (1947), pp. 5–22

Wasserstein, Bernard, *The British in Palestine: The Mandatory Government and the Arab-Jewish Conflict, 1917–1929* (2nd edn., Oxford, 1991)

Wavell, A. P., *The Palestine Campaigns* (London, 1928)

Weigert, Gideon, *Israel's Presence in East Jerusalem* (Jerusalem, 1973)

Weingrod, Alex, and Manna, `Adel, 'Living along the Seam: Israeli Palestinians in Jerusalem', *International Journal of Middle East Studies*, 30 (1998), pp. 369–86

Whitbeck, John V., 'The Road to Peace Starts in Jerusalem: The Condominium Solution', *Middle East Policy*, 3: 3 (1994), pp. 110–18

Wigoder, Geoffrey, *The Vatican-Israel Agreement: A Watershed in Christian-Jewish Relations* (Jerusalem, 1994)

Wilken, Robert L., *The Land Called Holy: Palestine in Christian History and Thought* (New Haven, 1992)

Wilson, Charles, *Ordnance Survey of Jerusalem* (London, 1965)

Zander, Walter, *Israel and the Holy Places of Christendom* (London, 1971)

Ze'evi, Dror, *An Ottoman Century: The District of Jerusalem in the 1600s* (Albany, NY, 1996)

Zunes, Stephen, 'US Policy Towards Jerusalem: Clinton's Shift to the Right', *Middle East Policy,* 3: 3 (1994), pp. 83–92

Index

A

Abbas, Mahmoud (Abu Mazen) 290–95
Abd Allah b. al-Zubayr, Caliph 10
Abd al-Malik b. Marwan, Caliph 10–11
Abd al-Qadar, Hatim 298
Abdeen, Sheikh Abd al-Qadder 341
Abdul Hadi, Awni 190
Abdul Hamid II, Sultan 320
Abdullah I, King 110, 132, 138, 141, 152, 154–7, 165, 169, 174–5, 180–84, 186–9, 197, 235, 281, 340
Abed Rabbo, Yasser 339
Abraham's Oak Monastery 286
Abramov, Alexander 199
Abu Dis 128, 186, 212, 291, 295, 299, 311–14, 352, 355
Abu Ghosh tribe 26
Abul Huda, Tawfiq 153
Abu Midyan *waqf* 322
Abu Tor 226
Abyssinians 28, 99–100; *see also* Ethiopians
Acheson, Dean 185
Acre 9, 23, 25, 110
Agnon, Shmuel Yosef 3, 326
Agudist movement 151
Ahad Ha-am 4
Ahd, al- 75
Ahimeir, Yossi 338
Ahmed I, Sultan 17
Ajamian, Archbishop Shahe 269–70
Alami family 66
Alami, Saad al-Din al- 222
Alawnah, Atef 299
Albert, King 86
Albin, Celia 346
Aleppo 11
Alexander, Bishop Michael Solomon 31, 33–5
Alexandria 240
Alexii I, Patriarch 278
Alexii II, Patriarch 286
Ali, Shawkat 106, 325
Allenby, General Sir Edmund 74, 78–80, 82–5, 90
Allenby Square 217
All-India Muslim League 325
Allon, Yigal 206

Alpher, Joseph 315
Al-Quds University 299
Alterman, Natan 5
America-Israel Public Affairs Committee (AIPAC) 247, 249
American Colony 50, 259
Amirav, Moshe 261, 289, 346
Amman 153–5, 165, 187–9, 191, 224, 227, 339
Ammunition Hill 206
Ananus 1
Anastasia, Grand Duchess 280
Anatot 247
Anglicans 30–35, 41, 58–9, 272
Anglo-American Committee of Inquiry 122
Anglo-Jordanian Alliance (1946) 198
Anglo-Palestine Bank 143
Antonii, Archimandrite 279
Aqsa, al- 10, 181, 183, 227–8, 251, 255, 300, 318, 326, 330–32, 336, 341–2, 344
Aqsa *intifada*', 'al- xiii, 317, 344, 350, 353, 359
Arab Club 88
Arab Higher Committee 110, 115–6, 126, 145, 147, 160
Arab League 124, 160, 174, 226
Arab Legion 132, 144, 153–8, 161–3, 183, 190
Arab-Ottoman Brotherhood 69
Arab revolt (1936–9) 108, 110, 115–16
Arafat, Yasir 227, 241, 256, 260, 264, 286–7, 289–90, 294, 298, 300, 302, 304, 306, 313–16, 339, 343, 347, 352
Aranne, Zalman 206
Araunah, King of the Jebusites 329
Aref, Aref al- 188–9, 222–3
Ariel, Rabbi Yisrael 336
Arlosoroff, Chaim 108
Armenia, Republic of 314
Armenian quarter 12
Armenians xii, 12, 17–20, 27, 38, 65, 79, 96, 99–100, 194–5, 266–70, 272–3, 314
Asali family 66
Asali, Shukri al- 69
Ashbee, C. R. 87
Ashkenazim 46, 253, 259
Ashrawi, Hanan 273, 298
Ashu, Mustafa 183

Association for the Protection of al-Aksa Mosque 325–6
Assumptionists 48
Ateret Kohanim 334–5
Auster, Daniel 116, 119, 143
Austin, Senator Warren 139
Australia 79, 127, 137
Austria 24, 27–30, 54, 70–71
Aviner, Rabbi Shlomo 335
Azariya, al- 212, 291, 295, 313
Azcárate, Dr Pablo 35–6, 138, 145, 157, 169

B

Babakhanov, Ziayutdin 285
Baker, James 261–2, 338
Baldi, Paschal 24
Balfour, Arthur James 245
Balfour Declaration (1917) 58–9, 75, 90–92
Balfour Street 196
Baqa 133, 163, 181, 338
Barak, Justice Aharon 237
Barak, Ehud 307, 309–10, 313–15; 343, 354
Barclay, Bishop 58
Barclays Bank 144, 148
Barlassina, Mgr Louis 94–5
Batei Mahseh 51
Batsh, Ahmad al- 298
Baybars, Sultan 102
Beckerman, Chaia 347
Beersheba 77
Begin, Benny 304, 335
Begin, Menahem 206–7, 212, 235, 237, 240–42, 244–7, 297
Beilin, Yossi 289–96, 311, 354
Beilin-Abu Mazen draft agreement 290–95, 309–10, 313–14, 358–9
Beirut 33
Belgian Congo 358
Belgium 27, 75, 86, 145
Beltritti, Patriarch Giacomo Giuseppe 273
Belzberg, Marc 335
Ben-Ami, Shlomo 310
Benedict XV, Pope 92
Benediktos, Patriarch 194, 269, 272
Ben Eliezer, Benjamin 339
Ben-Elissar, Eliahu 263
Ben Gurion, David xii, 5, 119, 125–6, 150–51, 162–5, 175–8, 200, 204, 218, 235, 242
Bentov, Mordechai 212
Benvenisti, Meron 215, 235, 254
Bentwich, Norman 87, 104–5
Ben Yehuda Street 134
Berlin 56, 116
Berlin, Treaty of (1878) 54

Bernadotte, Count Folke 158–62
Betar 326
Betar Illit 308
Bet Hanina 192, 257, 299, 314
Bethlehem 5, 9, 12, 22, 38, 40–41, 53, 72, 81, 93–4, 97, 100, 110, 117, 124, 128, 209, 212, 253, 267–9, 350, 357
Bevin, Ernest 125, 138, 162
Bialik, Haim Nahman 5
Bira, El- 247
Biran, Dr Avraham 171, 183
Bir Zeit University 273, 353
Boissanger, Claude de 169
Bolivia 135
Bombay 325
Bouillon, Godfrey de 8
Brabant, Duke of 319
Brémond, Consul 22–3
Brenner, Yosef Haim 5
Briand, Aristide 72
Britain: see Great Britain
Brookings Institution 233
Brotherhood and Purity 88
Brown, George 211, 232
Brunsson, Colonel Nils 158–9
Brzezinski, Zbigniew 233
Budeiri, Sheikh Musa 101
Bull, General Odd 205–6
Bunche, Dr Ralph 159, 162
Bundy, Rodman 345
Bunsen, Chrétien, Baron de 30–31
Buraq 324
'Burma Road' 158

C

Cadogan, Sir Alexander 139, 148, 153–4, 156
Cairo 97, 106, 118, 148, 157, 192, 250
Cambon, Jules 56
Cambrai 81
Camp, J. N. 88
Camp David Agreements (1978) 236–7
Camp David Conference (2000) 313–17, 342–3, 354
Canada 126, 136, 248
Canberra 347
Capitulations 17, 72, 95
Capucci, Bishop Hilarion 263
Caradon, Lord 232
Carey, Dr George, Archbishop of Canterbury 266
Carletti, Consul 56
Carlowitz, Treaty of (1699) 24
Carmelites 48
Carrington, Lord 244

Carter, President Jimmy 233, 237, 245, 248, 250, 313
Casaroli, Mgr 271
Casey, R. G. 137
Catherine II ('the Great'), Empress 25
Cave of the Patriarchs 287
Celli, Mgr Claudio 275
Chandigarh 347
Charlemagne, Emperor 7
Christopher, Warren 304
Church Missionary Society 52
Church of the Holy Sepulchre xi, 7–9, 12, 16–17, 20, 25–7, 41, 55, 59, 65, 89, 93, 96, 99, 126, 273, 294, 318
Church of the Nativity 9, 18, 38, 40, 93, 96, 100, 318
Church of the Redeemer 59
Churchill, Winston 118–19, 278
Churchill White Paper (1922) 59
Çiller, Tansu 300
Clarendon, Earl of 52
Clark, Joe 248
Clarke, Percy C. 148
Clayton, Gilbert 83
Clifford, Clark 169
Clinton, President Bill 286, 307, 313–16
Clive, Nigel 150
Coenaculum 86
Coghill, Sir Patrick 193
Cohen, Geula 242
Cohen, Saul 346
Cohen, Yehoshua 162
Colbi, Dr Saul 284
Comay, Michael 209
Combes, Emile 55
Conder, Claude 64
Connor, James 52
Constantine, Emperor 6
Constantinople 8, 18–19, 21, 27–8, 39–40, 42, 54, 64–6, 71, 75, 77, 97
Convent of Zion 16
Copenhagen 76
Copts 99–100, 165, 195
Cordeliers: see Franciscans
Costa Rica 243
Coupland, Sir Reginald 110
Cracow, Free City of 29
Crerar, Major-General Henry 137
Crimean War 42–4, 319
Crusaders 2, 8–10, 92, 102, 331
Cultural Club 69, 88
Cunningham, Sir Alan 139, 141, 148–9
Cust, L. G. A. 93
Cyprus 290

Cyril, Bishop of Jerusalem 6
Cyril, Bishop of Melitopolsk 60
Cyril, Patriarch of Jerusalem 35–6
Czechoslovakia 127, 135

D

Dagostino, Colonel 79–80
Daily Telegraph 115
Dajani family 66
Damascus 14, 66, 75, 77, 88, 101–2, 160
Damascus Gate 50, 62, 142, 150
Damianos, Patriarch 97–8
David, Ben 301
Dawn 242, 332
Dayan, Moshe 167, 180–81, 203–5, 207, 212, 235–8, 241–2, 328, 331
Dayan, Yael 261
Dead Sea 163, 191–2
Decentralization Party 69
Deir al-Sultan 93
Deir Yassin 144, 163
Denmark 27, 135
Derderian, Yeghishe 195, 269–70, 272–3
Deutsche Palästina Verein 57
Dinstein, Yoram 243
Diodoros I, Patriarch 273–4, 276
Disciples of Christ 77
Disraeli, Benjamin 50
Djemal Pasha 71, 76–8
Doar Hayom 326
Dome of the Rock 7, 10, 236, 318, 328, 335–6, 344
Dominican Republic 243
Don John of Austria 17
Dow, Sir Hugh 149–50, 164, 197
Draper, Professor Gerald 346
Drouyn de Lhuys, Edouard 39–40
Druzes 28
Dufferin, Lord 64
Dulles, John Foster 199–200
Dulzin, Aryeh 244

E

Eban, Abba (Aubrey) 180, 184, 210–11, 213, 215, 229, 242–3, 331
Eden, Anthony 118, 200
Edri, Oren 301
Edward VII, King 50
Edward VIII, King 50
Efrat 308
Egeria 7
Egypt 26–8, 69, 71–2, 74, 79, 124, 161–2, 183, 190, 201, 231–3, 235–41, 245–6, 279
Egypt-Israel peace treaty (1979) 240

Egypt-Jordan treaty (1967) 205
Ein Karem 128, 163, 204
Eisenhower, President Dwight D. 196
Eitan, Michael 311, 354
Eitan, Rafael 301
Ekrem Bey 68
Elad, Amikam 324
Elazar, Professor Daniel 346
Eliash, Mordechai 172
Elizabeth Fedorovna, Grand Duchess 277
Elon, Benny 312
El Salvador 243
Emadi, Eliahu 253
Eshkol, Levi 177, 205–7, 218, 227, 269, 272
Etheridge, Mark 168
Ethiopia 108
Ethiopians 195, 198
Etzion bloc 308
European Parliament 274
European Union 301
Eusebius, Bishop of Caesarea 6
Evans, Harold 148, 157
Evelina de Rothschild School 95
Eytan, Walter 174, 244, 251

F

Fahd, Crown Prince 250
Faisal, Emir 75–6, 86, 89–90, 101, 104, 152
Faisal, King of Saudi Arabia 233
Fajr, al- 226, 253, 256, 346
Fakhr al-Din 20–21
Falkenhayn, General Erich von 78
Faqih , Ibn al- 324
Farhi, Colonel David 224
Fatah, al- 75, 227, 253, 261, 298, 341
Fatat, al- 75
Fawzi, Dr Mahmud 201
Felici, Mgr Angelo 271
Ferrari, Cardinal 56
Finn, James 37–8, 48, 319
Fitzgerald, Sir William 120–22, 126, 137–8
Flandin, Etienne 62
Foreign Affairs 251
France 17–24, 27–9, 34, 38–43, 52, 54–62, 69,
    71–5, 77, 79–80, 82–6, 89–93, 95–6, 118,
    126, 145, 167, 178, 190–91, 202, 232, 267
Francis I, King 17
Franciscans 9, 17–23, 39–40, 61, 83, 126,
    170
Franz Josef, Emperor 51
Frederick II, Emperor 12, 165
Frederick William IV, King 29–31, 58
Freij, Elias 253
French Hill 206, 218

Fribourg 171
Friedman, Isaiah 76

G

Gabon 201
Galilee 162
Garden Tomb 65
Garreau, Roger 136–7, 146–7, 184
Gasparri, Cardinal Pietro 75
Gaza 68, 77, 151, 189, 226, 239, 251, 255, 260,
    262, 289–90, 302, 317, 336, 340, 342,
    347–8, 350, 353
General Islamic Congress (1931) 106–7
geniza 2
Georgians 16
German Colony 48, 133, 141, 163
Germany 56–9, 69–71, 75–8, 115
Gethsemane 61, 99, 196, 277, 279
Ghali, Butros 236
Giannini, Frediano 55
Gilman, Representative Benjamin 248
Gilo 212, 218
Giornale d'Italia 56
Givat Ram 204
Givat Zeev 291, 295, 314–15
Givon 291, 295
Gladstone, William Ewart 30
Glazebrook, Otis 71
Glubb, Brigadier John 144, 154–6, 190
Gobat, Bishop Samuel 35, 37–8, 48
Goitein, S. D. 11
Golan Heights 218
Goldberg, Arthur 231
Goldfoot, Stanley 334
Goldstein, Baruch 287
Goldziher, Ignaz 11
Goodman, Alan Harry 335
Gorbachev, Mikhail 285
Gorchakov, Prince Alexander Mikhailovich 60
Gordon, General Charles 64–5
Goren, Chief Rabbi Shlomo 328–9, 332–3
Gort, Viscount 119
Goût, Jean 84–5
Government House 51, 149, 161–2, 206, 229
Grady, Henry F. 124
Granados, Dr García 200–201
Granville, Lord 29
Graves, Philip 81, 133
Graves, Richard 122, 133–4, 140, 143–4, 147
Graves, Robert 133
Great Britain 27–38, 42–3, 52, 62–5, 69–70,
    71–151, 153, 160, 164, 167, 176, 178,
    184–5, 232; Cabinet 138; Cabinet Committee
    on Palestine 118–19; Colonial Office 106,

117–18, 141; Commonwealth Relations Office 137; Foreign Office 83, 118–19, 159, 180, 185–7, 191, 201, 230, 278, 325; India Office 106, 325; War Office 63, 81, 154
Greece 26, 97, 193
Greek Colony 141, 163, 181
Greek Orthodox Church xi, 8, 24–8, 35–8, 41, 53, 55, 60–61, 71, 77, 87, 92–3, 96–100, 137, 172, 193–5, 215, 266–9, 272–4, 276, 281
Greenberg, Uri Zvi 5
Gregory, Saint (of Nyssa) 5
Grey and Ripon, Earl de 63
Gromyko, Andrei 139–40, 149, 157, 159, 285
Guatemala 127, 200, 243
Guizot, François 28–9
Gulf War 260, 274
Gur, General Motta 207
Gush Emunim 334–5
Guttman Centre of Applied Social Research 355
Gvirol, Shlomo ibn 3

H

Ha-aretz 312
Habash, George 227
Hadassah Hospital 126, 144, 156, 159, 204
Haddad, Faiq, Bishop 272
Haifa 68, 110, 135, 150, 160, 317
Haganah 134, 142, 152, 154, 279
hajj 251, 322
Hakim, Caliph al- 8
Halaby, Najeeb 233
Halevi, Yehuda 3
Halevi, Justice B. 215
halukah 5, 49
Hamas movement 289, 302, 305
Hanieh, Akram 315–16
Har Adar 308
Haram al-Khalil, al- 173
Haram al-Sharif, al- (Temple Mount) xii, xiii, 8, 12, 23, 71, 103, 106, 115, 126, 142, 181, 207, 222–3, 225, 235, 255, 276, 288, 293–4, 305, 309, 311, 314–44, 348–9
Hardinge, Lord 83
haredim 258–9
Har Gilo 247
Har Homa 247, 307, 309–10
Harman, Abraham 214, 283
Harun al-Rashid, Caliph 7
hasidim 47
Hassan II, King of Morocco 241–2
Hauser, Rita 233
Havatzelet 49
Hayes, Louis des 19–20

Hebrew University of Jerusalem 87, 107, 126, 156, 159, 204, 209, 217–8, 321, 347, 355
Hebron 78, 102–3, 173, 186, 245, 285–6, 287, 296, 322
Hejaz 75, 89, 106
Helena, Saint 6–7, 65
Heller, Mark 346
Helm, Sir Knox 198
Herzl, Theodor 4, 49, 320
Herzog, Chaim (Vivian) 157, 208
Herzog, Jacob 171, 181
Hilton, John 122
Himmler, Heinrich 158
Holst, Johan Jurgen 303–4
holy places 6, 15–27, 54–5, 80, 85–6, 93, 117, 131, 137, 159, 162, 173, 189, 195, 203, 205, 211, 213, 227, 229, 232, 236, 251, 269–72, 274, 276, 292–4, 303, 309, 316–44; *see also* Church of the Holy Sepulchre, Church of the Nativity, Western Wall *etc.*
Holy See: *see* Vatican
Honduras 243
Hong Kong 249
Hospice of St John 273
Hovevei Zion 49
Hurva synagogue 51
Husayni family 26, 49–50, 66, 68–9, 88, 103, 105, 107–8, 119–20, 141, 188, 323
Husayni quarter 49
Husayni, Abd al-Kader al- 142, 261
Husayni, Hajj Amin al- 88, 100, 104–7, 110, 115–16, 124, 151–2, 165, 183, 192, 227, 323–5, 327, 340
Husayni, Faisal 261–2, 297, 300–302, 305, 310, 312, 339, 351
Husayni, Husayn al- 78–9
Husayni, Jamal al- 68–9, 147
Husayni, Kamil Bey al- 87
Husayni, Musa Kazim Pasha 101, 104–5, 142
Husayni, Said al- 69
Husayni, Shukri al- 69
Hussein, King of Jordan 183, 187, 192, 195, 205–7, 227, 239, 241, 259–60, 262, 339–41
Hussein, Sherif of Mecca 73, 75–6, 106, 110, 327
Hussein, President Saddam 274, 338
Hyderabad, Maharajah of 107

I

Ibn Abd Rabbihi 324–5
Ibn Saud 106
Ibrahim 26, 28
Ignatius Polikarp, Archimandrite 281
Independence Park 217
India 106, 126–7

Indonesia 242
In multiplicibus curis 170
International Jerusalem Committee 216
International Red Cross 148–9, 161, 279
intifada 239, 255–7, 275
Iran 126–7, 241, 246, 343
Iraq 90, 116, 136, 144, 191, 246, 274
Irgun Zvai Leumi 123, 144, 151
Isawiya 204
Isidoros, Archimandrite 193–4
Islamic Conference 241, 343
Israel: admitted to UN 169; administration of
    Jerusalem (1949–67) 202–4; armistice
    agreement with Egypt (1949) 163, with Jordan
    (1949) 203; Chief Rabbinate 328, 332;
    conquest of Jerusalem (1967) 205–8; Defence
    Ministry 199; establishment of 150; Foreign
    Ministry 2, 173–4, 199–200, 208–9, 243–4,
    250, 267, 280; Herut Party 206, 333; Housing
    Ministry 258; Interior Ministry 224, 307, 310;
    Kach movement 336; Knesset 167, 176–8,
    198, 213, 226–7, 236–8, 242–4, 299, 301,
    309, 313, 337; Labour Party 234, 242, 295,
    309, 354; Likud party 234, 242–4, 261, 264,
    289, 296–7, 301, 303–4, 311, 337, 354;
    Mapai party 177; Mapam party 212, 235;
    Meretz party 289, 309; National Religious
    Party 206, 309, 329; and partition of
    Jerusalem 179–86; peace treaty with Jordan
    (1994) 338–9; Police Ministry 307; relations
    with Vatican 270–76; Religious Affairs Ministry
    172, 209–10, 222, 273, 284; Shas party 332;
    Shinui party 346; Supreme Court 176,
    215–16, 245, 274, 279, 301, 333; war
    (1948–9) 151–63 (1967) 205–8, 328–9;
    Yahadut Ha-Torah party 289
Israel Electric Corporation 254
Israel Lands Administration 306
Israel/Palestine Centre for Research and
    Information 310
Istanbul Committee 3
Italy xii–xiii, 54–6, 71, 79–80, 83–6, 94, 96,
    108–9, 170, 274, 359
Itinerarium Burdigalense 7
Ivory Coast 201
Izzet Bey 78–9

J

Jaabari, Suleiman 340
Jacobites: *see* Syrian Orthodox Church
Jacotin, Pierre 62
Jaffa 4, 19, 25, 71, 77, 110, 225, 275, 317
Jaffa Gate 48–9, 51, 79, 134, 142
Jaffa-Jerusalem railway 50

Jaffa, Treaty of (1229) 12
Jaffee Centre for Strategic Studies 315
Jakobovits, Chief Rabbi Immanuel 249
Jamia al-Arabiyya, al- 325
Jarallah family 50
Jarallah, Sheikh Husam al-Din 105, 165
Jarallah, Salah al-Din 222
Jarjou, Emile 298
Jericho 78, 101–3, 165, 285–6
Jerome, Saint 5
Jerusalem: Arab education system in 225–6, 235,
    306, 340; Arab press in 226, 306; bombings
    123, 133–4; 296; Armenian quarter 314, 316;
    British rule in 79–149; Christianity and 5–9,
    90–100; Christian quarter 12, 59, 267, 309,
    314, 316, 351; Christians in 16–48, 52–62,
    71, 92–100, 192–5, 266–86; Crusader rule in
    8–9; demography 14–15, 45–50, 114, 117,
    121, 128, 186, 192, 203, 212, 266, 347, 351,
    355–8; Egyptian rule in 26–9; Islam and
    9–12; Israeli rule in 202–344; Jewish quarter
    12, 47, 49, 51, 87, 152, 157, 178, 180–81,
    210, 215, 314, 316; Jordanian rule in 186–92;
    Judaism and 1–5; Mamluk rule in 12–13;
    municipal council 68, 187, 65–6, 119–22,
    213; municipal elections 107–8, 221, 264;
    Muslim quarter 12, 14, 49, 50, 257, 288, 309,
    314, 316, 351; Ottoman rule in 14–79;
    Palestinian elections in 296–8; planning
    schemes 217–19; *see also names of districts,
    streets, institutions etc.*
Jerusalem Biblical Zoo 182
Jerusalem District Electric Company 254,
    299
Jerusalem Embassy Act (1995) 249
Jerusalem Foundation 216
Jerusalem Institute for Israel Studies 308–9, 315
Jerusalem Law (1980) 242–5
Jerusalem Temple Foundation 334
Jessey, Revd Henry 30–31
Jesuits 18–20
Jewish Agency 108, 110–12, 119, 124–6, 128,
    134, 136, 140–41, 151, 164, 279
jihad 12
jizya 23
John Paul II, Pope 274–6
Jordan, Hashemite Kingdom of 158, 165, 167–9,
    174–5, 179–98, 205–7, 223–8, 231, 233,
    250–51, 259–61, 338–40, 355; *see also*
    Transjordan
Jordan, River 72, 101
Joseph, Bernard: *see* Yosef, Dov
Josephus 1
Julian the Apostate, Emperor 7

K

Kahalani, Avigdor 307
Kahane, Rabbi Meir 336
Kahn, Chief Rabbi Zadoc 68
Kaiserin Augusta Victoria Hospital 51, 78, 159, 305
Kamel, Mohamed Ibrahim 236, 238
Karrazi, Kamal 343
Kashmir 332
Katamon 133, 141, 163, 167
Katz, Professor Elihu 355
Keffenbrink, Freiherr von 48
Keith-Roach, Edward 324
Kennan, George 139
Kennedy, Senator Edward 248
Kennedy, President John F. 196
Kerr, Malcolm 233
Khaled ibn Walid 107
Khalid, King of Saudi Arabia 250–51
Khalidi family 107, 119
Khalidi, Awni 136
Khalidi, Dr Husayn Fakhri al- 107–8, 116, 189
Khalidi, Mustafa Bey 116, 119
Khalidi, Rashid 324
Khalidi, Ruhi al- 69
Khalidi, Walid 251–2, 346
Khalidi, Yusuf Dia 68
Kharezmian Tartars 12
Khatib, Ali al- 226
Khatib, Anwar al- 222–3, 252, 263
Khatib, Rawhi al- 213, 220, 228, 263
Khomeini, Ayatollah Ruhollah 241
Khrapovitskii, Metropolitan Antonii 99
Khuri, Ahmad (Abu Ala) 298
King David Hotel 123, 169
King George V Avenue 110, 134
Kinglake, A. W. 47
Kirkbride, Sir Alec 155–6
Kisch, Colonel F. H. 323–4
Kissinger, Dr Henry 232–3
Kitchener, Herbert 63
Klausner, Joseph 326
Klutznick, Philip 233
Koestler, Arthur x
Kolchak, Admiral 277
Kollek, Teddy 213, 216, 218–21, 228, 232, 234–5, 243, 249, 256, 258, 264–5, 274, 288, 290, 333
Konstantin, Grand Duke 50
Kook, Chief Rabbi Avraham 334
Kook, Rabbi Zvi Yehuda 334
Kraus, Friedrich 71
Kressenstein, General Friedrich Freiherr Kress von 77

Küçük Kaynarca, Treaty of 25
Kutcher, Arthur 217

L

Lahore 407
Lantos, Representative Tom 248
La Rochefoucauld, Cardinal 19
Lash, Brigadier Norman 156
Lateran Treaty (1929) xii, 359
Latin Christians 8–9, 15–26, 28, 35–40, 43, 53–6, 60–62, 77, 83, 85, 88, 93–6, 99–100, 126, 170–72, 195, 266–7, 272, 275; see also Roman Catholic Church, Vatican, Franciscans
La Tour d'Auvergne, Princess 48
Latrun 158, 161
Lau, Chief Rabbi Yisrael Meir 276
Lausanne 169
Lawrence, T. E. 63, 76
League of Nations 82, 90, 93, 95
Lebanon 62, 115, 124, 174, 192, 246
Leeds Castle 236
Lehi (Stern Gang) 151, 159, 162, 334
Le Morzellec, Joëlle 345
Lempereur, Jean 18–21
Leonid, Archimandrite 281
Lepanto, Battle of (1572) 17
Lerner, Yoel 336
Le Strange, Guy 318
Levontin, Avigdor 209–10
Levy, David 262
Levy, Shlomit 355
Lewis, Samuel 244
Lie, Trygve 162
Lieberman, Senator Joseph 335
Lifta 48, 163
Lilienblum, Moshe Leib 2
Lin Chick, Dr 137
Linowitz, Sol 246
Lisicky, Karel 135, 158
Lloyd George, David xiv, 76–8, 80–81, 89
London 234, 244–5
London, Convention of (1840) 28–9
London Conference (1920) 89; (1946) 124–5
London Society for Promoting Christianity among the Jews 53
Louis, Emperor 7
Louis XIII, King 18–19
Louis Napoleon: see Napoleon III
Louis-Philippe, King 29
Lubianker (Lavon), Pinhas 177
Luke, Harry 94
Lundström, Colonel Age 161
Lutherans 30, 58–9
Lydda 117, 161

M

Maaleh Adumim 247, 291, 295, 308, 314–15, 357
MacMichael, Sir Harold 116–18
Madrid conference (1991) 231, 262–3, 274, 300
Magdalen College, Oxford 99
Mahane Yehuda market 228
majlis al-shura 65
Malaysia 332
Malha 163
Mamilla district 163
Mamilla pool 48
Mamilla Street 208
Mamluks 2–3, 12
Mandelbaum Gate 180
Manookian, Patriarch Torkom 270
Marshall, George C. 162–4
Marx, Karl 38
Mary Magdalene Convent 286
Massey, W. T. 81
Matza, Yehoshua 301
Mavromatis, Euripides 254
Maximilian, Archduke (of Austria) 50
Maximilian, Archduke (of Bavaria) 50
Mazzini, Giuseppe xii
McDonald, James G. 169
McGovern, George 248
McLintock, Robert 138
McMahon-Hussein correspondence 75
Meah Shearim 49
Mecca 9–10, 106, 251, 322
Medina 9, 70
Meir (Myerson), Golda 176–7, 280
Melville, Herman 1
Menshikov, Alexander Sergeievich, Prince 41
Mercier, Cardinal 86
Metternich, Clement-Wenceslas, Prince 29
Mevasseret Zion 258, 357
Milan 56
Miller, Haim 289
millet system 15, 37, 52
Milo, Roni 338
Mishkenot Shaananim 49
missionaries 52–3
Mokassad Hospital, al- 305
Moldavia and Wallachia 42
Monde, Le 180
Montefiore, Sir Moses 49, 319
Morgenthau, Henry 71
Morocco 241–2, 315
Morrison, Herbert 124
Morrison-Grady plan 124
Moskowitz, Irving 335
Mosul 11
Motza 131

Mount Carmel 176
Mount of Olives 26, 48, 61, 112, 186, 203, 207, 251, 256, 279, 283
Mount Scopus 51, 112, 144, 156, 159, 161, 167, 180–82, 185, 203–4, 206–7, 216–18, 245
Mount Zion 48, 99, 152
Moyne, Lord 119
Moynihan, Senator Daniel Patrick 248
Mubarak, President Hosni 240, 246, 343–4
Muhammad 9, 318, 324
Muhammad Ali (Egyptian) 26–8, 31
Muhammad Ali (Indian) 106
Muhtasib, Sheikh Hilmi al- 225
Mulqi, Fawzi al- 181
Münchhausen, Baron Thankmar von 57
Munich agreement (1938) 115
Muskie, Edmund 245
Muslim-Christian Society 88
Muslim Council (1967–) 222–5, 329, 331
Musrara 163, 316
Mussolini, Benito 108–9
Myerson, Golda: *see* Meir, Golda

N

Nablus 26, 68, 102–3, 209
Nabulsi, Sulayman al- 194
Nahmanides, supposed tomb of 312
Namari, Kamal 227
Napoleon I, Emperor 25, 62
Napoleon III, Emperor 39, 42–3, 54
Narkiss, General Uzi 207, 328
Nashashibi family 50, 105, 110
Nashashibi, Ragheb al- 69, 104, 107–8, 116, 183, 188–9, 197
Nazareth 12, 73, 110, 161, 273, 317
Nebi Musa festival 101–5, 188
Nebi Samuel 206
Negev desert 124, 162, 176
Nesselrode, Charles Robert, Count 41
Netanyahu, Binyamin 296, 303–4, 306–9, 335, 342, 350
Netherlands 27, 126, 174, 201, 233, 243
Neturei Karta 160
Neumark, Baruch 203
Neuville, René 145, 148–9, 197
Neve Yaakov 246
New Gate 48
Newman, John Henry, Cardinal 31–2
New York 177, 234, 315
New York Times 180, 241, 243, 274, 335, 336
New Zealand 137
Nicholas I, Tsar 40
Nicolayson, Revd John 53
Nieuwenhuys, Jean 145, 158

Nikolai Nikolaievich, Grand Duke 61
Nixon, President Richard 231
Noah, William Ewart Gladstone 324
Noble Rescript of the Rose Chamber (1839) 28, 52
Norway 27, 263, 303–4
Notre Dame de France 48, 208
Nur al-Din 11
Nusseibeh, Anwar 189, 222–3, 253, 261
Nusseibeh, Sari 261, 299, 346

O

O'Connor, John, Cardinal 274
O'Connor, General Richard 115
Odessa 59
Olmert, Ehud 264, 288, 298, 300, 303, 305, 311, 342, 344
Omariyya building 217
Operation Alpha 185–6
Operation Kedem 161
Operation Nahshon 142
Or, Ruth 333
Ordnance Survey of Jerusalem 63
Orient House 300–306, 306
Orthodox Palestine Society 61, 277, 280
Oslo 263, 298
Oslo Agreement 263–4, 287, 289–90, 295, 298, 300, 303–4
Osservatore Cattolico 56
Ottoman Empire 3, 14–79; see also Turkey
Ottoman parliament 68, 69

P

Pail, Meir 243
Pakistan 229
Palestine Broadcasting Service 114
Palestine Exploration Fund 63
Palestine Liberation Organization (PLO) 192, 227, 239, 247, 250, 252, 253, 255, 259–62, 290, 294, 298, 301–2, 304, 339
Palestine Police Force 146
Palestine Post 134
Palestinian Academic Society for the Study of International Affairs 303–4
Palestinian Authority 263, 275–6, 296–300, 302, 305–6, 308, 310, 340–42, 352–3; Force 17 Presidential Guard 306; General Security Service 306; Ministry of Education 306; Ministry of Health 305; Ministry of Jerusalem Affairs 300, 302; Ministry of Justice 306; Ministry of Religious Affairs 305, 330
Palestinian Broadcasting Corporation 300
Palestinian Council 264
Palestinian Covenant 304

Palestinian National Charter 250
Palestinian National Council 250, 260, 311
Palestinian Social Congress 252
Palmach 142
Palmerston, Lord 27, 29
Panama 135
Papen, Franz von 78
Paris 85, 92, 124; Peace Conference (1856) 43 (1919) 89, 92–3; Treaty of (1856) 51–2
Parsons, Levi 53
Passarowitz, Treaty of (1718) 24
Pattir, Dan 240
Paul VI, Pope 271–2, 274
Peel, Lord 110
Peres, Shimon 242–3, 262–3, 269, 289, 294–6, 302–4, 339
Perlmutter, Amos 241
Persia 27; see also Iran
Peru 126
Philaret, Metropolitan 283
Philippines 135
Picot, François Georges- 72, 74–5, 80, 83–5
Piépape, Colonel de 79
Pirie-Gordon, Harry 81
Pisgat Zeev 218, 246
Pius XI, Pope 93
Pius XII, Pope 170
Plaza Hotel 217
Plymouth 31
Poland 24, 47
Pollock, J. H. H. 99–100, 142
Polycarp, Archimandrite 193
Popular Front for the Liberation of Palestine 227
Porath, Yehoshua 112
Porphyrios, Bishop 87
Portugal 27
Pro-Jerusalem Society 87
Protestants xi, 28–35, 37, 43, 58–9, 65, 267
Prussia 27–35, 50
Psagot 247
Punch 51
Puritans 30–31
Pusey, Edward Bouverie 32

Q

Qaddumi, Faruq, 304
Qalandiya 189, 212, 314
Qastal 142
Quandt, William 233
Quds, al- 11, 292, 295; see also Jerusalem
Quds, al- 226, 256
Quq, Dr Zakaria al- 310
Quran 10

R

Rabin, Yitzhak 207, 239, 242–3, 256, 262, 287–8, 295–7, 300–301, 304, 339, 350, 359
Rabinovich, Rabbi Nachum L. 335
Rabinowitz, Rabbi Louis 333
Rafael, Gideon 346, 358
Rajoub, Colonel Jibril 306
Ram, a- 219, 291
Ramallah 117, 144, 150, 155, 167, 204, 219, 273, 295, 306, 316, 350, 357
Ramat Eshkol 218
Ramat Rahel 167, 175–6
Ramleh 25, 117, 161
Ramon, Haim 309–10
Ras al-Ain 144, 158, 161
Ras al-Amud 188, 288, 310
Ratisbonne, Abbé 58
Ratisbonne monastery 48
Rauf Pasha 65
Reagan, President Ronald 246, 248–9, 260
Redemptoris nostri cruciatus 170
Reedman, John 159
Reform Judaism 4
Rege-Donato, Consul 54
Rehavia 48, 133
Rehovot 177
Reynier, Jacques de 148–9, 161
Rhodes 162, 167
Rice, Tim 288
Richard I ('the Lionheart'), King 12, 316
Rida, Muhammad Rashid 107
Rifai, Samir 180–81
Riley, General William 161
riots (1920) 104 (1929) 326–7 (1982) 336 (1996) 342
Robinson, Father Paschal 95
Rogers, William 231
Roman Catholic Church 31–2, 92–3, 118, 270–76; *see also* Latin Christians
Romania 98
Rome xii–xiii, 7, 54, 95, 171, 270, 359
Romema 163
Rosenne, Shabtai 173, 279–80
Ross, Archie 185
Rostow, Eugene 214
Rothschild family 245
Rothschild, Baron Edmond 322
Rothschild Hospital 87
Royal Commission on Palestine (1936–7) 110–13, 115, 121
Royal Engineers 63
Ruppin, Arthur 4
Rusk, Dean 164
Russell, Lord John 42

Russia 23, 25, 27–30, 37–43, 47, 59–62, 69, 83, 118, 267, 276–86
Russian Orthodox Church 41, 60–62, 195, 276–86
Ryckmans, P. 137

S

Sabah, al- 323
Sabbah, Michel, Patriarch 272–3, 344
Sabri, Sheikh Ikrima 276, 341
Sadat, President Anwar 235–7, 240, 245–6, 251
Safed 3, 110, 223, 322
Safieh, Anton 143
Safran, Nadav 233
Sa'ih, Sheikh Abd al-Hamid al- 222–3
St George's Cathedral 59
St George's College 59
St Petersburg 60
St Stephen's Gate 142, 207
Saladin 11–12, 316, 331
Salesians 56
Salomon, Gershon 334, 337
Samaritans 28
Samuel, Sir Herbert 89, 92, 105, 108, 149, 325
Sanctuary of the Ascension 93
Sandström, Justice Emil 126
San Remo Conference (1920) 89, 95
Sardinia 27
Saudi Arabia 233, 250–51, 343
Saulcy, L. F. de J. C., 62
Schmidt, Edmund 71
Schneller, Johann Ludwig 48
Schneller's Orphanage 48, 142
Sea of Galilee 73
Sedan, Battle of (1870) 54
Semiramis Hotel 134
Sephardim 46, 253
Sergei Aleksandrovich, Grand Duke 61, 280
Seychelles 115, 116
Seymour, Hamilton 40
Shaab, al- 226
Shaftesbury, 7th Earl 27, 30–32
Shahaf, Brigadier-General David 299
Shahal, Moshe 301–2
Shamir, Yitzhak 162, 261, 273, 297
Shanghai 114
Shapira, Chief Rabbi Avraham 335
Shapira, Haim Moshe 206
Shapiro, Yaakov Shimshon 212
Sharansky, Natan 310
Sharef, Zeev 140
Sharett (Shertok), Moshe 108, 112, 140, 147, 151, 153, 160, 164–5, 169, 172, 175, 177, 199–200

Sharon, Ariel 257–8, 298, 304, 317, 335
Sheikh Jarrah 50, 167, 300, 309, 312
Shertok, Moshe: see Sharett, Moshe
Shilansky, Dov 337
Shiloah, Reuven 165–7, 180–81, 281
Shipler, David 336
Shlonsky, Avraham 5
Shuafat 128, 314
Shuckburgh, Evelyn 185
Shultz, George 249, 259
Shuneh 180
Shuqayri, Ahmad 192
Silberg, Justice Moshe 215
Silverthorn, General 146
Silwan 186, 258, 288
Sinai peninsula 62, 71
Siniora, Hanna 253, 256, 289, 346
Sinope, Battle of (1853) 42
Smith, Sir Sidney 25
South Africa 242, 289, 304
Spain 71, 83, 96, 102, 170, 230
Statute of Jerusalem 136, 146–7, 176, 184
Stavropoulos, Constantin 159
Stein, Cyril 335
Stephanopoulos, Sister Maria 286
Stern Gang: see Lehi
Stevenson, Frances 89
Stockholm 314
Storrs, Ronald xi, 80, 86–7, 94–6, 101, 103–4, 203, 323
Strachey, Lytton 64
Stratford de Redcliffe, Lord 42, 52
Suez Canal 50, 62, 63, 186, 190–91, 231
Sulayman I, Emperor ('the Magnificent') 14, 16–17, 102
Sulayman the Magnificent Street 216–7
Supreme Moslem Council (1921–51) 82, 105–7, 126, 188, 325, 327
Sur Bahir 247
Suwarha 313
Sweden 27, 126, 174
Switzerland 171
Sykes, Sir Mark 80–85, 94
Sykes-Picot Agreement (1916) 72–4, 82
Syria 28, 31, 33, 52, 62, 72, 89, 90, 101, 104, 145, 152, 174, 201, 232–3
Syrian Orthodox Church 99

T

Tahboub, Dr Hassan 305, 340
Talbieh 48, 134, 145, 163, 181, 196, 217
Tall, Abdullah al- 165–7, 183, 187, 203
Talmon, Shemaryahu 321
Talpiot 167, 326

Tamimi, Sheikh Tatzir 276
Tamir, Shmuel 240
Tanzimat 28, 52–3
Tashkent 285
TASS 284, 332
Tehran 241
Tel Aviv xiii, 4, 110–12, 142–3, 151, 199–202, 242–3, 248, 249, 294
Tel Aviv University 243
Temple 209
Temple Mount: see Haram al-Sharif, al-
Temple Mount Faithful 334, 337, 342
Templers 48, 57
Thalmann, Ernest 229
Thant, U 229
Thawra, al- 343
Thompson, William, Archbishop of York 63
Tiberias 110, 322
Tibi, Ahmad 346–7
Times, The 81, 133, 180
Timotheos, Metropolitan 276
Timotheos, Patriarch of Jerusalem 99, 193–4, 281–2
Tomb of Rachel 173
Tomb of the Virgin 93
Tombs of the Kings 62
Tractarians 31–2
Transjordan 102, 110, 126, 132, 138, 152–6, 163, 173, 178; see also Jordan
Truman, President Harry 156, 169
Tschoudi, Melchior 52–3
Tunisia 106
Tuozzi, Alberto 86
Tur, a- 186, 256
Turkey 14–79, 230, 243, 300; see also Ottoman Empire
Tuscany 21
Twain, Mark 47
Tyler, Samuel R. 196
Tzorbatzoglou, Consul 97

U

Ukraine 153
Umar, Caliph 9–10
Uniates 28; see also Greek Catholics
Union of Soviet Socialist Republics 139–40, 147, 174, 176, 184, 198, 232, 260, 266, 277–86; see also Russia
United Nations 119, 124–32, 134–41, 150, 163, 171, 173–7, 180, 184–5, 203–4, 223, 270, 285, 339; Ad Hoc Political Committee 176; Committee for the Exercise of the Inalienable Rights of the Palestinian People 252;

Educational Social and Cultural Organization 229; Emergency Force in Sinai 229; General Assembly 125, 128, 131, 136, 145–7, 158, 162, 168–70, 176–7, 198, 228–9, 252, 331; Palestine Commission 135, 139, 141, 145–6, 158; Palestine Conciliation Commission 168–9, 184; Relief and Works Administration 151, 159; Security Council 135, 139–40, 145, 153–4, 157–9, 161, 229, 231–2, 243, 307, 315, 332, 337–8, 343; Special Committee on Palestine 125–8, 131, 200; Truce Commission 145, 148, 157–8, 161; Truce Observer Organization 161, 182, 205; Trusteeship Council 131, 136–7, 138–9, 141, 146–7, 171, 173, 176, 184

United States of America 27, 71–2, 122, 124, 141, 145, 156, 163, 167, 176, 184, 189, 207, 229–33, 240–43, 247–50, 259–63, 307; Central·Intelligence Agency 139; embassy in Israel 177–8, 248–9; House of Representatives 248; Marine Corps 146, 161; Senate 156; State Department 130, 138–9, 164, 169, 171, 184–5, 196, 201, 241, 248, 274

Uruguay 127, 201
Uspenskii, Archimandrite Porfiri 35, 194
Utrecht, Peace of 23

V

Vaadat Ha-matzav 279
Valerga, Mgr Joseph 35–6
Valley of the Cross 177, 217
Vance, Cyrus 237
Vatican xii, 56, 75, 95, 126, 170–72, 175–6, 189, 251, 267, 270–76, 359
Vehementer Gratum 93
Venezuela 201
Venice 16–17, 21, 24
Vereté, Mayir 27
Victoria, Queen 31, 33–4, 63

W

Wadi Joz 186, 227, 288, 309, 316
Waldeck-Rousseau, René 55
Walker, P. W. L. 6
War of the Spanish Succession 23
Warhaftig, Zerah 212, 217, 329

Warren, Colonel Charles 63
Washington 250, 304, 338, 347
Wasson, Thomas 145, 157
Wauchope, Sir Arthur 106
Webster, George 122
Weil, Simone 301
Weizman, Ezer 241
Weizmann, Chaim 2, 76, 87, 89, 167, 171, 177, 245, 323, 325
Western Wall xii, 2, 12, 106, 115, 173, 175, 178, 181, 233, 242, 252, 294, 320–30, 349
Whitbeck, John V. 346
Wiesel, Elie 335
Wiet, Ferdinand 55
Wilhelm II, Emperor 50–51, 59, 75, 79
Williamson, Molly 250
Wilson, Captain Charles 63, 64
Wilson, Harold 232
Wolfson buildings 217
Woodhead, Sir John 113
Woodhead Commission 113–15
World Islamic Conference (1967) 227

Y

Yad Vashem 275
Yalçin, H. C. 169
Yediot Aharonot 253
Yemen 47
Yemin Moshe 134
Yosef, Dov 164, 169, 175
Yosef, Chief Rabbi Ovadia 332
Yost, Charles A. 231, 233
Young, W. T. 33–6
Yugoslavia 127–8

Z

Zaim, a- 291
Zander, Walter 24
Ze'evi, General Rehavam 211
Zenki 11
Zghayar, Ahmad Hasim al- 298
Zionist Commission 87
Zionist Executive 112, 244, 323
Zionist Organization 4, 76, 251, 325
Zion Square 228
Ziyad, Ziyad Abu 298